# Putti Names with Faces

## Women's Impact in Mission History

Christine Lienemann-Perrin,

Atola Longkumer,

Afrie Songco Joye,

Editors

Abingdon Press
Nashville

PUTTING NAMES WITH FACES

*Copyright © 2012 by Abingdon Press*

*This book is printed on acid-free, recycled paper.*

**Library of Congress Cataloging-in-Publication Data**

Putting names with faces : women's impact in mission history / Christine Lienemann-Perrin, Atola Longkumer, Afrie Songco Joye, eds.
    p. cm.
    ISBN 978-1-4267-5839-3 (book - pbk. / trade pbk. : alk. paper) 1. Women in missionary work—History. I. Lienemann-Perrin, Christine. II. Longkumer, Atola. III. Joye, Afrie S.
    BV2610.P88 2012
    266.0082—dc23

2012024966

Scripture quotations marked KJV are from the King James Version.

Those marked RSV are from the Revised Standard Version of the Bible, copyright 1946, 1952, 1971 by the Division of Christian Education of the National Council of the Churches of Christ in the United States of America. Used by permission. All rights reserved.

Those marked (GNT) are from the Good News Translation in Today's English Version-Second Edition © 1992 by American Bible Society. Used by Permission.

Those marked RSV are from the New Revised Standard Version of the Bible, copyright 1989, Division of Christian Education of the National Council of the Churches of Christ in the United States of America. Used by permission. All rights reserved.

12 13 14 15 16 17 18 19 20 21— 10 9 8 7 6 5 4 3 2 1

MANUFACTURED IN THE UNITED STATES OF AMERICA

# Acknowledgments

The book, which spans the continents in its content and through the contributors, has become a reality under the patient nurture and enthusiastic support of many people across the globe. The editorial team expresses deep appreciation and gratitude to all who have contributed to make this book possible.

We appreciate Fulata Moyo, Coordinator of Women in Church and Society, World Council of Churches, Geneva and Dietrich Werner, Programme Executive of Ecumenical Theological Education, World Council of Churches, Geneva, for organizing a much-needed consultation on Women and Mission, at the Ecumenical Institute, Bossey, in November 2008 and bringing close to thirty women from different countries to deliberate together. The consultation gave birth to the initial idea of a global theological resource book; here, too, the friendship of the editors was forged. The consistent commitment that Dietrich Werner shared toward the project is much appreciated. He provided space and funds for the preliminary meeting of the editors and connected us to potential donors for the project. Indeed, we are deeply grateful for his unstinting support.

The contributors to this volume have been most gracious in responding with enthusiasm to requests for their accompaniment in the journey; and their prompt deliveries of drafts have been nothing short of exemplary professionalism. For their shared commitment to the cause of women and mission, we are immensely grateful.

The book has become a reality through the generous financial support of organizations and church agencies who have believed strongly in the global, ecumenical book project on women in mission. These are: Ecumenical Theological Education Fund, World Council of Churches; Women's Programme Desk, World Council of Churches, Geneva, Switzerland; Edinburgh 2010 Fund, U.K.; Evangelisches Missionswerk in Deutschland, Hamburg,

Germany; Deutsche Gessellschaft für Missionswissenschaft (DGMW) Germany; Stiftung Historische und Ökumenische Theologie, Bern, Switzerland; Stiftung Dialog mit Kirchen, Religionen und Kulturen, Basel, Switzerland; and The General Board of Global Ministries, The United Methodist Church, USA. For their commitment to the need of such a resource book on women and mission, we graciously express our sincere and deep gratitude.

Kirsteen Kim, Maureen Trott, Carol von Gorp, Fulata Moyo, and Christoph Anders have all been immensely helpful with the procedures and communications with the donors. We are grateful to them all.

Our special thanks to Matthias Felder and Merve Rugenstein Itona, for the careful proofreading of the manuscript. Their support was a tremendous help to us. Also, we thank Begonia Rivera of the Ecumenical Institute for her most helpful assistance during the writers workshop at Bossey.

It has been a pleasure to work with Abingdon Press, our publisher, of Nashville, Tennessee. We are immensely grateful to all. Special thanks to Mary Catherine Dean for patiently shepherding the book through the publishing process, to Julianne Eriksen for copyediting and proofreading the manuscript, and to the entire production team for their prompt efforts toward a timely publication of the book.

May the collective efforts and shared vision of this book inspire and empower the readers to seek and participate in God's reign, where all are welcomed and recognized with their gifts and graces.

*Christine Lienemann-Perrin* (Bern, Switzerland)
*Atola Longkumer* (Jabalpur, India)
*Afrie Songco Joye* (Cavite, Philippines, and California, USA)

# Contents

# PART III: CONSEQUENCES FOR THEOLOGICAL REFLECTION ON MISSION

# Foreword

*Dietrich Wener, Ecumenical Theological Education (ETE)*

It is a privilege for ETE[1] to write a foreword to this innovative, highly scholarly and intercultural theological resource book on women and Christian mission. It is a unique and long-awaited treasure for further missiological research and theological education for many contexts.

Dana L. Robert in her famous introduction into the history of Christian missions has underlined the urgency to correct the one-sided attention of mission historiography on male missionaries in the past in the following statement:

> Around the globe, more women than men are practicing Christians. Measured by regular church attendance, pilgrimages, prayers at home, fundraising, and teaching children about the faith, Christianity is a women's religion. The ration of female to male Christians is approximately two to one. Within Catholicism, sisters outnumber brothers and priests by more than 50 percent. Yet because the priests, preachers, theologians, public leaders, and famous missionary entrepreneurs are typically male, the crucial roles of women in mission remain buried in the unwritten stories of human relationships. In the late nineteenth and the twentieth centuries, in both Catholicism and Protestantism, the majority of missionaries were women. However, until recently, overview histories of mission have scarcely analyzed women's roles or acknowledged that women typically make up the majority of active believers.[2]

It is the enormous merit of this book that it gives voice to women as both agents and subjects of missions in several regional contexts, some of which have rarely been published so far; as well as to the historical contributions of Christian women's mission in general as exposed in the unique history chapter of this book. The novelty of this book for theological education also lies in the format and the pointed study questions for practical reflections, as well as further readings/ explorations that are included in each regional survey article

and that make this book an asset for any theological and historical study.

The book owes its existence to an initiative that was developed
out of a joint consultation between the program on Ecumenical
Theological Education (ETE) and the program on "Women
in Church and Society" of the World Council of Churches on
"Women's Perspectives on Mission and Theological Education
in 21st Century," which was held November 24-28, 2008 in the
Ecumenical Institute of Bossey. Almost thirty leading women
theologians and scholars dealing with feminist theology, mission history, and theological research had come together to
reflect on women's role in Christian mission and in theological
education in the twenty-first century.[3] The seminar was planned
to articulate a distinct voice of women theologians within the
so-called Edinburgh 2010 process, which in looking back on
hundred years of Christian mission since 1910 had identified
nine global study themes on various aspects of the situation of
Christian mission one hundred years after Edinburgh 1910,[4] but
at that time did not foresee any distinct study group on women's
mission—this theme being regarded as a "transversal theme"
to be looked at throughout all the other themes. In consequence
this led to the fact that the final report volume of the Edinburgh
2010 conference does not show any specific entry and contribution on the role of women in Christian mission.[5] It is only
in the previous documentation of the reports of the Edinburgh
2010 study process that a distinct paper from Fulata L. Moyo on
the consultations around the "transversal" issue of women and
mission[6] was included, which also had a reference to the Bossey
consultation of women theologians and theological educators in
November 2008, the starting point for this resource book.

The sometimes overt, sometimes hidden lack of attention and
support to the role and concerns of women in Christian mission and the potential threat of the extinction of a distinct memory is further illustrated by an incident that was also directly
related to the Edinburgh 2010 conference. When searching for
a proper place for a pre-conference on theological education
in Edinburgh, Scottish friends advised to go to a place called
St. Colm's Missionary College, which was close to the Botanic
Garden and still offered very good accommodations. Arriving
and meeting there, participants surprisingly learned that they
had landed in the house that for one century had served as a center for women's mission: St. Colm's Women's Mission College
It was founded in 1908 as a Women's Missionary College of the
Free Church of Scotland[7] and had not only hosted a number of

key delegates of the Edinburgh 1910 world missionary conference (among them particularly the seventeen representatives
of the so-called younger churches from Asia), but was also the
house in which the famous Commission V report on "the training of missionaries" was drafted. It was at St. Colm's College
where the famous speech of the Indian Bishop Azariah "Give
us Friends" was written, asking for new ways of true equality and partnership between missionaries and indigenous
Christians, the younger and the older churches.[8] Unfortunately,
this famous place and institution, in which to some extend the
debate on theological education had started in the missionary
and the early ecumenical movement, just two weeks before the
solemn commemoration conference of Edinburgh 2010 was sold
in order to solve budget problems within the overall church and
because nobody could develop a sustainable concept of how to
raise the amounts needed for maintenance and upgrading the
building.[9] Within a few weeks, 100 years of a remarkable history
of women's involvement in world missions had lost its distinct
local place of historical memory without much public attention.
Although the immensely precious archives on the history of
St. Colm's could be rescued and are preserved, participants in
Edinburgh 2010 were somewhat puzzled and sad by this painful decision, which even after an additional petition of international participants of Edinburgh centenary conference[10] could
not be prevented.

It is well illustrated by this story that working against the trend
of sidelining the role of women and preserving and strengthening the memory of women's involvement in Christian mission
has to do with issues of power, finances, research grants made
available or refused, the presence of women and gender studies
in institutions of theological education, and not the least with
scholarly research work such as a resource book of this kind. It
will be of vital help for the future of curriculum development in
theological education that this new resource book will inspire
both teaching and further research for generations to come.

The world study report on theological education which has
been published as part of the Edinburgh 2010 study process
had stated: "While we can celebrate the significant changes that
have occurred in some contexts during the past decades with
regard to women in theological studies and teaching, it should
be emphasized that continuing efforts are needed. In most
regions of the world there is still an overwhelming task to be
accomplished in terms of encouraging, equipping, and enabling
young women theologians to gain access to degree programs,

teaching positions, and leadership in churches and educational institutions. As there is a backlash in many regions regarding the presence of women in church leadership and positions in higher education in general, it is very important that women receive strong support at every stage in theological education."[11]

The program on Ecumenical Theological Education of the World Council of Churches (ETE) is highly recommending this book to interested theologians, pastors, researchers, and historians, both men and women and for all regional associations of theological schools. This book is a must have for all institutions of theological education and their libraries in today's world, which want to contribute to correcting and deepening the picture, knowledge and commonly held perceptions on the significance and role of women in Christian mission, past and present.

*Dietrich Werner (Germany) is Lecturer in Missiology and Ecumenism, Program Coordinator of the Programme on Ecumenical Theological Education, WCC, Geneva, Switzerland.*

## Endnotes

1. The program on Ecumenical Theological Education (ETE) and its predecessor PTE for many years have been engaged in promoting women's leadership in theological education through publications, consultations, and special scholarships throughout the world. See PTE contribution to the Study of the Community of Women and Men in the Church, in *Ministerial Formation* (MF) 7, (1979): 12ff; theme issue on Women, Theological Education and Ministry in *MF* 33, (1986): 4ff, and also in: *MF* 38, (1987): 4ff. See also: Ofelia Ortega, Women and Theology: A Latin American Viewpoint, in Ministerial Formation Jubilee Issue No 110 (April 2008): 48-56.

2. Dana L. Robert, *Christian Mission. How Christianity Became a World Religion* (West Sussex: Wiley-Blackwell, 2009), 118.

3. The conference issued an important conference communiqué under the title "Women's Perspectives on Mission and Theological Education in the 21st Century—Mission for All:

Full participation in the mending of creation"; http://www.oikoumene. org/fileadmin/files/wcc-main/documents/p5/ete/Women%27s%20 Perspectives%20on%20Mission%20and%20Theological%20Education%20 in%20the%2021st%20Century.pdf (August 29, 2011).

4. See: http://www.edinburgh2010.org/?id=4643 (August 29, 2011).

5. Kirsteen Kim and Andrew Anderson, Edinburgh 2010. Mission Today and Tomorrow. Regnum Edinburgh 2010 series (2011).

6. "Who is not at the table?' Women's Perspectives of Holistic Mission as Mutually Inclusive," in Daryl Balia and Kirsteen Kim, Edinburgh 2010, Witnessing to Christ Today, Volume II (Oxford: Regnum Books International, 2010): 245ff. See also the website of Edinburgh 2010 process on women and mission: http://www.edinburgh2010.org/en/study-themes/transversal-topics/1-women-and-mission.html (August 29, 2011).

7. See: archives of St. Colm's and brief history: http://www.mundus. ac.uk/cats/48/1015.htm (August 29, 2011).

8. V. S. Azariah. "The Problem of Co-operation between Foreign and Native Workers" in: World Missionary Conference 1910. The History and Records of the Conference together with addresses delivered at the Evening Meetings, Vol. 9: To Consider Missionary Problems in Relation to the Non-Christian World (Edinburgh: Oliphant, Anderson & Ferrier; New York: Fleming H. Revell, [1910?]) 306-315, here p. 315. See also: Robert, Christian Mission, 55.

9. Ian Swanson, Church sells off missionaries' college in bid to save money. Decision to close St Colm's "reached with great sadness" (Published Date: 20 May 2010). http://www.scotsman.com/news/church-sells-off-missionaries-college-in-bid-to-save-money-1-1238050 (August 29, 2011).

10. Ian Swanson, Global funding plan could answer prayer for way to save Kirk college (Published Date: June 03, 2010); http://www.scotsman.com/news/scottish-news/top-stories/global-funding-plan-could-answer-prayer-for-way-to-save-kirk-college-1-1243668 (August 29, 2011).

11. See Short version of Global Study Report in Theological Education, in Edinburgh 2010. Witnessing to Christ Today, Volume II, Daryl Balia and Kirsteen Kim (eds.), 159. See also the two contributions on women in theological education in Dietrich Werner, David Esterline, Namsoon Kang, Joshva Raja (eds.), Handbook on Theological Education in World Christianity (Oxford: Regnum Publisher, 2010), 56-75.

# Introduction

*Christine Lienemann-Perrin, Atola Longkumer,*
*Afrie Songco Joye*

The beginning of this volume traces to an international consultation on Women's Perspectives on Mission and Theological Education in 21$^{st}$ Century, in November 2008, organized jointly by the Program on Women in Church and Society, and the Program on Ecumenical Theological Education of the World Council of Churches. Some participants continued the conversation and made explorations toward a publication that would serve as a bridge between theological education and concerns of women and mission.

Having the possibility of realizing the dream of an edited volume on the theme Women and Mission, the authors met in October 2010 Bossey, at the Ecumenical Institute of the World Council on Churches, located in the beautiful landscape on the lake of Geneva. While some of the writers were friends and colleagues, most of us knew one another only by name and by the drafts of our papers exchanged before the meeting. It was a promising experience when we met face to face at Bossey and were able to put faces to the names we have come to know over the months of email exchanges. To connect the names with the faces of our friends necessitated both to affirm and to correct our self-made images of the others.

This experience of connecting or putting a face to the names we have come to know can be said of women in mission. We know the names for some of the women who participated in Christian mission, and on the other hand we have only faces, unnamed as spouses or coworkers in mission. Hence the title of the book, *Putting Names with Faces*. Born out of the common experience of being women across a plurality of sociocultural loci, the title expresses the rationale and the objective of the present volume. Furthermore, it embraces well our common aspirations and aims: to do justice to at least some of the women who have contributed tremendously to the missionary endeavor in past and present times on all continents by way of putting faces to names; and to further contribute to the continuing task of teaching on women's impact in mission as a vital dimension of theological education and missional formation.

Uncountable are the women involved in the transmission and appropriation of the Christian faith who have never been mentioned by name in the historiography found in mission libraries. A few are known just as "wife of missionary XY" and some are known as "single women missionaries." Where, seldom enough, names occur, they are hidden in men's files, articles, or books, making it difficult to explore the traces of women's missionary agency. The recent developments in mission historiography and cultural studies have been encouraging, whereby women are beginning to be recognized as active agents as well as active recipients of Christian mission. These developments point to the need of more micro-historiography that takes into account the multiple meanings and practices each encounter and location generated, along with the macro and general statements praising women's roles in mission made in oral or written form persistently. Hence this volume is envisaged to fill some of the lacunae of micro context of women's experience and participation in Christian mission and to put faces and names to the many women who have communicated the gospel by word and deed throughout the whole history of Christianity across different contexts.

Since the beginning of Christian history, women have often, if not always, been part of mission, both as agents and as receivers. Again and again, women viewed conversion to the Christian faith as a return to God and as a way out of cultural and religious constraints. Women have regarded themselves as addressees of the Great Commission: "Go therefore and make disciples of all nations, baptizing them in the name of the Father and of the Son and of the Holy Spirit, and teaching them to obey all that I have commanded you" (Matt. 28:19-20 KJV). Women have known from the beginning that the great commissioning of Jesus, that is, to witness the Good News in various ways applies to them without reservations of gender, race, or class. However, many times women have experienced the exclusion from all four aspects of the Great Commission: making disciples, going out (working in the public space), and teaching (on pulpit and teacher's desk), and baptizing (celebrating the sacraments). The arguments to exclude women from crucial fields of mission have been gender-based over centuries and even continue today. On the one hand, women have been—and are—welcome to do missionary work, but on the other hand, their enthusiasm has been regarded as endangering the hierarchical order of the Church and the established local cultural traditions. Women, as both subjects and agents, had in many settings been controlled and excluded from involvement in the public sphere. They were either restrained to the household or—in the case of religious women—"encloistered" and made invisible and inaudible.

From the beginning, the transmission of the gospel has been a process of giving, bringing, and receiving. At no stage in the history of Christianity missionary have agents been *only* on the giving side; never and nowhere have the addressees of the message *only* been on the receiving side of the missionary process. Christian mission works as a two-way communication—although often imbalanced, it is sometimes also (unconsciously or as a policy) repressive. In tandem with the recently developed transcultural approach to mission history, this book looks at the interrelationships and mutual interaction between women missionaries and women converts as well as cross-gender relations within "contact zones" of colonial settings.

Arguably, it can be claimed that the historiography of Christian missions has contributed largely to efface the presence and tremendous contribution of women to the enlargement, consolidation, and deepening of world Christianity. Historiography has for a long time been interested mainly in the public aspect of world Christianity (history of mission institutions, leadership, and teaching in mission education, and written records of mission theology, control of mission power). Rarely has historiography shed light on the female face of Christian mission past and present. Women's enterprises in mission have constantly been kept out of the picture. Thanks to some missiologists—mainly women scholars—there has, however, been a change of mind, perspective, and method in recent times. The list of books on the history of women's mission is growing. They are beginning to fill the gaps of knowledge about women's mission past and present. But a lot of research work at many levels remains yet to be done. One of the much-needed texts is a resource book that will serve as study guide on women in mission for use mainly in theological institutions. It will hopefully stimulate further research on and by women in mission and lead to an inclusive understanding of mission across gender barriers, race relations, and cultural differences. Such discernment may inspire men and women to engage jointly and in mutual respect in the mission of the Church.

With these perceptions and reasons in mind, the aims of the book are mainly: (1) to continue, building on already existing resources, research on women's roles in Christian mission and thereby contribute to the overcoming of the paucity in this research area; (2) to draw renewed insights for the gendered aspect of mission and historiography of mission; (3) to create more awareness to readers of the gender aspect of mission and historiography of mission, as for instance the tension between emancipation and domestication in the field of mission; (4) to lay ground for the shaping of gender justice in mission theology and practice today; and finally (5) to make available an academic resource book that can be used as a study guide for use in spiritual and ministerial formation.

Asymmetries as well as egalitarian relationships in the women's mission past and present are addressed from women's perspectives. Therefore, the resource book and study guide is based on a cooperation of women scholars from the global North and the global South with global experiences and knowledge of women's context in various parts of the world. They bring into the conversation on the theme of women and mission both contextual and denominational diversities in reflecting and doing mission throughout world Christianity. Concerning the methodical approach, there was no single dominant scheme prescribed for every case study; it was instead left to the authors to decide according to the orientation of the case studies of the regions. Therefore, the chapters and the case studies rather mirror the great variety of research methods applied by the authors coming from different educational backgrounds, experiences, and cultural traditions. Hopefully, readers will appreciate the variety as a treasure rather than as a weakness.

The purpose of Part I (Foundational Perspectives) is twofold: It investigates, first, the biblical foundations of women's access to missionary work and serves simultaneously as a theological point of reference for the historical case studies of Part II. Theological criteria will be elaborated on the basis of various biblical passages (e.g., Gal. 3:26-28; Luke 4; John 4; and Matt. 28). The tension between different perspectives on women's roles in mission within the New Testament will be addressed explicitly. Second, it provides a historical survey on women in mission, showing women's absence *and* presence in the history of Christian mission. Given the limited space it is far from exhaustive, and does not account for the female face of mission throughout all centuries and all regions. It brings together, however, a selection of representative experiences of women in different periods of history and various parts of the world. Included in both chapters of Part I are bibliographical recommendations for further readings.

Part II is earmarked for deepening and concretising the role of women in mission through fourteen case studies from West Africa, Kenya, Ethiopia, Iran, India, Pakistan, China, South Korea, Japan, the Philippines, New Zealand, Mexico, Guatemala, and Europe. To ease and stimulate a comparative analysis of them in various respects, they have in general the same structure contending eight subchapters: Introduction; historical background; case study; analysis; conclusion; questions; recommendations; further readings. They deal with different periods of history: one that spans across 2000 years of women's presence in mission (Ethiopia), another analyzes women's roles at the turn of the sixteenth century (Japan); the majority of the case studies focus on the nineteenth and/or twentieth centuries (Korea; India; Iran; West Africa; Europe; Guatemala; Mexico), while some deal mainly with the present time (Philippines; Kenya; Pakistan; China). Obviously not all representative regions and denominations are included in the selected case studies. Unfortunately, it was not possible to find in due time authors from the Orthodox tradition in Middle East and Eastern Europe. In fact, valuable resources are available since recent times on women's roles throughout the history of Orthodox churches.[1] However, it is still a fact that written sources on women's role in Orthodox mission are either not yet available or not known to women interested in the topic—or simply not existing. To fill that specific lack remains a task for the future. Another lack of the book carries less weight: it includes no case study on North America since plenty of studies on American women in mission have been provided already and are easily available.[2]

Deriving from the results of the fourteen case studies, the main chapter in Part III develops and provides direction for a contextual missiology from a women's perspective that includes concerns and issues pertaining to women as both practitioners and receivers of mission. It outlines various contextual profiles of women's mission today. Furthermore, it retains the crucial issues, contents, and understandings of women's mission and missiology.

One of the features of the collected writings is that they bring to the fore some of the crucial tensions and negotiations of the gender aspect in mission. They demonstrate the so-called "gendered missions" in their close interrelationship with differences of race, class, and culture. Gendered missions and its historiography is most of all felt as an urgent need and relevant issue by women, and generally not by men. While it draws from women's experience, it should not remain exclusively female in its rationale and approach. It lies with women to take the initiative in "writing women into the history of mission." The task of overcoming the separation of mission contexts and agenda along the boundaries of gender requires that the conversation about mission has to take place across these lines—as well as across the boundaries of race, class, and culture.

## Endnotes

1. See the extended reading list in: Karla Koll, et al., "Women's Absence and Presence in the History and Records of Christian Mission—Historical Survey of Women in Mission," page 87, in this volume. It will hopefully assist in further interest and research.

2. See *North America*, page 89.

# PART I

# *Foundational Perspectives*

# Biblical Perspectives on Women's Impact in Mission[1]

*Christine Lienemann-Perrin*

The question of women's impact in mission in biblical times takes us back to the beginnings of Christianity in the first and second century, when the first Christian communities were starting to develop their religious and cultural identity and to gain an understanding of themselves as the Church of Jesus Christ. Just as the idea of being church was still in a state of flux, so too was the idea of what is called today "mission." What this concept comprised—who could participate in mission and help decide how it was to be done—differed according to the thinking of different local churches and itinerant apostles. The biblical foundations for mission are difficult to ascertain, because the relevant concepts[2] appear in the New Testament in connection with a variety of activities and groups of people. For example, they include such disparate things as the work of itinerant apostles among Gentiles in the known world at that time, as well as leadership tasks within local churches such as proclamation, teaching, responsibility for the sacraments, caring for the needy and for prisoners. But they also include standing up for one's faith under persecution, holding fast to the true faith, and transmitting the legacy of the faith to the next generation.[3]

The public dimension is the one characteristic that does stand out in the multifaceted subject of mission, in all the forms mentioned. Mission, at its core, urges Christians toward public activity, anchored as it is in the gospel of Jesus Christ. Jesus' own understanding of the purpose for which he was sent was as a public action carried out in the public sphere, in the streets, market squares, and the Temple. Called to account for it by the high priest at the beginning of his Passion, Jesus said: "I have spoken openly *(parrhesia)* to the world; I have always taught in synagogues and in the temple, where all the Jews come together. I have said nothing in secret *(en krypto)*" (John 18:20). From the beginning, the mission of Jesus' disciples involved active participation of church members in public tasks, in worship, communication within and beyond the congregation, as well as in public work outside the church among people of other faiths *(ethne)*. Did women take part in this? Could they actively and publicly participate in missionary tasks, and be involved in decision making, in view of the fact that in the Mediterranean world at that time, offices and functions in the public sphere *(polis)* were generally the affairs of men?[4] What follows is an exploration of women's role in mission in the early church, by asking whether, in what ways and to what degree, women participated in the public work of the early church.

The scope for women's mission activities basically depended on whether local churches, in ordering the way they operated within and beyond the congregation, held to androcentric and consequently unbalanced gender images, or whether and to what extent they thought up and realized alternative forms of community life. With that in mind, I will (1) sketch out the different ways in which Christian communities dealt with the issue; (2) outline an understanding of mission beyond established gender models based on Galatians 3:26-28; (3) explore the beginnings of "gendered missions," typified by hierarchical gender role stereotyping within the New Testament canon; (4) develop some perspectives, on the basis of four key biblical passages, for biblical perspectives on women's impact in mission; and (5) show how women took responsibility for mission beyond New Testament times with a few examples from the early church.

## 1. Women's Opportunities for Participation in the Early Christian Communities

In the period between the ministry of Jesus and the finalization of the Old and New Testament canons at the end of the second century, the degree to which women were able to participate in mission and the forms that this participation took place were exceedingly varied.[5] The local churches made no effort to make binding decisions to even out differences regarding women's participation. In the early church, under the sign of a new faith community, the relationship between the sexes was seen as a question of *discipline*, which allowed for some diversity. There was no overall binding decision between the local churches, as there was, for example, on the question of mission to the "nations,"[6] and whether Gentile Christians should be required to be circumcised or not. Thanks to this latitude in the rules, at the beginning women enjoyed a remarkable degree of participation in the public sphere of congregational life.[7] This was enhanced by the fact that the life of the congregation took place largely within what was in any case women's domain, namely the household of antiquity (*oikos*). "As the public gathering of the *ecclesia* of believers in Christ took place in homes and saw itself as a family-style community, its organization was well-suited to giving women the chance to actively participate."[8] However, care should be taken in drawing general conclusions from this openness regarding disciplinary issues. It is the specific period—the geographical, cultural, and religious contexts from which biblical sources come—that are the decisive factors. Do they come from the period of Jesus, the "generation of the Apostles," or a later period that continued to the end of the early church period? It makes a difference. Do the sources belong to Jewish or Gentile Christian communities? Do they come from rural or urban contexts? All these aspects are significant in dealing with the issue of gender in mission.

Some exegetes consider it unlikely that there were women in the itinerant group of disciples who accompanied Jesus in Galilee because it would have been culturally offensive, while others consider it a definite possibility.[9] In rural areas of Galilee, the sexes were less clearly separated at work and in living arrangements than they were in the town environment, so that there would be nothing unusual about men and women eating at the same table, or about the inclusion of women in Jesus' healing activities (Mark 1:29-31 & par.). Jesus did sometimes disregard Jewish customs with regard to relations between the sexes in rural areas, but it was not his general practice to disregard them. Most of all it is his preaching that shows a new attitude toward women. The relationship to Jesus and his message formed the basis for a new brotherhood and sisterhood; but a horizontal one, which flattened out the more usual hierarchical structure headed by the *paterfamilias*. Rulers and servants were viewed in a new way, so that equality emerged between all those who served.[10]

In Jerusalem the first Christians participated in worship at the Temple but also gathered for worship in private homes (Acts 2:42-47). It can be assumed that the prophecy in Joel 2:28-32, according to which all the members of a household in antiquity, both men and women, old and young, male and female slaves would be filled with God's Spirit and would prophesy, was well known to the early church in Jerusalem. Gender differences played no role in the experience of God's Spirit. The sources do not tell us whether women helped to plan worship services held in homes in Jerusalem, but in any case men and women took part together in home worship.

The Gentile Christian community in Antioch introduced something quite new by addressing the gospel directly to Gentiles, and by separating from the synagogue to build a new community that did not observe the Jewish law in every respect or practice circumcision. They gathered only in private houses, so that homes (*oikoi*) became both dwellings and the setting for worship.[11] Having separated themselves from the synagogue, full observance of the Torah, and circumcision, the church had to redefine its identity and its unity. Galatians 3:26-28 records a promise made to members baptized by the community gathered for worship. It indicates the essential characteristics of those whose life is "in Christ." We have here a summary of guidelines for the Christian life and their theological basis: all previous distinctions between human beings, whether in reference to God's plan of salvation, their place in society or anthropological characteristics, are eliminated through baptism. This is a sign of reorientation for the life of each individual, and a sign of their unity with one another "in Christ." For women this meant that in principle, participation in everything that happened in the community was open to them.

The various congregations that formed the background against which the Gospel of John was written, after they had been excluded from the synagogue by force, turned to the basic idea of Galatians 3.26-28 (see John 10:16; 17:20f), according to which the distinction between Jews and other nations was considered abolished in their unity with Christ. In no other Gospel are women so positively described in their missionary charisma and competence as in that of John. In John's Gospel, after the calling of the disciples, the Samaritan woman is the first to believe—the first missionary (John 4). Likewise, according to John, Mary Magdalene was the first witness to the Resurrection and the first to be charged by the risen Christ to carry the news of Easter to others. In the Johannine communities, female figures are found carrying out active and influential tasks, transmitting the basic idea of Galatians 3:26-28 and putting it into practice. This was taking place toward the end of the first century, at a time when, in other congregations, a restrictive attitude toward women's roles in the public arena of the community was already gaining ground (see 1 Timothy).

Later phases of early Christianity present a different picture altogether. For various reasons, during the second century three different types of local churches had emerged:[12]

1. Churches arising from a Jewish Christian milieu (cf. Matthew and the Didache), which took over the separation of the sexes from early Jewish society and banned women almost entirely from public life, which was ruled by men. In worship women played almost only a passive role;

2. Churches based on a post-Pauline conception of Christianity (see the Pastoral Epistles), in which women began to be stridently forced out from responsibility for worship and decision making in the congregation; women must henceforth keep silent during worship and leave leadership, administration of the sacraments, and public proclamation to men (1 Tim. 2:11-12; Eph. 5:22-24; Col. 3:18-20, 1 Pet. 3:1-6);

3. Churches with a concept going back to the old ideal of ancient Rome (cf. the letters of Ignatius), which successfully fended off tendencies in favor of "women's rights" in the urban society of the time.[13]

What does all this mean for a biblical basis for mission? What the New Testament has to say about women's role in mission is remarkably varied, yet contains tensions that cannot be resolved and even contradictions that exegetical interpretations cannot simply harmonize or cast aside. Taking the Bible as a whole, a fundamental hermeneutical decision has to be made, in the light of which individual texts are then read and interpreted. This procedure inevitably leads to a critique of the canon; meaning that, in the light of those biblical texts that are used as the basis for the hermeneutical key, it is only possible for other texts to be read critically and to interpret them in terms of a *contra textum*.

The history of interpretation assumed until well into the twentieth century that the Pastoral Epistles summed up and definitively established everything the Bible had to say about women's participation in public functions and offices. The admonitions to women in the Pastoral Epistles were to a certain extent made into the hermeneutical key on the issue of whether women should be allowed access to offices in the church and to public missions.[14] A theology of mission from a women's perspective would take a different path. Its key hermeneutical decision would be based on statements in the Bible that point to a reordering of gender relationships. This "new creation" is expressed especially clearly in Galatians 3:28.

## 2. Galatians 3:26-28 as the Hermeneutical Key for a Women's Perspective on Mission

"For you are all sons[15] of God through faith in Christ Jesus. As many of you as were baptized into Christ have clothed yourselves with Christ. There is no longer Jew or Greek, there is no longer slave or free, there is no longer male and female; for all of you are one in Christ Jesus" (NRSB, alt.).

There are four reasons for choosing this passage as the hermeneutical starting point for a missiology from a women's perspective:

1. Gender stereotypes that would prevent women from sharing in the responsibility for the whole of missionary theory and practice are declared invalid.
2. In Galatians 3, the problem of a gender-based hierarchy is explained as being closely connected with dominance and privilege based on religion, culture, and social and legal status.[16] It is impossible to use Galatians 3 to support the treatment of women's concerns in isolation from racial, religious, cultural and (post-) colonial, economic, and political problems.
3. Galatians 3 offers us a basic structure that is participatory. It therefore refuses to oppose a feminist exclusivity to the patriarchal exclusivity. The goal set by in Galatians 3 is that of women and men together in mission.
4. Of all the Bible texts that motivate women to accept the Christian faith and to join a local congregation, Genesis 1:27 and Galatians 3 are key passages. In many periods of Christian history, women have been more likely than men to accept the Christian faith on their own initiative, and have done so in greater numbers.[17] This step was often connected with women's hope for a concrete change in the situation of their lives. In the light of Galatians 3, they have expected a transformation of human relations within marriage and the family, but above all for the overcoming of gender barriers in the public sphere. The fact that women's experience in the church has often been, and continues to be, entirely at variance with these hopes is another matter altogether. But even within the churches women have drawn and continue to draw courage, by appealing

to Galatians 3 for the struggle against regimentation and restriction. This is another reason to choose this passage as the hermeneutical key.

"In the whole history of interpretation of Galatians, ever since the first Bible commentaries in the early church, only the slightest echo is found of the statement that in Christ's domain 'male and female' is no longer in force," says Thyen.[18] In Galatians 3:28 we meet "without doubt the most radical expression of the new relationship between the sexes which has been established by the Gospel."[19] Has there ever been a corresponding concrete reality in a local church, or has the formula "no longer male and female" been understood, from the beginning, only as a spiritual reality? Concrete historical experiences with the abolition of the three oppositions in Galatians 3:28 have been mentioned as having in fact occurred, in churches such as those in Antioch, Galatia, Corinth, Rome, Thessalonica, or Philippi,[20] although it must be admitted that the actual practice often did not live up to its ideals. As already mentioned, early Christianity in Antioch began by identifying itself as a community of Jews and Greeks, masters and slaves, men and women. The decision of the church at Antioch, moved by the Spirit to redefine theologically the traditional categories of male and female, opened the door to equal rights for women in leading worship, in the life of house communities, and also in spreading the faith beyond the city itself, as traveling missionaries, although to a limited extent.

In the Greek, unlike the nouns "Jew or Greek," the third pair of opposites does not say "man or woman," but rather "male and female." This is in order to take over the exact wording of Genesis 1:27 from its formulation in the Septuagint, thus emphasizing the "new creation" that has taken shape in Christ. The existing world becomes the "old creation," which is under the judgment of the cross on Golgotha (Gal. 6:14). In the exegetical literature there are widely diverging opinions as to how *no longer male and female* should be understood in relation to Genesis 1:27. While some see Galatians 3:28 as an eschatological statement, relating to the future and with no relevance for the present,[21] another line of interpretation sees the seed of the statement in the fundamental reshaping of the relationship between the sexes in the context of the churches being founded.[22] On the side of the latter it can be said that "no longer Jew nor Greek" does have the very concrete implication of giving up circumcision and religious rules about food (Rom. 14:17). What applies to the first opposing pair would have to be applied, by analogy, to the other two pairs.

There are grounds for believing that being baptized into a new humanity had concrete effects on the ways of life of Jews and Greeks, slaves and free citizens, men and women, as well as on community life overall, in the list of greetings at the end of Romans (Rom. 16). Paul sends greetings to people who carried public responsibility in the churches, not least among them those who had missionary assignments. The names in the list of greetings reflect the three pairs of opposites in Galatians 3:28. The functions of church members have been entrusted to them without regard for their religious or cultural background, their legal or social status, or their gender. They include both Jewish[23] and Gentile[24] Christians; those who are free[25] and those who are slaves[26] are mentioned in equal measure. In the same way, women as well as men shared in important functions in the communities. In the list of greetings in Romans 16, it is striking how many women are named: Phoebe, Lydia, Prisca, Mary, Tryphaena and Tryphosa, Persis, but especially the apostle Junia, whom Paul mentions together with the apostle Andronicus as "prominent among the apostles" (Rom. 16:7). In short, "in complete accordance with the tradition in Galatians 3:26-28, no specific gender distinctions were made in the distribution of tasks, either for proclamation of the gospel or within the community."[27]

The basic idea in Galatians 3 corresponds also to Paul's gender ethic as expressed in 1 Corinthians 7. The admonitions to husbands and wives are reciprocal, symmetrical, and egalitarian in their formulation. What is valid in the community should also have weight in the understanding of marriage. We have here horizontal partnerships, an understanding of marriage guided by relationships among brothers and sisters. However, the reciprocating gender ethic in 1 Corinthians 7 and the androcentric formulations in 1 Corinthians 14:33b-35 cannot be harmonized. The tension between these two statements points to a later insertion of 1 Corinthians 14:33b-35 into the text.[28] To sum up:

> The Gentile churches in the Hellenistic Roman cities (documented by name in Antioch, Corinth and Rome) of the first generation of early Christians had a concept of church, which came from the Pauline [...] mission, which treated women and men equally, from planning worship to leadership tasks in the community. This concept is based on the Spirit being given to all, and the concept of marriage as a partnership corresponds with it. The churches were living in a culture in which the image of women in particular was changing. The consequence of this development was that, to some extent, women were allowed more rights than

they had traditionally enjoyed. However, early Christianity does not just appropriate this cultural development, but also gives a theological basis for its position.[29]

## 3. The Ousting of Women from Public Functions and Mission (Pastoral Epistles)

What was it that led over time to the uniformity of the many different congregational structures that existed and at the same time to women being pushed out of public ministries and to their full participation in mission being most effectively curbed? This came about above all as a result of the critical situation early Christianity found itself in at this time of transition in its history. When changed circumstances made it necessary for church life, proclamation, and teaching to be restructured, women's retention of their right to participate in mission was especially endangered. I will give a few examples:

1. The transition from the generation of the apostles to the next generation in the "post-apostolic period" posed the question of whose legacy was to be preserved, by which followers in the Christian faith. During this phase, the change took place from equality of the sexes to the gender hierarchy dominated by men. The same care was not taken, nor interest shown, in transmitting the legacy of women apostles, prophets, and church leaders.

2. The recording of the tradition, that is, the compilation of the teachings and the canon, was entrusted exclusively to men, while women's traditions were increasingly pushed into the background, unseen and unheard, their witness destroyed. They thus gradually disappeared from the memory of church history.

3. A critical phase for the equality of men's and women's roles was the transition from house churches to the gathering of congregations in public buildings or basilicas, through which the *oikos* lost its public function.[30] The growth of Christianity made it necessary for the churches to move into public space. On being moved out of private homes, worship life had to adapt to the behavior expected by society, and especially to adapt to the rules of conduct of the public sphere. Now it became much more difficult for the churches to preserve the principle of equality of Galatians 3:26-28 than it had been in the discreet space of private homes.

4. In order not to endanger the spread of the faith, church officers sought to avoid everything possible that could cause offence in the society. This included especially offences against the well-established cultural rules on gender roles.[31] For the sake of expanding their mission, local churches decided to adapt to the surrounding culture and patriarchal gender stereotypes. Not least among the things that were sacrificed to this inculturation process was gender justice in the distribution of mission work; women had to withdraw from important areas of mission.

The combined effects of the different transitions brought forth the derogatory statements about women in 1 Timothy, which soon became the model for the relationship between the sexes in the lives of individuals and of the church. The post-Pauline congregational rule expressed here had serious consequences, not least of all for the role of women in missions (cf. esp. 1 Tim. 2:8-15, as well as 1 Cor. 14:33b-35). 1 Timothy tied the leadership and worship functions to the male sex, and these were then structurally anchored in the emerging order of offices in the church. Timothy appears in 1 Timothy as defender of the true apostolic teaching (1 Tim. 1:3-7, 18f; 3:14; 4:6, 12-16). In contrast, women are enjoined to submission and silence, forbidden to teach in the church. Their exclusion from responsibility in the church is substantiated by their alleged constitutional inferiority (1 Tim. 2:13-15; 5:2-16). This assessment of women corresponded to the role accorded to them in society, which was related to tasks in the home such as childbearing, bringing up children, keeping house, and in general, serving others. The household codes established in the post-apostolic period (Col. 3:18-4.1; Eph. 5:22-6.9; 1 Pet. 2:18-3.7) demand conduct of men and women which, in contrast to 1 Corinthians 7, is asymmetrical and irreversible; the wife is to obey her husband, while he is to exercise his superior rank lovingly (Col. 3:18-19). The social and gender image of the Pastoral Epistles corresponded to the ordering of congregational life—and vice versa.

A consequence of these developments was a gender-specific distribution of missionary work, which corresponded to the division in the ancient world between household (*oikos*) and public sphere (*polis*). Within the household, women received a specific mission, that of passing on the faith to their husbands (if they were not believers), their children and servants, and other women. In the public sphere, however, mission work took on a form that was accessible only to men, and was influenced and further developed only by their thinking. It included various mission areas: for example in encounters with other men in the marketplace (*agora*), in various occupational domains such as business, the military, and public office, and in all the extensive geographical areas where itinerant missionaries traveled and came into contact with people of other cultures, languages, and religions.

Increasingly during the later early Christian period and the beginnings of formal church history, there was an adaptation of church life and church order to the division of society in the ancient world, so that the churches too made an increasing distinction between their *public* life and the *private* life of Christians in house communities. Women were still allowed to participate in worship, but were no longer allowed to speak. What was especially fateful for women's mission was that their share in responsibility for *public* proclamation, the teaching of the church, baptism, and the Eucharist was, over time, taken away from them altogether. They no longer had any part in leadership. The only public task in mission that they retained was witnessing to the faith through service, practiced especially in caring for the sick, visiting people in prison, and ministering to the needs of the poor and hungry. Not least of all, the restriction on women's freedom of movement had a sustained effect on their mission activities. The condition of itinerant ascetic missionary, which had always been open to women only in exceptional cases, now became entirely the domain of men.

To sum up: the New Testament canon already shows the development of gendered mission, with the consequence that women were shut out of essential aspects of mission. Above all though, on the pretext of gender difference and the separation of the household from the public spheres, as prescribed by society, it was access to the *public* dimensions of mission that was largely closed to women. This process in turn had consequences for the understanding of mission, which was henceforth dominated by the male perspective. It led to the following:

- a one-sided orientation of mission thinking toward sending people out, spreading the faith, and winning new members, at the expense of practical missionary service, participation and just gender relations;
- a priority on control, regimentation, and discipline in the life of local churches, at the expense of diversity and letting the Spirit move, within Christianity; and

- primacy of men in training for church offices, at the expense of participatory concepts of ministry that could include women.

## 4. Biblical Perspectives on Women's Impact in Mission

Using four examples from the New Testament canon, in the light of Galatians 3.28 I shall sketch out some perspectives on a feminist, participatory theology of mission.[32]

### 4.1 Mary, Who Received the Message of Liberation and Shared It with Elizabeth in the Magnificat (Luke 1:25-56)

The logical reason for and beginning of mission is not the sending out of believing messengers, but rather the *receiving* of a liberating message. The first missionary "act" of Mary consists in receiving a great promise from the angel, and saying Yes to it: "Let it be with me according to your word" (Luke 1:38). Mary is called "Mother of the Church" among Christians above all because she trusted in this promise and said Yes to God's liberating message. The new thing that breaks into her life owes nothing to the will of any man, neither does she set it up herself as her plan for her life. It is a promise, coming from outside, and not one that either human beings or churches can give themselves.

After her first missionary act, Mary goes to see Elizabeth. In Elizabeth's house the first missionary conversation takes place, "woman to woman." The two women share their insights received from visions and appearances. Mary proclaims the mighty deeds of God. A conversation happening between women, entirely outside the public sphere, but of explosive political significance; its subject is no less than the turning upside down of social, economic, and political conditions, the lifting up of the lowly, and the preferential option for the poor. These are the politics of a new world order—today we would say, of global governance—that puts an end to the grasping of the power-hungry who want to rule the world. This women's discourse holds a vision of good governance under which justice and life in its fullness are made possible for all the needy.

## 4.2 The Samaritan Woman with a Message of Emancipation for Her World (John 4:5-42)

In the tradition of the ancient church, the woman from the Samaritan town of Sychar, whose name, according to Eastern Orthodox tradition, was Photeina, is revered as the very first person (not just the first woman missionary) to proclaim the gospel. Origen calls her an apostle; on fire with Jesus' words to her at the well, she proclaimed Christ to the inhabitants of her town. Even in the eleventh century, this Samaritan woman was still being called an apostle.[33] Theophylact describes her as receiving "priestly consecration" and as being the "teacher of the whole city."[34] Thus in the texts of ancient church fathers, the memory of women's mission as having a public character has been preserved, that is, at least a part of the church could later recognize, in the Samaritan woman's mission, public proclamation, teaching, and even priestly office.

The meeting of the Samaritan woman with Jesus at the well is the beginning of emancipation and a new way of life for this woman. Whatever her previous history may have been, it is certain that she was imprisoned within a culturally established, hierarchical gender system, which kept her in economic, bodily, and psychological dependence on men. Perhaps she was involved in institutionalized prostitution, but possibly also in the tradition of "chain marriage," in which a widow was married after her husband's death to a relative of his.[35] In the encounter with Jesus and in discussing the philosophy of life with him, she comes to a new insight about herself. This key experience awakens hidden capabilities in her. It is the beginning of an emancipated way of life, in which she makes use of her ability to think for herself and to act accordingly. She finds the courage to go and speak publicly in her home town. In her speech she passes on her insight to others, and moves them to go and see for themselves what they have heard, and to gain insight using their own intellectual powers.

## 4.3 Junia and Prisca with a Mission ad extra

Junia is the first in a line of women missionaries predating even Paul's time and continuing well into the history of early Christianity. Her tradition has been preserved especially by Eastern Orthodoxy and is still remembered today. It is about women taking part in the "first proclamation" of the gospel *ad extra*. In Romans 16:7, Paul mentions Junia from Jerusalem, who worked as a missionary together with Andronicus and helped to found new churches.[36] The women named in the New Testament as having worked in public, however, did not experience their public activity primarily as work done outside the already existing churches among the non-Christian nations. For them, to work outside meant mainly that they took the step outside the home, into the public space of the church community. It called on them to be present, visibly and audibly, outside the private sphere, to act in the face of well-established gender stereotypes, to proclaim their faith publicly, to teach in public, to take part in passing on the tradition, in administration of the sacraments and in church leadership tasks.

## 4.4 *Mary Magdalene with a Mission* ad intra (*John 20:11-18*)

What was the message that the risen Christ entrusted to Mary Magdalene, whom Augustine called the "apostle to the apostles"? "Go to my brothers and say to them, 'I am ascending to my Father and your Father, to my God and your God" (John 20:17). In the 1992 International Review of Mission concentrating on "Women in Mission," the African theologian Teresa Okure summarized the core message that the apostle Mary brought to the community, especially to its leaders, as follows:

> (But) now for the first time, the disciples are given to understand, through the message entrusted to Mary Magdalene, that they and Jesus now share the same parent or ground of being in God. [...] Equally importantly, the statement declares that in Jesus believers now have a new relationship to one another [...] They relate to one another in Jesus as blood brothers and sisters relate to one another.[37]

In John 20, the basic idea of Galatians 3 is made visible. Through their relationship to the risen Christ, those who were previously masters and slaves become sisters and brothers "in Christ," just as they become daughters and sons of God. The content of the mission of Mary Magdalene is the paradigm shift of brotherly and sisterly, egalitarian relations in the community. Thus she is the prototype of the missionary who is sent *ad intra*. The main thrust of her message, addressed to the responsible leaders of the community, is that they have to align themselves with the spirit of brotherhood and sisterhood. The meaning of *ad intra* is: "Take the message you are passing on to others seriously for yourselves as well." The consequences for the public life of the church, for the structure and the understanding of its ministries, are obvious. In order that a non-hierarchical understanding of its public existence can grow within the church, an understanding that includes issues of gender, there must not only be men who are active in mission, but women as well. In the above-mentioned issue, Aruna Gnanadason writes:

> Too often when women speak up, their voices are viewed as being confrontational or as demands for token representation in power positions. It becomes important for women to express more clearly whether this is in fact the case. Is it merely an attempt to get to centres of decision making and administration in order to play the role that men have been playing, or is it something more than that, that women are claiming? A reading of history underlines that at every stage. Women's cry for a more participatory and inclusive church and community rests on their longing for a church more responsive to the prophetic role it has to play in the midst of bleeding humanity. Women who have traditionally and willingly taken on a caring, nurturing role in the family, in the church, and in society, call for an evaluation of these roles in a church and society that so desperately needs them. There is a demand for setting the ecumenical house in order, stripping it of its hierarchical and crippling institutionalism, so that it could indeed be a movement of concerned and involved men and women engaged in a ministry of healing and reconciliation.[38]

The sending of Mary Magdalene "to the brothers of Jesus" has further consequences in regard to historical and contemporary mission. Sisterhood and brotherhood "in Christ" also applies to the way Christians live their lives in marriage and family, and to their dealings with employees in their homes and workplaces. It is not acceptable for their private conduct to be left to one side or to be kept separate from that which concerns the church community as a whole. When this is accepted, it leads to a double standard that is the source of unbearable situations for women, when members or clergy of the church keep up the appearance of respectability for public purposes, but at home are unfaithful to their marriages or use violence against their wives and children.[39] Violence in any form whatever should no longer be kept secret[40] but must be accounted for in the public space of the community. This also is part of women's mission *ad intra*, that they contribute toward keeping public awareness for injustice that takes place in private anchored in the consciousness of the church.

Thus, we arrive at the present day and at current perspectives of a women's missiology. In addition to the concept of public mission we also need a "missiology of the house." What might the cornerstones of an *oikos*-missiology be from women's point of view? One would be to rebuild the private sphere of the house upon the basis that, in the light of Galatians 3:28, it too should be free of the hierarchical gender stereotypes of "male and female." Another cornerstone is that the house and the public sphere need to be arranged in such a way as to be much more part of each other. Hermetically sealing off the private sphere from the outside does protect it from state interference and social control, from churches for example. It can however, also lead to increasing violence against the weakest in the household community. It is well known that in all world's societies of today, violence increases behind the excuse that what takes place in the home is of no public concern. The only thing that can help to bring about gender justice in the area of the *oikos*, is public scrutiny and raising the consciousness of the church in terms of its official awareness of the issues raised by wrongs that take place in the (Christian) house. Basic human rights concepts that were formulated in the twentieth century for individual states and the United Nations, in other words for the different spheres of public life, should not be left outside the front door with the result that the house degenerates into a space where laws do not apply.

## 5. Women in Mission in the Early Church

In discussion of the biblical basis for a women's theology of mission noncanonic texts of the second century and sources from post-biblical times should not be disregarded. This inevitably means confronting the basic issue of scripture and tradition. Surely on the question of women's missions, the gospel has something to say that goes beyond the canon and beyond the traditions of the institutional church, which asserted its authority over against alleged "heresies" and "false teachings" in this area. In the speeches of highly regarded church fathers reviling women who baptized, administered the Eucharist, taught, wrote and worked as missionaries, do we not hear a contempt for women, which contradicts the gospel? In the light of Galatians 3, I consider it imperative that we uncover the buried and often mutilated testimonies of women who functioned as missionaries, and recall them to mind.[41] Here are a few examples:

1. In the second century, Thecla traveled as a missionary to Seleucia-Ctesiphon,[42] where she "enlightened many

through the Word of God," as the *Acts of Thecla* says. In the basilica dedicated to her, she was revered for centuries as the founder of the Christian community.[43] The *Acts of Thecla*, written on the model of the Book of Acts, was already very controversial in the second century. Tertullian was annoyed "that women in Carthage appealed to this apostle and martyr to legitimize their activities as Christian teachers."[44] Thecla's missionary work in the public sphere offended against gender rules for women. To make travel easier, she dressed "in the manner of men"; she defended herself against sexual advances from an influential man, was then thrown to wild animals and was not devoured. She remained unmarried all her life.

2. A prophetic movement developed in the second century around the North African teacher Montanus, which appealed to Galatians 3:28 in allowing women access to all offices in the church, including those of priest and bishop. While the male-only episcopate was being established in the main church, the "New Prophecy" movement held to the charismatic order which assumed the equality of all members of the community, even though certain offices were only exercised by a few. In the mid-third century, a woman prophet of this movement whose name is not known managed to hold the community together as persecution was beginning. She also baptized and celebrated the Eucharist, and was recognized in doing so by those holding offices in the church. However, the "prophet church" finally broke with the main church over her. An indignant report on this event from the opposing side says:

3. "This woman [...] had often dared to act as though her invocation could not be disparaged as she blessed the bread and performed the Eucharistic celebration, bringing the sacrifice before God, (not) without the usual formulas of the sacrament; she also baptized many, using the right and customary words of interrogation, so that she was not seen to deviate from the rules of the church in any matter. What should we now say about these baptisms, in which the worst of demons was baptising, through a woman?"[45]

4. In the early Christian period, we continually come across women who were called "teachers" (*didaskaloi*)—despite the New Testament forbidding women's teaching. Even in the main church there were women teachers who were important for spiritual life, such as Macrina, the sister and teacher of the Cappadocians Gregory of Nyssa and Basil of

Caesarea. Philomena worked in Rome in the second century as female head of a school and was close to Gnosticism; her teachings have been recorded by a pupil, Apelles. Tertullian fought against her because she as a woman dared to teach and because he did not agree with her teachings. In the *Didaskalia* he said that if women did any teaching, it should be confined to other women. Jerome wrote polemics against interpreters of the Bible, "who—it's scandalous!—are learning from women what they ought to be taught by men."[46] The work of women as writers was also branded by the main church as an activity women should not be allowed to perform. As Christianization of the Mediterranean progressed, teaching women disappeared from the public sphere in the Christian communities. From then on, women could preserve certain autonomy in teaching only within women's monastic communities.

Women who wanted to participate in public missions developed new ways of living, together with other women or even with men. Traces of this can already be seen in the New Testament. There were communities of women, such as that of the sisters Mary and Martha (John 11:1-46)[47] or that of Tryphaena and Tryphosa (Rom. 16:12). That Junia is mentioned together with Andronicus (Rom. 16:7) indicates either a married couple who were missionaries or a missionary community of unmarried persons. Besides married couples who traveled on mission, there were also ascetically oriented couples who lived together freely, practicing abstinence.[48] The lifestyle of those known as *syneisacti*[49] was an attempt by both sexes to live together as sisters and brothers. The model for behavior of the sexes toward one another was Gal. 3:28, which was interpreted as anticipating the absence of sexuality in heaven.[50]

But these new ways of living, typified by participation in mission, were also resisted by the main church, for example by Chrysostom or by Cyprian, who accused the Bishop of Antioch of not fighting against the *syneisacti*, and even of living together with two of them. It was not that these two church fathers suspected those they were criticizing of being unchaste; they were more afraid of the scandal it might cause to the pagan public, and not least of the negative effects this might have on the work of spreading the faith, of mission.[51]

To sum up: Participatory mission in the spirit of Galatians 3 was, in the end, denied to women in the early church. They could not prevent the gender hierarchy of their time, in conjunction with the hierarchical division of public and private spheres, from finally putting an end to just gender relationships in mission. However, we may be grateful for the courage of women in the early church and afterwards who prepared the way for women's mission in the public sphere. Even in the ancient world there were women and also men who employed a liberation theology hermeneutic in reading the Scriptures. They received the message of the gospel with a critical approach to the Bible. They read the New Testament not only as a written witness to the incarnation of the Good News, but also as documentation for the fact that the Good News is not immune to betrayal. We today can pick up this (subversive) tradition in the biblical hermeneutic of the ancient church, and try to see the role of women in mission with new eyes.

## Further Reading

Anne Jensen, *God's Self-Confident Daughters: Early Christianity and the Liberation of Women* (Westminster: John Knox Press, 1996, translated by O. C. Dean).
Elisabeth Schüssler-Fiorenza, *In Memory of Her: A Feminist Reconstruction of Christian Origins* (London: SCM, 1983).

## Endnotes

1. This is a slightly revised version of the article: "The Biblical Foundation for a Feminist and Participatory Theology of Mission," published in *International Review of Mission*, vol. 93, no. 368 (January 2004), 17-34. I am grateful to the editors of IRM for the permission to reprint it in this volume.

2. For example: apostle, witness, sending, proclamation, toil (*kopian*: to labor hard in the context of mission).

3. The broad spectrum of meanings of the word "apostle" in the New Testament is revealing in this regard; see Jürgen Roloff, article "Apostel / Apostolat / Apostolizität I (Neues Testament)," in *Theologische Realenzyklopädie*, vol. 3 (Berlin: W. de Gruyter, 1978): 430-445.

4. Regarding the philosophical roots of the public sphere in antiquity, see Lucian Hölscher, "Öffentlichkeit" in *Geschichtliche Grundbegriffe. Historisches Lexikon zur politisch-sozialen Sprache in Deutschland*, vol. 4 (Stuttgart: Clett-Cotta, 1978), 413-467.

5. For the following, unless otherwise indicated, see especially Jürgen Becker, "Die Mitwirkung der Frau in den urchristlichen Gemeinden," *Materialdienst des Konfessionskundlichen Instituts Bensheim* (Germany), 2 (1999), 23-31.

6. Missions to the *ethne* (nations/peoples, or *heathens* [Gentiles]).

7. The Apostles' Council, see Acts 15; Gal. 2.

8. Ekkehard W. Stegemann and Wolfgang Stegemann, *Urchristliche Sozialgeschichte. Die Anfänge im Judentum und die Christusgemeinde in der Mediterrane Welt* (Stuttgart u.a.: Kohlhammer, 1995), 339.

9. In reference to Mark 15:40ff, see, for example, Luise Schottroff "Wanderprophetinnen. Eine feministische Analyse der Logienquelle,"

in *Evangelische Theologie*, 51, (1991): 332-344; Stegemann and Stegemann, *Urchristliche Sozialgeschichte*, 329. They do not think that women's participation in the wanderings of the Jesus movement would have been a breach of the patriarchal norms of Judaism.

10. See Mark 10:43f; cf. Becker, "Mitwirkung der Frau," 25.

11. For further information on house communities in early Christianity, see Roger W. Gehring, *Hausgemeinde und Mission. Die Bedeutung antiker Häuser und Hausgemeinschaften von Jesus bis Paulus* (Giessen: Brunnen-Verlag, 2000); Peter Wick, *Die Urchristlichen Gottesdienste. Entstehung und Entwicklung im Rahmen der frühjüdischen Tempel – Synagogen und Hausfrömmigkeit* (Stuttgart: Kohlhammer, 2002).

12. Becker, "Mitwirkung der Frau," 29.

13. Klaus Thraede, "Ärger mit der Freiheit. Die Bedeutung von Frauen in Theorie und Praxis der alten Kirche," in *"Freunde in Christus werden." Die Beziehung von Mann und Frau als Frage an Theologie und Kirche*, ed.; Gerta Scharffenorth and Klaus Thraede (Gelnhausen: Burckhardthaus-Verlag, 1977), 31-182; Hartwig Thyen, "nicht mehr männlich und weiblich, Eine Studie zu Galater 3:28," in *Als Mann und Frau geschaffen. Exegetische Studien zur Rolle der Frau*, ed.; Frank Crüsemann and Hartwig Thyen (Gelnhausen: Burckhardthaus-Verlag, 1987), 107-197.

14. See Thyen, "Studie zu Galater," 189ff. The history of women's missions in the nineteenth and early twentieth centuries shows that women's access to mission in the public sphere was usually denied on the basis of 1 Corinthians 14:34 and 1 Timothy 2:11. See Mary T. Huber and Nancy C. Lutkehaus, ed., *Gendered Missions: Women and Men in Missionary Discourse and Practice* (Ann Arbor: University of Michigan Press, 1999).

15. What Paul wants to try and express with the word "son" is the maturity of those who are freed from being under guardianship. Because of this liberation "male and female" are no longer valid definitions. Therefore believers of both sexes are "sons" for Paul. See Thyen, "Studie zu Galater," 127.

16. The distinction between slave and free implied a different legal status as well as a different place in society.

17. This was, however, not the case in the first wave of missionary activity in the nineteenth century. As long as only men did mission, then the majority of converts were men, as there was no access to those spheres of life where women were, for local cultural reasons.

18. Thyen, "Studie zu Galater," 116.

19. Ibid.

20. Ibid., 133-134; Becker, "Mitwirkung der Frau," 26; Elisabeth Schüssler-Fiorenza, *In Memory of Her: A Feminist Reconstruction of Christian Origins* (London: SCM, 1983).

21. " 'There is no longer man or woman,' does nothing to affect the natural order as such, but teaches an eschatological abolition of differences which happens 'in Christ,' in his body, with regard to salvation," says Conzelmann in Hans Conzelmann, *Der erste Brief an die Korinther* (Göttingen: Vandenhoeck & Ruprecht, 1969), 22.

22. Thyen, "Studie zu Galater"; Schüssler-Fiorenza, *Memory of Her*; Becker, "Mitwirkung der Frau" among others. As Brigitte Kahl says, "Paul gives Jewish monotheism a radical, universally-inclusive and anti-hierarchical definition. Christ becomes the 'germ cell' of a pluralist society of the children of Abraham, extending across the boundaries between old national, religious, social and gender identities." Brigitte Kahl, "Der Brief an die Gemeinden

in Galatien. Vom Unbehagen der Geschlechter und anderen Problemen des Andersseins," in *Kompendium Feministische Bibelauslegung*, eds.; Luise Schottroff and Marie-Theres Wacker (Gütersloh: Gütersloher Verlagshaus, 2nd ed., 1999), 603-611 (607).

23. Prisca, Aquila, Junia, Andronicus, Herodion. According to Becker it is possible to draw conclusions as to Jewish or Gentile origin from the names and other data. Becker, "Mitwirkung der Frau," 27.

24. Phoebe, Epaenetus, Ampliatus, Urbanus, Stachys, Apelles, among others.

25. Phoebe, Aquila, Prisca, Rufus, among others.

26. Ampliatus, among others.

27. Becker, "Mitwirkung der Frau," 28.

28. According to Thyen, "Studie zu Galater," 186f, as well as Becker, "Mitwirkung der Frau," 30.

29. Becker, "Mitwirkung der Frau," 29.

30. The first Christian basilicas were erected in the fourth century by Constantine. Before this Christians came together in private houses, which had been changed to accommodate meetings. On this subject, see Gehring, *Hausgemeinde und Mission*.

31. In the Epistles there are eloquent examples of admonitions to women to keep their appearance respectable at public worship, not to be conspicuous or expose their husbands: cf. 1 Cor. 11:5f, 13-16; 1 Cor. 14:33*b*-35.

32. For an overview of feminist biblical hermeneutics, compare Annette Noller, *Feministische Hermeneutik: Wege einer neuen Schriftauslegung* (Neukirchen-Vluyn: Neukirchener Verlag, 1995).

33. Cf. Theophylact, Archbishop of Bulgaria (ca. 1050–1108), in an interpretation of John 4.28ff (PG 123, 1241D).

34. Origen: *Comm. St. John* 4.26f (SC 222,126); 4.28 (SC222, 132); see also Ute E. Eisen, *Amtsträgerinnen im frühen Christentum. Epigraphische und literarische Studien* (Göttingen: Vandenhoeck & Ruprecht, 1996), 56.

35. The dominant interpretation prefers to describe the Samaritan woman as characterized by sexual greed and incontinence. Feminist biblical exegesis, however, rightly brings in other possibilities of interpretation, such as the seven-fold Levirate marriage mentioned in Mark 12:18-27, which legitimized "chain marriage" under the Torah; cf. Ruth Habermann, "Das Evangelium nach Johannes. Orte der Frauen," in *Kompendium Feministische Bibelauslegung*, ed. Luise Schottroff and Marie-Theres Wacker (Gütersloh: Gütersloher Verlagshaus, 2nd ed., 1999), 527-541 (531).

36. In a commentary by Chrysostom on Romans 16:7, we read: "Oh, and how great is this woman's philosophy, that she was deemed worthy to be counted among the apostles." Chrysostom, *In epis. ad Rom. homil.* 31,2 (PG 60.669f) quoted in Eisen, *Amtsträgerinnen*, 51. In the liturgy of the Byzantine church, Junia is revered to this day as an apostle, being included in the menology or lives of the saints along with fifty-six apostles and "two who were the equal of apostles," Mary Magdalene and Thecla.

37. Teresa Okure, "The significance today of Jesus' commission to Mary Magdelene," *International Review of Mission*, vol. 322 (1992): 177-188.

38. Aruna Gnanadason, "Women in the Ecumenical Movement," *International Review of Mission*, vol. 322 (1992): 237-246.

39. On the subject of violence in the private sphere, see, as representative of other research on the subject, Mary John Mananzan, ed., *Women Resisting Violence: Spirituality for Life* (Maryknoll: Orbis Books, 1994), 39-86.

40. Aruna Gnanadason, *No Longer a Secret: The Church and Violence against Women* (Geneva: World Council of Churches, 1993).

41. Most of the relevant sources were made available by Adolf von Harnack at the beginning of the twentieth century. See Adolf von Harnack, *Die Mission und Ausbreitung des Christentums in den ersten drei Jahrhunderten,* 4th edition (Leipzig: VMA-Verlag, 1924, 11912). On the following remarks, see esp. Anne Jensen, *Frauen im frühen Christentum* (Bern: Peter Lang, 2002); also Anne Jensen, *Gottes selbstbewusste Töchter. Frauenemazipation im frühen Christentum?* (Freiburg/Br.: Herder, 1992) the book has been published also in English: *God's Self-Confident Daughters. Early Christianity and the Liberation of Women* (Westminster: John Knox Press, 1996, translated by O. C. Dean); Anne Jensen, *Thekla – die Apostolin. Ein apokrypher Text neu entdeckt* (Freiburg/Br: Herder, 1995).

42. Today the town of Ayatecla/Meriamlik, about 30 km from Baghdad.

43. Jensen, *Thekla*, 117f.

44. Anne Jensen, "Die Theklageschichte. Die Apostolin zwischen Fiktion und Realität," in *Kompendium Feministischer Bibelauslegung*, ed. Luise Schottroff and Marie Theres Wacker (Gütersloh: Gütersloher Verlagshaus, 2nd ed., 1999), 742-747, 742.

45. Letter from Cyprian of Carthage, written after 250; cf. Cyprian, Epistle 75, 10ff., quoted in Jensen, *Frauen im frühen Christentum*, 63, 65.

46. Jensen, *Frauen im frühen Christentum*, XXXVI.

47. Mary and Martha may have held offices in the church, or worked together as missionaries; cf. Habermann, "Das Evangelium nach Johannes," 535.

48. Jensen, *Frauen im frühen Christentum*, XXX.

49. "Syneisacti" means, literally translated, those who are brought in together.

50. The abstinent lifestyles adopted by both men and women often took the form of "spiritual marriage" without sexual relations. However, this did not always indicate hostility to sex. A motive for abstinence was a decision not to have children, who would have been a hindrance to itinerant mission work. However, "there was room for loving one another" (Jensen, *Frauen im frühen Christentum*, XXXIf).

51. On this whole matter see Jensen, *Frauen im frühen Christentum*, XXXI (with the sources indicated).

CHAPTER 2

# Women's Absence and Presence in the History and Records of Christian Mission

## Historical Survey of Women in Mission

*Christine Lienemann-Perrin, Atola Longkumer, Marilú Rojas Salazar, Karla Ann Koll, Afrie Songco Joye, Cathy Ross*

In this introductory chapter we are adopting the concept of the *Historiography of World Christianity* as it has been developed by Andrew F. Walls.[1] The chapter may be regarded as a contribution to the Studies on World Christianity. Dale T. Irvin, another historian of World Christianity, explains the purpose and aspirations of the Studies on World Christianity as follows:

> The study of World Christianity is [...] an emerging field that investigates and seeks to understand Christian communities, faith, and practice as they are found on six continents, expressed in diverse ecclesial traditions, and informed by the multitude of historical and cultural experiences in a world that for good or ill is rapidly globalizing. It is concerned with both the diversity of local or indigenous expressions of Christian life and faith throughout the world, and the variety of ways these interact with one another critically and constructively across time and space. It is particularly concerned with under-represented and marginalized communities of faith, resulting in a greater degree of attention being paid to Asian, African, and Latin American experiences; the experience of marginalized communities within the North Atlantic world; and the experiences of women throughout the world.[2]

This chapter is aiming at a concise view of and introduction to the history of several hundred years of transmission and appropriation of Christian faith, focusing on the role of women in it. All six main world regions have been chosen for the following historical sketch: Europe, Africa, Asia, North America, South America, and Oceania. Some regions, however, are mentioned only sporadically or are omitted entirely because it was not possible to find authors ready to write a contribution. Negative answers were explained by the lack of written records. Orthodox Christianity in Eastern Europe and the Middle East is affected most by that lack. Investigation on women's missionary impact in the history of the Orthodox world is a task for future study and research.

# 1. Europe

Since concepts and strategies of mission in Europe have become a model for mission expanded to other continents, it is worthwhile to have a close look at the European mission history—even more so if we try to understand the impact on women's presence and absence in it.

## 1.1 Christianizing Europe in Fifteen Centuries

The Christianization of Europe has been accomplished only in the sixteenth century when the last parts of Lithuania became Christian.[3] From that time on, missionary endeavors in Europe shifted to other continents:[4] to the New World, as the Americas were called, and to Africa and Asia. Mission was thereafter embedded in, and to a great extent shaped by, colonial expansion—a context that will be looked at in the case study on Europe.[5] What follows here are some spotlights on the extension of the Latin Church from the fourth to the sixteenth century in Western Europe and some further remarks on Roman Catholic woman's mission in the seventeenth century.

When the Roman Empire expanded to the "barbarian tribes" in other parts of Europe, Christianity, too, reached the conquered regions, namely the territories of Ireland and the British Islands, France, Germany, Switzerland, and Austria. Many churches, chapels, and places of pilgrimage have been erected in these territories during the first four centuries of Christianity. The fall of Rome in A.D. 410 introducing the decline of the Roman Empire did not imply the end of Latin Christianity. In fact, the heritage of Rome as a ruling center continued to exist in the claim of the Roman church for spiritual leadership over the whole Christian realm—West *and* East.[6] The sixth to the eighth centuries were a time of political and social turbulence, caused by invading "barbarian" nations (Huns and Vandals) in the territories of Franks and Germans.

The period of turbulence, called Dark Centuries, ended with Charlemagne. His coronation in 800 by the Pope in Aachen, an old city on today's border between Germany and France, marked the beginning of the Holy Roman Empire of the German Nation, which lasted about one thousand years. After his death, the vast territories of Charlemagne's empire were split into three parts: France, Burgundy, and the German areas, whereupon Burgundy later was integrated partly into France, partly into Germany, Switzerland, and Italy. Throughout the Middle Ages, Christianity was further established in the cities but also extended to the countrysides by many monasteries erected in remote places. Local princes, kings, and other rulers opted for the Christian faith, followed by the subjects of their territories by mass conversions. Religious conversion of political subjects was neither a question of personal choice nor necessarily a case of coercion although violence and coercion have been executed in some cases as, for example, the Christianization of the Saxons, which was even extremely violent.

## 1.2 Difficulties of Recalling the Roles of European Women in the Transmission of Faith

"Women are lost in the androcentric readings of history," writes Mary T. Malone in her comprehensive opus *Women and Christianity*.[7] The chroniclers of the ancient church and the church in the European Middle Ages are providing sparsely— if any—information on women's role in mission. In 1924, the famous church historian, Adolf von Harnack, has contributed substantially to illuminate the women's part in the transmission of faith in Europe during the first three centuries.[8] European church history and European mission history have been treated for a long time as separate fields of research and teaching—the later treated as an appendix of the former. A new approach was launched in 1974, when three church historians started the project *Church History as Mission History*. After having reached the Early Middle Ages the project was, however, abandoned. Moreover, women are almost completely absent in these volumes.[9] Instead, the role of women in European's mission history comes to the fore in the publications by Mary T. Malone: *Women and Christianity* and Susan E. Smith: *Women in Mission*.[10] But even these books have their limitations since historical sources and records on women are limited, in most cases, on women of nobility who formed a small minority of the whole populace. Therefore wives, slaves, women of lower classes who were the main actors in the European mission field, will remain in the dark and unknown forever.

## 1.3 Mapping the Spaces of Ancient and Middle Age Societies

The constraints hindering women to participate in European mission throughout hundreds of years were a result of how the European society was shaped by different spheres of individual and social life. A dualistic divide of spheres of living, working, training, and leadership achieved, again and again, prevalence against the efforts of women to overcome these dualities. An oversimplified picture of the divide constituting the most serious stumbling block for missionary-minded women looks like this:

| Women's world | Men's world |
|---|---|
| Sphere of "the house" | Public sphere |
| Immobility | Mobility in public sphere |
| Invisibility to outside world | Visibility in public sphere |
| Inaudibility to outside world | Audibility in public sphere |
| No access to power outside the house | Access to power in politics, legislation, formal education |
| Wife's mission field: members of the "house" including children and domestic workers | Men's mission field: public spaces including the church |
| Nuns: cloister (separated from the public) as a substitute for "the house" | Monks: monasteries with open access to public space |
| Worship: Pews | Worship: exclusive access to altar and pulpit |
| Church leadership positions: absence from ruling positions | Church leadership positions: canon law, ordained ministry, clerical hierarchy |

The overall aim of women's missionary activities in Europe mission history was again and again to overcome these dualistic divides, to get access to the public sphere in society, church, and mission, and to explore forms of an encounter between men and women beyond sexual relations as a precondition for their cooperation in public mission. These aims were, according to women called to mission, non-negotiables for their own missionary involvement. What follows are some spotlights on women's absence and presence in European mission history. A combination of a typological and diachronic approach is most suitable for showing the characteristics of the achievements and constraints of women's mission in Europe.

## 1.4 Women as Martyrs (Deaconesses, Widows, Virgins)

The first and most famous faith witnesses in the Early Church were the martyrs who resisted apostasy. Remarkably, in being exposed to martyrdom by torture and killing, Christian witnesses of both genders, of all classes and nations were treated as equals by the authorities of the Roman Empire. Furthermore, martyrdom was carried out in public areas and exposed to the public. It is an irony that women got access to the public sphere only as martyrs. Contrary to the aims of their perpetrators, their witness contributed widely to the dissemination of the Christian faith. And—another exception in mission history—the life, torture, and death of women martyrs has been recorded together with male witnesses. Blandina, Perpetua, and Felicitas are well-known martyrs of the second and third centuries. They later became venerated as Saints in Orthodoxy and in the Latin Church.[11]

After the fall of Rome in A.D. 410 by the Visigoths and Alarich, the center of gravity of Christianity slowly "moved from the city to the country, from the palace to the monastery, from the south and east to the north and west, and from the Latins and Greeks to the Germans and Celts."[12] Throughout that period Christian women were expected to transmit their faith within the boundaries of their realm: among the (heathen) husbands, the children, and domestic workers. Their role in the transmission of faith in Europe cannot be overestimated. Some outstanding women of nobility were most important in the crosscultural mission of Europe. The Burgundian princess Clotilde (475–545) blending in her own person two cultures, two languages, and two faiths, moved her husband, the Frank King Clovis, to adopt Catholic Christianity as the first "barbarian" ruler in Europe. Clovis then introduced the Christian faith among his subjects during the fifth century. Likewise, Queen Berta of Kent (539–612) and Princess Ethelburga of Kent (d. 647) were influential Christians with a substantial share of shaping the Christianization of Europe and introducing Christianity in their context.[13]

The four centuries between the fall of Rome and Charlemagne were times of wars and social disorder. While "normal" structures of human living broke down, these Dark Ages brought a chance for women to explore new niches in social life. Since living as singles on their own was inconceivable in these times, they established new forms of community life. Following the model of coinobites,[14] unmarried women and widows of nobility lived together to fulfill charitable work among poor people. Later on, these communities found their way in monasteries. During the times of social disturbance, women living in monasteries were not prevented to fulfill their charitable work outside. Joining a monastery opened the opportunity for women to ameliorate their social status and to reach to a certain degree their intellectual, spiritual, and cultural autonomy. Even more rights were conceded to abbesses insofar as they were allowed to teach, to execute canon law, and to assign land titles to clergymen.[15] Some of them were even vested with the insignia of bishops: crozier and mitre. In some cases, abbesses ruled as heads of so-called double monasteries for nuns *and* monks. Hilda (614–680) became the first abbess of the double monastery in Whitby. It became a great center of learning and an essential feature for the rooting of the Christian faith in Britain. Hilda "was guided principally by the scriptures in the setting up of her monastery. The old egalitarian ideal of equality between women and men seemed to return for a while in this well-run double monastery."[16]

## 1.5 Beguines as a Missionary Movement of Laywomen

During the thirteenth century, the Latin Church passed a time of decadence and renewal. Reform movements gained momentum among the clergy as well as in the monasteries. Lay people and most of all laywomen who were gripped by the spirit of reform longed for a life in "holiness" outside the monasteries. But holiness was bound to the clergy and the religious. Beyond that, only women of aristocracy had access to a religious life. One of the most impressive efforts of women to overcome all these divides—gender, class, private-public, lay-clerical—was the beguine movement in the thirteenth and fourteenth centuries.[17] The beguine movement can be seen as a reconfiguration of out-dated concepts of mission in a changed context. It coped with new social challenges mainly in the growing cities where poverty exceeded to a high degree. Beguines usually lived collectively in clusters of houses arranged around a courtyard, called *beguinages*.[18] Some of the beguinages sheltered several hundred women—in Cologne, almost one thousand. The beguines practiced a very modest, spiritual, free and informal lifestyle—which was contrary to the ruling customs.

The main aim of the beguine's movement was to return, as lay Christians, to a biblical lifestyle by implementing a *vita apostolica*. They helped the poor in the cities, cared for the sick, and buried the death, especially those affected by the great pestilence during the fourteenth century. Furthermore, they taught in the vernaculars so that ordinary people, mainly women, could understand the scriptures in their own languages: French, Flemish, Dutch, Italian, or German. Many noneducated women got access to the Christian heritage. The beguine movement was emancipatory by being self-supporting financially and independent from clergy in spiritual matters. Beguines found in Eucharist devotion a way to experience being created in God's image as well as being themselves equal to males. Some of them were eager to participate fully at the Eucharist by getting both, bread and wine, and to incorporate in this way the body of Christ. Marguerite Porete (1250/60–1310), a famous beguine scholar and writer of many books, developed in writing and practice a mystic spirituality aiming at the decline of her will to the point where she could say: "It is now God who wills in my soul."[19] Marguerite Porete, while being a solitary beguine, was one of the rare itinerant missionaries traveling through France to transmit her message mainly to uneducated women. When she was accused of heresy she maintained a silence of eighteen months until she was burned to death in Paris in 1310.

## 1.6 Church Reactions to Women's Agency in Mission

Throughout the Early and High Middle Ages, the missional initiatives of women were regarded as a threat to clerical power, to the order of public and family life. Canon Law was used to gradually constrain concerned women in their ways of living and practicing mission. Between 800 and the Fourth Lateran Council in 1215, church legislation forced women to cut down, step by step, charity activities beyond their families as well as outside the monasteries. Pope Innocent III (1160–1216) argued that the only places suitable for women were "either marriage or strict enclosure behind convent walls" (*aut maritus aut murus*).[20] The "Sisters in Arms," as Jo Ann McNamara has coined Catholic nuns and religious laywomen, lost their struggle to make room in the Middle Ages society for developing a "third gender" according to their missionary approach.[21] How Canon Law led to a malorization of women's rights can be listed only very sketchily:[22] Women were finally excluded from services of liturgy, teaching, and leadership (exclusion from consecrating and being consecrated, from the ministries of an elder, deacon, priest, and bishop); women were forbidden to administer a confession and giving absolution, and to apply sanctions against wrongdoers in the church. Women were not allowed to witness in court for the prosecution of clergymen. When preaching in churches was limited to ordained men, and when celibacy became compulsory for priests, enclosure for women religious became a necessity "as a protection for men from the wiles of women, and as a necessary imposition on women, whose weakness and immorality endangered all."[23] It put also the end to the common missionary agency of monks and nuns in double monasteries. The beguine's movement became persecuted and was forbidden by the Council of Vienna in 1312. Beguines were forced to either opt for marriage, to become members of a "third order" (Tertiary) approved by the Pope, or nuns of an approved women's order.[24]

## 1.7 Itinerating Women Missionaries and Women in Foreign Missions After 1500

After the split of the Latin Church, Western Europe was divided in the Roman Catholic Church and various churches of the Reformation. During the sixteenth century, the Roman Catholic Church put all its efforts to foreign mission while most churches of the Reformation abstained more or less from it until shortly before 1800.[25] Based on the sixteenth-century colonialism, Catholic mission was a men's project—more precisely, a project of missionary orders for men, mainly Dominicans, Franciscans, and Jesuits. The Tridentine legislation, once again, confirmed the Bull Periculoso (1298) that women religious were not allowed to involve in missionary activities outside the monasteries. It insisted once more on the encloistering of women, declaring that nuns, more than monks, needed the safeguard of the cloister to protect their chastity.[26] Catholic orders for women joined the foreign missionary movement only in the nineteenth century.

Nonetheless, courageous laywomen of the Roman Catholic Church started mission overseas already in the seventeenth century. Among them was Marie Guyart, who started the transmission of faith to native women in Canada. Being a wife and mother, she opted for a non-encloistered life. By preaching and teaching, she explored a new type of Catholic women missionaries. But after her death her son identified women's mission as ancillary to that of male missionaries. Preaching, teaching, and other public tasks did not belong to women, he said, because of their lack of modesty and sinful propensities. According to him the title "apostle" was reserved for men only. Furthermore, he argued that women in positions of authority would not be accepted by the public opinion.[27] Mary Guyart's son successfully subordinated his mother's missionary endeavor to that of male missionaries.

Marguerite de Bourgeoys, another missionary in Canada, was ready for an itinerant life outside the protecting walls of a monastery, among natives. The narrative of pregnant Mary visiting her cousin Elizabeth (Luke 1:39-56) served Marguerite as a missionary model: mission from laywomen to lay women. She wrote:

> We are asked why we prefer to be wanderers rather than cloistered, the cloister being a protection for people of our sex. [...] Why do we go on missions which put us in danger of suffering greatly and even of being captured, killed or burned by the Indians? There are signs that the Blessed Virgin has been pleased that there is a company of women to honour the life she led in the world and that this company be formed in Montreal. The Blessed Virgin was never enclostered.[28]

The section on women's mission in Europe may be finished by glancing over the turbulent life journey of Mary Ward in whose life culminated the gender struggle over women's mission in the public arena.[29] Mary Ward was born 1585 in a Catholic family in Yorkshire. Shortly before, Queen Elizabeth I was excommunicated by Pope Pius V (1570), which turned into a severe persecution of Catholics in England. Mary's family had to flee from home to home and to celebrate Mass in hiding in fear of discovery. Mary's experiences during childhood marked her life by fearlessness and a driving sense of vocation to overcome any obstacles in her life. She accepted suffering and persecution as a distinct possibility to witness her faith. Never was she impressed or frightened by hostilities from the side of clerical hierarchy. At age twenty-four, Mary launched an Institute in St.

Omer, North of France, for Catholic migrants, mainly women and children, from England seeking shelter on the continent. The English Ladies' Institute, as it was called, was shaped by Mary according to the Jesuit community because Jesuits, as a missionary order, renounced a monastic life. Like Jesuits, Mary was looking for a missional model allowing free mobility to facilitate the public work of teaching, caring for prisoners, attending to the sick and dying. All these involvements were embedded in a profound spiritual lifestyle. The religious world of the time was ridiculing Mary's implementation of mission with comments like: "brain-sick English gentlewomen." But Mary and her companions were far from being discouraged. Additional houses of the Institute were founded with great success in Liege, Cologne, Trier, and Rome.

During the Thirty Years War, Mary and her sister colleagues were traveling as itinerant missionaries throughout Europe for thousands of miles, some of them starving from malnutrition. Several times in her life, Mary, a small, fragile, and unhealthy women, walked to Rome to get approbation for her Institute. While the Holy See was not altogether against Mary's plea, Jesuits distanced themselves from the English Ladies' Institute out of fear that their own reputation would be affected by sympathizing with her. Some of her adversaries in Rome even plead—in vain—for Mary's death by burning at the Campo dei Fiori where Giordano Bruno had been burned thirty years later. In 1624, Propaganda Fide voted to suppress the Institute, and the Congregation of Bishops added their condemnation. The English Ladies were to disband and close all theirs schools. But Mary, who then was on her way to establish new houses in Vienna, Pressburg, and other cities in Europe, was not informed about the decision. The final Bull of Suppression, Pastoralis Romani Pontificis, was decreed in 1631. It declared that the Institute was to be "suppressed, extinct, uprooted and abolished," because the sisters had "carried out works by no means suiting the weakness of their sex, womanly modesty, above all, virginal purity—works which men, who are most experienced in the knowledge of Sacred Scripture and the conduct of affairs, undertake with difficulty and not without great caution."[30] One house after the other was closed, Mary was arrested in Munich and imprisoned in a dungeon of a Convent of the Poor Clares. But even there, she contacted the sisters of the Institute by secret messages, and when she was released, she immediately turned back with other ladies to Rome, where the Pope summoned her. The charge of heresy was dropped, and she and her companions were allowed to live together in Rome. After 1639, Mary returned back to London to again set up a house "which quickly became a Catholic center in this most dangerous times for Catholics."[31] When the house in London was searched up to four times a day by police, Mary moved again and founded another house in the countryside of Yorkshire where she lived until her death in 1645.

Mary Ward's efforts of breaching the walls of gender typologies seemed to end in failure. However, a second Institute was established and approved by Pius IX in 1877, while the right to name Mary Ward as their founder was given to the Institute only at the beginning of the twentieth century. Today there are over four thousand women belonging to the English Ladies or Loretto Sisters, as they are called in North America, who continue women's mission in memory of Mary Ward.

*Christine Lienemann-Perrin*

## 2. Africa

### 2.1 Recording the History of Christianity in Africa: a Historiographical Remark

Before looking at Christianity in Africa itself, it is instructive to have a look at the various methodical shifts in "the making of history." They mirror the changing perspectives of historians, social anthropologists, church historians, and missiologists on Christianity, which has become the largest and most diverse religion on the African continent.

Several trends in historiography followed one after the other since the second half of the twentieth century. During the pioneer periods of European mission agencies coming to Africa in the nineteenth century, the emergence of Africa's Christianity has been recorded as a European endeavor. Reports on the growing plants of Christian life were written by missionaries themselves in the style of chronicles and aimed at finding financial and ideological support from the friends of missionary endeavors in their home bases. During decolonization of most of the African states in the 1960s, these idealizing chronicles came under severe critique of secular historians in Europe. In their anti-imperialist historiography the mission agencies were interpreted as ideological helpmates of European's conquest on the African continent. Many of them were secularists, criticizing religion in general. During the 1970s, a new generation of conscientized missiologists in Europe joined the anti-imperialist school of historiography by adopting the criticism of the missionary presence in Africa. A decade later, however, social anthropologists and religious scientists with expertise on African religion began to recognize and appreciate Christianity in Africa as an inherent element of Africa's religious and cultural landscape. This shift opened the way to interdisciplinary approaches to African Christianity, bringing together social anthropologists, church historians, and missiologists of Western and African background. Last but not least, the new interest in Africa's religious landscape was pushed by the postcolonial approaches to historiography from Africans and elsewhere, provoking a new critical discourse on the various acting forces of religious transformations on the continent.

While in the 1960s and 1970s Christian mission in Africa was mainly a much criticized project of European actors, later period showed changes. The mission has become a common endeavor of foreigners and local people. Such is a positive sign of progress. The Western transmission aspect is even losing weight vis-à-vis the African appropriation aspect in the process of Christianizing Africa. African initiatives in appropriating, transforming, and transmitting Christian faith on the continent had earlier started in Antiquity in Egypt and Ethiopia, continued in the sixteenth century in Congo, followed by the roots of African-initiated churches since the late nineteenth century in Southern Africa. African-sponsored mission work found its peak in transforming sub-Saharan Africa in a mainly Christian continent during the last decades. It has been stated many times that Africa has been Christianized by Africans mainly, and only to a much lesser degree by foreigners.

To what extent has the women's face of African Christianity been made visible in historiography? Are women researchers on African Christianity playing a role as actors in the scientific community? The answer is disappointing in both aspects. On the one side, women's impact in African churches is praised in generalizing words in missionary chronicles and historical records again and again.[32] On the other side, there is a disappointing silence what concrete investigations on female agency on the mission field is concerned. Christian Baëta, a famous first-generation theologian in Ghana, has been recorded to say that the impact of woman missionaries was more important for the indigenous church than the men's impact, because women lived close to the churches and together with them, not above them.[33] In the last two or three decades, a wave of women's research on women in African Christianity can be observed, partly by scholars from the USA and European countries like England, Netherlands, Sweden, Germany, and Switzerland who have spent some years in African countries,[34] and partly by African women researchers doing research work there or in the West.[35]

Since recently, the Internet and electronic communication have opened in a revolutionary way new opportunities for an interactive historiography on women's roles in African Christianity, which cannot be overestimated. It gives African women a direct access to participate in recording the great impact of their foremothers as well as their contemporaries on the emergence of Christianity in Africa. To give an example: in 1995,The *Dictionary of African Christian Biography* was launched as a modest project of the Overseas Ministries Study Center in New Haven, Connecticut by Jonathan J. Bonk, an American who has spent several years in Ethiopia.[36] Its purpose is to collect narratives of Africans and a few non-Africans who had an impact on churches in Africa. Several thousand biographical notes have been collected until 2008; some of them are only a few sentences, others, long articles. Some are collected from books; others have been written in English, French, Portuguese, or Swahili for the dictionary exclusively. The authors often are advanced students in theological seminaries throughout Africa to get their credits in church history. Information on about two hundred African women has been made available, beginning with women martyrs in the second century in North Africa until the present time. The *Dictionary of African Christian Biographies* has triggered similar projects in other continents of the Global South, mainly in Asia.[37]

## 2.2 *Two Thousand Years of Christian Life on the African Continent*

For two thousand years, Christian life has existed in Africa without interruption. In Bible readings we find Simon from the African town Kyrene who was the cross-bearer on Jesus' way to Golgotha (Mark 15:21); after the resurrection the apostle Philip baptized an Ethiopian who was treasurer of the King (Acts 8:26-40). Among the first women martyrs were Felicitas and Perpetua (d. 203) who were both church members in Karthago. The Coptic Church and the Ethiopian Orthodox Church are the churches with the longest continuous histories on the continent.[38] In sub-Saharan Africa, however, the transmission of Christian faith started only much later, in the 1480s when missionaries accompanied Portuguese traders along the coast of Western Africa and established a mission station first on the island Sao Tomé and then at the mouth of the Congo River. Manikongo, king of the Congo, was not only responding favorably to the Christian faith but imposed it also to the people of his kingdom.[39] The Portuguese missionary initiative was followed by Moravian missionaries during the eighteenth century. They worked among the Khoikhoi at the Cape of Good Hope where settlers from Netherlands and other European countries had already established their own Christian churches since the middle of the seventeenth century. When the "scramble for Africa" imposed colonization to the whole continent, except Ethiopia and Egypt, foreign mission organizations profited from political and military protection of the colonial powers to penetrate also the interior of the "dark continent." At the peak of imperialism between the 1880s and the beginning of World War I in 1914, Protestant denominations, Roman Catholics, and Anglicans established their mission churches in East, Central, West, and South Africa, introducing confessionalism according to their European traditions. This general picture, however, was perforated here and there by missionary individuals who countered the colonial and imperialistic missions, criticizing them and exploring alternative ways.[40]

Regarding the numerical extension and inculturation of Christianity in Africa, the last two hundred years has been the most important period. Again, the last three decades lead to an almost explosive growth of adherence in Christian churches as well as foundation of new churches. While 9 percent of the populace living on the whole African continent were Christians in 1910, it experienced an increase up to almost 50 percent in 2010.[41] One of the reasons of the fast growing trend has been the emergence of African Initiated Churches (AIC) since late nineteenth century and during the twentieth century. Even more important, however, are several generations of Pentecostal movements on the continent. To name African Christianity becoming an important element of World Christianity in the twenty-first century is no exaggeration.

In order to look now in more detail on the women's impact on African Christianity, three women from different periods, regions, and denominations are selected to illustrate *pars pro toto* how individuals have contributed to Christianity's growth on the continent, how they have shaped church life and were perceived by mission churches as well as their own adherents.

## 2.3 Individual Women Shaping African Christianity

*Kimpa Vita* (Ndona Beatrice), 1684–1706, was born and baptized in a family of Congo nobility at a time when Congo had
been a Catholic kingdom for two centuries.[42] Born and raised
during civil war she experienced visions since her youth. She
was trained as "a person said to be able to communicate with
the supernatural world."[43] When she got a message from St.
Antony of Padua through a vision she was persuaded that she
had died and St. Anthony had entered in her body and taken
over her life. A religious movement emerging from her activities was called accordingly Anthonians. It was a religious, pro-
phetical, and political movement aiming at the reunification
and peace of the Congo kingdom. The movement acknowledged the Pope as head of the Church but was critical about
the European missionaries in Congo. Kimpa Vita herself sent
out African missionaries in all parts of the Congo kingdom
and won converts from the Catholic Church among peasants as
well as among members, mostly women, of the nobility. While
she declared sacraments and good deeds as being irrelevant
before God, she gave priority to the inner persuasion of believers. According to her, Jesus and Mary were born in Congo and
were Congolese—a fact which was hidden to African converts
by European missionaries. Since Kimpa Vita was successful in
spreading her movement among the dissident provinces of the
Congo kingdom, she was captured, tortured, and punished by
death penalty at the order of King Pedro IV in 1706. The movement survived for a certain time until it was destroyed by the
king. But she has survived in the memories of the Bakongo people, especially among women. Several messianic movements in
the region of the Bakongo people in Northern Angola, Western
Congo-Kinshasa and Southern Congo-Brazzaville can be seen
as a late revitalization of Kimpa Vita's and the Anthonians'
heritage.[44] Kimpa Vita represents an early example of the so-
called "Ethiopianism" in African Christianity, meaning that
liberation and independence in religious and political terms
were in the center of its aspirations.[45]

*Christinah Nku* (1894–1980), a South African from the
Transvaal region, suffered from serious illnesses during her
childhood. In a vision, she received God's promise that she
would survive, an experience which led her later to focus on
the healing ministry. Having grown up in the Dutch Reformed
Mission Church, she has been rebaptized together with her
husband in the Apostolic Faith Mission in 1924; however,

after a dispute with the leader over personal and doctrinal questions she started her own church in 1939: the *St. John Apostolic Faith Mission South Africa*. Mother Nku, as she was called, started her ministry in the Johannesburg slums, "and crowds made their way each day to her two-room dwelling for prayer [...] Hundreds of persons reported being healed, and Christinah neither sought fame nor took money for her healing prayers."[46] She built seventy churches throughout the country, established schools, youth programs, bands and choral groups, which "expressed solidarity and affirmed personal and corporate worth and dignity in an otherwise harsh and restricted world."[47] The widely expanded movement split into about forty independent groups, but has entered a reuniting process after 2006.[48]

The name of *Alice Lenshina Mulenga Mubisha* (1924–1978) became famous in relation to an African independent movement, called *Lumpa* (meaning "better than all others" in the ChiBemba language), and founded by her with a religious center called *Zion* in Zambia.[49] Alice condemned shamanism, drinking alcohol, and polygamy. She was looking for a "pure" form of Christian communities throughout the country. Together with her adherents she was winning members by her sermons. She organized a church of fifty to one hundred thousand members who left the Catholic and Protestant churches to join her church. As the Antonians in Congo, Lumpa was also a religious movement of "Ethiopian" type since it supported the aspirations for national independence before 1964. Later on, it turned into an anti-state movement refusing to pay taxes. When the Lumpa Church founded its own villages, it was interpreted as a subversion of their power by local chiefs. Shortly after independence accompanied by civil war events in which Lumpa was involved, the Lumpa church was forbidden, Alice jailed, her main temple destroyed, while fifteen thousand flew to the Democratic Republic Congo. Alice died in house arrest in 1978. The Lumpa Church continues to exist today but is split into several groups.

## 2.4 African Christianity as a Women's Movement

Women are numerically and in agency surpassing men presumably in all churches around the world. This is true most of all in African Christianity, where the female face of worship, associations, religious orders, and diaconal work is visible everywhere. How to explain the appeal of Christianity to women? Why have many more women than men converted to

Christianity in Africa?[50] Two historical investigations may illustrate what can be found in similar form more or less throughout Africa.

Between 1876 and 1914, the *Church Missionary Society* (CMS) sent British married and later also single women in a mission field established in the Ukaguru region, Tanzania.[51] Founded by John Venn and Thomas Scott, CMS is an evangelical branch of the Church of England. It favored women embodying the domestic qualities of model wives, mothers, and homemakers. But increasingly it was obvious that CMS needed women also for working outside the domestic sphere to reach local women in their homesteads where missionary males had no access. Women were credited with their own inspiration by the Holy Spirit and therefore regarded as equal evangelists working side by side with men. Contrary to the High Church Anglicans focusing on hierarchy and clergy, low Church Anglicans including its CMS branch, estimated most of all qualities to which women as well as lay men had access: spiritual commitment, preaching, prayer services, Bible reading, revival, fellowship meetings, nursing, teaching, record keeping.[52] Acting in context of the Victorian era, CMS regarded women as human beings without sex and passion. "This desexualized character probably accounts for the ease with which unmarried women were sent abroad."[53] In the spirit of highly valued altruism, asceticism, and suffering, women missionaries of CMS were credited freedoms which otherwise were suspect. It was not seen as a risk to send them abroad to work eventually alone in a wilderness surrounded by native or unmarried European men. "Some women ran stations without the help of any men. [...] During one particularly difficult period, when the lone clergyman was sick for over a year, the various mission stations and services were entirely run by women."[54] As married women missionaries had to send their children to schools in England, and as they were expected to employ household servants at the mission compound to have the freedom of mobility and activity of missionary work, their lifestyle was teaching another ideal than the "Christian wife" preached to the local congregations in Ukaguru. Beidelman concludes that by 1900, CMS strongly advocated radical sexual equality between men and women missionaries. Evangelical missions, "such as CMS, which downplayed clerical roles and stressed instead the Holy Spirit, advanced women more than other Christian groups."[55]

Some eighty years later, a *Spiritan missionary project* was started also in Tanzania, among the Maasai people.[56] The mission church that emerged from that agency was called "Church of Women," a term coined by a young Maasai man in 1992, claiming that "there was in fact no church in Embopong, and what there had been was merely a 'church of women' (*kanisa oo ntasati*)."[57] The preponderance of female adherence was not at all intended by the Congregation of the Holy Spirit, called Spiritans, who spent several decades since the early 1950s in the Maasai district to convert first the male. Regarding the Maasai people as a patriarchal society, Spiritan missionaries in vain "tried to convert men first through schools, then in their homesteads, and finally in individual instruction classes. Maasai women were restricted from attending school, tolerated but not encouraged to attend homestead instruction and services, and dissuaded from holding formal leadership positions in the church."[58] The missionaries were disappointed to recognize that Maasai men did not respond to any of the missionary methods while women were eager to get baptized and become members of the Catholic Church. Local congregations turned out to be "incomplete," a failure in the eyes of the missionaries, and not attractive for Maasai men. A few male members got official responsibilities in the congregations as secretaries and catechists—responsibilities women were neither admitted to nor interested in. They rather ridiculed these "official" ministries and undermined male authority connected to them. What Maasai women were looking for by embracing Christianity was the improvement of their spiritual power and female fellowship. "By rejecting the authority of the *iloibonok*[59] and assuming the powers of healing for themselves and Christian missionaries, women challenged male assertions of power and authority."[60] Provided with an expanded spiritual platform women were enabled to reinforce their claims to spiritual, moral, and caring superiority in contrast to men's increasingly material interests. According to Hodgeson, gender inequalities were reduced in both Christian and traditional Maasai society due to the achieved negotiation of gender roles in this expanding and efficient "Church of Women."

## 2.5 Conclusion

Looking back at the history of Christianity in Africa, women's traces in mission are obvious in at least three ways: First, throughout mission history, women responded to the gospel transmitted by missionaries from abroad earlier and much more frequently than men. They perceived the gospel as a liberating and empowering force and in the Christian faith community a space to live according to the new freedom. Second, after having adopted the Christian faith, women were disappointed, again and again, by constraints they experienced as members not only of mission churches but also of African Initiated Churches run by African male leaders. Instead of keeping silent, some outstanding African women decided to break away to start their own movement or church. Such moves often split anew in many further branches. Third, by the enduring initiative of women converts, African Christianity turned the male and hierarchical church structures transmitted by many—although not all—mission agencies from Europe or North America into a largely female movement.

*Christine Lienemann-Perrin*

# 3. Asia

## 3.1 Introduction

The history of Christian mission in the continent is as varied and diverse as the continent itself. The cultures, religions, and historical developments of the continent of Asia cannot be written in monolithic terms. Asia is home to the world's most populous nation, diverse cultures, and multiple language groups. Major religions of the world, including Confucianism, Buddhism, Hinduism, Jainism, Shamanism, Sikhism, Judaism, Islam, Christianity and a myriad of indigenous religiosities trace their beginnings to the continent of Asia. In a recent book,[61] the authors have divided the continent into four regions: Eastern Asia, comprising of China, Japan, South Korea, North Korea, Taiwan, and Mongolia; Southeastern Asia, comprising of Vietnam, Indonesia, the Philippines, Thailand, Cambodia, Burma, Singapore, Malaysia, Laos, and Timor; South-central Asia, includes India, Nepal, Bhutan, Pakistan, Bangladesh, Sri Lanka, Afghanistan, Tajikistan, Kyrgyzstan, Kazakhstan, Uzbekistan and Western Asia, consisting of Turkey, Georgia, Armenia, Lebanon, Syria, Cyprus, Iraq, Palestine, Israel, UAE, Saudi Arabia, Jordan, Yemen, and Oman. While these regional categories are helpful in a general way, it is still difficult to describe Asia even in broad generalities, given its wide spectrum of diversity and each country presents its own multiple and plurality of cultures.

As much as there are regional diversities and plurality of cultures, the history of Christian mission in Asia is also multifaceted, with almost all the traditions and denominations of Christianity existing in the continent, spread over centuries. It is not only the continent where Christianity began, but also the encounter of Christianity beyond its homeland as early as in the first century, is claimed during the period of Jesus' own disciples. There are traditions that claim that Thomas, one of the disciples of Jesus, came to South India to the state of Kerala in the first century.[62] Asia is also the region where the Jesuit missions of the sixteenth century established Christian contacts, amid controversies pertaining to adaptation of local cultures, spanning from India, China, Japan, the Philippines, Burma, and Vietnam. For reason of orientation, the present focus of Christian missions in Asia is limited to the initiative of missions by Euro-American Christian mission societies.

Given the multifarious and heterogeneous culture and historical realities of the continent, this brief historical survey cannot pretend to be exhaustive. It will neither be a chronological history nor a country-wide narration of mission history; there are a plethora of excellent resources on Christian mission for each Asian country. Hence, drawing from these existing resources, the present historical survey will at best highlight some generalities and patterns with a large stroke of the brush pertaining to women's experience of mission.

Asia also presents one of the most complex contexts in Christian mission's relationship with women. Christian mission impacted women's lives tremendously by way of education, medical facilities, and social upliftment efforts, nevertheless there are qualms that Christian mission and its encounter with Asian women remains to be limited in relation to the patriarchal culture wherein women are not accepted as equals with their male counterpart both in the larger society and in the church. In a study of Christian mission and women among the Nadars of South India, under the Madras Presidency during the late nineteenth and early twentieth centuries, Eliza Kent had observed a "restricted form of femininity" despite the general consensus in mission studies that women's situation improved as a result of Christianization.[63]

Furthermore, in some contexts, it is argued that Christian mission ushered in patriarchal hierarchy wherein domestication of women took place. Mary John Mananzan pointed out this fact in the context of women in the Philippines, wherein, the imposition of a Western notion of feminine via the Spanish colonials and the Christian mission, inadvertently resulted in curtailing of the autonomy and freedom enjoyed by the women prior to the Christianization.[64] To argue this point that Christian mission in Asia in relation to women has to be understood both as an instrument of liberation and progress yet limited, examples and illustrations of women's experiences from different regions within Asia and from different mission societies will be presented. It should be noted that a discussion on women and Christian mission does not address only the recipients of mission but also the agents of Christian mission, that is, the women missionaries. These illustrations and examples from mission history will be presented within a schema of eight categories in four pairs: divisions and exclusions, motivations and negotiations, relationship and forms of organization, and transformation and Bible readings.[65]

## 3.2 Divisions and Exclusions

Women's experience, encounter, and participation in Christian mission are varied, although there is the tendency to conflate women's experience and role into one large perception, one such as liberation from clutches of oppressive cultural practices. Christian mission provided diverse opportunities as well as multilayered experiences for women varying from contexts to issues. A general experience and a degree of similar roles in participation in mission can be, however, observed across centuries and mission projects. It was more often that women, both as agents of Christian mission and receivers of mission, were second to the male members, who were most often the ones who set the agenda and priorities. Hence, it can be asserted that women experienced divisions and exclusions in comparison with men in the Christianization process.

A commonality observed among the diverse Asian cultures is the rigid division of the community along gender and class categories. These divisions legitimized by culture and religions further resulted in exclusions and marginalization of women. These exclusions were manifested in various practices and spheres. The division of the society impacted women most, and therefore, women in Asia in general have lived sequestered in the private space of home and family.

Women were excluded from the process of decision making, either as converts or missionaries. In many of the so-called mass movement conversions, the male's decision to change religion and embrace the new religion meant conversion for the whole family. In many villages in India, men and women sit in separate pews in the church services, most often the women folk occupying the back rows with the children. These practices go back to the beginning of mission, where church sitting was divided along gender lines and men and women were made to sit apart.

One example of how Christian mission created divisions and exclusions based on gender is vividly portrayed in the context of the Philippines during the Spanish conquest and Christianization. Mary John Mananzan describes the precolonial, pre-Christian Filipino women status that there were no gender disparities and in fact women were regarded as possessing "the greater intellectual superiority."[66] These earlier observations and descriptions of women's position and role were altered by the customs and ideas brought by the conquerors and the missionaries. Mananzan writes, "though the missionaries were forced to acknowledge the *mujer indigena's* superiority, which they could hardly deny, nevertheless, condemned as vice any behavior which they could not reconcile with the moral prescriptions for women in Spain. So they praised the woman's intelligence, strong will, and practicality, but they condemned her for being too sensual and too free in her behavior."[67] In other words, the very status and role of women noted as equal, independent, if not "superior" was condemned, since it was not conforming to the expected behavior and role of women in the Christian/colonial society. Paradoxically, the curtailment of women's freedom was initiated with the imparting of an appropriate lifestyle as befits a Christian woman, which indeed was patriarchal in its unquestioned organization of the society. Therefore, Mananzan writes, "the imposition of a strongly patriarchal system had decidedly negative consequences on the women."[68] Women who enjoyed equal freedom and opportunities became sheltered, timid women, thus "on the pretext of putting woman on a pedestal as an object of veneration, patriarchal society succeeded in alienating her from public life, decisions and significance."[69]

Divisions and exclusions imposed upon women were not limited to the women converts or the native women, it was simultaneously experienced by women missionaries as well as manifested in different mission societies. Here is an example from the Baptist Missionary Society (BMS) in China. Because of existing bias toward women, particularly single women as a source for potential "prejudice" against them by the native Chinese, BMS did not send single women as missionaries to China until the recommendations made by the deputation to China of two of its home board members. BMS revised its policy to send single women missionaries to China after observation of another mission society and their single women missionaries work in reaching Chinese women.[70] Both within the missionary community and the "receiving" community the divisions and exclusions between the genders are vividly portrayed in such attitudes and practices. Women were not valued as mission workers, rather held as potent distractions, yet the exclusions of women in the cultures they encountered required the reevaluation of such notions. In order to preach the gospel to the sequestered women, and to teach "civilizing" customs and norms to the new Christians, the role of both the women missionaries and the women of the household extended beyond the assigned boundaries.

## 3.3 Motivations and Negotiations

The divisions and exclusions kept women within patriarchal societies wherein they had no individuality, freedom, and choice. Women had to negotiate through the maze of male dominance that excluded and rendered them voiceless just as much in the Christianization project. While "native" women were constrained by the culture from acquainting with the new religion as individuals and curtailed from unfettered access to the education Christian mission invariably provided, women from the Christian mission community were constrained by their gender in responding to the evangelical fervor. Dana Robert perceptively writes of American women desiring to serve as missionaries in Asia or elsewhere, who had to "find" a husband who was a missionary himself. In other words, women who shared in the common evangelical motivation to save the souls of the "heathens" could not most often carry out their missionary zeal independently. Women who felt called for mission often had to marry a missionary husband, thereby living out their individual call only by assisting their husband in the mission.[71]

Christian mission activity among women also had to make strategic negotiation and accommodation with the prevalent cultures in their pursuit of the goal of evangelization. For instance, in China, missionaries had to accommodate the traditional outlook of Chinese society of keeping women in seclusion, away from the glare of public. In order to convince Chinese families to send girls to the Christian schools, education for women was in the boarding schools exclusively for women. Most important, the mission adapted Confucian teaching in the curriculum, which emphasized the docility and submissiveness for women in the Chinese cultures. Negotiating and accommodating the culture of gender seclusion "were adapted by the mission to convince the Chinese families that Christian schools were developing Chinese women as expected by the culture to be domesticate, submissive and loyal."[72]

Another example of negotiating the culture and norms can be drawn from Korea, as Hyaeweal Choi writes, "girls' mission schools were well aware of the importance of accommodating Korean customs for the sake of gaining Koreans' trust, and thus they required girls to cover their faces and bodies when they went off campus."[73] Only by 1908 did girls students of Ewha Girls' School stopped covering their faces. Interestingly, Choi points out the active agency of the Korean women for their freedom from the cultural practice of covering their faces, which was antithesis to their perception of modern women, was a result of the education imparted by the Christian mission.[74]

The development of Kobe Girls' School in Japan also provides an example of women missionaries' motivation to participate in mission and negotiate the challenges. During the tumultuous period between 1883 and 1909, when Japan was going through an identity formation as a nation, critical and antagonistic resistance toward Western culture and Christianity, women missionaries creatively "maneuvered" the circumstances to maintain the independent Christian character of the Kobe Girls' School. One of the ways of survival was acquiring a "collegiate status" for the school, since the prohibition against religious education applied only to secondary schools.[75]

## 3.4 Relationships and Forms of Organization

In spite of the divisions and exclusions, women surmounted the cultural obstacles inherent within the missionary community as well as the community they encountered. Subsequently, a negotiated space and activity for women either as agents of mission or receivers of mission were created. Their fervor for evangelization was best carried out in mission work among women in such space as *the zenanas in India* and with women such as the Bible women. Women's mission activity was carried out in and through a "web of human relationships."[76] Indigenous women from the mission regions were inducted to assist women missionaries, such women were called "Bible women." Bible women were given minimum training to assist in traveling, connecting with the local women, translation, and teaching about the Bible. This partnership between Western missionary women and native Bible women provided one of the earliest leadership roles for women in many parts of the world.[77] Primarily, Bible women's task was among their own people, yet, some became "foreign missionaries." Dana Lee Robert cites an example of Dora Yu, a Chinese medical doctor and a Bible woman, who became a cross-cultural missionary in Korea. In 1897, Yu and the American missionary Josephine Campbell opened the first women's mission of their denomination, Methodist, in Korea.[78] Among the Baptist Christians in India, it was a woman convert named Tongpangla from the first American Baptist mission station among the Ao Naga people, who was sent to the neighboring village as an evangelist.

Christian mission among women and by women required creative relationships and forms of organization as illustrated by the phenomenon of religious communities in the late seventeenth century in the Philippines. As noted earlier, women in the Philippines played an important role, such as priestesses in the pre-Christianity period; however, R. G. Tiedemann notes that "their transition into Christian institutional life proved difficult."[79] There were women converts who chose to live a pious life in solitude, akin to the religious communities of the established church such as the Royal Monastery of the Immaculate Conception of the Poor Clares. This was exclusively for women of Spanish heritage. Indigenous women and women of mixed ethnicity who had converted to Christianity and opted to live pious lives in contemplation and assistance to the church were known as *beatas* and their communities known as *beaterios*. Although they were permitted to wear a habit, they were "never recognized as religious congregations under canon law but were simply considered as 'pious unions,' for tasks of piety and charity."[80] The resistance of the Spanish church and the civil authorities to accept native women in religious orders was thus negotiated by the establishment of the *beates* as tertiaries attached to one of the mendicant orders. The earliest *beaterios* were organized by Antonio Esguerra and Francisca de Fuentes. It was not until the twentieth century that the native religious orders were recognized and given the status of regular religious congregations.[81]

Despite the exclusion of women, the process of Christianizing still presented circumstances that called for "untraditional" forms of organization and relationships as can be noted in the phenomenon of the "institute of virgins" in late seventeenth-century China in the Fujian province. Due to the paucity of missionaries, it was necessary to recruit Chinese lay persons for both evangelization and church management. Among these lay people was a group of single women known as the "institute of virgins."[82] The institute of virgins was akin to the *beatas* of the Philippines. These single women consecrated their lives for mission and carried out the tasks of instructing children and women.

Dana Robert also writes of the widow Xu Candida (1604–1680), who organized a group of Chinese women to raise funds for mission activities, such as: support missionaries and church buildings, print devotional materials, and assist the poor. These consecrated virgins later acted as leaders of the underground church, supported by their web of family relationships.[83] Women participated vigorously and with creativity in the mission enterprise, amidst state repressions, cultural constraints such as the house group of consecrated virgins in China.

## 3.5 Transformation and Bible Readings

Involvement and encounters with Christian mission led to the transformation of women in all spheres of life. Among the most vivid transformations experienced by the women were in the social practices that oppressed and excluded women, albeit it must be noted that social transformation *in toto* that ensures unhindered equality for women is yet to be achieved. That is, despite transformation of some oppressive cultural practices, it must be noted that in most Asian countries women continue to be discriminated in every aspect, social, political, economic, and religious. Undoubtedly, transformations and changes took place in almost every mission context, repressive cultural practices were overcome, education for women, and leadership development are areas of obvious changes achieved through mission. Local women who embraced Christianity often surmounted the cultural inhibitions and prohibitions as illustrated in the stirring response of Japanese *kirishitan* women martyrs during the Tokugawa persecution of the *kirishitan* in the late sixteenth century in Japan as Haruko Nawata Ward explored and unveiled in her study of women martyrs in Japan.[84] These women martyrs were transformed by the new religion and its literature, particularly on martyrs. According to Ward, images of "women as apologists, leaders of communities and leaders of resistance in imperial persecution" portrayed in three surviving collections of Stories of the Saints: *Santosu no gosagyo* (1591), *Santosu no gosagyu no ushi nukigaki* (1591), and *Maruchiriyo no kagami* (1596–1614), were instrumental in transforming Japanese women during the persecution.[85] In addition to the loyalty and leadership in the nascent Christian community, Japanese *kirishitan* women were also motivated by the "promise of union with Christ" and "freedom from the restraints imposed upon them by the patriarchal Confucian culture."[86] Ward summed up that the *kirishitan* stories of women martyrs during the persecution of Tokugawa demonstrated that women were able to overcome artificial social constructs such as class, ethnicity in order to exercise leadership and individual commitment.[87]

Ann Hasseltine Judson (1789–1826) and her mission activities illustrate the transformation of women in mission involvement. Most often she is only known as the wife of the famous Adoniram Judson, Baptist missionary to Burma. In recent years, historical studies that take cognizance of women's role in mission shed more light upon the life and work of Ann Judson. Anna May Chain asserts that Ann "was a scholar in her own right," learning Thai and translating catechism and the Gospel of Matthew into Thai. Ann is also known for her role in the translation work carried out by her husband while he was in prison. It is told that she smuggled the manuscript, hidden in a pillow cover. Her method of meeting regularly with small groups of women to study the Bible was continued by later missionaries. Subsequently, the first Burmese Baptist woman convert, Ma Min Lay, started a school for girls. The informal gathering of women to study the Bible eventually became a place for basic theological training, which went on to become Bible schools for the locals. The Karen Women's Bible School, Burmese Women's Bible School, and Bhamo Women's Bible School had their inception in small Bible study groups. These women schools have become seminaries and co-educational institutions.[88] Ann Judson also wrote letters that were published in mission journals; these letters influenced the American women and society of both the mission tasks and the ethnographic knowledge of the Burmese people and culture.[89] The biography of Ann Judson provides an example of transformation of both the missionary wife and the natives. A wife who was expected to maintain a Western-Christian notion of domestic life was transformed into a capable missionary in her own right, learning a foreign language and engaging in translation work.

Christian mission among women also brought about another sort of transformation as it is exhibited in the analysis of the life of Pandita Ramabai, the famous Indian convert, known for her work for the welfare of women. Conversion was more complex than just a change of religion, as Gauri Viswanathan unveils in her study of Ramabai. Christian mission also transformed an individual beyond a passive colonial subject, into a passionate, learned critic of established religions in the case of Ramabai: Hinduism and Christianity.[90]

## 3.6 Conclusion

Christian mission in Asia unfolded in diverse contexts, yet, certain large themes of experiences and participations can be noted. The undergirding vision was the evangelical fervor to share the gospel of Jesus, which included social upliftment and human dignity along with the salvation of souls. Women, both as agents of mission and as receivers of mission, have been active, albeit less acknowledged. That women hold up "half the sky" can be truly applied also to Christian mission as Dana Lee Robert commented "[t]he history of Christian mission must focus on women, for the majority of Christians in the world are women. If judged by numbers of members, Christianity is predominantly a women's movement."[91]

Christian mission has arguably been a positive force for women in Asia, giving them voice and agency. Having said this, the journey is far from complete, there continue to be more challenges, women experience new forms of exclusion and discrimination. It is heartening however, that there is growing awareness and conscious efforts to include women as equal partners, if not "principal agents" in the mission of the church. It is good to heed the direction of an Asian missiologist, Peter C. Phan, who underscored the need to recognize and include women's essential role in the church in discussing the concept of World Christianity and Christian mission in relation to Asian churches and their experience and resources, stating the "necessity of empowering women if the church is to become the church *of* and not simply *in* Asia."[92]

*Atola Longkumer*

## 4. North America

Women played a significant role in spreading the vision and mission of Christ in North America. Behind the scenes and in the forefront, women were a potent force in the survival and growth of Christianity, particularly in the nineteenth and twentieth centuries.[93] They exhibited competencies and skills in missionary work, social welfare reform, religious education, social justice advocacy, and human relationships, which attracted followers to the causes and to the Christian faith. Lucretia Coffin Mott, a Quaker minister from New York, once said, "If you want to get something done, ask a busy woman."[94] Although on a limited scale, the church created varied opportunities for women to use their skills to serve the church and church institutions with the supervision of male leadership.

Prior to the Reformation movement, women were accepted and encouraged to express their convictions courageously. The women joined forces with the great reformers in attacking and opposing some of the abuses and injustices in society. During the Reformation period in the sixteenth century, women were prohibited by the male authorities to do priestly work or conduct religious services. This was true in both the Old World and the New World. However, women of faith found other ways to do mission. They used their voices to support or oppose social and religious issues and concerns. Women who demonstrated greater competencies and more talents and who were seemingly frustrated on the patriarchal nature of church leadership chose either to continue fighting for their equal rights or to pursue missionary work in other countries. Elsie Thomas Culver, author of *Women in the World of Religion*, points out, "The thing that really hurt women was that leaders of the Protestant Reformation quite ignored the fact that women were of tremendous value to the life and work of the church and failed to provide for them [...] any challenging avenue of religious study and service."[95] In North America in the 1800s, the prohibition was not a deterrence to women's exercise of their rights and expressions of their capabilities. It is worth noting that a reformed type of Christianity—Protestant or Catholic—moved from Europe to North America.[96] The North American settlers or colonists protested the restrictions on women. Their missionary effort spread around the world, with many women serving as missionaries, with the aim to Christianize the natives of their host countries. Women excelled in mission in at least four areas: missionary work, religious education, social justice, and the ministry of healing and evangelism.

## 4.1 Missionary Work

The work of the church in mission to places other than the local church was done largely by women. They knew how to raise money for mission work operation, although final decisions came from the top male leadership. They were competent in relating to people, and to teaching and leading persons of different ages and stages. Women missionaries were invaluable, because they had gifts of human relations and linguistics and skill to communicate with native women. To serve as overseas missionary was an opportunity and challenge to the women in the Protestant churches.

At the end of the sixteenth century, a group of Roman Catholic American women started missionary work in Mexico with the responsibility to teach young girls basic Catholic tenets. It was during this period that the Franciscans and Jesuits formed Christian communities in the Americas. Other notable events, included the reading from the Book of Common Prayer by an Anglican church member, Robert Hunt, to colonists when they established Jamestown, the first successful colony in 1607. He later addressed colonists in New York and served communion in Virginia. In the 1600s and early 1700s, British missionary societies founded societies in the Eastern shores of the United States, such as the Society for the Propagation of the Gospel in New England in 1649, the Society for Promoting Christian Knowledge in 1695, and the Society for the Propagation of Gospels in Foreign Parts in 1701. In the 1870s, Congregational Missionary Societies began to be formed, while the Women's Baptist Home Missionary Societies were formed in Boston and Chicago. Women held executive positions on the International Missionary Council, which became a part of the World Council of Churches, and the United States Foreign Missions Conference, which was connected later to the National Council of Churches.

The enthusiastic effort of American women for overseas mission work led to the formation of missionary societies in the Eastern part of the United States. Notable beginnings were the Female Foreign Missionary Societies in Massachusetts and Connecticut in 1812.[97] The Baptists, Methodists, and other societies were founded, so were auxiliaries and associations for the cause of foreign mission with male and female members. Although women comprised a large majority of the missionaries, the men still led the decision making. The women's associations were "much more stable and active than those of the men,"[98] due to women's dynamic leadership and dedication. However, despite their effort and sacrificial personal giving of funds for mission, the women's associations experienced decline in the 1850s. It was assumed that due to control of policy decision making by men, women's voices were unheard, particularly in promotion and ways to use the funds they themselves raised.[99]

The Missionary Society of the Methodist Church, founded in 1819 and approved by the church the following year, helped reinforce the importance of mission work worldwide. The most successful Methodist women's organization was located in Baltimore, Maryland, where the first Methodist Conference in the United States was held 1848.[100] Besides raising funds and mission education awareness, the women missionaries recruited and trained girls and boys on the fundamental beliefs of the Christian faith, with the goal of preparing them to "Christianize" the unconverted souls.[101]

Dr. Hugh Vernon White, an authority on mission, pointed out that the accomplishments of women in mission work were innumerable. Historical accounts reveal the tremendous work of women in bringing the Good News to people of different cultures, races, and languages.

## 4.2 Education

Women excelled in education. Many women who were capable in leading societies and associations and served on committees and commissions within their religious denominations in the Protestant tradition became "leavening force" in the church. Women theologians, such as Dr. Mary Lyman of Union Theological Seminary of New York and Dr. Georgia Harkness (1891–1974) of the Pacific School of Religion in Berkeley, California, increased the credibility of women in religious and theological fields through their teaching and writings.[102] Places like salons, coffee shops, and women's homes were used as gathering sites for dialogues, literary, philosophic, and religious assemblies. Women organized them, which was significant volunteer work for them, and creative activities that the church did not and could not offer.

American women who became outstanding missionary educators included Isabel MaCausland, a sociology professor who taught at Kobe College, Japan; Lolita Wood, Old Testament professor who served in Poona, India; and Alma Locke Cook, who taught in China and later in South Rhodesia. In the late 1800s and early 1900s, women often initiated the formation of small independent groups called "peripheral groups," which aided in the growth of Christianity. A group of women gathered each week to reflect on and share the Sunday sermons, the content and context and the implications for them. Men frowned on the women's gathering and their purpose. The women, however, defended themselves by reasoning out their desire to understand the sermons and the application for Christian living.

## 4.3 Social Justice Advocacy and Action

Women's courage, conviction, and commitment won the hearts and minds of the people in the Eastern shores of the United States, as they struggled and fought for their rights to speak, to vote, and to learn. Despite the prohibitions imposed by them by the church hierarchy during the Reformation movement not to do priestly work or religious service, they expressed boldly their opposition to church and church authorities' abuses. The spread of Protestant beliefs and values from the Old World to the New World brought a genuine desire not simply to study the Scriptures, its meaning and implications for daily living, but also to manifest individual rights and freedom. The pursuit for social justice was evident in the women's causes for education, abolition of slavery, and the right to vote.

The nineteenth century was called a century of causes. Eleanor Flexner (1908–1995), author of *Century of Struggle*,[103] spoke of women's activities from 1800 to 1900 in the context of the women's rights movement. Congregational-oriented Oberlin College in Ohio championed women's education in the United States when the college became inclusive by accepting all students regardless of race, color, or sex in 1833. This was a breakthrough in women's education. Lucy Stone (1818–1893), an Oberlin alumna, "became an agent and lecturer for the Anti-Slavery Society" and for women's rights, legally, politically, morally, and religiously.[104] Antoinette Brown (1825–1921), a Unitarian female minister—the first ordained women minister in the United States—also advocated against slavery. She preached until she was ninety years old.

Women believed in their right to vote. Susan Anthony led the women's rights movement, particularly the exercise of the right to vote. Lucretia Coffin Mott of Seneca, New York, was determined to urge women their "sacred duty" to fight for the "sacred right to the elective franchise."[105] Along with her husband, Mrs. Mott founded Swarthmore College in 1864. Other notable women who helped spread Christian virtues and values included Frances Willard, Dorothea Dix, and Harriet Tubman. Frances Willard led women's causes for temperance, purity, and peace, and women's rights. While Dorothea Dix pushed for prison and hospital reforms and advocated for mental health, Harriet Tubman, an escaped slave, secured the release of many slaves. These and other women contributed significantly in freeing the slaves. Thus, in 1863, the Emancipation Proclamation was signed (180). Harriet Beecher Stowe's *Uncle Tom's Cabin*, a now classic book filled with religious images, was considered the most influential anti-slavery publication of its period.[106] Behind Christianity's survival were courageously confident and confidently courageous women of faith.[107] Their feet and hands moved along with their mouth as they shared their conviction of gender equality and human rights.

## 4.4 *Healing Ministry and Evangelism*

Women were influential in taking the initiative in establishing healing ministries in the United States, particularly in the nineteenth century. As early as the seventeenth century, however, women had spearheaded such form of service. Anne Hutchison (1591–1643), in particular, reached out to the sick and spread her conviction on God's love that won many followers in the Bay Colony, the Eastern coast of the United States. She was described "a woman of ready wit and bold spirit," and the "American Jezabel."[108] It was noted that women gathered in her home to hear her commentary on the weekly sermons preached by John Cotton and John Wilson. She believed on Rev. Cotton's message of a "covenant of grace" more than on Rev. Wilson's "covenant of works." Her church authority, however, denounced her views as dangerous. One belief that Hutchinson upheld was that God's revelation to humans could be over and above what the Bible conveyed. The other belief Hutchinson taught was that one's personal inner assurance of God's grace would justify and validate one's relationship with God. The conservatives assumed that her views undermined the authority of the Bible and human effort to work out one's salvation "with fear and trembling." Evidently, Ms. Hutchinson's progressive religious views were far ahead of her days. Her tragic death in 1643, along with seven of her eight children, was a great loss for the advancement of a more open, nontraditional view of the Christian faith.[109]

Another noted woman who formed the most significant of the religious communities in North America was Ann Lee, originally from England who moved to New York in 1776 with a few faithful followers. Imprisoned and persecuted in England for her religious beliefs, she continued spreading her message of human iniquity and divine healing in the United States, particularly in New York and New England. Ann Lee felt God's power and was filled with visions and divine revelations and other gifts from God; as were her followers.[110] The Shakers Society or The United Society of Believers in Christ's Appearing was formally organized in 1787, three years after Ann Lee's death.[111] The Shakers grew with religious revivals and emphasis on withdrawal from the world, celibacy, and perfection."[112]

In the latter 1800s mind-care movements blossomed. The movements focused on healing through prayer and meditation, without using medicine and different forms of drugs. Interest in spiritual healing began possibly with Melinda Cramer, who formed a group along with some other leading women of the movement. Mary Baker Eddy (1821–1910), one of the women, taught and practiced the New Testament ministry of spiritual healing. She wrote the step-by-step healing process and published her writings. She discovered the laws of health and applied those same laws to material prosperity. She founded the Christian Science Church in the 1870s. After her death in 1910, she left to the churches, her publications, an estate of over two million dollars. Her influence spread as a large following of Christian practitioners grew around the world.

New England, site of the beginnings of mind-care movements, produced female writers, like Julia Anderson Root, author of the *Healing Power of Mind* and Helen Bigelow Merriam, *What Shall Make Us Whole?*[113] Myrtle and Charles Filmore, founders of Unity School of Christianity in the late 1800s, kept the mind-care movement alive. They emphasized positive thinking and mind over matter. Among the many women evangelists by the end of the 1800s and the beginning of the 1900s, Aimee Semple McPherson and Ellen White (1827–1915) stood out. Ms. McPherson led the Four Square Gospel, a charismatic, speaking-in-tongues-centered church. With her husband James White, Ellen White founded Seventh Day Adventists; she purported the values of fresh air, sun, and a simple vegetarian diet for good health. She spoke to large crowds of up to two thousand people, and established schools and colleges. In 1880, with the leadership of General William Booth and his wife Catherine, the Salvation Army came to the United States from England. They were known for their evangelical approach, great support for women and charitable work for the less fortunate. The religious body gave importance to women and their place in the structure and organization around the world, until these days.

Indeed, women in North America shared their gifts and graces for the spread of Christ's mission in the midst of patriarchal domination in the church and society. They manifested genuine commitment, deep compassion, confident courage, and courageous confidence in fulfilling the work of Christ, the work of love and service especially to the powerless and marginalized people. R. Pierce Beaver once exclaimed, "their (women's) religious zeal exceeded that of men generally."[114] They tread on hot water with male dominance in leadership and male monopoly in decision making; yet they emerged stronger and bolder in meeting the educational, physical, moral, and spiritual needs of persons of all ages and stages. Those women deserve grand commendation and deep gratitude from women and men around the world.

*Afrie Songco Joye*

## 5. South America

### *5.1 Roman Catholic Women in Mission*

In Latin America, Christian history and mission can only be understood along the lines of the Conquest, this latter understood as invasion, occupation and colonization of a continent by European powers (Spain, Portugal, England, France, and Holland) during the fifteenth, sixteenth, and seventeenth centuries. This domination was justified by three great principles: "No one's land," as the right of Europeans to appropriate the lands by not recognizing the property rights of the indigenous peoples; "Lands for Christianity," with the mission of spreading Christianity, even by force, in which the new religion did not believe indigenous people to have a soul; and, finally, the so-called "Rights of Conquest," which meant the right to impose a culture, religion, and society over others and to use the indigenous peoples as forced labored hands.[115]

Colonization was performed between the cross and the sword, with the consequent demographic collapse or genocide. There are three different ways of reading the history of colonization and Christianity: (1) The so-called "black legend," which upholds that the genocide of the inhabitants of America was carried out exclusively by the Spaniards. It is believed that such legend was promoted by the British and the Protestants who were fighting Christian Spaniards for the dominion of the new lands.[116] (2) The "white legend," which maintains that the Conquest was a civilizing process that allowed the Christianization of indigenous peoples, and that the death of the indigenous population was due to the new diseases to the continent brought by the Europeans. Those who uphold this viewpoint do not believe that there was such a thing as the genocide of the indigenous peoples but a peaceful process of civilization and Christianization.[117] And finally, (3) The one called by León Portilla "the vision of the defeated," which upholds that the Conquest was a physical, cultural and religious genocide by the hands of Europeans and which was continued by the hands of the American States.[118] According to this viewpoint, the indigenous population was terminated, forced to do hard labor, and indigenous women were sexually abused being exposed to the process of *mestizaje*.[119] This last viewpoint is the one I will follow in this historical framework since history is not neutral. The *mestizaje* was the result of violence brutally exercised by Spanish men over against indigenous women.

Christianized Latin America went from colonial to post-colonial, and, finally to neo-colonial times, keeping the oppression and violence against women, indigenous and African peoples. Toward the end of the nineteenth century and the beginning of the twentieth century, with the initiative of Pope Leo XIII to make of the laity an active organization, lay and consecrated women were also integrated to the missionary and apostolic work with more strength in the Catholic Church and in society: "In many Latin American nations feminine Catholic organizations were born that gave space to women to act in society in the name of the Church and in defense of their proposals, such as the Social Catholic Action in Columbia in 1908, or the Union of Catholic ladies in Mexico in 1912, in the midst of an extremely conflictive contact."[120] In other places, such as Chile, the organization of Catholic Chilean women was founded in 1921, and in Brazil in 1922 the associations of Catholic women played an important role in the catechesis and evangelization. By 1930, a women's branch of the Catholic Action was established along the whole continent and was one of the movements with greater strength in the catechesis and evangelization with a liberal tendency in that time, even amidst religious women.[121] I could affirm that these movements were some of the predecessors that gave way to what was later known as liberation theology.

Despite the historical load of triple discrimination and marginalization that women underwent in history in Latin America by reason of their sex, their race, and their economic status of poverty, they have been the basis and foundation of the experience of faith of Christianity. After the Vatican II Council and since 1970, missionary women support and are responsible for small base communities, and catechesis in parishes, and exercise well-defined leaderships in solidarity with the poor. Several congregations of Catholic religious missionaries started to live at the margins of the cities accompanying process of liberation such as: human rights groups, citizen solidarity networks, caring of the sick using the indigenous traditional medicine, and the creation of diverse study centers for biblical and theological reflection.

In the field of the defense of the rights of women, there is a variety of groups where lay and religious women work in the search of the victims of violence, in particular the "disappeared" during military dictatorship. An example of those groups is the Mothers of Mayo square in Buenos Aires. Other more recent examples are the groups of Women of Juarez who look for their disappeared daughters, and the movements in favor of indigenous women.

The reality of poverty and suffering in Latin America, the birth of liberation theology, the documents of the Latin American Episcopate, especially Medellín (1969) and Puebla (1979), and the struggles of Latin American peoples against dictatorships and poverty, are the reasons to awaken a political and social commitment as Christians in Latin America. In this process, women are playing a fundamental role as subjects of a new theological reflection based on a concrete Christian praxis: that the Gospel be Good News of liberation from any oppressive situation, especially for women. From this perspective, the Latin American Christian cannot be alien to the Christian prerogative of political, economic, and social transformation. Not all Catholic Christians, however, keep this commitment, and many prefer to maintain a more conservative stand, creating, thus, a slow process of involution, especially in regard to the ecclesiastical patriarchal structure.

*Marilú Rojas Salazar*

## 5.2 Protestant Women in Mission in Latin America

As Latin American republics gained independence from Spain beginning in the early nineteenth century, the Roman Catholic Church remained the official state church and the only permitted religious institution. Protestant presence in the region grew slowly during the nineteenth century as state policy was changed to first tolerate and then encourage Protestant groups. During the later decades of the nineteenth century, liberal parties came to power in most of Latin America and promulgated constitutions that established lay governments and allowed freedom of worship. These liberal governments welcomed the presence of Protestants as they sought to limit the influence of the Roman Catholic Church and expand trade relations with Europe and North America.

Often the first Protestants on the scene were colporteurs who traveled from place to place selling Bibles and tracts. Though the early colporteurs were usually men, Melinda Rankin (1811–1888) was possibly the first female Protestant missionary to work among Latin Americans. Without the support of a particular mission society or denominational board, she worked in education and Bible distribution among Mexicans from 1850 to 1871. The congregations she organized laid the foundations for the National Presbyterian Church of Mexico.[122]

Building on the work of early colporteurs, North American mission societies and denominational boards looked increasingly to the continent to the south as a mission field. Historic Protestant missions presented Protestantism as a form of thought and religious practice that would contribute to the modernization of the continent. Educational institutions, which would disseminate Protestant values beyond the churches founded by the missionaries, played a central role in efforts to reform Latin American societies. Between 1880 and 1920, Methodists, Presbyterians, Baptists, Congregationalists, and Quakers built a network of primary and secondary schools, many of which were schools for girls. Brazil, Cuba, and Mexico had the greatest concentration of Protestant schools.[123] Single women missionaries, many sent by women's societies or boards, served as teachers and directors in these schools.[124]

Latin America was excluded from consideration at the International Missionary Conference held in Edinburgh in 1910 because the continent was viewed by the organizers as already Christianized. Yet the historic Protestant mission boards working in Latin America argued that the Roman Catholic Church had failed to meet the spiritual needs of the population. In four hundred years, the Roman Catholic Church had not given the people access to the Christian Scriptures nor promoted high moral standards. The Protestant missions saw most Latin Americans as only nominal Roman Catholics.[125] Despite the fact that none of the justification for Protestant mission activity focused on the needs of women in Latin America, women missionaries outnumbered the men, not only in historic Protestant missions but in other Protestant mission efforts as well. Neither historians of Protestantism in Latin America nor those writing on the history of women in mission have paid much attention to the contributions of women to this movement.[126]

Faith missions gave many North American and British women the opportunity to serve in Latin America. Susan Beamish (1874–1950) of Ireland was sent to Argentina in 1901 by the Regions

Beyond Missionary Union. In 1903, she married the Scottish missionary Harry Strachan. After fifteen years of service in Argentina, the Strachans founded their own mission agency, later known as the Latin America Mission, with its headquarters in Costa Rica. In 1921, Susan started a Bible institute for women. Two years later, men joined the student body. This institution, today the Latin American Biblical University, has trained women and men from throughout the continent as evangelists, pastors, Christian educators, and seminary professors.[127]

Early Pentecostalism also provided new spaces for women to exercise gifts in mission. Alice Christi Wood (1870–1959) from Canada founded the first Pentecostal mission in Argentina. Raised among Quakers, Wood had already served as pastor of a Friend's church as well as a missionary with the Christian and Missionary Alliance in Venezuela and Puerto Rico before she experienced Pentecostal renewal in 1907 in Ohio. In her ministry in Argentina from 1910 to 1959, Wood promoted the full participation of women in the leadership of the church, though the movement of which she was a part was not always open to women's leadership gifts.[128]

The case of Mary Ann (Hilton) Hoover, who served in Chile with her husband, Willis Hoover, demonstrates the transnational nature of the Pentecostal movement and the role women played in its spread. The Hoovers, missionaries with the Methodist Episcopal Church from the United States, learned of the Pentecostal revival at the Mukti Mission, founded in 1905/06 by the famous Indian convert Pandita Ramabai, through the letters of Minnie F. Abrams, a training school classmate of Mary Ann's. In 1909, the Hoovers established the Iglesia Metodista Pentecostal, later renamed later as Iglesia Evangélica Pentecostal. Today, the IEP is the largest Pentecostal church in Chile. Mary Ann became a role model for women's leadership within the church. [129]

Protestant churches, especially Pentecostal congregations, have grown rapidly in Latin America, especially in the last decades of the twentieth century. More than a quarter of the population in countries such as Brazil and Guatemala now identify themselves as Protestant. Though some recent studies have focused on women and gender roles in Latin American Protestantism,[130] much more research needs to be done to recover the history of women as protagonists of this movement.

*Karla Ann Koll*

# 6. Oceania

## 6.1 Introduction

The area known as Oceania covers a large area and has many islands in the vast Pacific Ocean. It is normally divided into three sub-regions described as Melanesia (the black islands) in the southwest with New Guinea being the largest; Polynesia (the many islands) in the central and southeastern region; and Micronesia (the small islands) in the northwestern part. From the sixteenth century, European sailors gradually mapped this enormous ocean called "Mar Pacifico" by Ferdinand Magellan. But it was not until the end of the eighteenth century that the English explorer James Cook began mapping the Pacific in earnest. His three voyages to the Pacific (1768–71, 1772–75, and 1776–80) led to an increased awareness of the Pacific Islands and also coincided with the rise of the British evangelical missionary movement that was to prove influential for the rooting of Christianity in these islands.

The London Missionary Society (LMS) was founded in 1795 and chose the Pacific as its first missionary field. In 1797, twenty-six lay artisans and four ordained clergy arrived in Tonga, Tahiti, and the Marquesas with the aim of "civilizing" the people by introducing European skills combined with Christian teaching. The Anglican Church Missionary Society, founded in London in 1799, started work in Aotearoa/New Zealand on Christmas Day, 1814, along the same lines. The Methodists subsequently arrived in 1822. The pattern was similar to that elsewhere in the Pacific—initial resistance followed by widespread acceptance of Christianity. The Roman Catholics generally arrived after the Protestants and sometimes found their converts among those who were enemies of people aligned with the Protestants. The rapid spread of Christianity owed much to the work of indigenous people who took the gospel with them on their travels.

## 6.2 Women in Mission

As the story of the European settlement of Aotearoa (New Zealand) has been told, golddiggers, missionaries, pastoralists, soldiers, adventurers, and agricultural laborers have been brought into view. It is the men who settle the country and break in the land. Women are viewed only in terms of their relationship to men: "the pioneers and their wives." They are mute appendages, unnamed and therefore unidentified.[131]

Women have been seen as adjuncts to men and "have been systematically written out of historical and anthropological records"[132] so it is harder to find information on the early women in mission in Oceania. Australian historian, Hilary Carey offers this helpful analysis of the role of missionary wives. They have been seen as helpmeets, as heroines and as partners.[133] First, most missionary wives were helpmeets to their husbands, enlisted to join in their husbands' work and to support their husbands in their high calling. Second, missionary wives were portrayed as heroines, "fighting the hostile forces of paganism in dangerous and exotic locations, bringing their feminine virtue to transform the domestic and gender arrangements of natives everywhere."[134] Third, they were also seen as partners whose labor was essential to the work of the mission. They performed and directed the practical tasks such as teaching, nursing, cooking, and other tasks normally assigned to the women's sphere as well as providing the role model for a Christian family life. The Christian home became a conscious and intentional missionary strategy so the women had the central goal of reforming the family by role-modeling pious domesticity and a Christian family life. The Christian home became the missionary goal but its relationship to colonialism was often unquestioned and indeed even sanctioned. The focal point of a Protestant mission station was the mission home and this offered "the object lesson of a civilised, Christian home."[135] Conversion and civilization were often seen as a unitary process and that domesticating indigenous women according to English middle-class ideals was part of the early CMS missionary strategy.

However, many missionary wives were involved outside the home in such endeavors as education, health care, advocacy issues, land rights, setting up organizations, and Bible translation. Their personal vocations and evangelical spirituality meant that they had a vital interest in the salvation of the local people. Women as "mother educators" were seen as both agents and disrupters of colonialism. While they were agents of the Empire, they were also dismantlers of the Empire by educating local women and so giving them the inklings of liberty and equality.

Roman Catholic women religious, especially the Sisters of Mercy, made valuable contributions in the area of education. Sister Mary Joseph Aubert (1835–1926) is a notable example of a woman engaged in educational and charitable work, eventually founding a new Order, "Daughters of our Lady of Compassion."[136] Florence Young (1856–1940), who had Brethren connections, is another example of a woman who started a mission organization. She founded the Queensland Kanaka Mission in order to convert Melanesian laborers in the Queensland sugar plantations—it was later renamed the South Sea Evangelical Mission. Elizabeth Colenso (1821–1904) worked as a missionary teacher and Bible translator both in Aotearoa/NZ and on Norfolk Island for most of her life.[137]

Henry Williams, one of the first CMS missionaries to Aotearoa/ NZ, may have been unusual in his view which he stated to the CMS Committee in London, "With regard to Mrs Williams, I beg to say, that she does not accompany me, merely as my wife but as a fellow-helper in her work."[138] However, this does seem to be nearer the reality of women's involvement in mission in the early days in Oceania. The women were as fully involved as they could be in God's mission in Oceania and certainly the development and spread of Christianity in this region would have been very different without them.

*Cathy Ross*

## 7. Conclusion

1. Through all centuries and continents various *divisions* have been the core stumbling block for women seeking access to the transmission and/or appropriation of Christian faith. They were caused, among others, by culture, Bible interpretation, gender rules, class barriers, and labor rules.

2. Divisions produced various *exclusions*: from agency in the public sphere, from church leadership, from power in decision making regarding finances and church laws.

3. Women's motives to get involved in the transmission of faith as missionaries and in the appropriation of faith as converts were to overcome all kinds of exclusions, that is, to get *access* to education, ordained ministry, and to public space.

4. On the way to become either missionaries or converts they had to *negotiate* viable solutions—be it by standing firm, by compromising, or by exploring new ways serving all sides. Sometimes, negotiated solutions were later revoked so that women had to start again from the beginning. This was often happening in processes of institutionalization of mission initiatives following the pioneer period.

5. Women involved in mission (at the Western home base of a missionary organization and in the "mission fields"; transmitters as well as appropriators of faith) were exploring their ways

of communication either beyond male-shaped forms or within the limited spaces of given structures. They developed specific *relationships*: sometimes egalitarian, small, rule-less, and sometimes chaotic. Relationships were often based on local ground and were self-supporting, sometimes they were crossing boundaries of space, culture, gender, class, color, and religious communities.

6. Women missionaries and women converts were exploring and establishing their own ways of communication and cooperation. Sometimes they invented alternative *forms of organization*: networking, low level and flexible structures, egalitarian instead of hierarchical structures and processes of decision making. These forms reflect relationships as a highly appreciated value in women's perspectives throughout the past.

7. Women's agencies in the transmission and appropriation of faith are all aiming at *transformation* and renewal in the sense of the new creation: transformed gender relations and cross-cultural relations, new forms of being church, and of doing mission.

8. *Bible readings* are regarded as a means to look critically at ideologies legitimizing harmful cultural structures, church forms, marriage forms, church (canon) laws, as well as to find new ways of shaping culture, marriage, Christian home, and church laws.

*Christine Lienemann-Perrin*

## Further Reading on Women in Mission History

### Books on Women's Role in Orthodox Churches[139]

Elisabeth Behr-Sigel and Kallistos Ware, *The Ordination of Women in the Orthodox Church* (Geneva: World Council of Churches Publications—Risk Book Series No. 92, 2000).

Deborah Belonick, *Feminism in Christianity: An Orthodox Christian Response* (Syosset: Dept. of Religious Education, Orthodox Church in America, 1983).

Christina Breaban, Sophie Deicha, and Eleni Kasselouri-Hatzivassiliadi, eds., *Women's Voices and Visions of the Church: Reflections of Orthodox Women* (Geneva: World Council of Churches, 2006).

Sebastian P. Brock and Susan Ashbrook Harvey, *Holy Women of the Syrian Orient: The Transformation of the Classical Heritage* (Berkeley: University of California Press, 1987).

Sarah Elizabeth Cowie, *More Spirited Than Lions: An Orthodox Response to Feminism and a Practical Guide to the Spiritual Life of Women* (Salisbury: Regina Orthodox Press, 2001).

Kyriaki Karidoyanes FitzGerald, *Orthodox Women Speak: Discerning the "Signs of the Times"* (Brookline: Holy Cross Orthodox Press, 1999).

Kyriaki Karidoyanes FitzGerald, *Women Deacons in the Orthodox Church: Called to Holiness and Ministry* (Brookline: Holy Cross Orthodox Press, 1998).

Kyriali Karidoyanes FitzGerald, ed., *Encountering Women of Faith* (Berkeley: InterOrthodox Press, 2005).

Ellen Gvosdev, *The Female Diaconate: An Historical Perspective* (Minneapolis: Light and Life Publishing, 1991).

Kyriak Leonie Liveris, *Ancient Taboos and Gender Prejudice: Challenges for Orthodox Women and the Church* (Aldershot, Hampshire: Ashgate Publishing Ltd., 2005).

Frederica Mathewes-Green, *The Illumined Heart: The Ancient Christian Path of Transformation* (Brewster: Paraclete Press, 2002).

Brenda Meehan, *Holy Women of Russia: The Lives of Five Orthodox Women Offer Spiritual Guidance for Today* (Crestwood: St. Vladimir's Seminary Press, new Edition 1997).

See also: http://www.orthodoxwomensnetwork.org/ (November 03, 2011).

## Books Relevant for Several Continents

Fiona Bowie et al., eds., *Women and Mission. Past and Present: Anthropological and Historical Perceptions* (Oxford et al.: Berg Publications 1993).

Mary T. Huber and Nancy C. Lutkehaus, eds., *Gendered Missions. Women and Men in Missionary Discourse and Practice* (Michigan: University of Michigan Press, 1999).

Dana L. Robert, *American Women in Mission: A Social History of Their Thought and Practice* (Macon: Mercer, 1997).

Susan E. Smith, *Women in Mission. From the New Testament to Today* (Maryknoll: Orbis Books, 2007).

Andrew Walls, *The Missionary Movement in Christian History: Studies in the Transmission of Faith* (Maryknoll: Orbis Books, 1996).

## Europe

Anne Jensen, *God's Self Confident Daughters: Early Christianity and the Liberation of Women* (Kentucky: Westminster John Knox Press, 1996).

Mary T. Malone, *Women and Christianity* (Dublin: Columbia Press). *Vol. I: The First Thousand Years* (Dublin: Columbia Press, 2000); *Vol. II: From 1000 to the Reformation* (Maryknoll: Orbis Books, 2002); *Vol. III: From the Reformation to the 21st Century* (Maryknoll: Orbis Books, 2003).

Jo Ann Kay McNamara, *Sisters in Arms: Catholic Nuns through Two Millennia* (Cambridge, MA and London: Harvard University Press, 1996).

## Africa

Dictionary of African Christian Biography: http://www.dabc.org/ (November 3, 2011).

Dorothy L. Hodgson, *The Church of Women: Gendered Encounters between Maasai and Missionaries* (Bloomington and Indianapolis: Indiana University Press, 2005).

Brigitta Larsson, *Conversion to Greater Freedom? Women, Church and Social Change in North-Western Tanzania under Colonial Rule* (Uppsala: Uppsala University, 1991).

## Asia

Virginia Fabella and Mercy Amba Oduyoye, eds., *With Passion and Compassion: Third World Women Doing Theology* (Maryknoll: Orbis Books, 1988).

Evelyn Monteiro, SC and Antoinette Gutzler, eds., *Ecclesia of Women in Asia: Gathering the Voices of the Silenced* (New Delhi: ISPCK, 2005).

Limatula Longkumer, "Women in Theological Education from an Asian Perspective," in Dietrich Werner, David Esterline, Namsoon Kang and Joshva Raja (eds.), *Handbook of Theological Education in World Christianity* (Oxford: Regnum Books International, 2010), 68-75.

Wong Wai Ching, "Engendering Christian Mission in Asia: Understand Women's Work in the History of Mission," in *Asian Journal of Women's Studies* (2003): 38-66.

Sun Ai Lee Park, "Asian Women in Mission," in *International Review of Mission*, (April 1992): 265-280.

## North America

Pierce R. Beaver, *American Protestant Women in World Mission: History of the First Feminist Movement in North America* (Grand Rapids: Eerdmans, 1968, rev. ed. 1980).

Elizabeth A. Clark and Herbert Richardson, eds., *Women and Religion: The Original Sourcebook of Women in Christian Thought* (San Francisco: Harper 1977).

Elsie Thomas Culver, *Women in the World of Religion* (Garden City: Doubleday, 1967).

Dana L. Robert, *American Women in Mission: A Social History of Their Thought and Practice* (Macon: Mercer, 1997).

Shelton H. Smith et al., eds., *American Christianity: An Historical Interpretation with Representative Documents. Vol. II, 1820–1960* (New York: Scribner's Sons, 1963).

## Latin America

Virginia Navarro and Marysa Sánchez Korrol, *Women in Latin America and the Caribbean* (Indiana: University Press, 1999).

Ana María Bidegain, *Participación y protagonismo de las mujeres en la historia del catolicismo Latinoamericano* (Buenos Aires: San Benito, 2009).

Elizabeth E. Brusco, *The Reformation of Machismo: Evangelical Conversion and Gender in Colombia* (Austin: University of Texas, 1995).

## Oceania

Cathy Ross, *Women with a Mission: Rediscovering Missionary Wives in Early New Zealand* (Auckland: Penguin, 2006).

Mark Hutchinson and Edmund Campion, eds., *Long Patient Conflict: Essays on Women and Gender in Australian Christianity* (Sydney: Macquarie University, 1994).

# Endnotes

1. Andrew F. Walls, *The Cross-Cultural Process in Christian History: Studies in the Transmission and Appropriation of Faith* (Edinburgh: T&T. Clark, 2002); Walls, *The Missionary Movement in Christian History: Studies in the Transmission of Faith* (Edinburgh: T&T. Clark, 1996); Walls, "Christianity Across Twenty Centuries," in *Atlas of Global Christianity 1910–2010,* ed. Todd M. Johnson and Kenneth R. Ross (Edinburgh: Edinburgh University Press, 2009), 48f (*short and excellent*); Sebastian Kim and Kirsteen Kim, *Christianity as a World Religion* (London/New York: Continuum, 2008). Kim and Kim show in an exemplary manner how it is possible to focus on the most relevant events and thoughts in Christian (mission) history in five world regions.

2. Dale T. Irvin, "World Christianity: An Introduction," *Journal of World Christianity* 1:1 (2008): 1-26 (1f).

3. For further reading on the mission history in Europe, see David J. Bosch, *Transforming Mission: Paradigm Shifts in Theology of Mission* (Maryknoll: Orbis Books, 1992); Stephen B. Bevans and Roger P. Schroeder, *Constants in Context: A Theology of Mission for Today* (Maryknoll: Orbis Books, 2004).

4. Exceptions: Franciscans went to China in the thirteenth century; Portuguese mission was started in Congo in the fifteenth century, and so on.

5. Heike Walz, "Swiss-German Protestant Women in Mission: The Basel Mission: Nineteenth to Twenty-First Century," in this volume.

6. During that crucial time, Augustine developed his theological and philosophical opus, *City of God,* discerning the Civitas Dei from the Civitas Terrena.

7. Mary T. Malone, *Women and Christianity* (Dublin: Columbia Press); *Vol. I: The First Thousand Years* (Dublin: Columbia Press, 2000) (=Malone I); *Vol. II: From 1000 to the Reformation* (Maryknoll: Orbis Books, 2002) (= Malone II); *Vol. III: From the Reformation to the 21st Century* (Maryknoll: Orbis Books, 2003) (=Malone III); quotation here: Vol. I, 186.

8. Adolf von Harnack, *Die Mission und Ausbreitung des Christentums in den ersten drei Jahrhunderten* (Wiesbaden: VMA-Verlag, 1924). The large volume remained for several decades the benchmark in the historiography of mission.

9. Heinzgünter Frohnes, Hans-Werner Gensichen and Georg Kretschmar, eds., *Kirchengeschichte als Missionsgeschichte,* 2 Vol.s (München: Kaiser, 1974–1978).

10. Malone I-III; Susan E. Smith, *Women in Mission: From the New Testament to Today* (Maryknoll: Orbis Books, 2007); Jo Ann Kay McNamara, *Sisters in Arms: Catholic Nuns through Two Millennia* (Cambridge and London: Harvard University Press, 1996). My short comments on women's mission in Europe are mainly referring to Malone, in some cases also to Smith and McNamara.

11. For more details on women martyrs, see Anne Jensen, *God's Self Confident Daughters: Early Christianity and the Liberation of Women* (Kentucky: Westminster John Knox Press, 1996; translation from German: Gottes selbstbewusste Töchter. Frauenemanzipation im frühen Christentum? Freiburg i. Br. et al.: Herder 1992).

12. Malone I, 176.

13. Ibid., 180.

14. In the Ancient church, coinobites were practicing—differently from hermits—a community life. Later on, coinobite communities of the Latin Church often belonged to a religious order and observed its rules.

15. So, for example, the abbesses of monasteries in Ely, Coldingham, Oxford, Essen, Fontevrault, Göss, Heidenheim, Hildesheim, and Quedlinburgh.

16. Malone I, 193f.

17. Beguines were called according to the beige color of their dresses.

18. Similar to the women's movement, however smaller in size and relevance, a movement of lay males, called *begardes*, arose at the same time.

19. Malone II, 182. Because mystic spirituality was beyond clerical control, the clergy became suspicious of losing spiritual power over mystics like Marguerite Porete. One of her famous books is titled: "The Mirror of Simple Souls." It is a guide for uneducated women to achieve mystical union with God.

20. Malone II, 128.

21. "Religious women and men represented a lay alternative to the hierarchical church [...]. Renunciation of sexual activity enabled them to maintain a spiritual parity, [...] a third gender." McNamara, *Sisters in Arms*, 148-175 (148).

22. R. Puza, article 'Frau' B (II: Kanonisches Recht) in *Lexikon des Mittelalters,* Vol. IV (München: Deutscher Taschenbuchverlag, 1992), 855f.

23. Malone I, 216.

24. It saw a timid revival in later centuries. Today there still exist six beguinards in Belgium and sixteen in Germany—many of them founded in the twentieth century by contextualising the original model in today's world; see: http://de.wikipedia.org/wiki/Beginenhof; http://www.beginenhof.de/basics/aktuelles.html (both September 19, 2010).

25. Exceptions: Baptists, the Moravian Church, and the Lutheran missionary enterprise in South India (Tranquebar) initiated by the Danish King in 1706.

26. Smith, *Women*, 97. Pope Pius V decreed in 1566 that strict enclosure was even required of Tertiaries.

27. Malone III, 134; Smith, *Women*, 117.

28. Quoted according to Smith, ibid., 118.

29. For the following, see Malone III, 104-112; Margaret Mary Littlehales, *Mary Ward: Pilgrim and Mystic* (London: Burns & Oates, 1998).

30. Quoted in Malone III, 109.

31. Malone III, 110.

32. See, for example, Adrian Hastings in his seminal opus on *The Church in Africa 1450–1950* (Oxford: Claredon Press 1994); regarding lay movements arising in the 1950s, he states that "women were important—more important than within the Church's missionary-shaped structures. Such movements [...] all constituted a degree of threat [...] to clerical and missionary control." (603). See also by Adrian Hastings, "Were Women a Special Case?" in Fiona Bowie, ed., *Women and Missions: Past and Present: Anthropological and Historical Perceptions* (Providence: Berg, 1993), 109-125.

33. Christian Baëta in an interview with Waltraud Haas, a former missionary in Cameroun; cf. Waltraud Haas, *Erlitten und erstritten* (Basel: Basileia Verlag, 1994), 47.

34. To name just a few: Waltraud Haas; Andrea Schultze; Brigitta Larsson; Dorothy L. Hodgson; Phillys M. Martin; T.O. Beidelman; Dana L. Robert. Women theologians are joined by religious scientists in this field of research, among them Rosalind I. J. Hackett; Gerrie ter Haar, and Jean Comaroff.

35. Mercy Amba Oduyoye; Nyambura Njoroge; Isabel Phiri as well as many other members of the *Circle of Concerned African Women Theologians.*

36. Homepage of the Dictionary of African Christian Biography: http://www.dacb.org/ (September 28, 2011).

37. See *Biographical Dictionary of Chinese Christianity,* launched in April 2006, www.bdcconline.net (September 29, 2011).

38. Elizabeth Isichei, *A History of Christianity in Africa: From Antiquity to the Present* (London: SPCK Publishing, 1995); see also Belaynesh Bekele Abiyo on Ethiopia in this volume. Church Fathers in Northern Africa were Tertullian (d. after 220), Cyprian (d. 258), and Augustine of Carthage (d. 430).

39. "In the mind of the Portuguese and in the mind of the people of Congo religious conversion was dependent upon a royal decision." Hastings, *Church in Africa*, 75. For Congolese Catholicism under Afonso I and his successors, see ibid., 79-86.

40. Hastings, ibid.

41. Todd M. Johnson and Kenneth R. Ross, eds. *Atlas of Global Christianity 1910–2010* (Edinburgh: Edinburgh University Press, 2009). North Africa, with its Muslim majority, is included in these figures: 40 percent of Africa's population is Muslim, compared to 48 percent of Christians, ibid. yxz.

42. http://www.dacb.org/stories/congo/kimpa1_vita.html/ (September 28, 2011).

43. For Kimpa Vita, see http://en.wikipedia.org/wiki/Kimpa_Vita (July 28, 2011).

44. The most famous example is the Kimbanguist church (Eglise de Jésus Christ sur la terre par son envoyé spécial Simon Kimbangu), founded as a messianic movement in 1921 in Nkamba, a place called the New Jerusalem by his adherents.

45. "Ethiopia" has been coined by liberation movements throughout Africa as the only African country which has resisted successfully colonialism. Ethiopian type of African Independent/ Instituted Churches have, therefore, nothing to do with the age old Orthodox Tewahedo Church or other churches *in* Ethiopia.

46. Frederick Quinn, "Christinah Nku 1894 to c. 1980 St. John Apostolic Faith Mission South Africa," see http://www.dacb.org/stories/southafrica/nku_christinah.html (September 28, 2011); Linda E. Thomas, "Christina Nku: A Woman at the Center of Healing Her Nation," in *Embracing the Spirit*, ed. Emilie M. Townes (Maryknoll: Orbis Books, 1997).

47. Quinn, ibid.

48. Christine Landman, "Christina Nku and St John's: A Hundred Years Later," see http://www.christina-landman.co.za/nku.htm (September 28, 2011).

49. For further information and bibliographical references on Lenshina and her Lumpa Church, see Norbert C. Brockman, "Lenshina Mulenga Mubisha, Alice c. 1924 to 1978," http://www.dacb.org/stories/zambia/lenshina1_alice.html/; also http://en.wikipedia.org/wiki/Alice_Lenshina (both July 28, 2011).

50. "Again and again in a mission history, the early significant baptisms were mostly women," notes Adrian Hastings, "Were Women a Special Case?" 112.

51. T. O. Beidelman, "Altruism and Domesticity: Images of Missionizing Women among the Church Missionary Society in Nineteenth-Century East Africa," in *Gendered Missions. Women and Men in Missionary Discourse and*

*Practice,* eds. Mary Taylor Huber and Nancy C. Lutkehaus (Michigan: University of Michigan Press, 1999), 113-143.

52. Ibid., 117.

53. Ibid., 124.

54. Ibid., 123.

55. Ibid., 133.

56. Dorothy L. Hodgson, *The Church of Women. Gendered Encounters between Maasai and Missionaries* (Bloomington and Indianapolis: Indiana University Press 2005). Hodgson has spent several years among the Maasai to investigate in the Spiritan's mission policy.

57. Ibid., 205.

58. Ibid., 1.

59. Male leaders in the Massai society.

60. Ibid., 257.

61. Todd M. Johnson and Kenneth R. Ross, eds., *Atlas of Global Christianity* (Edinburgh: Edinburgh University Press, 2009).

62. Leonard Fernando and G. Gispert-Sauch, *Two Thousand Years of Faith: Christianity in India* (New Delhi: Viking, Penguin Group, 2004), 55ff.

63. Eliza F. Kent, *Converting Women: Gender and Protestant Christianity in Colonia South India* (New York: Oxford University Press, 2004), 9.

64. Mary John Manazan, "The Filipino Woman: A Historical Perspective," in John S. Pobee, *Culture, Women and Theology* (Delhi: ISPCK, 1994), 49-64.

65. This orientation and the pairs are drawn from a schema prepared for the present chapter by Christine Lienemann-Perrin.

66. Mananzan, "The Filipino Woman," 49-64.

67. Ibid., 60.

68. Ibid., 63.

69. Ibid., 64.

70. Brian Stanley, *The History of the Baptist Missionary Society 1792–1992* (Edinburgh: T & T Clark, 1992), 198.

71. Dana L. Robert, *American Women in Mission: A Social History of their Thought and Practice* (Macon: Mercer University Press, 1997), 32.

72. Li Li, "Christian Women's Education in China in the Nineteenth and Early Twentieth Centuries," in http://www4.samford.edu/lillyhumanrights/papers/Li_Christian.pdf (August 9, 2010).

73. Hyaeweol Choi, *Gender and Mission Encounters in Korea: New Women, Old Ways* (Berkeley: Global Area, and International Archive, University of California Press, 2009), 69, in www.escholarship.org/uc/item/0q65z7q9#page-69. (June 11, 2011).

74. Ibid., 70ff.

75. Noriko Kawamura Ishii, *American Women Missionaries at Kobe College, 1873–1909: New Dimensions of Gender* (New York: Routledge, 2004), 109.

76. Dana L. Robert, *Christian Mission: How Christianity became a World Religion* (Oxford: Wiley-Blackwell, 2009), 141.

77. Ibid., 139.

78. Ibid.

79. R. G. Tiedemann, "Christianity in East Asia," in *The Cambridge History of Christianity,* Vol. 7 (2006): 451-474.

80. Ibid., 453.

81. Ibid., 454.

82. Ibid., 465.

83. Dana L. Robert, "Christendom and Colonization," in Howard Clark Kee, et al., *Christianity: A Social and Cultural History* (New Jersey: Prentice Hall, 1998), 536.

84. Haruko Nawata Ward, "Women Martyrs in Passion and Paradise," in *The Journal of World Christianity*, Vol. 3, No. 1 (2010): 44-66.

85. Ibid., 56.

86. Ibid., 65.

87. Ibid., 66.

88. Anna May Chain, "Wives, Warriors and Leaders: Burmese Christian Women's Cultural Reception of the Bible," in *SBL* Archive, http://www.sbl-site.org/publications/article.aspx?articleId=455 (June 10, 2010).

89. Susan Hill Lindley, *"You Have Stepped Out Of Your Place": A History of Women and Religion in America* (Louisville: Westminster John Knox Press, 1996), 72.

90. See, Gauri Viswanathan, *Outside the Fold: Conversion, Modernity, and Belief* (Princeton: Princeton University Press, 1998), 118-152.

91. Dana L. Robert, *Christian Mission*, 141.

92. Peter C. Phan, "World Christianity and Christian Mission: Are They Compatible? Insights from the Asian Churches," in *International Bulletin of Missionary Research*, Vol. 32, no. 4 (October 2008): 193-200.

93. Elsie Thomas Culver, *Women in the World of Religion* (Garden City: Doubleday, 1967), 184. Figures in brackets in the main text refer to that book.

94. Ibid., 174.

95. Ibid., 112.

96. Ibid., 123.

97. Pierce R. Beaver, *American Protestant Women in World Mission: History of the First Feminist Movement in North America* (Grand Rapids: Eerdmans, 1968, Rev. 1980), 35.

98. Ibid., 37.

99. Ibid., 38.

100. Ibid., 4f.

101. Ibid., 44.

102. Pierre Dubois (1255–1321) suggested that girls be trained in theology and medicine to win others "by spirit and service." His voice was several centuries ahead of his time (Culver, ibid., 123f).

103. Eleanor Flexner, *Century of Struggle: The Woman's Rights Movement in the United States* (Cambridge: Belknap Press, 1959).

104. Ibid., 172.

105. Ibid., 179.

106. Adrian Hastings, "Latin America," in Adrian Hastings, ed., *A World History of Christianity* (Grand Rapids: Eerdmans, 1999), 328-368 [438].

107. Culver, ibid., 184.

108. Shelton H. Smith, Robert T. Handy and Lefferts A. Toetscher, *American Christianity: An Historical Interpretation with Representative Documents. Vol. II, 1820–1960* (New York: Scribner's Sons, 1963), 114.

109. Ibid., 115.

110. Ibid., 590.

111. Ibid., 563.

112. Ibid., 587.

113. Julia Anderson Root, *Healing Power of Mind* (Whitefish: Kessinger Pub, 2010); Helen Bigelow Merriam, *What Shall Make Us Whole? (1890)*, (reprint: Whitefish: Kessinger Pub, 2009).

114. Beaver, *American Protestant Women*, 17.

115. Virginia Navarro and Marysa Sánchez Korrol, *Women in Latin America and the Caribbean* (Indiana: University Press, 1999), 77- 122.

116. Bartolomé de Las Casas, *Brevísima Relación de la destrucción de las Indias 1542*. (*A Brief Account of the Destruction of the Indies*) In this book, Las Casas denounces the situation of abuse of the Spaniards upon the indigenous. Even though the Crown implemented new laws that penalized the abuse, there were some, however, who considered the accusations to be exaggerated and denounced them as a "black legend" against the Spaniards.

117. Bernal Díaz del Castillo, *Historia verdadera de la conquista de Nueva España* Vol. I 1492–1581 (Alicante: Biblioteca Virtual Miguel de Cervantes, 2005).

118. La cumbre continental de Pueblos y Organizaciones indígenas de América, Quito 2004 and Cumbre Continental de Pueblos y Organizaciones indígenas del Continente de Abya Yala, Mar de la Plata, 2005; See Miguel León Portilla, *La visión de los vencidos* (México: UNAM, 1959) ; Leonardo Boff, *Quinientos año de Evangelización. De la conquista Espiritual a la Liberación Integral* (Santander: Sal Terrae, 1992).

119. The Mexican-American theologian, Virgilio Elizondo, defines the term *mestizaje* as follows: "a mixture of personal groups in the biological, cultural and religious sense" (una mezcla de dos o más grupos de personas biológica, cultural y religiosa). See Virgilio Elizondo and Janette Rodríguez, *Our Lady of Guadalupe: Faith and Empowerment Among Mexican-American Women* (Austin: University of Texas Press, 1994).

120. Ana María Bidegain, *Participación y protagonismo de las mujeres en la historia del catolicismo Latinoamericano* (Buenos Aires: San Benito, 2009), 34-35. "En muchas naciones latinoamericanas nacieron organizaciones católicas femeninas que dieron espacio a las mujeres para actuar en la sociedad en nombre de la Iglesia y en defensa de sus planteamientos, como la Acción Social Católica en Colombia en 1908 o la unión de Damas católicas en México en 1912, dentro de un contacto extremamente conflictivo."

121. Ibid.

122. Melinda Rankin, *Twenty Years among the Mexicans: A Narrative of Missionary Labor* (Cincinnati: Chase & Hall), 21875, see http://www.archive.org/details/twentyyearsamong00rankrich (August 5, 2010). *Christian Work in Latin America: Report of the Congress on Christian Work in Latin America held in Panama, February 1916*. Volume II (New York: Committee on Cooperation in Latin America and Missionary Education Movement, 1917), 115-118.

123. Jean Pierre Bastian, *Historia del Protestantismo en América Latina* (Mexico: CPUSA, 21990), 143-150.

124. *Christian Work in Latin America: Report of the Congress on Christian Work in Latin America held in Panama, February 1916*. Volume III (New York: Committee on Cooperation in Latin America and Missionary Education Movement, 1917), 463-470.

125. For an example of this line of argument, see Robert E. Speer, *South American Problems* (New York: Student Volunteer Movement for Foreign Missions, 1912), 141-164.

126. For example, Dana L. Robert's seminal work, *American Women in Mission: A Social History of Their Thought and Practice*, does not give any examples of Protestant women working in Latin America.

127. W. Dayton Roberts, "The Legacy of Harry and Susan Strachan," in *International Bulletin of Missionary Research* 22:3 (July 1998): 127-131. http://

www.internationalbulletin.org/system/files/1998-03-127-roberts.pdf (September 20, 2010).

128. Kathleen M. Griffin, "La 'Cuestión de la Mujer' en el pentecostalismo del centenario argentino: Gualeguaychú, 1910–1917," forthcoming.

129. Mary's schoolmate, Minnie F. Abrams (1859–1912), joined the Mukti Mission in 1898. She reported in detail on the revival movement and sent the book to Mary and her husband.

130. For example, see Elizabeth E. Brusco, *The Reformation of Machismo: Evangelical Conversion and Gender in Colombia* (Austin: University of Texas, 1995).

131. Bronwyn Labrum, *Women's History, A Short Guide to Researching and Writing Women's History in New Zealand* (Wellington: Bridget Williams Books, 1993).

132. Fiona Bowie, "Introduction: Reclaiming Women's Presence," in *Women and Missions: Past and Present Anthropological and Historical Perspectives,* eds., Fiona Bowie, Deborah Kirkwood and Shirley Ardener (Oxford: Berg, 1993), 1.

133. Hilary Carey, "Women's Peculiar Mission to the Heathen, Protestant Missionary Wives to Australia 1788–1900," in *Long Patient Conflict, Essays on Women and Gender in Australian Christianity,* eds. Mark Hutchinson and Edmund Campion (Sydney: Macquarie University, 1994), 26.

134. Carey, "Women's Peculiar Mission," 33.

135. Diane Langmore, "The Object Lesson of a Civilized Christian Home," in *Family and Gender in the Pacific,* eds. Margaret Jolly and Martha Macintyre (Cambridge: Cambridge University Press, 1989), 84-94.

136. See Jessie Munro, *The Story of Suzanne Aubert* (Wellington: Bridget Williams Books, 1996).

137. See Cathy Ross, *Women with a Mission: Rediscovering Missionary Wives in Early New Zealand* (Auckland: Penguin, 2006).

138. Henry was a former naval officer and arrived in Paihia on 3 August 1823 to be the head of the CMS mission in New Zealand. Henry Williams, "Algar Williams Collection, Williams Family Papers," (Auckland War Memorial Museum Library, Te Papa Whakahiku, MS91/75, 1783–1965), Henry Williams, 6 August 1822.

139. Since neither a section on women in the mission history of Orthodox churches, nor a case study on Orthodoxy is included in the volume, bibliographical references on women's role in the Orthodox churches are included here.

# PART II
# *Case Studies*

# CHAPTER 3

# Mothers for All: The Missionary Impact on Models of Femininity and Maternity in West Africa

*Amélé Adamavi-Aho Ekué*

## 1. Introduction

When by the end of the nineteenth century, women were assigned specific roles by Western missionary societies within the missionary enterprise in the so-called missionary fields, no one thought of the repercussions this encounter between European and indigenous women would have.

Today, memory about this distant history is pale. However, knowledge about the missionary impact on role models for women in both church and society would contribute to a more differentiated understanding of the current societal changes impinging on gender relations. The theme of women and mission is thus not only a subject of historical-missiological interest, but one that reaches to the most actual and controversial dimensions of global Christianity. How did Christianity, in the course of its inculturation in diverse contexts, contribute to cultural, social, and religious change? Where did the encounter between foreign and indigenous people give rise to mutual enquiries about the underlying structures, motives, and stories?

In answering these questions the present article seeks to offer first a theme-oriented contextual introduction that explores the encounter between female European and African missionaries on the late nineteenth- and early twentieth-century Gold and Slave Coast. A subsequent case study located in the sub-region will develop on local role models for women on both a diachronic and synchronic level, and the changes that can be noted in this respect in confrontation with external role models. Specific attention will be paid to religious functional roles, as the deaconesses of the European missionary societies, the *hamedadawo* (parish mothers) of the local missionary church, and in the modern times, to the prophetesses of Pentecostal-charismatic churches, and the models of femininity and maternity they convey.

In a critical analysis the focus will be laid on the internal management of this confrontation between different functional roles and role models. Three lines of analysis will be particularly developed. First, the ambiguity of the missionary presence with regard to its impact on indigenous women's adoption of role models will be scrutinized. Second, light will be shed on the intertwining of social, political, and religious aspects, which over the course of time contributed to the development of preferred models of femininity and maternity. Third, with the discussion of the distinctive yet interrelated layers of history of missions, societal organization and religious innovation a systematic review of the main findings of the case study will be offered, in view of highlighting the contemporary ramifications of the historical antecedents. The evolvement of alternative models of femininity and maternity, religious innovation as catalyzing factor for female versatility, and the impact of aspirations to power on fostering asymmetric gender relations will be themes that deserve attention in this section. These themes will receive a more conceptual framework in the last paragraph where the implications of the analysis for missiology will be discussed.

## 2. Missionary Christianity on the Gold and Slave Coast

The encounter of the population on the ancient Gold and Slave Coast with Christianity reaches as far back as the end of the fifteenth century when, among other Europeans, the Portuguese explored the West African coast in search of suitable places for slave trade. The fortifications, like *Sao Jorge da Mina* (Today Elmina), which served them as stations for trading and expeditions into the inner-land, as well as the temporary home for clergy[1] are until today reminders of this era.

It is, however, only in the mid-nineteenth century, when especially Protestant missionary societies sent missionaries in the region, that the history of Christianity in this part of West Africa has been genuinely institutionalized. The missionary initiatives from Europe were primarily led along distinct ethnic boundaries. The Basel Mission started their activities in 1845 among the *Akan* in today's Ghana, the North German Mission (Bremen Mission) in 1847 among the *Ewe* of present Ghana and Togo, and the Wesleyan Methodist Mission in 1840 among the *Ge* and *Ga* of the actual Southern Togo and Ghana. It has to be noted that although the period was characterized by accentuated Protestant missionary initiatives, the Roman Catholic Church also has been present in the region throughout the end of the nineteenth century contributing to the implantation of Catholic Christianity.[2]

The most pertinent question underlying the subsequent encounter and confrontation between European missionaries and African population was: Is it possible to be both African and Christian at the same time? The missionaries attempted not only to enhance a process of religious change, but also made an effort of evangelizing and civilizing a population which they deemed "lost in the darkness of heathenism."[3] The encounter centered thus not only about a possible change of religious affiliation but more fundamentally about the (in)compatibility of Christianity with the indigenous worldview and cultural traditions. This can be further illustrated by three dimensions that are also related to the understanding of the changes introduced by missions in the field of gender relations and role models.

The first dimension of the missionary encounter between Europeans and the local population is marked by a serious conflict of loyalty related to conversion. The social organization of the local population being traditionally tied to the performance of certain rituals that would assure the continuity of the community, the adoption of Christianity to the detriment of the ancestral religion was marked by high levels of uncertainty on the side of the African population. What would be the consequences for the family, the clan, and the entire ethnic group if the habitual ceremonies were no longer performed? Hesitation, fear, at times even pressures and official prohibition, determined individual reflections on conversion.[4] Conversion was considered a valid option only if the traditional religious system could no longer offer plausible responses to individual problems and biographical turning points. Several motives, like issues of recovery of health and survival after serious sickness, the attractiveness of the biblical narratives and the missionary preaching on them, as well as the overcoming of distress were thus paramount for the consideration of daring the transition from one religion to the other.[5]

It is interesting to note that conversion was also a key theme for the missionary engagement in favor of women, through whom the missionaries expected to be able to win over larger strata of the local population for Christianity.[6] Deaconess Hedwig Rohns, in charge of the missionary work among women in Southern Ghana around the turn of the nineteenth century, reported of incidents with African women, which reflect precisely this conflict of loyalty felt between the traditional religion and Christianity.

"I want to see, if your God is more effective than our idols, therefore I offer you my daughter for his service, with the hope that my youngest child will thus survive."[7] Even more so the conflict becomes apparent when potential converts vocalize their fear directly when called to consider conversion: " 'You have experienced the power of our God, don't you want to become a Christian?'—'My mother, I would like to, but I am afraid of the demons.'"[8]

As a second dimension, it is important to note the attention given to the presence of evil forces as part of the local African worldview, intertwined with the aspiration for a protected life. In this context it deserves to be highlighted that the missionaries' understood the local religious system with spiritual forces, both good and evil, witchcraft, fetishes, and divinities as superstitious and irreconcilable with Christianity. The external symbol of conversion and the readiness to lead a Christian life was thus, in the missionary view, the converts' abandonment of all rituals and signs of the fetish (In Ewe *trowo*, in Ge *legba*), translated by the missionaries as "demons."[9] The intercultural communication operated thus along a double line. On the one hand, the missionaries viewed traditional religious practice as superstition that needed to be eradicated. On the other hand, they introduced images of the devil and demons as standing behind the evil forces experienced as real and life-threatening by the local population, which reinforced the belief in witchcraft.[10]

In the perspective of the African converts, Christianity stood in concurrence with the traditional religious system and had to "prove" its plausibility. Was the Christian God "powerful" enough to provide security, health, and communal longevity? However, there was also the recognition that conversion demands an inner preparation and change of attitude, as an Ewe woman's answer to Hedwig Rohns' question on becoming a Christian reflects: " 'I still want to wait, right now there is too much hate in my heart. I have an enemy and I hate her'."[11]

Against this background it becomes understandable how the

process of conversion was accompanied by a cognitive rear-rangement by which the converts were able both to integrate the worldview and ritual framework of the new religion and to adapt it to their realities.[12] For the deaconesses the educational work with indigenous women constituted a possibility to counter what they identified as the "vicious influence," as integral part of an elaborated missionary education system with an early childhood school, a girls' school, and a young women's association.

Education can thus be considered as the third dimension of importance in the European-African encounter. The mission-aries and deaconesses emphasized the educational mandate among indigenous women as the key for the solidification of the missionary endeavor.[13] The missionaries thereby pursued the intention to contribute to both their young female pupils' formal instruction and to their inner transformation. This can be illustrated by the curriculum offered in the missionary schools, ranging from reading, writing, counting, vernacular and for-eign languages, singing and needlework. The most important aim, however, was to enable them to read the Bible and to incor-porate the message of the biblical narratives to their own lives.[14] This existential appropriation of the Christian message through female missionary education is an essential feature for the understanding of the inculturation of Christianity in the local context.

## 3. Indigenous Interpretations of Missionary Gender Models—Three Case Vignettes

The missionary encounter did not take place in a neutral sphere. Both missionaries and indigenous population had partic-ular views of each other, and carried expectations and aspirations along with their interaction. To note this is particularly important with regard to the different gender roles prevalent in this context. The traditional societies located on the former Gold and Slave Coasts were organized according to diverse political, social, and religious structures. The continuum of *Ewe*-people were charac-terized by an acephalic organization with several decentralized chiefdoms, whereas the ethnic groups of the *Ga* and *Ge* have tra-ditionally been kingdoms with a centralized leadership of several affiliated clans and families.

Women, especially in the coastal region occupied central religious, economic, and political roles. As *queen-mothers* of the Akan in Southern Ghana for instance, they performed rit-ual as well as representative and status-bearing roles for the ethnic group. Women were also at the forefront of local trade and commerce, securing more often than not the survival of the entire family. The dual-sex organization of the traditional society[15] offered women the possibility of gaining recognition by taking on roles in public life and for the benefit of the entire community. Ritual communication was one important sphere in which women played a crucial role, as according to the traditional belief women were the appropriate media of the divinities. Interestingly, the traditional ideology provided a relative flexibility of gender construction. This is for instance mirrored in the absence of gender prefixes and the use of a neuter particle as object and subject pronouns in the vernacular languages. Also, women could be conceptualized as taking on male functions for ritual purposes without any discriminatory distinction. Moreover, the eligibility of women for these roles was not made dependent on their maternity.

There is still insufficient information about the way traditional African societies functioned in respect to these flexible gender constructions. How did the social and political organization influence the way women achieved and exerted public, including religious roles? And how did the confrontation with foreign worldviews and the introduction of social systems through colonization and mission impact the local gender construction? The following case vignettes seek to offer insights into these questions, especially with regard to West African women's religious roles in mission. Both historical and contemporary examples are taken as illustration to shed light on the continuity and discontinuity of the motives at stake in this cross-cultural discourse. However, one methodological problem needs to be considered here, namely the scarcity of sources, and among the few existing most are documents written by missionaries, deaconesses, and male indigenous missionary assistants.

## 3.1 Case Vignette 1: Local Deaconesses and Female Assistant-teachers

The relationship between the missionaries and the local population can be characterized as an asymmetric one, in which the European missionaries, as well as the deaconesses, adopted a paternalistic attitude. Not only did they hold the conviction that the "heathens" need to be converted to Christianity, but also that they would have to be civilized and led to a lifestyle devoid of the traditional practices viewed as demonic and indecent. This was particularly valid for the perception of women:

The woman in heathenism is subject to foreign forces. She is not master of herself, and can therefore not develop herself to gain individuality, she remains more or less a non-personal representative of a mass. Most of all she is the property of her tribe and remains [...] very fondly linked with it.[16]

This view stands not only in contrast to the social and economic autonomy of women in the region, but seems to be dominated by the religious judgment offered by the missionaries around the turn of the last century. The work of the deaconesses was oriented toward the preparation of indigenous women for the enhancement of the missionary endeavor from within the local context. Education and evangelization among women and children were understood as the stepping stones for the implantation of Christianity in the region.

It is interesting to note, that the European deaconesses encountered local women with perceptions marked by the nineteeth-century bourgeois society with distinct gender roles,[17] restricting the possibility of women to gain public recognition to the private sphere and the role of maternity. The deaconesses, recruited by the missionary societies among single women constituted thus both within their own society and in West Africa marginal role models. They were able to provide leadership in a professional field outside the private domain, yet were dependent on male missionaries, and—most remarkable in a context that emphasizes the reproductive capacities of women—were not mothers.

The recruitment of indigenous women as deaconesses and assistant teachers at the missionary stations in the *Ewe-* and *Ga*-region was subject of a controversy among the missionaries themselves.[18] What has been initially envisioned as a pragmatic step to enhance the missionary work and to ameliorate the cultural translation of the gospel in the region, turned out to unveil a disparity in the conception of gender roles in the perspective of the local population. The example of Mercy Baëta,[19] who became the first indigenous female teacher and deaconess of the Ewe-Church, gives indications for this observation.

Born in 1880, Mercy Baëta was trained at the missionary station of Keta. First, she attended the boys' school, later, after the foundation of the girls' school she joined classes for early childhood learning. After completion of her formation, she was recruited as teacher at the girls' school from 1894 to 1903. Her biography is certainly an outstanding example of how the local population aspired to the deaconesses' educational proposals, but also how the proposed gender role model generated individual conflicts. Mercy Baëta quit working in 1903, when her family insisted on her marriage. Although the sources are tacit about the precise circumstances, one could presume that on the one hand the expectation to fulfill the conventional female role of maternity, and on the other hand the incompatibility of marriage and maternity with her function as teacher and deaconess, may have contributed to this decision.

Mercy Baëta returned to serve the deaconesses in Keta in 1906 as she finally did not get married at this time; this only happened in 1916, one year prior to her death when she wedded Thomas Acolatse, but her story initiated an indirect discourse on the flexibility of gender roles within the local setting: How can the traditionally transmitted role of women as religious function-bearers be reconciled with maternity? And how can the role model of European deaconesses become reinterpreted within the indigenous Christian worldview?

## 3.2 Case Vignette 2: "Hamedadawo" or Mothers for All

The creativity, which indigenous women used to integrate the foreign role model of a deaconess into the local, flexible gender system can be illustrated by the office of a parish mother (*hamedada*), introduced officially in the constitution of the Ewe-Church in 1933.[20] Elderly, married women were appointed as parish-mothers to complement the clergy's pastoral work. The tasks assigned to the parish-mothers impinged clearly on the missionary field as Luise Funke's differentiated description shows:

> It is not the duty of the parish-mothers to preach or to offer baptismal instruction, for these pastors, teachers and church elders are responsible. However, what an indispensable help does a loyal parish-mother constitute for a pastor when she accompanies the women to be baptized, offers pastoral care to them, gives them indications for their behavior, when difficulties arise from their heathen parents.[21]

Three aspects seem to be significant here. First, the parish-mothers are married, which means that they have, according to the prevalent traditional worldview, at least potentially fulfilled their roles as biological mothers and are now appropriate models for the flexible gender role construction in the region, allowing women to be both active in the private and public sphere. Unlike the single and childless European deaconesses and the first indigenous deaconesses, they were not exposed to the conflict of loyalty between the expectation to become mothers and thus to ensure the continuity of the community, and the possibility to gain recognition through an official role.

Second, being elderly, menopausal women the parish-mothers, having accomplished their biological role as mothers, were in a phase of life allowing them to dedicate time and commitment to take on the social role of mothers—mothers for all—within the missionary work of the parish.

Third, in such a phase in which the transition from the traditional religious system to Christianity was accompanied by high levels of individual and collective rearrangements, the presence of the parish-mothers as interpreters for the experienced changes was of utmost importance. The *hamedadawo*, with their double belonging to the indigenous community and the missionary church parish, represented also the cultural translatability of Christianity on the local terrain. This is particularly important in a period of the missionary history when the local church parishes started to consolidate their communities with new converts.

## 3.3 Case Vignette 3: Ritual and Power among Christian Prophetesses

In this third case vignette attention will be given to a third phase in the history of Christianity in the context studied. Interestingly, we are able not only to witness the genesis of African Instituted Churches (AIC), and the implantation and spread of evangelical and Pentecostal-charismatic churches,[22] but also a new type of missionary active women even within the now autonomous missionary churches.

The first type is represented by women in the missionary churches, both in the Protestant and Catholic churches of Ghana and Togo. *Dada Akofala* ("Mother consoler") is an example for a woman who, after a life-long membership in the Evangelical Presbyterian Church of Togo (*Eglise Evangélique Prébytérienne du Togo*, EEPT), experienced in the 1950s a vision—"she saw the light"[23]—which encouraged her to gradually split off the EEPT and to found initially a prayer group within the EEPT and later, when excluded from the missionary church, an independent church, *L'Eternel est mon Berger* ("The Lord is my shepherd"). The missionary church observed with much suspicion the way *Dada Akofala* attracted particularly women with particular health concerns or problems to bear children into her community in Lomé, for whom the reported stories of spontaneous healing and childbirth after the encounter with Akofala and prayers with her were attractive.

Followers of *Dada Akofala* formed a congregation similar to a base community in her house in Lomé,[24] where they would live during the day before returning to their own households in the evening. The structure of the day was determined by regular and extended devotions, which followed specific liturgies developed by Akofala, based on verses of the Bible, songs from the Hymnbook of the EEPT, as well as hymns with lyrics adapted to Akofala, prayers and meditations. Adherents of the community were also exhorted to a strict spiritual life with fixed times for specific prayers, for instance praying Psalm 23 whenever one leaves the house, and with periods of fasting and reclusion.

*Dada Akofala* would also practice "prayer-healing" in receiving solicitors with special individual concerns. These healing sessions reposed on the personal encounter between the believer and *Akofala*, and the prayers formulated at this occasion by her and the solicitor. The characteristic of these prayer-healing sessions is a three-layered procedure comprising the individual healing session with *Akofala*, the private continuation of the prayers she indicated to the believer, and the testimonial of successful healing after the recovery.

Whereas *Akofala* remains rather a singular figure in the setting of local missionary churches, another type of missionary women has emerged within the African Instituted Churches of the region. The spiritual dimension of healing plays a prominent role in the AICs. Health and well-being is considered as a divine benediction according to the local worldview,[25] it is thus not surprising that the quest for maintenance and restoration of health still constitutes a primal motive for adherence to these churches and impregnates the spiritual practices of the communities to a great extent. Particular attention is given to the domain of maternity, childbirth, pregnancy, sterility and child care.

The Celestial Church of Christ,[26] with congregations along the West African coast and strong branches in Benin, Togo, and Ghana may serve as an empirical example. The church, which lays emphasis on the manifestation of the Holy Spirit and the practice of rituals depending on it, like prophecy, healing and glossolalia, is composed of a large female membership. Women feel attracted to the church not only because their physical and spiritual concerns as well as their needs for ritual accompaniment are taken seriously here, but also because their spiritual capacities are embedded into the hierarchical system of offices open to them.

Women in the Celestial Church of Christ can occupy all charismatic-spiritual offices in the congregation, for example as a prophetess, able to receive visions and to interpret them as well as to heal and to prophesy. Women occupying these positions receive the title of "honorable mother," which indicates the specific dedication and functional role these women take on particularly for female congregation members. Female members of the congregations, especially pregnant women, may spend a limited time in the church premises and receive both spiritual and physical accompaniment until the delivery.

However, it is important to mention that women cannot be pastors and preach in the Celestial Church of Christ. Their role is rather highlighted in another field of importance for the ritual practice in this church, which is purity and impurity in relation with sexual intercourse, menstruation, and childbirth. After the delivery a woman remains forty days impure, has no access to the church building ("temple"), is prohibited to touch any sacred object, and may not take part in congregational meetings. She is not even allowed to take part in the ritual of outdooring (*videto*), celebrated by the relatives without the child's mother, during which the child receives his or her first name. During the entire period the woman is considered impure, she has to follow extended purification and cleansing rituals offered by the *honorable mothers*, before she will be allowed to return amid the church congregation to present herself with her newborn and give thanks to the Lord.

## 4. Critical Analysis from Women's Perspective

In the three case vignettes different types of female missionaries were presented, who each in her own way brought to the fore specific themes relevant for the missiological discussion of gender roles within the selected context.

First, the local deaconess as a female role model seemingly fitted into the exported gender role model of the European missionaries and deaconesses. Young girls and women who successfully attended the missionary schools were selected to assist the deaconesses in their missionary work amidt the local women. Celibacy, moral decency, and servitude were considered as the key features of potential indigenous deaconesses, standing thus in perfect consistency with the exigencies for the European deaconesses. However, the assigned role model collided with the local representation of women's roles and with a generally more flexible gender system, allowing women to take on functions both in the private and in the public spheres.

Whereas indigenous deaconesses, like Mercy Baëta, integrated the expectations of their European counterparts regarding moral decency and servitude without difficulty, celibacy constituted a serious challenge for them as this lead into a conflict of loyalty between their families, the larger community, and the missionary community. The deliberate denial of maternity was according to the traditional worldview not a valid female option as this endangered the continuity of the lineage.[27] It is thus not surprising that precisely at this turning point of her biography Mercy Baëta obviously hesitated between the conformity with the traditional local and the missionary role model for women. It would certainly be a simplification to state that individual choices, all the more in such rather rare cases of indigenous deaconesses, were merely determined by functional options. It is important, however, to underline the personal, institutional, and communal dimensions of this conflict.

The missionary interface did in this early period of mission in the region lead to a dual adoption of the gendered expectations. On the one hand, the European missionaries and deaconesses succeeded in implanting solidly the image of the morally decent and subordinate woman in a Christian household. On the other hand, African women, while adopting this role model, remained loyal to the traditional gender expectations. The ideal of maternity and the importance of reproduction in the local worldview hindered local women from adopting divergent role models, like the celibate deaconess, which would have constituted a sharp rupture with the communal linkage.

Undoubtedly, education plays an important role in the missionary encounter, and its impact on gender roles and relations has so far certainly been underscored. In the present case vignette education plays a double role. First, it correlates with the institutionalization and professionalization of the missionary work with women at the end of the nineteenth century in West Africa. Second, and most importantly, it is the field in which the cultural and religious encounters were negotiated.[28] In as much as Mercy Baëta and other indigenous adopted the role model assigned by the missionaries and deaconesses, they were, at the same time, able to use their own education and their position as assistant teachers at the missionary schools as vehicle for the translation between the role models.

Education as mode of translation between different cultural gender arrangements is a theme, which became even more apparent with the autonomous Ewe-Church in the region, and the introduction of the *hamedadawo*. The parish-mothers, entrusted with a distinctive missionary role for the benefit of newly converted women, served as the interpreters of the new religion by offering guidance for an adequate life conduct as well as models for women who fulfilled traditional gendered expectations—especially maternity—alongside a public religious function.

These "mothers for all"[29] were thus not only of significance for the individual but also collective transmission of a gender role model. Maternity was henceforth no longer only the marker of communal recognition and individual valorization of women, but gained within the new social organization of the Christian parishes a religious meaning.

The parish-mothers' task to accompany newly converted women and to mediate between them and their families, who possibly complicated the choice of their relative and enforced the conflict of loyalty, constituted thus—even though in a new religious setting—a familiar role model which was highly valuated.

At the same time, and this is significant for the consideration of implications on the local gender relations, the institutionalization of the *hamedadawo* in the Ewe-church constituted the beginning of asymmetric gender relations and unequal representations of women in the official hierarchy. The parish-mothers were not part of the church elders' meeting, and could not take on pastoral tasks nor did they have the opportunity to be consecrated as pastors of the church.

The female prophets of the African Instituted Churches, and the same may be valid for women in the contemporary Pentecostal-charismatic churches and to a lesser degree for female charismatic personalities within missionary churches, occupy frequently much higher religious positions than women in the missionary churches. Women as preachers, healers, prophetesses, and evangelists are current in these congregations. However, this does not eradicate an evident distinction made between the valorization of women's contribution in the ritual practice of the churches and the factual recognition with the assignment of official pastoral positions. The case vignette on prophetesses in the context has shown that women alongside, or even against, the collectively attributed role, may individually opt for a "spontaneous," but not institutionally supported, missionary role.

Both the examples of *Dada Akofala* and the prophetesses of the Celestial Church of Christ illustrate how the missionary role is intricately centered about gender. On the one hand, the religious practice is organized around a charismatic leadership personality who uses her femininity as a medium for healing (*Dada Akofala*), and on the other hand around the collective experience of ritual accompaniment of maternity (Celestial Church of Christ).

In the cases presented, power, status, and ritual are paradoxically intertwined with the perception of gender. Whereas both in the diachronic and synchronic perspective, on the one hand, women have gained access to official religious positions, on the other hand they have been restricted in the exertion of these functions. The status and power women achieved, either through the deployment of individual efforts and capacities or through the entrustment of collective tasks, only reached to a certain extent. This paradoxical intertwinement merits further discussion in order to understand the role of gender as factor in religious and social performance in the region.

## 5. Questions for Discussion

All illustrated case vignettes made evident that women were and are considered as actors within the local social and religious setting. Their participation in public ritual performances and their insistence on selected themes, as religious and social cohesion of female converts, healing and fertility, stresses their importance for the larger society and renders their status plausible. At the same time the exclusion from distinct positions or spheres of activities is in a subtle way linked with gender. The underlying reasons however are complex.

For the "missionary generation" of parish-mothers the exclusion from the presbyters' council was the attempt to limit their potential aspiration for clerical roles, only open to men. This did not constitute a diminishment of their impact on the missionary endeavor, but rather the institutionalized attempt to maintain the status quo of gendered role divisions in the missionary church,[30] attributing clergy positions to men and diaconal functions to women. Individual personalities, in the missionary as well as in Pentecostal and charismatic churches could, as the example discussed shows, claim clerical roles, and eventually resume to split off if this opportunity was not realizable within the limits of their church of origin.

Gender does obviously not only play a role for their recognition as religious leader figures capable to attract a number
of people, but also as one reason for their exclusion from the
mainline churches. As founders of new communities growing
out of the missionary churches, they create thus environments
for the performance of new gender role models alongside the
articulation of themes suppressed or only sparingly touched
upon in the church of origin. Akofala responded, on an individual level and certainly not devoid of personal ambitions, to
the popular longing for the experience of wholeness and salvation as both spiritual and physical momentum. In doing so she
transcended existing boundaries in her church of origin both in
terms of assigned gender roles as well as in accepted theological paradigms.[31] Her femininity served as a vehicle to extrapo-
late healing as a feature of the local religious-cultural universe,
which has been suppressed in the *praxis pietatis* of her reformed
church of origin, but resonated much with the local worldview
and the need to experience the divine also physically.

In legitimizing her healing mission through divine visions
and through years of prayerful life she became transformed in
the eyes of her followers into a person with obvious charisma
and power, a status which at the same time caused the schism
from the Protestant church. The official church considered her
community as a sect and stigmatized her healing rituals as
incompatible with the official church teaching, condoning her
behavior as personal cult. On the surface and in the official comments her womanhood played no significant role; however, on
the level of indirect discourse femininity was influential in this
case, as the community attracted primarily women for whom
the female leader and prophetess represented a role model of
a woman gaining status through religious capacities and functions.

Yet the question remains how the ritual performance of
women, and the potential social recognition derived from it,
interplays with the way in which they deal with procreation.
The issues of reproduction, pregnancy, and childbirth, as suggested earlier, play a paramount role in the self-definition of
women in the region under study and cannot be detached from
collective cultural images of women, which in turn are intertwined with a host of historical, social, and economic factors.
The interesting process of relevance in this respect is the fact
that the traditional flexible gender-system, allowing women
the exertion of roles both within and outside the private sphere
while being biological mothers, was accompanied over the time

by two crucial restrictions. The first is related to the prevailing ideology of seeing women temporarily as polluted because of menstrual blood and the second to the perception of impurity caused by childbirth, and therefore excluding them from ritual places and performances for which they were traditionally pre-destined.

The theme of pureness/impurity, familiar from the traditional cultural-religious setting, reoccurs, as described previously, within the religious practice of the AIC. A stereotyped conclusion that women are excluded from cultic functions because of these restrictions, at least prior to the menopause, should not be drawn lightly. Principally women are highly respected for their religious roles within the instituted churches. As prophetesses and healers, as matrons for maternity care they take on official functions not only valued within their church congregations, but also in the wider community.[32] Limiting this social function of women would be detrimental to the collective interest of the local population of securing the continuity of the population. It is also interesting to note that the "honorable mothers" of the African Instituted Churches, serve as interpreters of mother-hood and sterility. The life-giving role of women is interpreted as the fulfillment of an obedient and prayerful female life-conduct, whereas sterility—the greatest fear and at the same time most serious social stigmatization for local women—is viewed as the absence of divine benediction and adequate reli-gious behavior. Therefore sterile women receive utmost atten-tion and guidance from the prophetesses in order to regain social recognition. Many women in this situation, experiencing high levels of social pressures and stress, seek advice and opt for a temporary communitarian life in the AIC congregations. The "honorable mothers" are thus not only midwives and child-care advisors, but on a symbolic level of action important duty-bearers for the religious embedding of socially relevant themes.

Viewed against the background of the overriding comple-mentary and flexible gender system, based on male and female reciprocal action, one may suspect that the preponderance of women in the ritual interpretation of fertility, life giving and vitality needed to be balanced. The only possibility of con-trolling women's access to power—which challenges men's status—is located in the realm of their biological determina-tion. Consequently, the periodical ritual restrictions serve as a method to limit disproportions in gender relations, and do not work to exclude women categorically from ritual performance. The African Instituted Churches, by contrast to the missionary churches, offer institutionalized opportunities for women to take on religiously and socially significant roles.

The second, more principal question to ask is, whether Christian missions in this part of West Africa contributed to the emancipation or to the subordination of indigenous women. The answer to this question will have to be formulated in a distinctively differentiated manner.[33] On the one hand, missionary societies contributed to a general emancipation of the local population. The translation of the Bible and the appropriation of the biblical narrative within the universe of their own stories had an irreversible liberating impetus, especially when seen within the colonial setting and the aspirations for freedom and independence.[34] This is undoubtedly equally valid for women, especially those who have been socially marginalized, for instance as witches, women without children and otherwise culturally marginalized people, who felt particularly attracted by the universal and inclusive salvific message of Christ.

On the other hand, the advent of Christianity also contributed to a confrontation between different cultural systems and patterns to which the gender configuration belongs, which resulted in severe conflicts of loyalties and processes of adaptation. The changes in local marriage patterns constitute an illustration for this. Women traditionally remained located in their paternal compound after marriage and paid more or less extended periods of visits to their husbands, whereas the missionary ideal of a Christian marriage was based on the expectation that the couple would reside in the groom's house in order to found a "Christian household" with the man as its head.[35] The missionary expectation of a rearrangement from patrilocality to marital residence has resulted in a fluid practice. Today, married women in the context of the study alternate their residence between their husbands' and parents' house, and thus maintain a balance between the traditional societal organization and the missionary expectation.

The complexities of the data are evident. The answer to the question of the impact of Christianity on the emancipation of women is thus ambiguous. As Elizabeth Isichei states, "the decline of these patterns may well be experienced by women as a loss,"[36] but it also opened new avenues for creative female action.

## 6. Recommendations

Against the presented background of female missionary activity as prominent feature of the history of mission as well as contemporary missions in West Africa, one has to ask the question on the theoretical implications for missiology. To ask this question means first to acknowledge the over-proportionally high presence and activity of women in this field, a fact that has been seldom recognized, as Dana L. Robert accurately states: "until recently overview histories of mission have scarcely analyzed women's roles or acknowledged that women typically make up the majority of active believers."[37]

As the case vignettes showed and has been further explored on in the analysis the dimensions of maternity, purity, and power through ritual performance play an important role in the understanding of the local religious landscape, gender relations and the social structure as a whole. It is thus crucial, not only to highlight the inner-contextual plausibility of these aspects, but more so to expand on their significance for the understanding of missions as cross-cultural enterprise.[38]

In light of the findings presented it is paramount to offer a terminological and methodological reflection, before embarking on the thematic features as indicated previously. First, the notion of gender has to be explored with regard to its implications for missiological research and secondly, the methods of research applied in missiology have to be evaluated in relation to their capacity to shed light on the way gender influences the religious, cultural and social structures in a given context.

The introduction of the notion of gender as a historical-social category in the academic discourse during the 1970s,[39] helped to raise the awareness for the differentiation between the biological *sex* and the socially constructed *gender*. The gender perspective does not imply an a priori oppression of women, but rather takes into consideration that gender functions as a key element in societal structures, their description and theories. It bears thus a double perspective: on the one hand, the factual differentiation and hierarchical distinction between women and men in a given society according to the prevalent worldview which renders this distinction plausible from the insider's view, and, on the other hand, it means the conception through which these structures are unveiled, described, and critically analyzed.

With the beginning of the period of slavery and most extensively with the era of colonization of Africa the interest of travelers, traders, administrators and missionaries focused also on the description of gender relations and the respective roles of men and women, as they expected valuable information on the social organization, also useful for the colonial administration. However, these ethnographic portraits need to be scrutinized carefully if used as missiological sources. They constitute frequently the sole available sources on the societal composition, including gender relations, but they are often ideologically biased, and impregnated by the worldview and interest of the authors. In the case of missionaries' reports, for example, the documents were also guided by the concern to attract potential supporters and sponsors for the missionary societies.

The reports written by indigenous evangelists and catechists constituted commissioned topical dissertations that dealt with specific issues of interest for the European missionaries, who wanted to gain knowledge about the cognitive arrangement concerning core themes of the local religious practice and worldview, for instance on the indigenous understanding of the soul, witchcraft, the devil, or practical and sociopolitical issues, like chiefdom, festivals, marriage, and widow customs.

## 7. Conclusion

In the course of the present study different aspects of the indigenous configuration of gender have been explored against the background of their missionary impact and vice versa. Three dimensions of relevance for a missiological discourse came clearly to the fore.

First, the nineteenth-century history of mission on the West African coast bears indications for an influence on the local gender configuration and gender relations, on a much deeper level than presently acknowledged in missiological research. The intentional missionary work in a cultural milieu marked by a flexible gender system, allowing both men and women to exert societal and religious roles beyond those determined by their biological sex, has resulted in a decisive cross-cultural exchange between male and female missionaries, who separated strictly roles in relation with reproduction and religious functions, and the local population with a more flexible arrangement of responsibilities women and men could respectively and interchangeably take on.

This allowed at the same time the creation of role models of femininity—and one could also state the same for masculinity—which have been, if not deviant, rather untypical within the respective milieu. European deaconesses being "mothers for all" and indigenous female missionaries represent such forms of intercultural adaptations. Therefore, paying attention to the gender dimension of mission means more than an addendum to the study of the missionary impact. Second, it reveals important and cross-cutting insights in the inculturation process, as for instance the relation between gender, gender-related role models, and conversion. Changing the religious milieu implied not only a cognitive rearrangement with regard to loyalties between the old and the new religious system, but simultaneously also the creative adaptation of culturally mold expectations related to maternity.

Third, on the socioreligious level, the analysis of the contemporary case studies showed that the religious communities, especially of the Charismatic and Pentecostal type, serve as arenas in which societal key themes as reproduction, child care, but also religious expertise and power,[40] are named, explored and interpreted within a framework, with sometimes seemingly contrasting concepts, for instance of maternity and purity.

A missiology that takes account of these processes of religious, intercultural, and societal modes of transmission, benefits undoubtedly from the inclusion of the gender perspective, as this contributes to make apparent inner-societal underpinnings of the contextualization of Christianity in a given culture, which would otherwise remain veiled.

## Further Reading

Miriam Adeney, "Do Missions Raise or Lower the Status of Women? Conflicting Reports from Africa," in *Gospel Bearers, Gender Barriers: Missionary Women in the Twentieth Century*, ed. Dana L. Robert (Maryknoll: Orbis Books, 2002), 211-222.

Fiona Bowie, Deborah Kirkwood, and Shirley Ardener, eds., *Women and Missions: Past and Present. Anthropological and Historical Perceptions* (Providence/Oxford: Berg, 1993).

Marie-Thérèse Maleissye, ed., *Femmes en mission. Actes de la XIe session du CREDIC à Saint-Flour (Août 1990)* (Lyon: Editions Lyonnaises d'art et d'histoire, 1991).

Sarah Namusoke, "African Women's Participation in God's Mission for Justice and Dignity," *International Review of Mission* 87/347 (1998): 480-484.

Simone Prodilliet, *Wider die Schamlosigkeit und das Elend der heidnischen Weiber: Die Basler Frauenmission und der Export des europäischen Frauenideals in die Kolonien* (Zürich: Limmat Verlag, 1987).

Jane E. Soothill, *Gender, Social Change and Spiritual Power: Charismatic Christianity in Ghana* (Leiden/Boston: Brill, 2007).

## Endnotes

1. For examples of the early European-African missionary encounter in this sub-region. see Wilhelm Johann Müller, *Die Africanische auf der Guineischen Gold-Cust gelegene Landschaft Fetu* (Graz: Akademische Druck- und Verlagsanstalt, 1968), which offers one of the rare reports of a preacher

attached to the Danish African Company, living in the seventeenth century for eight years on the former Gold Coast.

2. See, for an overview on the history of Christianity and early missionary endeavours in the region: J. Kofi Agbeti, *West Africa Church History. Christian Missions and Church Foundations 1482–1919* (Leiden: E. J. Brill, 1986); Peter Bernard Clarke, *West Africa and Christianity: A Study of Religious Development from the 15th to 20th Century* (London: Edward Arnold, 1986); Ralph M. Wiltgen, Gold Coast Mission History 1471–1880 (Techny: Divine World Publication, 1956); Bernard Salvaing, *Les missionnaires à la rencontre de l'Afrique au XIXe siècle* (Paris: L'Harmattan, 1994).

3. A recurrent motive for the evangelization of the local population was borrowed from Acts 26:18: "to open their eyes, that they may turn from darkness to light and from the power of Satan to God, that they may receive forgiveness of sins and a place among those who are sanctified by faith in me" (RSV).

4. See Salvaing, *Les missionnaires*, 165-167.

5. Hedwig Rohns, *Die Schwesternarbeit der Norddeutschen Mission im Ewelande* (Bremen: A. Guthe, 1912), 3-7 (All quotations from German books are translated by the author). Rohns refers to several of these motives with regard to female conversion. She mentions that childbirth resp. survival in families with high child mortality rates, healing after illness, appealing character of the gospel and the missionary predication, as well as dreams and other individual motives.

6. The missionary work with women in the region started officially in 1889 with the sending of the first deaconesses of the North German Mission Society in Bremen. Although the missionaries showed interest in reaching out to women in evangelizing the local population from the outset, it was only at this time that the female missionary work was institutionalized. See Hedwig Rohns, *Bilder aus Ketas Schwesternhaus* (Bremen: Verlag der Norddeutschen Missionsgesellschaft, 1932), 3.

7. Rohns, *Die Schwesternarbeit*, 6.

8. Ibid., 7.

9. Ibid., 1, 7: "Tote Götzen" ("dead idols"), or more explicitly, 4: "Dämonen" ("demons"). However, in the local understanding *trowo/legba* are the material representations of divinities which cannot be equated with the demon or devil.

10. See, with regard to the introduction of images of the devil into the worldview of Ghanaian Christians the work of Birgit Meyer, *Translating the Devil: Religion and Modernity among the Ewe in Ghana* (Edinburgh: Edinburgh University Press, 1999); Id., "Commodities and Power of Prayer: Pentecostalist Attitudes towards Consumption in Contemporary Ghana," *Development and Change* 29 (1998): 751-776. Id.: "'If you are a devil, you are a witch and, if you are a witch, you are a devil.' The Integration of 'Pagan' Ideas into the Conceptual Universe of Ewe Christians in Southeastern Ghana," *Journal of Religion in Africa* XXII, 2 (1992): 98-132.

11. Rohns, *Die Schwesternarbeit*, 5.

12. In Hedwig Rohns' collection of conversion stories the association of women's conversion to Christianity in the early missionary period with gender-specific experiences of childbirth, childcare, and prevention of early child mortality as well as healing comes to the fore as a prominent feature.

13. See Rohns, *Die Schwesternarbeit*, 16f.: "the more we succeed to impregnate the children's hearts with the eternal truth contained in the biblical narratives, the more our girls' school will contribute to the larger work of the mission, and the more, through her, Christianity will be spread among the people."

14. Ibid., 23.

15. See Ifi Amadiume, *Male Daughters, Female Husbands: Gender and Sex in an African Society* (London: Zed Books, 1987).

16. Dorothea Sarasin, *Der Dienst der Frauenmission* (Stuttgart/Basel: Missionsverlag, 1938), 3.

17. See Simone Prodolliet, *Wider die Schamlosigkeit und das Elend der heidnischen Weiber: Die Basler Frauenmission und der Export des europäischen Frauenideals in die Kolonien* (Zürich: Limmat Verlag, 1987).

18. Whereas Martin Schlunk, Inspector of the North German Missionary Society, was able to recognize the utility of local assistants in the missionary work, especially with regard to the intercultural communication, Luise Funke remained hesitant to call indigenous women 'deaconesses' as this would be a term associated with "higher perceptions". See Luise Funke, *Erste Schritte zur weiblichen Diakonie* (Bremen: Bremer Missionschriften, n.d.), 28 and 21.

19. For details, see Charles M. K. Mamattah, *The Beginnings of the Y.M.C.A in Ghana* (Achimota, mimeo., 1952), 19. Mercy Baëta was the elder sister of the first synod secretary of the Ewe-Church, Robert Baëta (1883–1944), whose son Christian Baëta (1908–1994) was a renowned professor of theology and leading figure of the ecumenical movement.

20. Church Constitution of the Ewe-Church in Togo of 1935, 8-9: § 14,6. The office of a parish-mother (*hamedada*, plur. *hamedadawo*) was designed in analogy to the function of the male church elders. By contrast to the latter the *hamedadawo* were not part of the church council, but were organised in a separate section.

21. Luise Funke, *Die Mitarbeit der afrikanischen Frau am Gemeindeleben der Ewe-Kirche* (Unpublished communication, mimeo, 1939), 3.

22. The origins of AIC, as the Church of the Lord (Aladura) or the Celestial Church of Christ can be traced back to the influence of local preachers and their adherents arriving on the territory of Togo and Ghana from Nigeria and Benin where they have been founded. For further background to the Aladura Movement, see Harold W. Turner, *History of an African Independent Church 1: The Church of the Lord (Aladura)* (Oxford: Clarendon Press, 1967), especially: 10-26.

23. See Paul Wiegräbe, *Ein seltsamer Ableger der Ewe-Kirche in Paris. 21.10.93* (Unpublished report. Bremen State Archives 7/1025: 124.8).

24. In 1974, Dada Akofala also founded a community— "Gilgal"—with an orphanage, school, and social welfare department in the central region of Togo.

25. The AICs reinterpret the value of healing against the background of the biblical narrative and the message and practice of Jesus and distance themselves from the traditional practices of healing.

26. The Celestial Church of Christ is a prophetic African Instituted Church of the Aladura-type, founded in 1956 by Samuel Bileou Oshoffa in the Republic of Benin and spread thereafter along the entire West African coast. See the church's own publication *Lumière sur le Christianisme Céleste*, n.d., s.l.

27. See Joan F. Burke "These Catholic Sisters are all Mamas! Celibacy and the Metaphor of Maternity," in *Women and Missions: Past and Present:*

*Anthropological and Historical Perceptions,* ed. Fiona Bowie et al. (Providence/ Oxford: Berg, 1993), 251-266: 256.

28. Rhonda Anne Semple, *Missionary Women: Gender, Professionalism and the Victorian Idea of Christian Mission* (Woodbridge: The Boydell Press, 2003), 17ff., 190f., expands on this aspect and draws attention to the influence of mission women on the "creation and maintenance of boundary markers that indicated a professional mission identity" (193).

29. Burke, "These Catholic," 257; 263 mentions the term of "mothers for all the people" as the recurrent description of African women's alternative maternity upon opting for a consecrated life as religious sisters in Congo.

30. Hanna Mellemsether, "African Women in the Norwegian Mission in South Africa," in *Gender, Race and Religion: Nordic Missions 1860–1940,* ed. Inger M. Okkenhaug (Uppsala: Studia Misionalia Svecana XCI, 2003), 157-173: 166-167, reports of similar mechanisms for the Norwegian Lutheran missions in South Africa, stating that "there is no evidence that these Bible-women took part in the annual evangelists meetings, nor were they elected to the parish councils" (167).

31. Michael A. Williams, Collett Cox and Martin S. Jaffee, "Religious Innovation. An introductory essay," in *Innovation in Religious Traditions. Essays in the Interpretation of Religious Change,* ed. Michael A. Williams, Collett Cox and Martin S. Jaffee (Berlin and New York: Mouton de Gruyter,1992), 1-17 (9), explain how influential "genius" or "charisma" can be for the development of religious innovation from within what is referred to as tradition, and in reference to Marilyn Robinson Waldman and Robert Baum they ascribe importance to the ability of such religious personalities to sensitively "read" the cultural system and to adapt or to create roles for a new self-definition.

32. This is particularly relevant for the AICs as they transcended the classical pattern of religious affiliation installed by the missionaries with a rigid system of *Volkskirchen* (ethnic churches), as the example of the Reformed Ewe-Church which grew out of the North German Missionary Society shows, and are reaching out to people with diverse social and ethnic affiliation within the local context.

33. See Miriam Adeney, "Do Missions Raise or Lower the Status of Women. Conflicting Reports from Africa," in *Gospel Bearers, Gender Barriers. Missionary Women in the Twentieth Century,* ed. Dana L. Robert (Maryknoll: Orbis Books, 2002), 211-221; Elizabeth Isichei, "Does Christianity Empower Women? The Case of the Anaguta of Central Nigeria," in *Women and Missions: Past and Present. Anthropological and Historical Perspectives,* ed. Fiona Bowie et al. (Providence/Oxford: Berg, 1993).

34. For the impact of Christianity on the emancipation of African populations, see Lamin Sanneh, *Translating the Message: The missionary impact on culture* (Maryknoll: Orbis Books, 1989), who states that Africans became missionary agents of change through the missionary encounter.

35. The practice of polygamy was another important challenge for European missionaries, which was considered as moral deviation to be imperatively corrected.

36. Elizabeth Isichei, "Does Christianity Empower Women," 227.

37. Dana L. Robert, *Christian Mission: How Christianity Became a World Religion* (Malden/Oxford: Wiley-Blackwell, 2009), 118. Dana Robert herein dedicates a whole chapter to the role of women in mission, "Women in World Mission: Purity, Motherhood, and Women's Well-Being": 114-141. By contrast in the significant more recent missiological studies of Andrew F. Walls,

*The Cross-Cultural Process in Christian History* (Maryknoll/Edinburgh: Orbis Books/T&T Clark, 2002), and Id., *The Missionary Movement in Christian History* (Maryknoll/Edinburgh: Orbis Books/T&T Clark, 1996), one cannot find any distinct reference to women's commitment in missions.

38. Robert, *Christian Mission*, 119, hints to the often neglected factor in missions that women "have deliberately crossed cultures to witness to their faith" and in doing so interpreted gender and social roles differently than traditionally prefigured in their own context.

39. See Randi R. Warne, "Gender," in *Guide to the Study of Religion*, ed. Willi Braun and Russell T. McCutcheon (London/New York: Cassell, 2000), 140-154. In academia the development of the gender discourse and the epistemological interest therein can be traced in the emergence of university and college departments, first in the USA and in Britain, in the meantime also in other regions of the world, for women's or gender studies alongside the institutionalization of disciplines dedicated to the research in gender and gender relations. This constitutes the broad contemporary trend, from which one cannot fail to dissociate feminism, as mainly a Western approach aiming at the ideological critique and overcoming of patriarchal structures, as well as the American *womanism* with its critical stance vis-à-vis a Western, white-dominated, and thus biased feminism.

40. See Stephen Ellis and Gerrie Ter Haar, *Worlds of Power. Religious Thought and Political Practice in Africa* (London: Hurst & Co., 2004), 98-100.

CHAPTER 4

# Gendered Charisma: Women in Mission in the Neo-Pentecostal Churches and Charismatic Movements in Kenya

*Philomena Njeri Mwaura*
*and Damaris Parsitau Seleina*

## 1. Introduction

Scholars of African Christianity have acknowledged the tremendous growth of the church in Africa in the twentieth century, a consequence of the modern missionary movement and local agency. The *World Christian Encyclopedia* observes that in 1900, Kenya had a Christian population of 5,000. By 2000, they were 23 million and were projected to grow to 34 million or 90 percent of the total population by 2050.[1] Male and female missionaries from a variety of Christian traditions from Western Europe and North America prosecuted the modern missionary movement. Whether as wives of missionaries or single, women missionaries were involved in the social and charitable dimensions of mission as evangelists, teachers, trainers of Bible women, in medical and pastoral work, and accompanying the poor. Dana L. Robert observes that after the Second World War, American women missionaries began to excel in specialized forms of ministries such as gospel recordings, Bible translation, and the training of pastors.[2] Women missionaries are credited with providing role models to local women, equipping them for ministry and transforming their lives.

Today, the church in Kenya has a feminine face and also owes much of its growth to the agency of local women who were among the pioneer converts and have been the most ardent adherents and enthusiastic evangelists to the present day, often sacrificing their resources in propagating the gospel. Christianity gave women autonomy and a place on which to stand and challenge the male-dominated sacred world and negative traditions that impinged on their well-being and dignity.[3] Very often, women were driven to the church by suffering and misfortune or seeking protection against witchcraft accusations.

Although women have been the pillars of the mainline churches in both colonial and postcolonial times, they were and have been excluded from positions of power and key areas of decision making. This is however not so in the spiritual[4] group of African Instituted Churches (AICs) where they have been agents of religious innovation, founding churches and functioning as leaders, healers, prophetesses, evangelists, and hymn composers. Spiritual AICs just like Pentecostals recognize that the Spirit was poured out on women just as on men and that charismatic gifts can operate freely in women and men equally. Reference to Acts 2 and Joel 2:28-32 confirms to them the significance of charismata in the life of today's church. Prominent women founders of AICs in Kenya include Gaudencia Aoko of the Legio Maria Africa Church, 1963, and Mary Akatsa of the Jerusalem Church of Christ 1985.

The AICs are not the only obvious factor in the new face of Africa's Christianity. The various "waves" of Pentecostalism are another—even more important—element changing its face continuously. African Pentecostalism has found the interest of many academics within and outside Africa who have described and analyzed that recent religious phenomenon in a long list of articles and books.[5] Therein, several waves of Pentecostalism are usually distinguished, among them the classical Pentecostal churches (1920s to 1950s), the non-denominational churches, charismatic fellowships, and charismatic renewal within the mainline churches (from the 1950s to the 1970s), and the neo-Pentecostal churches, ministries, and international organizations (since the 1980s). The latest churches are described quite often by critical connotations due to religious business and market-oriented aims, strategies of exploiting adherents, a wealth and prosperity theology, and a lack of diaconical commitment. Since overlaps in terms of content, shape, and time between these waves are not excluded, the terminologies are quite often inconsistent so that a definition of the use of these terms in this case study is necessary. "Pentecostalism" is used as an all-embracing term for all types of Pentecostalism. "Neo-Pentecostalism" and "neo-Pentecostal" churches refer to churches and movements established by Africans—men or women—since the 1970s in Kenya. Neo-Pentecostal churches and organizations founded by women are either branches within an already existing neo-Pentecostal church or have separated themselves from a male founded and male led neo-Pentecostal church. "Charismatic" churches or movements are used as synonyms of neo-Pentecostal churches. The term "ministries" is often preferred by neo-Pentecostals over against the term "churches." It refers to cross-denominational movements with a low or soft structure offering diverse programs that cater for spiritual, emotional, psychological, economic, and social needs of the followers. The same is true for the term "organizations" founded and led by women. In many cases, they operate in a trans-denominational way and understand themselves as cross-national self-help networks for women in and outside the country. Organizations do not compete against established (neo-Pentecostal) churches.

While women were prominent already in the revival movements of the colonial period and in the 1970s, they currently feature prominently as founders, pastors, evangelists, and teachers in the Pentecostal and charismatic churches that emerged in the 1990s. Women's involvement in mainline churches, charismatic and AICs, also takes the form of the innumerable church women's organizations.[6] In the Roman Catholic Church, African congregations of nuns were founded in various dioceses like the Assumption Sisters of Eldoret and Nairobi, Little Sisters of St. Francis, and Congregation of the Sisters of Mary Immaculate in Nyeri and Sisters of St. Mary Mukumu among others. Their achievements in education, pastoral work, health care, justice and peace advocacy is remarkable. Women organizations in mission churches have played significant roles in mission.[7] These mission activities of women have contributed to the creation of new forms of being church through the women's associational and devotional life and Christian communities that have led to the evaluation of the church in Africa as a woman's church.[8]

The focus of this paper lies on the neo-Pentecostal churches, charismatic movements, and ministries that have enlarged both theological and missiological space for Kenyan women. In these churches that begun in the 1970s and early 1980s, women are increasingly taking up leadership positions and roles hitherto denied to them. They act and function in their own churches as general overseers, bishops, pastors, teachers, evangelists, prophetesses, and healers. They baptize, administer communion, perform and officiate marriages and funerals and all other ministerial functions normally performed by male ministers.

The paper investigates their understanding of mission, their roles, and how they have contributed to the creation and or promotion of Christian communities. It will use three case studies of women founders of charismatic churches and ministries to demonstrate how neo-Pentecostal churches, charismatic movements, and ministries are engaged in mission. These are Jesus Is Alive Ministries (JIAM), Faith Evangelistic Ministries (FEM) and Ladies Homecare Spiritual Fellowship (LHSF). These ministries lay emphasis on new salvation and new birth, evangelism, faith healing, deliverance, prophecy, transformation, and charismatic gifts. Bishop Wanjiru of JIAM is selected on the basis of her success story, that reads like the dictum "from grass to grace" in which she overcame both personal and social limitations to emerge as a founder and presiding bishop of one of Nairobi's most successful ministries, legislator, a cabinet minister, and an entrepreneur. Teresia Wairimu of FEM is selected not just for her ministry to single women but for encouraging women to rise above culture, patriarchy, and exposing practices that discriminate against women and girls. Rev. Judy Mbugua of LHSF has been instrumental not just the ministerial formation of women and their responsibilities in the family but as an author, theologian, and holder of many international offices where she highlights women's voices in the church. These female religious who call their organizations "ministries" prefer this term because they view their organizations as offering diverse programs that cater for the spiritual, emotional, psychological, economic, and social needs of their followers. The term has missiological connotations since it encompasses engaging in proclamation of and witness to Christ in their context.

## 2. Historical Background of Kenyan Christianity in General, Neo-Pentecostal and Charismatic Christianity in Particular

Kenya is a profoundly religious nation with a rich diversity of cultures and different religious traditions dotting its landscape. Its religious landscape is highly complex and dynamic, comprising a multiplicity of religious traditions, including African indigenous religions, the various strands of Christianity and Islam as well as some small faith communities. Demographically, Kenya is a predominantly Christian nation. According to the findings of the Kenya Population and Housing Census 2009, Christians make up 31.8 million of Kenya's 38.6 million people, representing 82.6 percent of the population.[9] Roman Catholics are the single biggest denomination accounting for 9 million people. Protestants stand at 18 million people whereas other Christians account for

4.5 million. It is further estimated that 4.3 million of the population are Muslims. There is an even smaller numbers of Hindus (estimated at about 500,000) mainly from the Indian subcontinent who settled in Kenya before and after colonialism. At the same time, there are also significant populations of Sikhs, Buddhist, Confucian, Baha'i, Jews and other such minority faiths. The non-religious population though small may signify some level of irreligiousness probably due to effects of secularism.[10]

While women form the majority of the population in Kenya (51 percent) and play active roles in the development of society, Kenya remains a very patriarchal society, and the status of women remains relatively low with inequalities prevailing in many aspects of life: social, economic, power and decision making and control of family, community, and national resources.[11] Women are largely marginalized and discriminated against even in Christian circles and the situation is worse for single women: divorced, separated, widowed, and spinsters. These women are castigated and sometimes referred to as home wreckers, husband grabbers, and other demeaning words. Yet, emerging trends in contemporary Kenya show that more than one-third of Kenyan households are female headed, a trend that has heavily impacted on family life.

Christianity was first founded along the Kenyan coast in the nineteenth century through the work of Anglican, Methodist, and Holy Ghost Fathers missionaries before spreading into the interior of the country by 1914. This mission encounter was followed by the African Instituted Churches (AICs) that are described as a movement representing an African response to the missionary movement in Africa. These churches emerged most clearly where the missionary presence was strongest, and where scripture was translated into African mother tongues earliest. AICS offered an enlarged ritual space for women who were prominent in faith healing and deliverance. African Instituted Churches are said to comprise a quarter of the Christian population in Kenya.[12]

## 3. Women's Roles in Neo-Pentecostal Churches and Charismatic Movements

The most recent development within Kenya's diverse Christianities is the emergence of neo-Pentecostal churches and charismatic movements particularly from the 1950s, 1960s, and 1970s onward. Since the 1970s, Kenya has experienced a phenomenal growth of neo-Pentecostal churches and charismatic movements that cut across social, ethnic, and gender lines in both urban and rural areas of the country.[13] They are characterized by emphasis on personal salvation in Christ as a transformative experience wrought by the Holy Spirit; and in which pneumatic phenomena such as glossolalia, healing, miracles, visions, prophecies, and signs and wonders are sought and encouraged.[14] In Kenya as elsewhere in Africa, there has been a shift in religious affiliation away from mainline churches toward Pentecostal and charismatic groups. According to the *Pew Forum on Religion and Public Life,*[15] the Pentecostal and charismatic movements account for more than half of Kenya's population and have impacted on both the Catholic and Protestant Christians. The character of this growth is evidenced by the number of registered churches and groups, pending registration and monthly applications for registration.[16]

Neo-Pentecostalism has created an enlarged space for women, single and married, who have become visible in religious and public life. Women have been able to exercise their gifts for the benefit of the church and society and they perceive themselves as God's instruments in his mission of salvation. Neo-Pentecostalism has contributed to women's emancipation from oppressive cultural practices and their culturally prescribed gender roles. They have feminized the religious landscape and altered dominant discourses and practices in religious authority in domestic spheres as well as on the level of the nation state.

In many Christian churches, both mainline Protestant and Catholic, women remain excluded from key ecclesial and ministerial positions. Their roles and positions continue to be debated in church circles. On the contrary, Kenyan Pentecostalism has brought about the advent of women in mission and leadership into the fore. Increasingly these churches are seen to be promoting women to leadership positions hitherto denied to them. Yet, contradictions and paradoxes still exist in regular Pentecostal churches. While Pentecostalism has been lauded as possessing both liberating and empowering consequences for women, many established Pentecostal churches do not recognize or give women space to lead these churches. It is for these reasons that Browning and Hollingsworth critically point out that "Pentecostalism has the dubious and paradoxical character of being at once liberating and disempowering for women seeking equality in spiritual matters."[17]

For example, the Deliverance Church, one of the largest Pentecostal churches in Kenya with over a thousand church congregations spread all over the country is a male-dominated Pentecostal church. Its local, regional, and international congregations are all led by men. Even the Deliverance Church Council (DCC), the highest decision-making body as well as its twelve administrative units have no female member at all sitting in it. Except for Pastor Jennifer Kahare, the only female leader in this church, all other major Deliverance Church congregations are led by men who co-pastor with their wives. Thus, in one sense, these churches have enlarged the place for pastors' wives who are co-leaders and co-founders together with their husbands. Yet, many of these wives occupy ambiguous positions in these churches as most of them are career women and, as one pastor put it, *men are the head and women are the neck.*[18] Men are also the head of the household and women are to submit both to God and men. Women's access to leadership in the DCC as in many other mainstream Pentecostal churches is therefore restricted despite the fact that they form the bulk of membership in these churches. These churches reinforce women subordination, particularly by excluding them in church leadership.

Although the Pentecostal churches seem on the surface to uphold gender hierarchies, a closer look at the gender discourses and practices found within these groups shows both accommodation to and resistance against patriarchal values. Bishop Arthur Kitonga of Redeemed Gospel Church for example has ordained several prominent female clergy such as Bishop Margaret Wanjiru of JIAM, and Rev. Judith Mbugua of LHSF; yet women who could not cope with this kind of patronage have left to found their own ministries. Initially, women-led ministries did not enjoy respect from male-led Pentecostal churches. However, the very successful ones such as JIAM, FEM, and LHSF have changed the initial prevailing biases toward churches led by single unmarried women. Today, these female-led ministries enjoy significant levels of respect from a variety of mainstream Pentecostal churches. It seems to us that we shall focus on these special women ministries because women have a marginal place in regular Pentecostal churches. We shall now briefly discuss the mission roles of three neo-Pentecostal female-led ministries.

## 3.1 *Margaret Wanjiru of Jesus Is Alive Ministries (JIAM)*

Born in Nairobi on December 22, 1961 as the third child of casual workers, Wanjiru is a single mother of three children and one of the few women bishops in Kenya. Her early life was characterized by poverty, hardships, and an unstable upbringing. Her father was a hopeless drunk while her mother brewed illicit brew to feed the family. Wanjiru dropped out of school after falling pregnant when she was seventeen years old,[19] but her determination to make something out of her life led her to undertake a variety of manual jobs to enable her to finish school and college. She worked as a toilet cleaner, hawker, house girl, office cleaner, and later earned herself a job as a sales girl. In her efforts to escape poverty, she got involved in witchcraft. However, her association with witchcraft was short-lived.[20] She became born again at a crusade in 1990 and thereafter started preaching on the streets of Nairobi. This experience marked her spiritual and social transformation and the beginning of a life of mission, evangelism, and commitment to serving God in every way possible. She is currently the Presiding Bishop of Jesus is Alive Ministries, an international Christian organization with headquarters in Nairobi and one of the fastest growing churches in Kenya. The church has branches in the United Kingdom, the United States of America, South Africa, and Uganda. Her church's mission is achieved through a variety of ministries that include a dynamic media ministry, a welfare ministry dubbed as the Good Samaritan project, hospital and prison chaplaincy, children's ministry, youth evangelism, public transport, micro-finance (Glory Development), a bookshop and a Bible school. Wanjiru has facilitated the empowerment of women and men in her church through these ministries. She views the mission of her church as reaching out to the world with the gospel of Jesus Christ. According to JIAM website, this mission is fulfilled through "evangelizing the unsaved, setting the captives free, and teaching Christians worldwide how to live a victorious life through the word of God."[21] The church is further called to "bring salvation, healing, deliverance, prosperity, redemption and righteousness to all the nations of the world."[22]

Wanjiru claims that several years ago, the Lord took her through a nine-hour vision in which he revealed to her the vision "Africa Shall be Saved." This is the vision that drives her and her church and has inspired the mission to other parts of the globe. Her media ministry entitled "The Glory Is Here" also serves the goal of evangelism cross-culturally and virtually. Her vision for global evangelism is based on Matthew 24:14, "All the gospel shall be preached in the entire world for a witness unto the nations and then shall come the end." During the celebrations of JIAM's 10th anniversary in 2003, Wanjiru rolled out a plan for the evangelization of Africa and the world and even launched special buses for this endeavor.

From 2003 onward, Wanjiru began to spread her influence beyond the ministry and its related business ventures. A culmination of this expansion was her candidacy in the Kenyan parliamentary elections of 2007, which she finally won, becoming a member of parliament. Announcing her decision to stand in the elections to thousands of jubilant church members, she said that God had given her a prophecy through a visiting American preacher, Prophetess Brenda Todd. Todd had told Wanjiru that although she had been prodded by God from time to time to join politics, the appointed time had come and she could not disobey God any more. Wanjiru justified her entry into politics by likening herself to Esther in the Bible who rescued her people from destruction.[23] Todd likened Wanjiru to King David who was chosen by God and anointed by Samuel, as explained in 1 Samuel 16:1-13. After the anointing ceremony, Wanjiru asked the crowd to vote for her, saying that when the righteous are in authority, as Proverbs 29:2 puts it, people rejoice. Wanjiru's entry into politics had already started with opposition against a draft constitution proposed by the government. It was at this time that she and many other Pentecostals mobilized Kenyans to vote against the proposed draft during a national referendum that was held in November 2005. One of the provisions of the proposed constitution that irked Pentecostals in particular was to allow Muslims to have Kadhi courts, known elsewhere as Sharia courts, which decide on Muslim private issues of marriage, divorce, and inheritance.[24] Pentecostals argued that the provision seemed to elevate Islam, which is a minority religion in Kenya. A broader constellation of Christians advocated for a secular constitution that would treat all religions equally. Wanjiru thereafter successfully stood for parliamentary elections in Nairobi's Starehe Constituency, which houses her church, parliament itself, and central government offices. She justified her entry into politics with the need to combine evangelism with social action for the total transformation of society. She was also irked by the corruption in government and the lack of political goodwill to bring about change in society.

Bishop Wanjiru simultaneously appealed to an audience far wider than Pentecostals; this is because she has become a role model to thousands of women who throng her monthly meetings. Despite the generally traditional teachings of her neo-Pentecostal church ministry, she has advocated a greater empowerment for women. She has wielded to great effect her identity as single mother, a consummate urbanite, a self-made businesswoman, and a rare Kikuyu member of Orange Democratic Movement.[25] Despite her career being filled with scandals and controversy, Wanjiru continues to be viewed by many not only as a ground breaker in Kenyan sociopolitical history but also as one who upgraded the roles of single women in religion and politics, all in a society that frowns upon female leadership, particularly where the said woman is unmarried. Wanjiru combines church and politics and has built an illustrious career as a minister of the word of God and a cabinet minister.

Since her election to Parliament, her vision for her Starehe Constituency is to promote development and empowerment. She plans to bring prosperity to her constituents by reaching out to them economically, socially, and spiritually. Wanjiru believes that for women to contribute to their own development and that of their communities, they need to be empowered holistically. She hopes to harness women's strength through supporting local groups, networking, and tapping women's collective energy to improve the lives of all. The church has a membership of over 20,000 members and uses other media for evangelism like crusades, local and international conferences, DVDs, CDs, audio tapes, and a monthly magazine called *Faith Digest*. All these ensure that her message reaches many people.

## 3.2 Teresia Wairimu of Faith Evangelistic Ministries (FEM)

FEM, one of Nairobi's best-known Christian ministries, was started in 1989 by Teresia Wairimu who was born on November 13, 1957. She started with a group of seventeen women, most of whom were single. A mother of two, Wairimu says that God called her to evangelism in 1985. In the 1990s, she became the first female preacher to hold regular revival crusades at Uhuru Park grounds in Nairobi. FEM has consolidated its position among Kenyan Pentecostal and charismatic churches and ministries through its monthly crusades. Each month, the ministry also holds seminars, luncheons, and conferences for women in major towns such as Nairobi, Nakuru, Mombassa, and Eldoret. These meetings focus on women's spiritual, economic, and social empowerment. Wairimu owns *Ebenezer Magazine*, an annual publication that highlights the activities of her ministry. She also runs ministries for the youth and a mercy ministry for those living in the slums such as Korogocho in Nairobi. She proudly claims to have preached in over twenty countries.

Like many other charismatic ministries, FEM started as a seventeen-women prayer fellowship mostly comprising of single women who used to meet at Huruma residential estate for prayer and fellowship in 1985. But soon the house was too small for them and Wairimu was forced to look for a bigger venue. In these prayer meetings, they fasted and prayed for revival and fire, both needed for evangelistic missions. In 1989, it became clear to her that there was need to organize the activities of her ministry and she founded Faith Evangelistic Ministries International, registered by that name. Over the years, FEM has metamorphosed into a larger church, the Four-Square Church, which was established to cater to the needs of a larger and growing church.

Wairimu has a mission to evangelize Africa, from Cape Town to Cairo and to the rest of the world. She has worked closely with Reinhard Bonnke to spread the gospel to all corners of the world. Under the banner of Bonnke's mission, "Africa Shall Be Saved," the two have evangelized many parts of Africa, including Ethiopia, Uganda, Nigeria, and South Africa. She has also preached in India, Austria, Canada, Jamaica, Denmark, Norway, Germany, Poland, and Portugal. They have also held conferences together—for example, the Euro-Fire Conference in Birmingham and Germany at the dawn of the new millennium. Her European ministry office is based in London, and she also has a US-FEM chapter called Teresia Wairimu Evangelistic Ministry (TWEM), based in Dallas, Texas. TWEM was founded in 1998 and coordinates her transnational networks in Europe, the USA, and other locations. The objective of the ministry, according to her website, is to reach out to people in the United States "by facilitating conferences in various cities throughout the USA [and to] provide outreach to our partners throughout the United States through our office in Dallas, Texas."[26]

FEM has myriads of different and diverse ministries that target various groups of members. It runs ministries for single women and the youth. It is, however, her ministry to the youth and single women that have had the greatest impact in terms of spiritual and material empowerment. Wairimu holds interactive audience with women throughout the year and is therefore able to personally understand their issues first hand. While she obviously appeals to a wider audience nationally and internationally, she has always remained attached to her female members and followers. Besides, Wairimu has always imaged herself as a dignified person with a great personality and has not been involved in scandals. This has earned her tremendous respect both locally and abroad.

Her ministry has changed the lives of many single women in a patriarchal society. Besides being a role model to many single women, she has also mentored, empowered, and trained a significant number of them for ministry. Female leaders such as Cathy Kiuna of Jubilee Christian Centre; Rev. Elizabeth Wahome of Single Ladies Ministries International; the Rev. Nancy Gitau of Deborah

Arise Africa; and Evangelist Alice Mugure of Zion Prayer Mountain and Kenya House of Prayer have been mentored by the evangelist as most of them served as ushers and organizers in her ministry before founding their own churches or ministries.

FEM is also engaged civically and politically in the public sphere through prayer and intercession. Intercessory prayer groups such as "Fourth Watch," "Watchmen," "Gatekeepers," and "Prayer Warriors" all join together with Evangelist Wairimu to pray not only for Kenya but for the African continent and the world. FEM undertakes various humanitarian missions and charities labeled mercy ministries, to the less fortunate members. For example, since 2005 it has been operating a feeding program for orphans in Nairobi and famine-stricken victims in Killifi and Kwale districts at the coastal region of Kenya. She also runs a number of mercy ministries such as for those living in Nairobi slums like Korogocho and Kibera. Other ministries include prison ministries, hospital, and homes for the elderly.

During the crisis that followed the disputed presidential elections in Kenya in 2007–2008, Wairimu distributed relief food and materials to the displaced victims in the volatile Rift Valley Province; and at the risk of her safety, urged conflicting communities to live in peace and seek reconciliation. Her spiritual interventions of prayer and healing resulted in many of them getting saved. In recognition of all these efforts, on May 9, 2008, Wairimu was honored with the Martin Luther King Jr. Peace Award for her humanitarian service and for her vocal campaign among church leaders during the post-election violence.

Since the inception of her ministry, Wairmu has been shepherding her flock and commands respect as a healer, a prophetess, philanthropist, and peace builder. She believes that God has divinely mandated her to reach out to women to embrace and promote self-actualization in the wider society so that they can take up leadership positions and roles in the church and mission. In her sermons, she locates women preachers within the biblical tradition even as she draws both examples and inspiration from biblical female heroines such as Deborah, Esther, Mary Magdalene, and others. Wairimu further believes that women are mandated to preach the gospel and that not to do so is in fact contradicting scriptures.

For these reasons, she has developed strategies for changing the conditions of women within the church. She makes use of audio-visual media and recently she wrote an autobiography to encourage women to rise above victimhood, personal limitations to make a difference.[27] She privileges the Holy Spirit for breaking a culture of women's subordination. While she is not a feminist by Western standards, this woman visionary promotes the rights of women and girls in the Kenyan society by highlighting those aspects of culture that discriminate them.

## 3.3 Rev. Judy Mbugua of Ladies Homecare Spiritual Fellowship (LHSF)

Ladies Homecare Spiritual Fellowship (LHSF) is a faith-based organization founded by the Rev. Judy Mbugua. This interdenominational and holistic ministry seeks to build a nation of healthy families with strong moral values. According to Rev. Mbugua, LHSF was founded and registered in 1985 as "an interdenominational Christian fellowship for ladies with a mission to improve the quality of life in their families."[28] In its website, it is also indicated that the mission and vision of LHSF is "to raise strong women who are committed to praying for the salvation of their families." These strong women are equipped with spiritual and practical resources to raise strong and healthy families, an undertaking that is hoped to translate into building an even stronger nation. Since its inception, LHSF (Kenya) has been reaching out to these families with a holistic ministry, addressing various social, economic, and spiritual needs.

The Rev. Mbugua, a head of this charismatic ministry, is an accomplished woman. She was born to wealthy and educated parents in 1947 in Limuru, Kenya. Mbugua, a trained secretary, went on to marry Richard Mbugua, a high school teacher, and together they have three children and four grandchildren. Although she grew up in a wealthy home, she dropped out of school before she completed her primary school education and got married while still a teenager. Mbugua explains that she was ill-equipped to carry out heavy marital and parental responsibilities as she lacked the necessary home management skills. Yet she managed to overcome a traumatic teenage marriage because her husband supported her and the children.

She claims to have undergone a tremendous spiritual transformation when she got "born again" in 1967. Thereafter and in 1974, she was baptized in the Holy Spirit, a baptism she credits for her spiritual growth and one that would later lay the foundation for the task ahead of her, particularly the founding of the LHSF. In 1980, Mbugua joined the Nairobi Pentecostal Church (NPC) Valley Road, an affluent and well-known Pentecostal church in the city of Nairobi but with dozens of branches in various parts of the country. Mbugua credits the NPC for equipping her with the necessary spiritual resources that would later on enable her to found and lead a women's ministry. It was while at the NPC that she started preaching and ministering, a venture that sharpened her public speaking skills, self-confidence, and other qualities such as leadership and management. Yet, NPC could not ordain her let alone giving her any leadership roles. However, she was ordained as a full minister in 1991 by Bishop Arthur Kitonga of a different Pentecostal church, the Redeemed Gospel Churches of Kenya (RGC). She nevertheless remains affiliated to her own church, the NPC.[29]

In 1985, Mbugua founded and registered the Ladies Homecare Spiritual Fellowship in Nairobi. To date, this charismatic ministry remains affiliated to the Nairobi Pentecostal Churches (NPC) although it has recently acquired its own facilities such as the Homecare Karen Retreat Centre.[30] LHSF first started as a women prayer fellowship. Rev Mbugua explains that she desired to bring women together to talk, pray, and fellowship with one another. So she invited women to her house for prayer and fellowship. These home-to-home prayer meetings were held every first Saturday of the month. The first meeting attracted twenty women who committed to praying for their families and the nation. The second meeting attracted 40, then 60, and within a year, 200 women were attending the monthly meetings. Within five years, the numbers had risen to over a thousand women from different denominations. The growth in numbers necessitated the need for adequate and spacious facilities. It is at this point that the meetings were then moved to the Nairobi Pentecostal Church Valley Road. Today, meetings are held at the Homecare Retreat Centre in Karen, Nairobi. While the ministry originally started in Nairobi, they have long spread to various parts of the country. Today, it has a total of about twenty local branches. Each branch builds a home called a prayer tower consisting of a hall, a prayer room, retreat facilities, and a counseling room with telephone help lines operating 24 hours. Thus, from a small home-based prayer fellowship, LHSF has grown to become an interdenominational religious organization with over twenty branches in the country and one in Zimbabwe. The ministry has also become a vibrant charismatic ministry that caters for the spiritual and physical needs of women from all walks of life. However, the ministry focuses on very poor and vulnerable women, especially those living in informal settlements such as Kibera in Nairobi.[31]

Since its mission is to "bring holistic ministry to women," LHSF runs a shelter for women who have suffered various forms of abuse. These women include those who are victims of Gender Based Violence such as rape, incest, and crisis or teenage pregnancy. It also has programs to cater for women and children, particularly those orphaned by the HIV and AIDS pandemic. It does this by providing food (there is a feeding program in Kibera), shelter, clothing, counseling and education to these women and children. Several families living in this informal settlement and those who were affected by the post-election violence that rocked Kenya after the disputed 2007 presidential elections have been resettled back with the help of the ministry. This is because LHSF runs a project called Group Savings and Loans, a micro-finance facility that operates as a partner of local banks such as Barclays Bank to provide loans for needy and vulnerable women members to start small businesses. Women in this ministry are therefore involved in the arts and craft and detergent-making small scale industries; ventures that have significantly transformed the lives and families of these vulnerable women.[32] Several attest to the transformative nature of her ministry. For example, Mary Anyango was living in a ramshackle hut in the Kibera informal settlement after her husband died of HIV-related complications. Anyango, who is also HIV positive, was severely ill and malnourished. She joined LHSF and got free antiretroviral drugs and food. Within a couple of months, she felt better and learned how to take care of herself. Besides, she learned new skills such as tailoring, dressmaking, and handicrafts. She soon begun to make dresses and earned enough to eat and rent a small but descent house. She is also able to feed and send her two children to school and save a little money for a rainy day. Anyango claims that LHSF has transformed her life and given her hope and a reason to live. Scores of other women living with HIV and AIDS are supported and assisted with food, antiretroviral drugs, and other medical needs. The organization also operates a Voluntary Counseling and Testing Center, and offers a variety of counseling services such as trauma and psychological counseling. At the same time, the ministry has several other programs that are meant to cater for the needs of its members. For example, they have a Mentors Programme that works with leaders not only to contribute to the spiritual and physical needs of orphaned children and vulnerable women but also to mentor young girls and women.[33]

Rev Mbugua is politically and publicly engaged in national issues through prayer and intersession. For this reason, she helped found the National Interdenominational Women Prayer Network, an outfit consisting of women networks established to bring together all Christian women ministries to pray for the country. This network, which comprises of more than 150 women leaders from various Christian denominations, also mobilizes women leaders and their followers to pray and make intercession for the family unit and the nation at large. This Christian women's initiative further maintains a database of all relevant women Christian ministries in the country, communicates to them on topical issues affecting the nation for immediate intercessions, holds national prayer conferences, and keeps in touch with the government and church leaders for prayer issues. This ministry appropriates mass media technologies to disseminate information about important national happenings, events and activities that require prayer and intercessions. Mbugua herself is a televangelist who preaches on television and produces an annual newsletter, LHCF News, which addresses current family-related issues besides highlighting her ministry's activities. Mbugua is an opinion shaper both nationally and internationally by virtue of the fact that she is a holder of various national, regional and international offices. In 1987, she was elected the Pan African Christian Women Alliance (PACWA) continental coordinator at the fifth General Assembly of the Association of Evangelicals in Africa, held in Lusaka, Zambia. She holds this position to this day. This continental body requested her to help establish a women's affairs desk mandated to look into issues affecting women members of the association. On a regional level, PACWA searches for models and resource persons and establishes relationships with major women groups in Africa and beyond. PACWA also provides information and training for women in social, economic, political and legal issues as diverse as land use, bank loans, gender-based violence, and female genital mutilation. PACWA also facilitates development projects among women all over Africa, which includes a tailoring and sewing school in Zambia, training for self-help projects in Madagascar, micro-business classes such as dressmaking, vegetable selling and crafts, adult literacy classes among the Maasai women in Kenya and Tanzania, tie and dye projects[34] in Mali and the Gambia, single mothers projects in Ghana, chicken projects in Botswana, teenage pregnancy support programs in Sierra Leone, girls hostels projects in Nigeria and nutrition centers for street children in South Africa. PACWA is therefore a regional women's body that draws membership from thirty countries including the USA and the Netherlands.

Mbugua is also an accomplished woman who holds varied offices. Besides being the founder of the Ladies Homecare

Spiritual Fellowship, the co-coordinator of the National Interdenominational Women Prayer Network, and PACWA she is also a lecturer at the Haggai Institute for advanced leadership and the international chairperson and President for AD 2000, a ministry to encourage Christians to reach all the unreached people or groups worldwide with the gospel of Christ by the year 2000.[35] Besides, she is also the author of *Our Time has come: Christian Women and Politics, Women Ministry in Church.*[36] She is an accomplished public speaker who speaks and ministers in various national and international forums and conferences. Her ministry and lectureship has taken her to Europe, Asia, Australia, the USA, and many African countries. In her works as a theologian and scholar, Mbugua interrogates not only issues of women leadership in evangelical churches but also issues of patriarchy and the roles of men in marriage and family. She advocates for partnership with men and stresses the need for both genders to work together for the benefit of the family, the church, and the nation. Though Mbugua may not consider herself a gender activist or feminist, she has helped highlight and to some extent address issues affecting women in Kenya and Africa. She has immensely contributed to improving and transforming lives of vulnerable women in urban informal settlements in Nairobi and elsewhere.

All these three women religious visionaries view their mission as God ordained to bring social, spiritual, missiological, and gender transformation to their members and the larger society. The ministries have not only redefined missiological space but have also had significant impact not just on their members but also on the Kenyan society more generally. This has missiological implication in the sense that there is urgency for women to take up and reclaim their position in the Kenyan society. Besides, they are powerful role models who have inspired and mentored other women to found their won charismatic ministries thus further widening space for women and promoting their agency.

How do these Pentecostal women view their mission? What impact have they had in the church and society? What are the implications of their involvement for the future of mission in Kenya?

## 4. Pentecostalism as Women's Space: Missiological Insights from (Neo-) Pentecostal Mission Agency by Women

From the case studies, it is evident that evangelism, social welfare, and action are important foci of their mission work. The goal of evangelism is spiritual conversion, moral and social transformation. The mission initiatives are local, cross-cultural and global, directed to not only those who have not heard the gospel but also to Christians in other denominations. The purpose is to create awareness of salvation by exposing people to gospel values and realities. Women are major agents in this endeavor and they have always carved out space for themselves seeking their liberation and that of others. But while there is no uniform pattern of Pentecostal liberation, there are three identifiable pathways to greater equality. First, Pentecostal women may have greater opportunity in the life of their local church than they enjoy in the larger society. Second, they might also enjoy greater opportunity in public life, and third, the collective status of women in a community or nation may benefit from Pentecostalism. JIAM, FEM, and LHSF provide a fascinating window into how these women have resisted patriarchal structures and also provide us with important insights into these questions as the most prominent female-led movements in Kenya.

The case studies have shown how religious communities and personal religious commitment offer women opportunities for self-determination as well as leadership experience— both of which help them become agents of change. Wairimu and Wanjiru have risen to prominence as leaders in the neo-Pentecostal movement, despite the stigma typically attached to single or divorced women. Despite being married, Mbugua too has struggled to curve a space for herself in a male-dominated church. Acclaimed as role models, these leaders have encouraged single women, and indeed all women, to rise above cultural inhibitions and to overcome gender-based discrimination in church and society. The egalitarian theology implicit within Pentecostalism provides space in the church and in ministries where women can exercise their spiritual gifts.

The three case studies present a different leadership pattern, where women are the dominant heads of the churches, and not mere adjuncts to dominant males. All three of these women present another pattern, at least in part because Wanjiru and Wairimu are single and Mbugua is married. Unlike Reconstructionist feminist theologians who would want to see a more egalitarian church leadership that eliminates all kyriarchal hierarchies[37] these women leaders are not critical of traditional church structures but do challenge gender stereotypes and prejudices in African patriarchal cultures and would want to see liberating gender relations in church and society. They exhort women to circumvent such limitations through the power of the gospel, using their spiritual gifts to rise to their full potential.

The three women have challenged the conservative segment of Pentecostalism that restricts the level of a woman's ritual status. The ministries they are involved in serve a variety of roles and functions. Some ministries emphasize healing and deliverance, which they interpret as part of the divine plan of God for them and are legitimized by an encounter with God through a conversion with divine power that manifests itself in the ability to heal and deliver from demonic powers. Still others emphasize women's empowerment, and the ministry to single women as well as mercy ministries. Others establish international networks and media ministries and business enterprises. These women leaders are particularly zealous in evangelism, especially in transnational mission within Africa and abroad. In mission fields they have untrammeled space to exercise full responsibility.

As far as relationships of power between "born again" women are concerned, we argue that leading female figures such as Wanjiru, Wairimu, Mbugua, and many others exert authority over other women, including young girls and men by drawing on traditional sources of power. These sources include personal charisma, the accumulation and dissemination of financial resources through patron client networks, and the ability to demonstrate privileged access to spiritual forces.

Does the fact that Pentecostal women enjoy some measure of equality in the life of a church create positive changes for them outside that church? One measure of this is whether or not Pentecostal women behave in ways that create more alternatives for them in society than their culture would traditionally grant them. One area in which these Pentecostal female clergy and leaders have benefited women is in the area of mentorship to fellow women and girls. The story of Margaret Wanjiru's rise to public leadership is inspiring to thousands of women who aspire to rise above victimhood and patriarchy and to make something out of their sometimes difficult challenges and circumstances. Evangelist Wairimu is a role model to many single women and to other female preachers. She has equally empowered and trained a significant number of women for ministry. Most of them served as ushers and organizers in her ministry before founding their own churches or ministries. Because of her integrity and her political prophecies, she is considered and respected as a prophet to the nation in Pentecostal church circles.

## 5. Questions for Discussion

1. Women's agency transcends all facets of African Christianity but is most dynamic among neo-Pentecostals. It even generates

new forms of cross-cultural, trans-denominational, and international Christianity. What are the markers of these initiatives?

2. Can you discern some impacts deriving from (neo-) Pentecostal women's movements on the Roman Catholic Church, Protestant churches, and other churches in Africa? What are—or what should be—the mayor issues on the agenda of a trans-denominational women's network?

3. At least two of the presented women (Wanjiru and Wairimu) have an emancipatory profile regarding women's roles in marriage, family, and church leadership, but adopt a conservative stance in various issues of public life. Do you observe similar behaviors in other countries inside and outside Africa? Make comments on both aspects from your own contextual experiences.

4. Missionary outreach, crusades with the aim to win all African peoples from Cairo to Cape Town for Christ have been criticized many times outside and inside World Christianity. Pleading for political and juridical means (e.g., constitutional law) to hinder the growth and strength of Muslim peoples (as suggested by Wanjiru) can increase religious conflict and strife. Should such "unethical means" for mission purposes not be renounced? Are there safe spaces for women from different religious, cultural, and geographical backgrounds to start a conversation on that contentious issue?

## 6. Recommendations

The following recommendations are limited to two proposals for further research on women in mission:

1. In religious science the rise of women leadership, its role vis-à-vis men's leadership, and its impact on neo-Pentecostalism are still to be explored in further studies. Since neo-Pentecostalism is a controversial phenomenon from the point of view not only of mainline churches, but also of evangelical churches as well as in human sciences, it would be most interesting to know if women make a difference by transforming the criticized aspects of neo-Pentecostalism as for instance the lack of diaconial engagement, materialistic aims, and exploitation of adherents.

2. While women's movements as described in the case study are powerful forces in the society, they are quite often perceived as dissenters if they act against Roman Catholic canon law or Protestant church laws. They are sometimes also criticized within the Pentecostal churches as the case study shows. This may be the reason why women and their adherents rather break

away from mother churches—be they mainline or Pentecostal—than renouncing their theological, structural, and practical essentials. The exploding church fragmentation challenges the ecumenical existence of the church. Fresh efforts are needed to bring again to the table those willing to end the marginalization of women by church law or cultural reservations, and ecumenically concerned women of autonomous movements.

## 7. Conclusion

The paper has shown how the neo-Pentecostal churches and Charismatic movements have enabled women to impact the religious landscape of Kenya by feminizing it and empowering hordes of marginalized women and girls. Unlike in mainline churches where women still decry their absence in key areas of decision making, in the neo-Pentecostal churches women have not only ritual power but authority to lead due to the democratization of charisma in Pentecostalism. Their talents have been utilized for the benefit of the people of God. Pentecostalism appears to realize that the mission of the church demands the full mobilization of all sectors and that to ignore any would diminish the full potential to work with Christ in reconciling a lost world unto the Father. By enlisting various categories of women (wives of pastors, single, divorced, separated, widowed, young and old) and by recognizing charismatic gifts and the presence of successful female-led ministries, neo-Pentecostalism has opened space for women to make an impact in the church, in wider society, and in the country even transnationally.

Pentecostalism offers its adherent's access to the Holy Spirit, and many Kenyans feel empowered by this promise. It is, after all, spiritual gifts and not gender that qualify individuals to be delivered and valued. This understanding of the priesthood of all believers has legitimized women's aspirations for top leadership in the church.

The major shift in ideology from mainline Christianity to Pentecostalism has heralded a new phase that has significantly affected the status of women, not least single women. And while the role of women in church ministry and leadership remains a contentious issue within Pentecostalism, women have made progress in challenging patriarchy in the church and in public culture. We argue that the conversion experience does lead to a valuing of the self in relation to God and others that increases women's autonomy and undermines patriarchal public culture. This feature of neo-Pentecostalism will continue to impact and influence the church and shape mission in the twenty-first century. Women in Nairobi neo-Pentecostal churches have contributed to the evolvement of other ways of being church.

## Further Reading

Phyllis M. Martin, *Catholic Women of Congo-Brazzaville: Mothers and Sisters in Troubled Times* (Bloomington: Indiana University Press, 2009).

Philomena N. Mwaura, "A Stick Plucked out of the Fire: The Story of Rev. Margaret Wanjiru of Jesus is Alive Ministries," in Isabel Apawo Phiri, et al., eds., *Her Story: Hidden Histories of Women of Faith in Africa* (Pietermaritzburg: Cluster Publications, 2002), 202-224.

Philomena N. Mwaura, "Gender and Power in African Christianity: African Instituted Churches and Pentecostal Churches," in Ogbu U. Kalu, ed. *African Christianity: An African Story.* (Trenton, NJ: African World Press, 2007), 410-445.

Nyambura J. Njoroge, *Kiama kia Ngo: An African Christian Feminist Ethic of Resistance and Transformation* (Ghana: Legon Theological Studies Series, 2000).

Isabel A. Phiri, et al., eds., *Her Story: Hidden Histories of Women of Faith in Africa* (Pietermaritzburg: Cluster Publications, 2002), 202-224.

Jane E. Soothill, *Gender, Social Change and Spiritual Power: Charismatic Christianity in Ghana* (Leiden and Boston: Brill, 2007).

## Endnotes

1. David B. Barrett, George T. Kurian and Todd Johnson, eds., *World Christian Encyclopedia: A Comparative Survey of Churches and Religions in the Modern World* (New York: Oxford University Press, 2001), 429.

2. Dana L. Robert, *American Women in Mission: A Social History of their Thought and Practice* (Mercer University Press, 2005), xix.

3. Elizabeth Isichei, *A History of Christianity in Africa: From Antiquity to the Present* (London: SPCK, 1995), 31.

4. Spiritual AICs are the African churches that were founded in the early twentieth century as a result of the outpouring of the Holy Spirit and African quest for self-determination in church and society. They emphasize the gifts of the Holy Spirit such as prophecy, speaking in tongues, visioning, healing, and preaching. The churches also allow women leadership and some of them have women founders. Other AICs include the so-called Ethiopian churches that broke away from mission churches in a quest for African self-determination in church and society and were generally similar to the mission churches in polity, liturgy, and theology.

5. Among many other books see: Harvey Cox, *Fire from Heaven: The Rise of Pentecostal Spirituality and Reshaping of Religion in Twenty-First Century* (Cambridge, Mass: Da Capo Press 2007, 11994); David Westerlund, ed., *Global Pentecostalism: Encounters with Other Religious Traditions* (London and New York: Macmillan, 2009); Ogbu U. Kalu, *African Pentecostalism: An Introduction* (Oxford and New York: Oxford University Press, 2008); Cephas Omenyo, *Pentecost outside Pentecostalism: A Study of the Development of Charismatic Renewal in the Mainline Churches in Ghana* (Zoetermeer: Uitgeverij Boekencentrum, 2002); Kwabena J. Asamoah-Gyadu, *African Charismatics: Current Developments*

*within Independent Indigenous Pentecostalism in Ghana* (Leiden: Brill, 2005); Allan Anderson and Edmond Tang, eds., *Asian and Pentecostal: The Charismatic Face of Christianity* (Oxford: Regnum Books International, 2005).

6. These associations include: the Catholic Women Association; Mothers' Union (Anglicans), Woman's Guild (Presbyterian Church of East Africa); Mothers' Council (African Independent Pentecostal Church of Africa).

7. It is, however, beyond the scope of this paper to deal with all these important issues.

8. See Phyllis M. Martin, *Catholic Women of Congo-Brazzaville: Mothers and Sisters in Troubled Times* (Bloomington: Indiana University Press, 2009) 96-101.

9. Compared to 78 percent in 1998. For these figures, see Kenya Population and Housing Census 2009, http://www.scribd.com/doc36670466/ Kenya Population and Housing Census-PDF (April 15, 2011). See also Pew Forum on Religion and Public Life documents: Historical Overview of Pentecostalism in Kenya www.pewforum.org/doc (April 15, 2011).

10. Accurate statistics for minority faiths are difficult to come by and are largely a matter of conjecture.

11. Federation of Women Lawyers-FIDA-Kenya (2008), report titled "Kenyan Laws and Harmful Customs Curtails Women's Equal Enjoyment of International Covenant on Economic and Social and Cultural Rights" (*International Covenant* on *Economic, Social* and *Cultural Rights* - ICESCR), 1.

12. John Padwick (2008), "Focus on African Instituted Churches and Development in Kenya," in *Global Development and Faith –inspired Organizations in Europe and Africa*. Berkeley Center Report Hague, June 24-25, 17.

13. Parsitau, D.S and Mwaura, P.N (2010) "God in the City": Pentecostalism as an Urban Phenomenon in Kenya, in *Studia Historiae Ecclesiaticae*, Journal of the Church History Society of Southern Africa, University of Pretoria 36. (2): 95-112.

14. See Kwabena J. Asamoah-Gyadu, " 'Born of Water and the Spirit': Pentecostal and Charismatic Christianity in Africa," in Ogbu U. Kalu, ed. *African Christianity: An African Story* (Trenton, NJ: Africa World Press, 2007), 340.

15. The Pew Forum on Religion and Public Life, *Spirit and Power: A 10-Country Survey of Pentecostals* (Washington 2006), for the Kenyan Pentecostalism, see http://pewforum.org/Christian/Evangelical-Protestant-Churches/Historical-Overview-of-Pentecostalism-in-Kenya.aspx (March 6, 2010).

16. In 2007, the Kenya Attorney General decried the increasing demands for registration of churches. By then, there were 8,520 registered churches, 6,740 pending applications and 60 applications that were filed every month. See *The Standard* 4th September 2007, 6.

17. Melissa D. Browning and Andrea Hollingsworth, "Your Daughters Shall Prophesy (As Long as They Submit): Pentecostalism and Gender in Global Perspective," in *The Liberating Spirit: Pentecostals and Social Action in North America*, ed. Michael Wilkinson and Steven M. Studebaker (McMaster Divinity College Press: Pickwick, 2010), 161.

18. This is attributed to Pastor J. B. Masinde of Deliverance Church who made this statement in 1997 while delivering a sermon at a church in Nairobi.

19. JIAM Website: www.jiam.org (March 6, 2010).

20. Philomena N. Mwaura, "A Stick Plucked out of the Fire: The Story of Rev. Margaret Wanjiru of Jesus is Alive Ministries," in Isabel Apawo Phiri et.al., eds., *Her Story: Hidden Histories of Women of Faith in Africa* (Pietermaritzburg: Cluster publications, 2002), 202-224.

21. JIAM Website: www.jiam.org (March 6, 2010).

22. Ibid.

23. Oral Interview, Bibiana Chege, Nairobi April 2009.

24. The Constitution was finally adopted on August 27, 2010 after it was voted for overwhelmingly at a referendum on August 4, 2010. Kadhi Courts are now enshrined in the Constitution.

25. Orange Democratic Movement (ODM) is the name of the main opposition political party in Kenya.

26. Faith Evangelistic Ministry: www.Evangelistwairimu.org. / (April 8, 2009). See also: http://twem-usa.org (April 8, 2009).

27. Teresia Wairimu, *A Cactus in the Desert, an Autobiography of Teresia Wairimu with Anne Jackson* (Revival Spring Media, 2010).

28. Personal interview and interactions with the Rev. Judy Mbugua by Damaris Parsitau in Nairobi on May 5, 2009.

29. Bishop Arthur Kitonga who served as the Presiding Bishop of the expansive Redeemed Gospel Churches of Kenya for over four decades has had a reputation of ordaining female clergy from other Pentecostal churches, such as the Hon. Bishop Margaret Wanjiru of JIAM, and the Rev. Elizabeth Wahome of Single Ladies Ministries International (SLIM). It would seem that Bishop Kitonga is open and respectful toward female leadership in Pentecostal churches and has acquired a reputation for this move.

30. This extensive facility which is one of the ministry's income generating facilities was opened in January 2009. It is open to both local and international visitors and can accommodate fifty people. LHCSF members often gather here for both physical and spiritual nourishment.

31. The sprawling Kibera slum is said to be one of the largest informal settlements in Africa.

32. Oral interviews of LSHF members by Parsitau, May 9, 2009.

33. Homecare Spiritual Fellowship's Newsletter, 3rd Quarter 2008-1st Quarter 2009, 1.

34. Tie-Dye is a process of dyeing textiles made from knit or woven fabric usually cotton and typically using bright colors. The process is accomplished by folding the material into a pattern, binding it with a string or rubber band. Dye is then applied to only parts of the material. The ties prevent dyeing every part of the material. Designs are formed by applying different colors of dyes to different parts of the material. Tye-Dye has become a cottage industry especially for many women's groups in various parts of Africa.

35. Francis Manana, "Mbugua, Judy Wanjiru," in *Dictionary of African Christian Biography*: http://www.dacb.org/stories/aa-print-stories/kenya/mbugua_judy.html (May 6, 2011).

36. Judy Mbugua, ed., *Our Time has Come: African Christian Women Address the Issues of Today* (Grand Rapids, MI: Baker Book House, 1994).

37. The term *kyriarchy* deriving from the Greek word for "Lord" has been invented by Elisabeth Schüssler-Fiorenza to characterize interdependent and collaborating systems of domination and submission where one person might be oppressed in one context but favored in another. For a more detailed definition, see Elisabeth Schüssler-Fiorenza, *But She Said: Feminist Practices of Biblical Interpretation* (Boston: Beacon Press, 1992), 115-117, 122-125.

CHAPTER 5

# Women in Ethiopian Christianity: An Appraisal of their Impacts Past and Present*

*Belaynesh Bekele Abiyo*

## 1. Introduction

"But you, who do you say that I am?" Jesus asks his disciples (Mark 8:29). To bring Christ in to one's own context, every generation must answer for itself what it means to witness Jesus as the Christ. The answers are inevitably shaped by historical, cultural, social, and political contexts of a certain community. It is essential, therefore, to identify the context out of which any Christology or theological reflection on Jesus Christ emerges.[1] Likewise, one has to consider which images of Jesus Christ are favored in connection with a specific Christological definition.

Emerging Christologies of the twentieth and twenty-first centuries have challenged the relevance of more traditional images of Christ for today's Christians. Contemporary analysis by theological movements such as feminist liberationist Christologies have demonstrated an ability to actively engage with the memory and traditions of the historical Jesus, who is portrayed in the Scriptures as the Christ, in order to re-interpret his message for the globalized community today. Feminist liberation theologians and scholars have actively sought to transform traditional images of Christ for contemporary society.

*At the time of completing this article the author Ms. Belaynesh Bekele Abiyo is living at a home for asylum seekers in Schaffhausen, Switzerland. Ms. Abiyo had no access to a library and had to work with Internet resources only. This is the reason why main parts are quoted from Internet pages.

Creative dialogue with the memory of Christ and Christological traditions can create an image of Christ as liberator that people from different backgrounds and nations can connect with on a personal level. Jesus' concern for liberating people from their poverty, suffering, and sin is emphasized by feminist liberation theologians in their search for a Christ that is relevant to contemporary society and to women in particular. "For African women, the Jesus of the gospel comes through as the friend, healer, advocate, and source of transformation of which we are critically in need. Further, Jesus 'the boundary breaker' is a source of hope for women bound on all sides by religions and cultures of Africa. This is the Christology that stimulates women's 'protests Theology.' Empowered by the Holy Spirit, they risk announcing the good news of God's Jubilee."[2]

In this paper I will focus on Ethiopia, a country with a Christian tradition reaching back to Antiquity and Early Christianity (2). Women's roles in Ethiopian history, political life, society and churches will be portrayed (3). Today, Ethiopian society believes that women are created to serve their fellow male human beings in full submission. In addition to patriarchal culture, Christian teaching on Christology is exclusively androcentric. Through its interpretation and imagery it has legitimated the oppression of women. Therefore, the need for feminist liberation Christology for Ethiopian women is outlined whereby its Christological imageries deserve closer attention (4). Ethiopian Christian teachings of Christology seem "too high" that they are beyond the reach of ordinary people in general, of women in particular. One of the main reasons for that is the miaphysite Christology of Ethiopian Orthodox Tewahedo Church (EOTC), which emphasizes the divine nature of Jesus Christ and gives less attention to his human nature. Males have the right to represent God, not females; women's status is absorbed into the male fellows' status. So women are regarded as invisible. They are, in general, assumed to be less clean, less intelligent, and not worthy to represent God the creator and Jesus Christ who died on the cross to save the world.

## 2. History of Christianity in Ethiopia

"Ethiopia, through its unique political independence and its venerable indigenous Ethiopian orthodox church, represents an impressive continuity in the history of the church in Africa."[3] Moreover, familiar texts in the Bible such as the narrative of the baptism of the Ethiopian eunuch (Acts 8:26-39) and the promise

proclaimed in the Psalms: 'Ethiopia shall soon stretch out her hands unto God' (Psalm 68:31 KJV), offered points of identification for African Christians."[4]

However, "the Ethiopians date the coming of Christianity to Ethiopia to the fourth century A.D., when a Christian philosopher from Tyre named Meropius was shipwrecked on his way to India. Meropious died, but his two wards, Frumentius and Aedesius, were washed ashore and taken to the royal palace. Eventually they became King Ella Amida's private secretary and royal cupbearer respectively. They served the king well and Frumentius became regent for the infant prince Ezana when Ella Amida died. Frumentius and Aedesius were also permitted to transmit the new religion (Christianity) in Aksum. Frumentius and Aedesius returned after some time to the Mediterranean Sea, traveling down the Nile through Egypt to do so. When they reached Egypt, Frumentius contacted Bishop Athanasius of Alexandria and begged him to send missionaries back to Aksum, since the people there had proved so ready to receive the gospel. Athanasius agreed that the need was urgent and immediately appointed Frumentius to the task, which needed someone fluent in the language and sensitive to the customs of Aksum. He ordained Frumentius the first *Abuna* (Bishop) of the Ethiopian Orthodox Church. Frumentius has since come to be known as the Abuna salama (Abba salama) or bishop of peace. His mission was successful and, with the support of king Ezana, Ethiopia became a Christian nation.

The link between the Ethiopian church and the patriarch of Alexandria was not broken until the twentieth century, since the Coptic patriarch of Alexandria has sent to Ethiopia each of its succeeding Abuna."[5] "This meant that Egyptians ruled the Ethiopian church for sixteen centuries. At the end of the fifth century, nine monks arrived probably from Syria, though perhaps from Egypt, and introduced monasticism into Ethiopia. Monasticism has remained a dominant feature of the Ethiopian church to this day. It is assumed that these monks may have been driven out of Syria after the council of Chalcedon for being Monophysite Christians. Monophysites believe that the divine and human natures of Christ were fused in to a single nature at his birth. On the other hand, the ecumenical council of Chalcedon distinguished between the divine nature of Christ and his human nature, declaring the monophysites heretical. At any rate, whether or not it was due to the nine saints, the ETOC, along with the Coptic church of Egypt, and smaller churches in Syria, Turkey, and Armenia, have remained non-Chalcedonian.

These non-Chalcedonian churches have formed a distinctively oriental orthodox branch of the worldwide church. The nine monks also encouraged the translation of the Bible into Ge'ez, which was the language of the people at that time. The Ethiopian church continues to use Ge'ez as its liturgical language, though it is no longer a spoken language."[6]

"During the seventh century the Muslim conquests cut the Ethiopians off from the rest of the Christian world, except for the Ethiopian monastery in Jerusalem, while a continuing thread of contact with Egypt was maintained because the Coptic patriarch of Alexandria supplied the Ethiopian church with its Abuna."[7] At first, "the relation between the Ethiopians and the Muslims was cordial, with mutual trade and mutual religious toleration, some of which grew out of real religious similarities. Since Ethiopians had been kind to several of Mohammed's companions who had fled there, the prophet Mohammed also instructed his followers to be kind to the Ethiopians. Eventually, however, relations deteriorated and Ethiopia slid into its dark ages,[8] retreating into the security of the mountains to defend themselves against the Muslims. They did, however, maintain their independence, their culture, their identity, and their faith."[9]

"In twelfth century, Ethiopia emerged from the dark age under the leadership of a new Zagwes dynasty. The Zagwes were from central Ethiopia and of dubious backgrounds. Later ecclesiastical texts accuse them of not being the pure Solomonic lineage. That is, they did not descend from Menelik, the son of the biblical king Solomon and the queen of Sheba, who supposedly founded the royal house of Ethiopia."[10] In 1543 a Portuguese musket killed Ahmed Gragn, a militant Muslim who had tried to destroy Ethiopian Christendom. Afterward Islam fell apart. At that time John "Bermudez took advantage of the death of the Abuna (Bishop) to claim that the dying patriarch had appointed him as his successor, and that Pope Paul III has appointed him as Archbishop of Ethiopia when John Bermudez had been in Europe. There was, however, no evidence that either claim was true, but the Portuguese in Ethiopia believed him and pressured King Galawdewos to adopt the Latin Roman Catholic liturgy. A delegation of Jesuits was sent out to further pressure the Ethiopian court, which resisted, but at the same time, thought of joining the Roman Catholic Church. In 1607-1632, King Suseynos became Catholic (Latin Roman) in the hope of an advantageous military alliance with the West, but his successor drove the Catholic missionaries out of Ethiopia again when they tried to assert full blown Catholicism."[11]

"Ethiopia has historically been an empire, expanding in area and incorporating new groups into the population. The greatest expansion of the empire in the second half of the nineteeth century took place under the sovereign rule of Menelik II, and incorporated new peoples in the west, south, and east, so that, in the end, the country knew a population of great diversity."[12] "Menelik II, who succeeded in holding off and defeating the Italian attempts to colonize Ethiopia, started another clandestine mission to people living southwards."[13]

His first goal was to unite the old Ethiopian empire, which had been disbanded since the Oromo movement in the sixteenth century. "He wanted to re-establish the ancient frontiers of Ethiopia up to Khartoum and as far as Lake Nyanza where the Galla tribes lived."[14] Second, he wanted to acquire control over the valuable trade resources of the south. The rich sources of the gold, ivory, coffee, spices, and slaves were very much in his interests. Therefore he sent his soldiers to the south and southeast to secure his interests and hinder the powers from intruding into the old Solomonic empire. He wanted to defend the Ethiopian territory against the European colonialists.

Menelik II was the defender of the Ethiopian Solomon dynasty. He was in his right to unite the Christian kingdom that had been spilt into pieces during the era of princes. From his point of view his policy of incorporation of the kingdoms and chieftains into the empire was justified. "Kebire Negast" is the name of the famous epic work from the fifteenth century. Its primary goal is to legitimize the authority of the legendary Emperor, Yekuno Amlak, who had restored the Solomonic empire. Thus the book is devoted mainly to defending the lineage of Menelik I who is perceived as the son of biblical King Solomon and Queen of Sheba. So the aim of Menelik II was to restore the glory of the Solomonic dynasty and revitalize the magnificent deeds of his forefathers.[15] He was very much aware of his historical obligations.

From 1889 to 1909, when Menelik II became the sovereign ruler of the Ethiopian kingdom, he conquered many people and incorporated them in his empire: chieftainships and nations like the Afar people, the Somali people, and other southern people like the Sidama, Kambata, and Hadiya. That colonial rule—or inner colonization—has been regarded as a milestone in Ethiopian history. In this period of time Menelik II the EOTC gained strong position in the country and expanded to the colonized parts of the country. The Ethiopian Orthodox Tewahedo Church was the official state religion until the fall of Emperor Haile Selassie, the last king of the so-called Solomonic monarchy, in 1974.

"Protestantism came to Ethiopia through mission societies beginning in the nineteenth century. Their impact bore some fruit in the twentieth century, but did not create a large following. The three churches that have shaped Ethiopian Protestantism are the Lutherans, Sudan Interior Mission, and the Mennonite Mission. The earliest presence of Protestantism was the Lutheran mission work that has later become the Mekane Yesus (dwelling of Jesus). This church is mostly found in the southern and western areas of Ethiopia due to the weak presence of Ethiopian Orthodox Church there."[16]

## 3. Women in Political, Social and Religious Life of Ethiopia's History

When we refer to history we can observe that from antiquity on not only men struggled for the better, but also women contributed a lot in their part being on the side of men. "More than in any other country, women in Ethiopia fought as courageously as men in the battlefield."[17] This may be illustrated by women of leadership families as well as by common women.

### 3.1 Queen of Sheba

"A large part of the history of Ethiopia is centred on the legend of the Queen of Sheba of Ethiopia and the biblical King Solomon of Israel. Many Ethiopians believe that the relationship between Queen Sheba and King Solomon resulted in a son who founded the Solomonic Dynasty in Aksum,"[18] in the northern part of Ethiopia. Surprisingly, the current movement of "Rastafarianism," a Jamaican movement, has pushed the world to rediscover the Queen of Sheba's story. "According to an Ethiopian legend, the Queen of Sheba learned about the wisdom of King Solomon from a merchant called Tamrin, how he worshiped God, and of his skills in building a great Temple in Jerusalem. The Queen of Sheba she decided to visit and see for herself King Solomon's wisdom, how he worshiped God and his many skills. When the Queen of Sheba visited King Solomon in Jerusalem she gave him many gifts and asked him many questions, which he was able to answer."[19] Even if there is no evidence about her giving birth to King Solomon's child, we will find the evidence of the Queen of Sheba's visit to King Solomon in Jerusalem in the Old Testament (1 Kings 10:1-10).

"According to the Ethiopian national epic, Kibra Negast, compiled in the fourteenth century, the Queen of Sheba, who visited

King Solomon in the Old Testament time, came from Tigre in Northern Ethiopia. She made the arduous journey across the desert and the Red Sea with her retinue and rich gifts to learn wisdom from the great King Solomon. Later, he beguiled her into sleeping with him and on her return she gave birth to a son, Menelik I. According to the legend he was the founder of the Ethiopian Solomonic dynasty, which supposedly ended only with the deposition of Emperor Haile Selassie in 1974."[20]

As legend says, the town of Aksum was established during the reign "of the Queen of Sheba in 500 B.C. And then Aksum became the ancient city of Ethiopian civilization and a powerful kingdom. Aksum remained the capital where the coronations of emperors and empresses were held until the reign of Emperor Haile Selassie. [Aksum] has become Ethiopia's most important centre of the Orthodox Tewahedo Christian faith with many archaeological remains of interest and historical significance."[21]

The legend of the Queen of Sheba is also well known in popular culture. Be it joke or serious talk, many people are referring to her story. Many songs, movies, and books are produced based on her legendary story. She was the hero figure who took action to learn more from the wise king. She was the bold type and brave leader of the country. She could be the representative of both spiritual and political leaders. "Biblical texts like 1 King 10:1-13 and 2 Chronicles 9:1-12 tell about the Queen of Sheba's gifts of spices, gold, precious stones and beautiful wood. The Queen of Sheba was awed by Solomon's wisdom and wealth, and pronounced a blessing on Solomon's God."[22] She understood that God put him in a position to do justice and righteousness. She could be the good example for both spiritual and religious leaders in Ethiopia.

Even at the time when women in most parts of the world were relegated to household chores, the number of Ethiopian women in the late seventeenth century participating in war expeditions against foreign aggressors was on the rise. "According to historian Richard Pankhurst between 1464 and 1468, under the leadership of King Zere Yakob, women's expansion into political positions became more evident, and as the report continues Zere Yakob established a women's administration by appointing his daughters and relatives to key provinces."[23]

## 3.2 Empress Taitu

In the nineteenth century, the most famous queen involved in military affairs was Empress Taitu, wife of Emperor Menelik II.

"One of the most important accomplishments of Menelik II was the defeat of the Italians in 1896 at the Battle of Adwa."[24] Adwa is the historical place in the northern part of Ethiopia where Italians and Ethiopians fought and Ethiopians defeated Italian invaders in 1936-1941. For such a great accomplishment his wife is the first person to be appreciated. "Historians have estimated that an average of 20,000 to 30,000 women have participated in the campaign of Adwa alone. While the majority served in non-violent chores such as food preparation and nursing of the wounded, a significant portion served as soldiers, strategists, advisors, translators, and intelligence officers. Women from the aristocracy worked alongside maids and servants thereby breaking norms in class separation."[25]

"In the battle of Adwa Empress Taitu is said to have commanded an infantry of no less than 5,000 along with 600 cavalrymen, accompanied by thousands of Ethiopian women. Her strategy to cut off the invading Italian armies' water supply led to the weakening of the enemies' warfront. Following her example, Empress Mennen avidly participated in battles"[26] taking place during the Ethio-Italian war (1936-1941). While women of higher class participated in military activities, the women from lower class accompanied them as maids and servants. They served as cooks and in other administrative roles. As many said Ethiopian women worked so hard, seldom resting till late at night, even at midnight grinding, and frequently went up before 'cockcrow.' Tired from the march, no matter how late, water had to be brought, fuel collected, supper prepared by the soldiers' wives before daylight, and with a huge load, they had to march again the next day.

## 3.3 Empress Zewditu

Another important woman in Ethiopian history is Empress Zewditu, the daughter of Menelik II who stayed on the throne for thirteen years. As Ethiopian history points out she didn't come to the position soon after the death of her father, Emperor Menelik II; according to the tradition[27] access to the throne was given to the so-called Lij Iyasu, the grandson designated heir of Emperor Menelik II, in 1913. "But because of his endless and special relationship with Muslims in the Eastern part of Ethiopia, Lij Iyasu was never officially crowned and recognized as Emperor."[28] There was another grandson of emperor Menelik II, Ras Tefari (Haile Selassie), who was at the time too young to be crowned. Then "the nobility of Shewa, a place in the central Ethiopia, and the clergy of EOTC officially crowned Zewditu,"[29] as Empress of Ethiopia, in 1916. Her leadership was successful.

## 3.4 Empress Menen

Following the example of Empress Taitu, Empress Menen, the wife of Haile Selassie had a tutor "at home like the former Lords' and Dukes' sons and daughters. Beyond academic education she was taught home economics and spinning in line with Ethiopian tradition. Since she had the best knowledge of household management people called her the head of women. In 1928 when her husband went to the battlefield she administered the people in the capital city."[30]

Although the EOTC does not mention much about women's participation in the construction of church buildings there are some records from history. Empress Taitu told Empress Menen to complete the construction of a church founded by her in 1910 at the eastern part of Addis Ababa around Entoto Mountain. "Keeping that the promise, Empress Menen invested a lot of money and completed which served as a monastery. Empress Menen gave her estate to the monastery and helped those who gave service to the church. This monastery is still a shelter for many Christians."[31]

According to Yared Gebre Michael, "in March 1915 Empress Menen had travelled to Jerusalem to visit the place where Jesus Christ was born. After she visited every part of Jerusalem, she went to Egypt to visit holy places. On May 28, 1919 she donated a large amount of money to construct schools for the poor children and freed slaves. On September 24, 1923 she founded a new school for girls near to Genete Loul palace. At that school a great number of ladies of the higher classes have got a chance to learn. Besides that many students received scholarship to foreign countries."[32] This school fulfilled its objectives and helped at least some women to participate in the sphere of knowledge and technology equally with men. These are some of the remarkable works of the late Empress Menen in the Ethiopian history.

## 3.5 Common Women

When we come to the real situation of common Ethiopian women apart from royal family, we see that traditionally women have suffered sociocultural and economic discrimination and have had fewer chances for personal growth, education, and employment in comparison to men.

Women's ownership rights are very limited in Ethiopia, even though land reforms enacted in March 1997 tried to improve access to land by stipulating that women have the right to lease land from the government. In fact, during the land redistribution exercise carried out in the Amhara Region, almost 130,000 poor rural women became landowners. Despite these reforms, it is frequently the case that women's only chance to access land is through marriage. It is generally accepted that only the head of the household—typically the husband—can be a landowner. Women who separate from their husbands are likely to lose their houses and property, and when a husband dies, other family members often claim the land over his widow. A study by Gebreslassie identifies two main factors that work against women's legal right to control land: lack of ownership of oxen with which to plough the land and cultural taboos that constrain women from the work of ploughing and sowing. According to statistics, only about 20 percent of households are currently "female-headed families," many of which are headed by widows. The Civil Code remains discriminatory in regard to access to property other than land. It grants husbands control of common property and allows them to make all decisions related to such property. Ethiopian women have only limited access to bank loans. Public financing for women may be granted to female heads of households who own land; by contrast, married women who wish to obtain loans must first seek permission from their husbands.

"In Ethiopia even the revolution of 1974, which ended the Empire of Haile Selassie and brought a socialist government in power had little impact on the lives of rural women. Land reform did not change their subordinate status, which was based on deeply rooted traditional values and beliefs. An improvement of economic conditions would improve the standard of living of women, but real change would require a transformation of the attitudes of governments and men regarding women."[33]

## 3.6 Women in Ethiopian churches

### 3.6.1 Ethiopian Orthodox Tewahedo Church (EOTC)

Even though there are some women who participated in constructing church buildings and establishing Orthodox Church historical and spiritual centers, the EOTC is paying little attention to women. Conform to cultural traditions the church regards women as subservient to men. The strong patriarchal and hierarchical leadership of the EOTC has closed the doors for ministry by women in the church. Biblical references, as for example, 1 Timothy 2:13-15; 5:2-16; Colossians 3:18-4:1; Ephesians 5:22-6:9, and the gender of Jesus Christ are the main weapons which are used by the church in order to exclude women from the priesthood. Women in EOTC are also confronted with the andro-centric bias and the misogyny that have informed Christian theo-logical tradition for centuries. Ethiopian Christendom has been, however, no exception given that occidental Christendom and theological thinking have been shaped by Tertullian's descrip-tion of women as the "devil's gateway" and Thomas Aquinas' characterization of women as "misbegotten men."

Women are only wanted for making bread for the count-less celebrations of the church during the year in the EOTC. As the Third World women theologians, Virginia Fabella and Mercy Amba Oduyoye, state, "This church, the male-dominated church, *wants* women but does not *need* them."[34] The women are not needed but only their effort, their unconsidered contri-bution. In general Ethiopian women whether they are from a higher or lower class, are the victims of patriarchal Christianity. EOTC by reflecting male dominance in different ways made women invisible figures within the church based on gender typologies expressing that women are absorbed into the male in the same way as Jesus was absorbed into the divine and became "one Nature" (Tewahedo).[35] Women are thought of as lesser human beings than men, and regarded as second-rate citizens. And I would say that EOTC did hardly bring much change to Ethiopian women's life; instead it put another burden in addi-tion to the cultural one being already there.

### 3.6.2 Women in the Ethiopian Evangelical Church Mekane Yesus (EECMY)

The Ethiopian Evangelical Church Mekane Yesus is one of the strongest Protestant churches in Ethiopia, which grew out of the works of the different Lutheran missionary societies from Germany, Sweden, and other Scandinavian countries like Norway and Finland. The missionaries who came to preach the gospel in the nineteenth and twentieth centuries were active also in the social services and development projects like build-ing schools for girls and boys, building health centers, literacy education centers for adults, and so on. The church has a women ministry's office under the department of mission and theol-ogy or the evangelism department. Each and every synod of the church office has its own women ministry's office coordinator. The Mekane Yesus Seminary in Addis Ababa is also providing some scholarship opportunities for women for theological and leadership studies. In spite of all these efforts, the strong influ-ence of patriarchal religion of the past and the traditional culture are still playing a great oppressive role in women' life in EECMY.

From the beginning the church had great women like Aster Ganno who was the wife of late Onesimus Nesib, the translator of the Bible in to the Oromo language. In 1886, when Onesimus Nesib decided to teach and to translate the whole Bible into the Oromo language, he faced difficulties because "he did not have an adequate knowledge of his mother tongue in terms of vocabulary and idioms, as he had not lived in the Oromo culture since his childhood. Luckily for him, Aster Ganno was able to come to his rescue. After finishing school she was assigned the task of composing a dictionary of pure Oromo words by listing derivatives of every particular root and removing dialectical and alien's forms. Even though she was a constant source of material for Onesimus' work as he worked on the New Testament, which was revised and published by the Imkullu press in 1893, she was not acknowledged for her contribution."[36]

Even the missionary societies did not consider women as missionaries. Women accompanied them as wives and helpmates of the missionaries.[37] Those among the missionaries' wives who were not considered as missionaries on their own started the women's ministry or holistic mission work for women and continued serving women. Especially in the southern and western parts of Ethiopia missionaries' wives did a great job by reaching Ethiopian women at home. They taught them some skills like home economics, handcrafting, and so on. That helped many women to become familiar with house management. The Ethiopian women valued such kind of missionaries' wives' concern toward women. But that should be seen only as the beginning of access to the restricted public places for Ethiopian women. EECMY women who are still the victims of most patriarchal culture and religion are looking forward enjoying total liberation for themselves and for other women throughout the country and beyond.

## 4. Toward Ethiopian Women's Christology

Surprisingly, in Ethiopia the whole history of the church, which was focused on the relationship of a biblical king, Solomon, and the Queen of Sheba, became more oppressive for Ethiopian women. The imprint of the colonization period, which had given a hard time for women who were from lower classes is still causing to them double oppression.[38] The women who stayed without education under such a system are victims of other cultural pressures today. EOTC's teaching that lays more emphasis on the divine side of Jesus Christ influences also most of the Christologies in

other churches in Ethiopia. Therefore women have deeply internalized the meaning that only men can represent Jesus Christ.
But there is still a need to meet the God who can understand their
real situation. In their disturbing situation the introduction of
feminist liberation Christology from Ethiopian perspective could
be helpful in order to empower them to see things in a new and
different way.

Ethiopian Orthodox Christians and some others Christians
from Protestant mainline churches, who are influenced by
EOTC make literal interpretation of the historical Jesus. He was
incarnated as male human being. From a feminist perspective
this might lead to the misleading view that only the male is
close to the divine, that there is no room for women in the incarnation, and that the body of the woman is unclean. EOTC also
teaches that Mary is *theotokos* (giving birth to God). There is no
relation for other women to see her as one of them: an example
of the faithful servant of God. She is in a position too high to be
connected to women's lives. As the Ghanaian theologian, Mercy
Amba Oduyoye says: "the Mariology of Orthodox Christianity
put Christian women on pedestals and viewed them as 'the
neck that turns the head,' but their roles were fixed and could
not be modified even by individual talents. Ethiopian monks
put their monasteries in the far recesses of their mountainous
country partly to isolate themselves from women."[39]

According to my theological perception, the Christological
teaching, which mainly focuses on the divine nature of Jesus
Christ and gives less weight to the human side of Jesus, is oppressive to women. Thus, I want to propose some relevant feminist
images of Jesus Christ, which might help toward the liberation of
women from the dominance of patriarchy and hierarchical religion and culture. My base for constructing the following feminist
images of Jesus Christ for Ethiopian women is mostly derived
from Third World feminist articulation of Christology. And I think
that these images could be also the best models for Ethiopian
women's Christology as they would help them to come closer to
Jesus as a participator in their life or as accompanying them in
their hard life situations. That could give them the hope of resurrection and lead them to freedom from different patriarchal and
hierarchical religious and cultural bondages and practices.

## 4.1 Jesus Christ, the Homeless Wanderer (Migrant)

Musimibi R. A. Kanyoro, a Kenyan woman theologian, suggests that cultural hermeneutics is an important first step toward

an African women liberation theology. She also notes that, "[all] questions regarding the welfare and status of women in Africa are explained within the frame work of culture."[40] According to some African cultural traditions women cannot inherit land or own property. They themselves are considered as the property of the men. In African culture both ownership and leadership belong to the domain of men. According to cultural and religious tradition women in Ethiopia should be always dependent from and submissive to men. As we go through the Gospel records of Jesus' life and ministry in this world, we do not find any information about Jesus' ownership of a house. He has been wandering his whole life while serving those people who had houses to live in and something to live on. He made himself the poorest among the poor. In Ethiopia, especially according to my own ethnic group, Kambata,[41] the person who does not have his own house to live is regarded as the poorest among the poor. For Kambata people, the "home" means the whole household and all persons living in it. When they ask about home they are asking about property and settlement. Among my community the homeless person could be considered as a stranger, needy or dependent.

According to Kambata people's interpretation of home and homelessness, Jesus of Nazareth who had no home could be seen as needy. When we come to Ethiopian women they too, like Jesus, neither own property for themselves nor their own homes and houses. Throughout their whole life they are homeless wanderers and considered always as needy ones. Jesus became a homeless pilgrim because of the sociopolitical and religion-cultural situation of his time right from the beginning from his early age, when his parents took him to Egypt to save his life from the hand of Herod. Likewise Ethiopian women's homelessness also starts from their very moment of birth. From that very moment on she will belong for all her life to someone else, she will have no share in her father's house, or later in her husband's house. In some areas and ethnic groups, if the husband dies, and in case the widow had no son, her fate immediately will change to homelessness and wandering.

In such situations the homeless pilgrim's image of Jesus Christ can and will give hope for homeless and wandering women. It gives consolation or the feeling of knowing that God is in solidarity with them, that they are not alone with their fate as Christ participates to their fate. It leads them to the message of resurrection in order to transform their oppressive situation in both church and society. Both church and society have to give a place for women to rest from their wandering, and homelessness. I hope and believe the powerful transformation will come from Jesus Christ himself who passed through this path in order to save, and give rest and peace for those who were and still are in a wandering and hopeless situation.

## 4.2 Jesus Christ, the Servant of All

Like families in many other African countries, most of the Ethiopian families prefer having a son instead of a daughter. By the time of birthing the women who are surrounding the mother give the joy signal by shouting "Ululation."[42] In such performance there are symbolic numbers indicating the gender of the babies. At the birth of a girl it should be three times, and four or seven times at the birth of a boy. Intentionally or ignorantly from this very moment of such performance, the community starts discriminating against a newborn girl. The mother of a newly born girl herself abuses her daughter, because the whole culture is abusive toward the female gender. In contrary the boys receive good treatment from every member of the community because they are assumed to be future heroes, kings, chiefs, and so on. Girls however will face many problems. They are predestined by the society to be the servants of all, being good for nothing but only for fetching water, collecting fire wood, and cooking meals for the whole family. Beginning from their early childhood until their death, they give forced and imposed oppressive service for the entire community. Women are predicted to serve the whole society, which may be called "unconsidered sacrificial service."[43]

Women in Ethiopia serve clean and unclean members of society just as Jesus dealt with clean and unclean people in his ministry. Girls serve their brothers who look down on them because of their female gender. They are washing the feet of the whole family every night; they are made weak and unfit for the public, but they are connected very strongly with the "kosha."[44] Nowadays, it is sometimes named kitchen, especially if it has a modern interior. In most of Ethiopian families and society women and girls cook for all, feed all, try to make all happy, but because of their gender the community members always despise them despite their countless services.

When we compare their life to that of Jesus of Nazareth who served all, he served the weak and sick, the so called clean and unclean, he served the wicked and innocent, he served men and women, He served his own betrayer, washed Judas' feet.

Therefore we can say that Ethiopian women have something in common with Jesus of Nazareth because both serve their oppressors or betrayers. Ethiopian women serve their Judases; they serve the clergy who refuse to greet them in public. Particularly lower class women were or in some areas still are not welcomed to kiss the cross in the hand of the priest. He would not allow them to do so because those women are categorized as unclean and unworthy. Surprisingly the clergy, priests, the so-called clean group, and other church ministers, enjoy the meal which is prepared by those the so called unclean maids.

As Jesus fed the masses without separating enemies and friends Ethiopian women too are serving the whole society while the latter is ignoring them instead of appreciating them. Concerning our colonial history country-women were regarded as inferior beings, they worked without rest, they accepted unconsidered service, and some of them were transferred from one lord's house to another to perform more service.

The "servant of all" image for Jesus Christ could be a relevant metaphor for Ethiopian women who have been serving their entire community. Males are willing to appropriate for themselves leadership roles of Christ, but refuse to adopt the servant role of Jesus. As long as this partition of Jesus Christ along gender lines is practiced, the servant metaphor remains oppressive to women. The church is fulfilling its mission in the world only when Jesus Christ is mirrored in it, where there are neither Jews nor Greeks, neither masters nor slaves, not man and woman (Gal. 3:28).

## 4.3 Jesus Christ as a Compassionate Provider

Jesus Christ is a compassionate provider who knows the needs of people. Jesus nurtures and feeds the hungry; the Ethiopian women also do so. The story of Mark 6:30-42 bears many similarities between Jesus' compassionate feeding of the crowd and Ethiopian women mass feeding during the feasts. When we see the story in Mark, Jesus fed the five thousand men, and numberless women and children. He himself was from the uncounted group because even at the end of service or feeding all, he didn't take any fragment of basket with him. Only his twelve disciples took twelve basketfuls of broken pieces of bread and fish. As he stood up and fed the masses countable and uncountable, Ethiopian women feed the masses during the feasts. They spend most of their energy in preparing food and feeding the masses standing by fully devoted for that service until all have taken enough. Most of the time they will be left empty handed without any remaining basketful of broken pieces of bread. Here also we can see a lot of similarity between Ethiopian women's devotion in their compassionate provision and Jesus' compassionate service and ministry for all.

Mercy Amba Oduyoye and Elizabeth Amoah in their writing on "The Christ for African women" emphasize his servanthood metaphor and portray Jesus of Nazareth as the caring, and compassionate nurturer of all.[45] Serving, caring for the weak, sick, and aged, nurturing the whole family is daily experience for Ethiopian women as mothers. It is good and appreciable serving others with such devotion, but most of Ethiopian women are serving the society because it is a must for them to serve the community. It is considered as their fate whether they are tired or hungry; very little attention is given toward them. Service to one another in the society and elsewhere should be the duty of everybody in spite of gender differences. Human beings are created to live in relationship through helping and serving each other. But serving becomes oppressive when some are considered as servants against their will, while others act as honored masters who think and believe they are superior. This is exactly what is happening in Ethiopia: gender relations are a "servant-master relationship."

Thus, Ethiopian female theologians should be strongly critical toward such an attitude in church and society. By choosing to be a servant, Jesus indicated that this work is not to be despised and disregarded, but to be seen positively as a divine work. Our savior Jesus' servanthood ministry was willingly done for the benefit of all including women, not to make some servants and others bosses or masters over others, but to serve each other. We can find its climax in Jesus washing the feet of his disciples in John 13; which is a strongly provoking symbol, teaching that every human being is created to serve one another. That is the great mission given to the sons and daughters of God.

# 5. Questions for Discussion

1. Why has Christianity as Ethiopia's main religion for more than 1600 years failed to bring much change in women's lives?

2. Compare the outstanding women in Ethiopia's political and religious history with similar figures in other countries described in this volume. Did they become a source of liberation and empowerment for women? If not, why?

3. What is the relationship between traditional gender typologies and mainstream Christology in Ethiopia?

4. A Christology focusing on the homeless and serving aspects of Jesus' life has been used in different ways in church history: on the one hand, it was used to legitimize the serving roles of women, slaves, and oppressed ethnic groups; on the other hand it has given and still gives strength to oppose every kind of oppression. How would you deal with the problem of such contradictory interpretations?

5. Which lesson do you learn from the Ethiopian case for doing mission in your own context?

## 6. Recommendations

Low Christology would help to balance the role of women and men in every aspect of life; especially it will teach them to serve God, and one another with mutual love and with full submission. It will remind Christians in Ethiopia and elsewhere that both women and men are created in the image of God, and Jesus Christ has died for both genders. So both, women and men, should be treated as equals in his kingdom ministry and in every other activity; and both should get access to the blessings of a 'life in fullness' (John 10:10).

High Christology or divine-centered Christology being coupled with the cultural background of the country, which is extremely hierarchal and patriarchal, is too oppressive for Ethiopian women. Thus it is a must to revisit Ethiopian Christological teachings from feminist perspective toward inclusive, empowering, and liberating mission work in Ethiopia.

Giving equal opportunities and considering women as fully human beings and as equals to their men fellow human beings will contribute a lot to the entire mission work in the church and society. And it could help in every generation anew to act in the transformative ways in doing mission work for the benefit of entire humankind without any discrimination. That is all about transformative mission work in the church and society.

## 7. Conclusion

According to the Gospel of Luke, mission is all about healing, restoring, saving, liberating, comforting, saying no to injustice, oppression, dehumanizing, hatred, and discrimination. Thus mission in the twenty-first century should be revisited in such context in order to reach all in a successful way! Some people might ask me what feminist Christology has to do with mission work. Is it not so holy and far away from human beings day-to-day life? Indeed, it seems silly for some, but holistic mission should serve both body and soul. Liberation and empowerment for women's body and soul is expected. Therefore the androcentric historiography of Ethiopian Christianity as well as Ethiopian Christology should be examined critically, and it is a must to introduce new approaches toward Ethiopian Christological imagination in order to bring a new approach to the entire Christian mission in Ethiopia.

## Further Reading

Bahru Zewde, *A History of Modern Ethiopia 1855-1991* (Ohio: Ohio University Press 2nd edition 2002).

Belaynesh Bekele Abiyo, *Who is Jesus for Ethiopian Women? Introducing Feminist images of Jesus Christ towards Liberating and Empowering Ethiopian women*. A master thesis submitted to the Protestant Theological University Kampen, the Netherlands, 23. August 2007.

*Women in Ethiopia, National Policy on Ethiopian, Implementing the Ethiopian National Policy for Women, Institutional and Regulatory Issues* (Washington D.C, The World Bank, 1998).

## Endnotes

1. Kelly Brown Douglas, "Christ, Jesus," in *Dictionary of Feminist Theologies*, eds. Letty M. Russell and J. Shannon Clarkson (Louisville: Westminster John Knox Press, 1996), 38f.

2. Letty M. Russell and J. Shannon Clarkson, in ibid., 113.

3. uu.diva-portal.org/smash/get/diva2:169585/FULLTEXT01 (August 24, 2011).

4. Staffan Grenstedt, Ambarcho and Shonkolla. From Local Independent Church to the Evangelical Mainstream in Ethiopia. The Origins of the Mekane Yesus Church in Kambata Hadyia (diss. theol., University of Uppsala, 2000), 16-17.

5. http://www.ethiopiatravel.com/religion_in_ethiopia.htm (August 24, 2011).

6. http://www.voiceofmaranatha.net/Ethiopia.htm (August 24, 2011).

7. http://fatherstephen.wordpress.com/2007/12/20/and-now-for-something-completely-different-music-from-the-ethiopian-orthodox/ (August 24, 2011).

8. The so-called *Dark Age* refers to a difficult and tragic past in Ethiopia, especially in the life of many EOTC monks.

9. http://www.utoronto.ca/aidsethiopia/Church3.html (August 24, 2011).

10. http://www.igougo.com/story-s1220132-Ethiopia-Islam.html (August 24, 2011).

11. http://www.utoronto.ca/aidsethiopia/Church5.html (August 24, 2011).

12. http://www.falasha-recordings.co.uk/teachings/ethist.html (August 24, 2011).

13. http://www.utoronto.ca/aidsethiopia/Church5.html (August 24, 2011).

14. http://www.biyokulule.com/Which_Way_to_the_Sea.htm (August 24, 2011).

15. Africans often call Ethiopia the only country on the African continent, which has never been colonized by the West. They ignore that Ethiopia has experienced a different kind of colonization when southern Ethiopia people like the Afar, Sidama, Kambata, and Hadiya were colonized and Christianized at the same time by Menelik II. In my view, Christianity was transmitted to peoples in the southern parts of Ethiopia through colonial mission.

16. http://worldmap.org/maps/other/profiles/ethiopia/ET.pdf Page 11 (August 24, 2011).

17. http://eabicbahamas.ning.com/profiles/blogs/empress-menen-the-wife-of-his (August 24, 2011).

18. http://www.ethiopiantreasures.co.uk/pages/aksum.htm (August 24, 2011).

19. Ibid.

20. http://www.oneworldmagazine.org/focus/etiopia/women.html (August 24, 2011).

21. http://www.ethiopiantreasures.co.uk/pages/aksum.htm (August 24, 2011).

22. http://www.mosthigh.co.za/rastafarian-woman.htm (August 24, 2011).

23. http://www.tadias.com/index.php?s=digg (August 24, 2011).

24. http://www.everyculture.com/multi/Du-Ha/Ethiopian-Americans.html (August 24, 2011).

25. http://www.tadias.com/07/23/2007/queens-spies-and-servants-a-history-of-ethiopian-women-in-military-affairs/ (August 24, 2011).

26. Ibid.

27. The ruling position primarily belongs to the son or grandson, not to the daughter whether she is elder than her brother or not. "Maleness" matters a lot in Ethiopia to have a throne, position, leadership, ownership, etc.

28. http://www.ethiopiantreasures.co.uk/pages/iyasu.htm (August 24, 2011).

29. Ibid.

30. http://www.houseofbobo.com/Empress%20Menen.htm (August 24, 2011).

31. Ibid.

32. Ibid.

33. http://genderindex.org/country/ethiopia (August 24, 2011).

34. Dorothy Ramodibe, "Women and Men Building Together the Church in Africa," in *With Passion and Compassion. Third World Women Doing Theology*, eds. Virginia Fabella, M.M. and Mercy Amba Oduyoye (Mary Knoll: Orbis Books, 1988), 14-21 (17).

35. Tewahedo means "two natures became one."

36. http://www.dacb.org/stories/ethiopia/onesimus_nesib.html (August 24, 2011).

37. Arne, Tolo, *Sidama and Ethiopia, The Emergence of The Mekane Yesus Church in Sidama* (Uppsala: Studia Missionalia Upsaliensia, 1998), 72.

38. Those women who served as house maids and mistresses during that time are called slaves or servants by the society even today. Their status has never changed even since the end of the colonization system.

39. Mercy Amba Oduyoye, *Hearing and Knowing, Theological Reflections on Christianity in Africa* (Mary Knoll: Orbis Books, 1986), 25.

40. Musimbi R. A. Kanyoro, *Introducing Feminist Cultural Hermeneutics. An African Perspective* (Sheffield: Academics Press, 2002), 18.

41. For basic information on the Kambata people and further references see http://en.wikipedia.org/wiki/Kambaata_people (July 15, 2011).

42. "Ululation" is a shouting for joy (cf. Jeremiah 31:12). In Ethiopia women from all ethnic groups can do it at the birth of new babies.

43. Their effort is not considered and appreciated. Thus it is so painful for women who are doing such unconsidered and not appreciated work in church and society.

44. "Kosha" is the place where women cook, put their things, most of the time kosha, is hidden and invisible, their destined place, a refuge where they can express their feelings such as agony, sorrow, and pain. Maybe if it happens in their life, they do express their joy too, but it is so rare!

45. Elizabeth Amoah and Mercy Amba Oduyoye, "The Christ for African Women," in *With Passion and Compassion. Third World Women Doing Theology*, eds. Virginia Fabella, M.M and Mercy Amba Oduyoye (Maryknoll: Orbis Books, 1988), 35-46.

# A Passion for Evangelism and a Heart for the Women of Iran

*Gulnar Francis-Dehqani*

## 1. Introduction

This chapter seeks to outline some of the complexities under-lying the relationship between Victorian Christian mission-ary women and the Islam and Muslims of Iran at the end of the nineteenth and beginning of the twentieth centuries.[1] During this period Iran was a land of diversity and upheaval. Geographically it covered a vast area of the Middle East and its climate was varied, according to the seasons and the differ-ent regions. By 1900 its population was around twelve million, made up of an amalgam of different cultures and races ruled by a weak and ineffective Qajar dynasty. Local leadership operated in towns and villages, co-existing alongside tribal communities each with its own systems of governing. With a dysfunctional Qajar dynasty at its helm, the country survived on minimal government and the real power shifted between tribal leaders, *ulama* (religious leaders) and foreign nations.

Iran was never colonized, nor did it come under direct impe-rial rule. Its location between East and West meant the coun-try was strategically important to a number of external nations, most especially Russia and Britain, and this ensured a kind of uneasy independence. Nevertheless, the impact of imperialism was strong and the British especially had considerable influence politically, economically and culturally.[2] The *ulama* and foreign powers, in particular, were extremely significant components in the development of late-Qajar Iran as well as its relationship with missionaries of the Church Missionary Society (CMS).[3] The tolerance of local authority figures and the people generally toward the mission was co-dependent upon the relative popularity of the British and the strength of the Muslim clergy at any given point.[4]

Despite Iran's multi-racial and factional nature the country remained an integrated whole throughout the Qajar period. This was largely due to the unifying influence of Islam operating across sub-sections of society. Other minority religious groups did exist but they had little influence and accounted for only 3 percent of the population. Islam in Iran, as elsewhere, was more than just a faith and acted as the ultimate basis of identity, providing a primary focus of loyalty and a supreme source of control. Kings and sovereigns attempting to limit the authority of Islam or the *ulama* did so at their peril. Crucially however, and unlike most other Muslim nations, the people of Iran adhered to the Shi'a branch of Islam rather than the more widespread Sunni group. And perhaps even more important, Iranians retained a strong sense of their own pre-Islamic past, never losing their Persian identity by total submersion into Arabic culture.

## 2. Iran and the History of Christianity

Christianity has existed in Iran since the earliest days. Traditionally, the three magi were from "Persian lands" and later legends suggest that either St. Thomas or St. Simon the Zealot brought Christianity to Iran. In any case, by the fifth century, there was an organized form of Christianity in the region and Assyrian and Armenian Orthodox and Roman Catholic communities still exist in Iran today. Numbers are very small, however, despite many restrictions, these groups have always been recognized as religious minorities living in cultural pockets maintaining their own customs, languages, and religious practices.

During the nineteenth and twentieth centuries many new churches and Christian groups mushroomed across Iran. The period witnessed the arrival of several foreign individuals and organizations eager to embark on evangelistic activity. Crucially these groups, eager to convert Muslims, encountered greater resistance and even hostility. Missionary activity was regarded as an arm of imperial invasion threatening Persian identity and culture. Moreover, in Islam apostasy is considered a crime as well as a sin and is punishable by death. Whilst missionary welfare work through educational and medical projects was often welcomed, the number of converts remained few and the sense of mistrust and suspicion would always remain.[5]

The Church Missionary Society (CMS) officially opened a station in Iran in 1875, beginning its efforts in the Armenian quarter of Isfahan, known as Julfa.[6] Compared with many CMS mission fields it was a small venture with efforts resulting in few converts and the work eventually came to an abrupt end almost exactly 100 years after it began. After the Islamic Revolution swept through Iran in 1979, all missionaries left the country and to date none have returned. By then, however, the efforts of CMS had resulted in the inception of a Persian church: an Anglican community with its own Bishop and governing structures. Tiny and severely persecuted, this group is still a presence in Iran and has survived against all odds.[7]

## 3. Mary Bird and the Work of CMS Women Missionaries in Iran

Among those who played a part in the early years of CMS in Iran were a number of significant women missionaries, the most famous of whom is undoubtedly Mary Bird (1910–2002). She enjoys this reputation partly because she was one of the earliest single women to work for CMS in Iran. Also, she is one of very few women from the Persia mission who wrote a book about her time in Iran.[8] Consequently, a little more is known about her than other female missionaries. She was a colorful and potent personality, deeply committed to her vocation and much loved by colleagues and Persians alike. In the CMS archives, though her writings are not as prolific as some, she stands out as an extraordinary woman, determined and strong, yet with a gentle disposition. Compared to many, her time in Persia was short but her impact was keenly felt and her influence long lasting. She paved the way for later work among Muslim women and as such was a true pioneer.

My aim in studying Mary Bird and her female colleagues is first to make them more visible by highlighting their presence. The official history of CMS in Iran, like that of many other missions, is heavily male biased. Yet the early women in particular, while they had limited roles in terms of the formal structures and decision-making bodies, were nonetheless extremely influential in the day-to-day running of the mission and encounters with the Persians of Iran. Second, my aim is to understand Mary Bird as a woman within her own time and context rather than judging her by our contemporary standards. It is all too easy to condemn missionary women of the past, for their methods were often guided by the ideologies of their time from which they cannot be divorced. It is far more helpful to study them with a critical mindset which seeks to understand and learn from them rather than to judge them for their mistakes.

Mary Rebecca Stewart Bird was born the fifth of six children on June 23, 1859 in County Durham, England. Her father, Reverend Charles Bird, was Rector of Castle Eden and her mother, Harriet Oliver, was the daughter of a doctor from whom she learned elementary medical skills. The Bird family was well connected, including such names as Isabella Bishop (nee Bird)—the travel writer—who was a cousin of Mary's father, and the famous religious figures, Archbishop Sumner and William Wilberforce. Mary's credentials for missionary work, therefore, were in place from an early stage. But it was not until after her father's death that in April 1891 Bird was formally approved as a CMS missionary. Africa was the land which had sparked her interest in mission, and it was there she hoped to work. However, Persia became her destination in an appointment considered by CMS to be a dangerous and risky experiment. It was with a sense of uncertainty about the future that on April 18, 1891, Mary Bird set out on her voyage which lead eventually to Julfa in Persia.

The journey took her and a colleague, Laura Stubbs, via Berlin to Odessa, where they crossed the Black Sea to Batoum. They traveled through Russia to Baku and boarded a steamer across the Caspian Sea to Enzelli, where another boat took them along the lagoon to Resht on the northern edge of Persia. Having already journeyed 2,000 miles, they still had a 500-mile trek across Persia, taking a further 21 days on horseback. According to Chappell, "the journey was a tedious one, though they experienced several modes of transit."[9] Mary herself does not speak of tedium though she writes graphically about the experience of traveling in Persia, mentioning in particular, the overnight accommodation, very far from standards to which she had been accustomed in England. The rooms were "built of mud, festooned with cobwebs and soot, a hole in the roof to let out the smoke of the fire, a lattice, sometimes no opening but the doorway to admit light and air, which is the more easily done when the door is missing!"[10]

When she finally arrived in Julfa it was a small group that Mary joined, yet her early years were an important and formative time in the mission's development. CMS, now more established, had begun shifting its emphasis to work more directly with Persians rather than through the Armenians of Julfa. Within this broad agenda, Mary was assigned to pioneer work among the women of Iran. Her priority on arrival was to learn the language so most of her time was spent studying. However, always anxious to be active, Mary taught English classes in the Armenian Girls' School and gave Bible lessons on Sunday afternoons. As soon as possible she began visiting Persian women wherever she found a welcome. Her efforts to form friendships with the rich were occasionally successful, but generally she found the poor more accessible. Nonetheless, contact with all women was more difficult than Bird had expected and she soon realized she would be received more readily if she had something to offer.

Mary began by teaching a number of girls and women to read and knit in the few homes where she found a welcome. Returning from one such visit, she noticed a woman crying in the street because her son was ill and she could not afford the doctor's fees. The woman eventually agreed to Mary's proposal that they should pray together, before willingly accepting the quinine that Mary hoped would cure the boy of what she believed was malaria. The boy's health was restored and "no sooner was he better, than the mother told all her neighbours [Mary] was a doctor."[11] Bird soon found women and children visiting her daily in the hope she could cure their physical ailments. Despite her concerns, senior missionaries encouraged Mary, assuring her that the women were safer in her hands than many of their own superstitious doctors.

Very quickly Bird's work and reputation grew. A room was rented in Julfa, acting as a dispensary for two or three days each week. Mary studied any medical books available and soon women began to trust her, coming to the dispensary in increasing numbers and begging her for home visits. She became affectionately known as *Khanum Maryam* (Lady Mary) or *Hakim Maryam* (Dr. Mary) and the mission soon understood the significance of her accomplishments. Despite the success of her unconventional medical work, evangelism remained at the center of Bird's agenda and her efforts were never isolated from an opportunity to spread the gospel message. Unlike Persian doctors, Bird accepted no money from patients but they soon understood that the Christian message was a component in the package she offered.

Growing confidence from achievements in Julfa soon convinced Mary to venture into Isfahan, hitherto closed to missionary activity and foreign presence generally.[12] Despite initial problems, Mary's open personality and persistent character, together with the medical advantages she offered, gradually broke down barriers. As the women began to trust her, relationships were formed and friendships created. The fame of the mission's small medical team spread far and wide and patients traveled great distances in the hope of receiving a cure. Concurrently, however, as she won the confidence of women, Bird also attracted growing hostility from the Muslim leadership in Isfahan. Soon *mullahs* were preaching openly against her and forbidding women from attending the dispensary. Many persevered, however, coming either at daybreak or in secrecy across the flat rooftops of neighboring houses.

This scenario depicts the ambiguous feelings of Persians toward Mary Bird in particular, and the mission and Britain in general. On one hand, she was loved, or at least respected, by those visiting the dispensary despite warnings, threats, and physical retribution. On the other hand, opposition grew both toward the mission and herself.[13] For *Khanum Maryam*, as well as being a friend to many, came to be perceived as a threat to Islam and the Persian way of life.

In 1901, Mary Bird was transferred to work in Kerman in southern Iran. As the following account shows, much of her time was spent alleviating the suffering caused from widespread opium addiction and long hours of enforced carpet weaving among children in particular.

> On Friday I saw a poor wretched woman leaning against the doorway.... As soon as I went near I knew by her contracted pupils that she had had a large quantity of opium ... Throwing back her *chadar*[14] [sic.] I found such a fine boy of about a year old dying in her arms ... we tried all we could, but in vein: the little pet died in my arms ... the baby, [the woman] remembered, was playing with pellets of opium; more she did not know. She died the next day, leaving three tiny children, all opium inhalers from birth.[15]

Bird's time in Kerman was brief, for in 1903 somewhat reluctantly she returned to England to care for her aging mother. Upon her departure a testimonial of gratitude was written by the leading inhabitants of Kerman (including the chief *mullah*), which spoke of "Her Highness the English Mariam Khanum,"[16] and her care for the sick of Kerman.

Eight years later in 1911, at the age of 52, and twenty years after she first arrived in Iran, Birdie, as she had come to be known, was welcomed back once more. Work had expanded considerably. The mission boasted thirty-two women, of whom nineteen were single. The CMS medical team included several nurses as well as four male and four female doctors. Mary clearly had a lower profile, but both colleagues and Persians were glad to have her back. For the first two years she was posted to Yezd where her time was spent visiting in the town and surrounding villages. She continued to have little practical help for her work as the small band of missionaries was already overstretched and numbers of converts were too low for any support from local Christians.

At the end of 1913 Bird returned to work in the surrounding villages and city of Kerman. Still remembered by many as *hakim*, she continued caring for the sick when she could, though the emphasis of her work shifted more towards teaching and evangelism:

> No notice of my coming had been given but the next day by 8.00 A.M. women were beginning to gather to enquire if I knew Persian and whether I had brought medicines for them. Only 35 came and were willing to listen to the Gospel. During the two weeks I was there numbers steadily grew, the highest being 157 in one day. On Sunday I had told them there would be no dispensary but many came to hear the Gospel.[17]

And it was not only women whom she impressed. Persian men, who seldom had contact with European women, often treated Maryam Khanum in a very different way. One of her colleagues, Clara Rice, a CMS missionary wife and contemporary of Mary's, explains how many took her seriously, willing to listen and argue with her.[18] On one particular occasion, some of the village women had assembled while Mary spoke of her faith. "Suddenly," Bird wrote, "I heard a man's voice behind me and saw that the village men had gathered behind a mulberry tree and said they were glad to listen."[19]

Her death, when it came, was sudden and unexpected. By mid-July 1914 all missionaries had left Kerman for their customary summer break except Bird who intended joining them at the end of the month. In the wake of a typhoid epidemic, she was determined to keep open the dispensary for two convalescing patients. Eventually she left Kerman on August 3. The following day Bird had a fever and it soon became apparent she herself had contracted typhoid. She died peacefully on Sunday August 16, 1914. Mary's memory and influence, however, did not die with her. A grave on the outskirts of Kerman still stands witness to her life and work. As a forerunner of work among women, she remained an inspiration to those who followed. For Persians there may have been "but one Khanum Maryam,"[20] however, other missionaries, both men and women, continued to receive a warm welcome in many remote villages in her name and for her sake.

## 4. An Evaluation of Mary Bird's Life and Work

Women's work within CMS in Persia during the late nineteenth and early twentieth centuries may be described in terms of three primary categories: evangelism, education, and medicine. Though the three areas seem distinct and self-contained, there was considerable overlap between them. Ultimately, the primary aim of each missionary was evangelism and all strove to spread the gospel message of salvation as the basis of social improvement. Theoretically, therefore, the practical work of teachers, doctors, and nurses was set within the context of the missionary task to evangelize and remained subordinate to it. However, the paucity of workers and the physical needs of people they encountered meant in practice, time was often unevenly divided between explicit evangelism on one hand and the exercise of professional skills on the other. Those set aside as evangelists frequently found themselves drawn into the realm of more practical activities. Meanwhile, educationalists and medical workers struggled to maintain the required balance between welfare work and spiritual responsibility. The theory of pure evangelism remained at the heart of mission ideology and continued infusing the evangelical language it relied upon. However, its application expanded to incorporate practical elements in an effort to improve social conditions.

This tension between the words and actions of missionaries, or their "sayings" and "doings," is an underlying element within the work of the CMS women in Iran, and nowhere is it more obvious than in the person of Mary Bird. Her language consistently conforms to the standards of nineteenth-century evangelicalism at its starkest.[21] She wrote, for example, of the influence of the "false prophet Mohammed" as responsible for turning Persia into "this seething mass of moral and social corruption."[22] Yet her conduct presents a notion of mission far greater than the narrow confines her words might present. Eager to win individuals for Christ in an effort to procure their salvation after death, she also represents an ardent desire to work for the redemption of whole *people*, not merely souls, in terms of all their relationships. Her concern was for salvation here and now, as well as in the life to come. Mary expressed this as a desire to "tell the sick ones of the Great Physician who still, though now invisible, goes about doing good to *soul* and body."[23]

Bird's love for the women of Iran, combined with intense commitment to evangelism, render her a fascinating and important figure in the overall evaluation of the CMS Persia mission and its female missionaries. More than that, however, Bird's life issues a challenge to late twentieth-century feminism. For it would be easy to dismiss her as a woman of restricted vision, enslaved by linguistic, religious, and ideological expectations of her day. The challenge, however, is to look beyond the superficial, in a willingness to see positive elements without expecting to endorse all her ideas and the manner in which she expressed them.

Her methods would be unacceptable today, but considered within the context of her time, she is impossible to dismiss. Bird combined genuine humility with utter confidence, and an unfailing spirit of adventure led her into new possibilities that extended the boundaries of acceptable behavior for British women. She represents a religious strand within the nineteenth-century women's movement whose expression was somewhat contorted due to the language and influence of evangelical Christianity and orientalist ideologies. This strand did not motivate women toward active involvement in organized politics or the fight for equality. Nevertheless, it grew from a similar concern for the well-being of womankind. Mary struggled to secure a better life for the women of Iran, intending to improve their immediate conditions as well as their spiritual life after death. Ultimately, she was concerned for the well-being of *whole* women, perceiving no need to dismiss either spiritual or physical needs and her achievement was in the love and affection returned to her by the Persians she encountered.

Theological assumptions meant Bird associated the suffering she encountered with the religion of Islam while confidently presenting Christianity as the solution to all social problems. In addition, appropriation of the imperialist agenda meant she regarded herself as part of a superior group, able to provide the necessary help. "We are 'put in trust with the Gospel,'" she wrote, "dare we hold it back from those who are perishing for lack of it?"[24] However, it was the woman-centered approach to her work, emanating from the same concern for female progress in Britain, which convinced Mary of the need to improve the condition of women in Iran. All these factors combined to ensure Bird willingly provided for the physical needs of Persian women, while never relinquishing the longing to accommodate their spiritual needs through the hope of salvation now and after death.

The physical problems of Persia through poverty, lack of education, and poor health care were too immense even for the best and most motivated philanthropic will in the world. This left only the spiritual dimension, both as a reservoir to encourage the missionaries themselves and as a source of hope to offer the women they encountered. The hopelessness of the social reality made it difficult for the missionaries to maintain ceaselessly the impetus for continuing work. But assurance of eternal life, together with the inner peace that faith could give, provided an underlying framework for the CMS women's motivation. Mary believed that if she could guide Persian women toward personal faith, then she had helped them find something greater than the possibility of temporal alleviation in this life. For inner joy and comfort were realities that no one could take away and, if sustained from within, would ultimately lead to the possibility of social change for women. Regarded in this way, Bird's life can be interpreted in a more rounded manner. The dualistic separation of spirit and body, apparent in much of her writings, becomes less difficult from a twenty-first-century perspective when considered within the context of her entire contribution.

In his study of women's roles in the modern missionary movement Sean Gill makes a passing reference to Mary Bird as just another example of how Islam was viewed in "stock Victorian terms as a religion of the sword whose precepts had little practical effect."[25] Certainly, Bird was extremely critical of Islam and its social manifestations.[26] In light of later developments in the theology of religions, Bird and her attitude toward Islam and Muslims can hardly be regarded as innovative or forward-looking. However, it is a more fruitful exercise to evaluate Bird's life contextually; without judging her merely on the strength of her written words or from the position of our contemporary values. In a sense, Mary Bird represents her age *fully*, for her life is an example of the best *and* the worst of late-Victorianism. For sure, she had little positive to say about Islam, yet as a deeply religious woman she fearlessly followed her calling and paved the way for others to come. Moreover, Mary was not a negative person. Everything she did emanated from a strong and earnest belief in the positive power of Christianity. She sincerely believed that Christ was the only solution for the problems of Persia and it was that belief which gave meaning to her life and inspired her to help others find meaning for theirs.

Recognizing the constraints of Victorian evangelicalism and orientalism that limited her, three things in particular may be said of Mary Bird. First, in her day, she was not looked upon as narrow-minded or prejudiced.[27] Notwithstanding her evident zeal for spreading Christianity, she was considered open-minded and tolerant, always willing to acknowledge nobility and truth wherever she saw it. Second, it must be noted that her writings, which often adhered to the strongly anti-Islamic tone typical of the time, were aimed at a *Christian* audience. She wrote not even for the general British public but for a specific group of CMS enthusiasts, expecting to be regaled by details of missionary success if they were to continue financially supporting the work. Evidence suggests that in conversation with Muslims her theology was much more abstract and inclusive. On one occasion Mary Bird recalled debating Christianity for three hours with a village governor near Kerman. At its conclusion she was eager for them to arrive at a point of mutuality and "proposed that we should pray that He who is the Truth should guide us into all truth." Put this way, "he at once agreed, and told all the servants present to bow for prayer."[28]

Third, Bird's life in action does not bear witness to the negativity portrayed in the unpalatable evangelical and orientalist language she used. Unable to express herself in terms of any other framework, it was for her deeds she came to be known, and for those, Mary was motivated by much more positive factors. Letters and articles may suggest a missionary motivation based on anti-Islamic fervor but considered in its entirety, her life reveals actions that sprung from an earnest and positive desire to share the most valuable gift she believed could be offered. Clara Rice describes her thus: "She reproved sin and its consequences, and deplored the darkness of the hearts of men [sic], but more by holding forth the true Light than by seeking to make darkness visible. There was more in her teaching that was positive than negative. It was for building up, not casting down."[29]

Bird was not afraid to criticize social norms where she believed it necessary but for that she should not be condemned. All cultures have elements worthy of rebuke and Persia at that time was no exception. While speaking against social ills when necessary, Bird—energized by her Christian faith—tried to ease suffering wherever possible.

The difficulty from a twenty-first-century perspective, and where it is possible and indeed necessary to be critical of Bird, is that while she was alive to the wrongs of Islamic Persia, she remained blind to the evils of her own culture in Christian Britain. "The very backbone of English greatness is its Christian home-life," she wrote, "look what this land is without that!"[30]

Unable to identify her experience of relative freedom as the result of living abroad, she rendered invisible the problems of women in England. Discovering her own potential away from Britain she displayed a kind of irrational loyalty to the land of her birth, recreated through distant memories and wishful thinking. It was this that gave Mary and indeed others among her contemporaries the belief that a transfer of Christian culture from West to East could bring about the end of Iran's social problems and that as such they were the catalysts change. Certainly, the freedom she enjoyed to work, travel and pursue a life outside the home, could be compared favorably with much that she witnessed in Iran. However, it hardly justified the glorified portrayal of her homeland or the position of women there, nor how marvelously God had prospered England since it became a Christian nation.[31]

Exceptional in many respects, Mary was unable to dispute the nationalist agenda within the ethos of the British Empire. Willing to challenge sexual stereotypes in Persia, she seemed unaware (or uncritical) of those operating at the heart of English society. Her achievements were in spite of such restricting ideologies and should not be denied because of them. Nevertheless, Mary and many of her colleagues fell prey to the temptation of whole scale comparison, by associating the social ills of Persia with Islam, while losing sight of the evils in Victorian Britain, in particular regarding its attitude toward women.

Many today will not understand Mary Bird, as countless Persians could not fathom her then. Some, of course, will believe she was misguided and wrong, and with the benefit of historical hindsight, there is indeed much to criticize. Nevertheless, amongst her contemporaries Mary Bird was an outstanding example of courage, determination, commitment, and love. Entirely a product of Victorian attitudes, she overcame many restrictions without disturbing the accepted boundaries of female behavior which would have rendered her work impossible. In a secular book on women travelers Jane Robinson writes of Bird and how Persian women's "curiosity soon turned to trust, and trust to love," for, "Mary was not one of the betrousering and civilizing brand of missionary: at home in her Jolfa dispensary and on her extensive travels [...] into the outlying areas, she grew to respect (if not condone) the Muslim traditions of the Persians, and was able to explain the Christian faith with a potent mixture of deference and authority."[32]

She grew to understand Persians perhaps better than any of her colleagues. Experiencing the extremes of their temperament, from great warmth to violent opposition, she was always eager to make friends and was moved by expressions of friendship shown toward her.

Above all, Bird passionately believed that Christ could offer the women of Persia comfort in the suffering that no one else could alleviate. In a mysterious way this touches on something significant. Countless came and went without ever becoming Christians, yet clearly Mary made a strong impact on the lives of many such Persians. Her success is ultimately incalculable for no one will ever know how many found solace through her vision of a loving savior, caring for them as friend and brother in their often unhappy and lonely lives.[33] But "results ... are more than those that are measurable,"[34] and once more Mary evades being judged by definable criteria.

Eager to speak of her faith whenever possible and rejoicing at individual baptisms, Bird remained aware of the complexities in converting an entire country. She understood that "foreigners can never evangelize a nation," but trusted they had a part to play in "train[ing] the first generation of workers."[35] She may have disapproved of prolonged missionary presence in Persia, for perhaps she had greater faith in the power of God and the wisdom of local Christians. Such notions are mere conjecture, but Mary's part in laying the foundations for the growth of an indigenous church community remains indisputable. While weeping for the plight of many Iranian Christians today, Mary would also rejoice at their perseverance and commitment. She would not doubt for one moment that her life's work had been worthwhile, even in the face of such small and apparently insignificant results. For Mary Bird believed in the value of each individual, body and soul, and her passion remained undiminished by the numerically small number of respondents.

## 5. Questions for Discussion

1. As Christian women (and men) how can we find the right balance between the valued traditions we have received and openness to new perspectives for change?

2. In our encounters with people of other faiths, how important is it that we stress our own beliefs and how much should we be open to the truth as others perceive it?

3. Should mission societies still send Christians from the West to work in other parts of the world?

# 6. Recommendations and Conclusion

My approach to Mary Bird has been to regard her as representative of her female colleagues who worked in Iran. Evaluating her role provides an appreciation of the part that CMS women generally played in the developing approach to the theology of religions and the growing women's movement of the time. They participated in the only way they knew how in the move towards gradual change in the religious and orientalist outlook. Increased contact with the people of Iran brought growing familiarity and acceptance of diversity. Despite their lack of a language to describe this development and their apparent enslavement to evangelical ideologies of the time, their experiences and actions betray a gradual shift that helped in the early tentative steps which led to growing familiarity between peoples of different faiths and opened the way for dialogue and understanding.

For this reason I have attempted to be *sympathetically critical* of Mary Bird by trying to appreciate her within the context of her own age while at the same time analyzing her contribution with the benefit of current historical tools and critical questions. I have followed this method because I believe it to be the most successful way of understanding women of the past and also the only way we can hope to learn from them. But I have followed this method also because I hope that future generations will judge us in the same way.

We struggle in our contexts to respond to the dominant discourses of our time and we each do that according to the cultural, religious, and other environments in which we find ourselves. Christians generally are still searching for the right way to approach the priorities of a secular culture on one hand and the realities of a multifaith world on the other. As if this were not complicated enough we burden ourselves further by an inability to accept differences in our own faith community so that dissension and diversity threaten to pull us apart.

While in so many ways we are worlds apart from Mary Bird and her colleagues, there are also similarities that may at first seem unobvious. Therefore, as I reflect on their historical significance I am challenged by their extraordinary achievements as well as angered by their blind spots and sympathetic toward their failures. For I cannot help wondering what our blind spots are, how we fail to see the priorities more clearly; and I cannot help wondering how we will be judged by future generations. Despite their many shortcomings the CMS women are the forebears in faith of Christian women today. Now the baton has been handed on and it is up to a new generation to do its part in passing on that which has been received. How will we choose to shape the present and how successful will we be in ensuring that the future is a better place for all?

If they were nothing else, Mary Bird and her colleagues were women of immense spiritual strength. They were adventurous, courageous and dedicated, willing to give their lives to the service of others. In the process they pushed forward the boundaries of acceptable female behavior by participating in activities hitherto the domain of men alone. Certainly they were shortsighted in many ways and from our perspective they may have lacked vision. But they succeeded in defying many of the obstacles in their way and as such they are role models for women of today and women of faith in particular. To move forward, we too must overcome the ideological, theological, and gender restrictions of our time. Perhaps patience, ingenuity, courage, spiritual autonomy, and humility will be some of the components that will serve us well just as they did Mary Bird and many of the other women who came before us.

## Further Reading

Sarah Ansari & Vanessa Martin, eds., *Women, Religion and Culture in Iran* (Surrey: Curzon Press, 2002).

Hassan Dehqani-Tafti, *Masih va Masihiyat Nazd-e Iranian*, volumes 1-3. London: Sohrab Books, 1992, 1993, 1995. (Christ and Christianity Amongst the Iranians: 3 Volumes, text in Persian.)

David Kerr & Kenneth Ross, eds., *Edinburgh 2010: Mission Now and Then* (Oxford: Regnum, 2009).

Alan Race & Paul Hedges, eds., *Christian Approaches to Other Faiths* (London: SCM, 2009).

Kevin Ward, *A History of Global Anglicanism* (Cambridge: University Press, 2006).

## Endnotes

1. For a more comprehensive study of this subject see, Guli Francis-Dehqani, *Religious Feminism in an Age of Empire: CMS Women Missionaries in Iran, 1869–1934* (Bristol University PhD, 1999.)

2. For more on the history and interpretation of imperialism see ibid., 19-20; and C. Eldridge, *Victorian Imperialism* (London: Hodder & Stoughton, 1978); A. Thornton, *The Imperial Idea and its Enemies* (London: McMillan, 1959); Edward Said, *Orientalism: Western Conceptions of the Orient* (London: Penguin, 1978.)

3. The Church Missionary Society (now known as the Church Mission Society) was an Anglican British organisation founded in 1799. For more on its history and work see Kevin Ward & Brian Stanley, eds., *The Church Mission Society and World Christianity, 1799–1999* (Surrey: Curzon Press, 2000).

4. For more on the history of Iran during the Qajar period see, Ann Lambton, *Qajar Persia* (London: Tauris, 1987); Malcolm Yapp, "1900–1921: The Last Years of the Qajar Dynasty," in Hossein Amirsadeghi, ed., *Twentieth Century Iran: An Interpretation* (Cambridge, Massachusetts: Harvard University Press, 1977.) For more on the history of Iran generally see, Roger Stevens, *The Land of the Great Sophy* (London: Methuen Co. Ltd, 1962); Ervand Abrahamian, *Iran Between Two Revolutions* (Princeton, New Jersey: Princeton University Press, 1982); Mehrzad Boroujerdi, *Iranian Intellectuals and the West: The Tormented Triumph of Nativism* (NY: Syracuse University Press, 1996); Nikki Keddie, *Roots of Revolution: An Interpretative History of Modern Iran* (New Haven: Yale University Press, 1981).

5. For more on the history or Christianity in Iran see, Robin Waterfield, *Christians in Persia* (London: George Allen & Unwin, 1973); Hassan Dehqani-Tafti, *Christ and Christianity Amongst the Iranians: Volumes I & II.* (London: Sohrab Books, 1992 & 1993, text in Persian).

6. CMS was always interested in working amongst Muslims in Iran rather than Orthodox Christians. However, in the early days it was not possible for non Muslims to reside in the cities of Iran so the mission made Julfa its base.

7. For more on the Anglican Church in Iran since the Islamic Revolution see, Hassan Dehqani-Tafti, *The Hard Awakening* (London: Triangle, SPCK, 1981); and Hassan Dehqani-Tafti, *The Unfolding Design of My World: A Pilgrim in Exile* (Norwich: Canterbury Press 2000).

8. Mary Bird, *Persian Women and Their Creed* (London: CMS, 1899).

9. Jennie Chappell, *Three Brave Women: Stories of Heroism in Heathen Lands* (London: Partridge & Co., 1920?), 123.

10. Bird, op. cit., 25.

11. Ibid., 39.

12. In 1891 Isabella Bishop wrote about her brief journey through Isfahan and the anti-foreign sentiment of the people, describing the experience as a "bad half-hour." See Isabella Bishop, *Journeys in Persia and Kurdistan* (London: John Murray, 1891), 244.

13. There was, for example, an attempt to poison her by the wife of a local *mullah*. For details, see Jessie Powell, *Riding to Danger: The Story of Mary Bird of Persia (Iran)* (London: The Highway Press, 1949), 62-3.

14. A chador is a long veil covering the body worn by Muslim women in Iran.

15. Quoted in Clara Colliver Rice, *Mary Bird in Persia* (London: CMS, 1916), 129-130.

16. CMS Archives, reference G2/PE/O 1904: 60.

17. Mary Bird, "Village work amongst women in Persia," in *Mercy and Truth* 18 (1914): 140.

18. Rice, op. cit., 103.

19. Bird (1914) op. cit., 141.

20. Chappell, op. cit., 160.

21. For more on Victorian Evangelicalism see, David Bebbington, *Evangelicalism in Modern Britain: A History from the 1730s to the 1980s* (London: Routledge, 1989).

22. In Bird (1899), op cit., 2 and Rice, op. cit., 174.

23. Ibid., 39.

24. Ibid., 103.

25. Sean Gill, *Women and the Church of England: From the Eighteenth Century to the Present* (London: SPCK, 1994), 195.

26. She, for example, devotes a chapter in her book to disproving and undermining the five pillars of Islam. See Bird (1899), op. cit., 5-15.

27. Rice, op. cit., 6.

28. Mary Bird, CMS *Annual Letters* (1903), 141.

29. Rice, op. cit., 136.

30. See ibid., 161.

31. Ibid., 142.

32. Jane Robinson, *Wayward Women: A Guide to Women Travellers* (Oxford: University Press, 1990), 154.

33. On rare occasions Mary heard of the effects of her work. After the death of one patient, a message was brought to Bird, asking that she visit the deceased woman's daughter and read to her from the Bible. Apparently hearing the Christian gospel had comforted the patient, and her dying wish was that her daughter also should hear the message of hope. Bird (1899), op. cit., 78-9.

34. Kenneth Cragg, *The Call of the Minaret* (London: Collins, 1985 rev.), 324.

35. In Rice, op. cit., 193.

CHAPTER 7

# Tetsur Tesayula: Christian Mission and Gender Among the Ao Naga of Northeast India

*Atola Longkumer*

*"The lack of gender analysis in this major survey for charting Christian world mission is symptomatic of the serious lack of awareness about the centrality of women in world mission from the early church to the present."*[1] *Dana Robert*

## 1. Introduction

Writing about the Indian context poses a daunting task due to the quintessential Indian plurality of contexts and circumstances in every possible aspect of the society. India is a country with contradictions. India is known to produce world-class skilled laborers for the global information technology, while it still lacks in providing basic education to millions of its rural children. India has a considerable global wealth, while it ranks among the bottom, in the list of nations, where children die of malnutrition and hunger.[2] India is known for its ideals of non-violence and tolerance, while there is simmering communal tension and violence.[3] India is listed among the nations that count having a woman as head of the state, while female-infanticide and bride-burning related to the practice of dowry take place on a regular pattern.

According to a survey conducted by the Thomson Rueters Foundation, India is among the five nations that are most unsafe for women.[4] Amidst impressive progressive intellectual activism, there exists also an alarming social conservatism, most tellingly manifested in relation to women and caste.[5] India is not a homogeneous culture; it is at best a hybrid of cultures and at worst a contesting, conflicting society with a "clash within" to use a term from Martha Nussbaum.[6] India is a nation of diverse social, religious, and economic layers and therefore a narration of India's history and social realities cannot be without qualifiers, such as region, language, historical period, ethnicity, religion, and economic status.

The paradigm of diversities and contradictions is also relevant in a discussion on women and Christian mission in India. Similar to the larger Indian society, the Indian Christian context comprises of a multiplicity of contexts with diverse church traditions, different historical periods and a myriad of sociocultural locations. For instance, there are progressive churches in the urban areas with members that can be described as elite as well as thriving charismatic churches; on the other hand, there are rural churches that can hardly pay the pastors' salary regularly. It is, therefore, important to underline that the history of Christianity in India and the Indian Christian community cannot be discussed in one voice with a single perspective.

Despite being a minority religion in the country, Christianity in India with all its myriad expressions enjoys certain recognition in the global context, from a population perspective as well as its leadership in contextual theology that reckons seriously cosmologies from religions that differ from Christianity.[7] India is also one of the earliest nations among the "mission fields" where women colleges were established during the heydays of Western missionary movement that have been in the forefront of providing modern and professional education to women, subsequently giving them agency.[8] Furthermore, Christians in India can also claim of having Indian woman leadership at the global level, such as Aruna Gnanadason, the former Executive of Women's Department in the World Council of Churches.

Despite such vibrancy of Indian Christians, there still persist daunting challenges for women in the church. Not only within church structures and practices, but even in the larger Indian society women are disadvantaged, marginalized, and oppressed by the patriarchal gender hierarchy across different social and cultural sections. The situation of women in India is more complex than what meets the eye, for instance, in modern India women are visible in every aspect of society as active participants and not less in the Christian community. Outwardly women in the Christian community appear to enjoy relative freedom socially and economically. Nonetheless, a stripping away of the veils of such general perceptions reveals deep-seeded discrimination, exclusion, marginalization, and violence against women. A critical feminist analysis reveals the true reality behind the façade of a progressive community. This paper will highlight some of the areas and issues of marginalization of women in the Indian Christian context. As noted earlier, India being a multi-language, multiculture country, the paper can only be selective of a specific context for a detailed study. A brief general survey of Christian mission in the country will suffice. Considering that there is a paucity of studies pertaining to women in North India and Northeast India Christians, centered on the Ao Naga Baptist Church in Northeast India as the specific case study the paper will also weave in relevant information of women in the Christian community of central-North India.[9]

## 2. Historical Setting: Christian Mission and Indian Christians

A brief survey of Christianity and its beginning in India is provided here to orient the selected case study. There are rich and a growing numbers of excellent resources of both micro and macro history of Christianity in India, which highlight the diverse voices, sources and dynamics of encounters between Christian mission and the existing local cultures. Drawing from these resources the historical orientation lays out a general frame of reference for the beginning of Christianity in India in its various stages with different cultural interactions.

Christianity in India is said to be as old as the time of Jesus' disciples. Certain Christian traditions claim that one of the disciples of Jesus, Thomas, arrived in the southern region of the country in the first century and established a nascent Christian community in Kerala.[10] This Christian community is known as the St. Thomas Christians and is a thriving community in the country.[11] The next arrival of Christianity in the country took place with the advent of the Portuguese traders in the late fifteenth century (1498). Their motive was not so much to make Christians but they had most of all commercial interests particularly of the spice trade which was under the monopoly of the Muslims until their arrival.[12] The arrival of the Jesuit Francis Xavier in 1542 initiated the third phase of Christianity in India. This period saw conscious efforts of Christianizing the people, not without controversy.[13] The Jesuits initiated lively religious discourse at every level, most famous being at the court of the Muslim King Akbar.[14] The Jesuits learned and translated Indian languages and also established Christian communities and educational institutions that are valuable legacies of this period that thrive even today.

The Protestant Christian mission in India began in the eighteenth century. Bartholomaeus Ziegenbalg and Henry Pluetschau were the first Protestants missionaries to arrive in 1706 at Tranquebar, locally known as Tarangambadi in South India. Their most notable contributions were mastering the local language Tamil, translation of the New Testament and parts of the Old Testament into Tamil and setting up a printing press. Along with establishing Christian communities notably among the lower strata to the people, they also established one of the first seminaries to train the natives.[15]

The arrival of the Protestant missionaries also coincided with the colonial interest and expansion in the country by Western countries, France, Portugal, the Netherlands, and England. The East India Company of England was established by the seventeenth century solely for trading purposes. Nonetheless Christian mission also followed, although not directly related with the Company. In fact, William Carey, the Baptist missionary from England first began his mission work in Serampore, a town under the control of Danish merchants. Despite the initial interest of commerce only, the relationship between Christian missionaries and the imperial power of the West presented a complex situation; with varying degrees of friendship, collaboration, and hostility.[16] The mission work of the evangelically inclined chaplains and William Carey presents one of the most exhilarating, complex, and fruitful chapters of Christianization in India.

Up until this period there are apparently no concerns or issues directly related to women in the missionizing project both as agents and receivers at least till the mid-nineteenth century in the encounter between Christian missions and the native cultures. The women question in Christian mission enterprise was a later development, beginning mid-nineteenth century. Women's activities, as both agents of mission and subjects of mission, become prominent only from the beginning of the modern missionary movement.

The arrival of William Carey[17] in Serampore in eastern India initiated the most exciting and influential mission enterprise in the country.[18] From a women's perspective, the establishment of the Serampore mission was crucial. While Carey and his colleagues, Joshua Marshman, and William Ward, known as the Serampore Trio did not engage in exclusive mission among women, their activities of discourse and criticism against the existing social evils related to women, arguably created awareness for social improvement of the women folks among the *bhadralok* in Bengal. Practices such as child marriage, widow remarriage, *sati* (the burning of the widow upon the pyre along with the deceased husband) that dehumanized women in the Hindu community, were challenged and reforms were initiated.[19] The mission activity of the Serampore Trio included learning native languages and translation, teaching the local language to the colonial officials, education, arguably generating interests among the learned native communities, and providing information regarding the "heathen ways" of local people to the eager Western audience.[20]

By the eighteenth century, Christianity in the West had gone through tremendous upheavals, reformations, and a revival phase, each attempt of reforms can be said as the church's assessment and development of self-identity.[21] Each historical event added a new dimension to the understanding of the church and its mission. The modern missionary movement of the West was one such event that witnessed the formation of mission societies[22] and proliferation of mission activities represented from all existing denominations to evangelize almost every region of the world. In India, this period presents the most exhilarating period of mission and women in terms of women participating as missionaries and women's sociocultural locations as mission tasks.

The Serampore Trio was followed by a plethora of mission societies representing the different church traditions and from different parts of the Euro-American world.[23] Medical mission, educational institutions, literacy endeavors, social improvements were undertaken as vehicles for evangelizing the natives.[24] The Zenana[25] mission, medical mission, and women institutions that enjoy renowned reputation are all products of this mission period in India, which continue to impact and serve contemporary Indian society.

The history of Christian mission is analyzed today from a variety of perspectives, no less from the post-colonial, post-modern lens. While these theoretical locations have made valuable contributions and provided concepts to critically assess knowledge and perceptions beyond the sweeping representations, narratives and monologues, there still exists a commonality of being women missionaries and a commonality of being women in society, almost always the "second sex" within male-centric, social-religious structures. In other words, despite the diverse social contexts, cultural locations, different historical periods, and mission societies, women across these categories share a commonality: discrimination and oppression within patriarchal social structures. This culturally imposed condition of being women cut across cultures and religions with variations in the degree of marginalization and exclusion.

For women in India, it can be claimed that their social uplift, by creating an environment of enlightened awareness, was the most significant result of Christian mission. Education initiated the journey for human dignity and agency for women in India in almost all the communities that encountered Christian mission, albeit limited and the project of complete emancipation remains unfinished,[26] as a cursory glimpse at the women situation in Indian churches indicates to this limited inclusion and empowerment of women.

In contemporary Indian society, women in the church have diverse status and roles depending on the denominations. Women are ordained for the Eucharist ministry in the following churches: the Church of North India (CNI), Church of South India (CSI), and United Evangelical Lutheran Churches in India (UELCI), Methodist Church of India (MCI), and some Baptist churches in the Northeast. The Presbyterian Church of India (PCI), Marthoma Church, Orthodox Church, Roman Catholics and the many Pentecostal/Charismatic/Indigenous churches do not ordain women for the Eucharist ministry. While ordination of women does have a symbolic significance and is indeed a significant step toward inclusion and gender equality in the church, it would be naïve to surmise that ordination is the sole objective of Christian feminist critique. Although, ordination of women is not common to all denominations, women from almost all the denominations in India pursue theological education. Furthermore, despite the fact that women form a vital section of the churches membership and also participate in the lay ministries of the churches, the decision-making authorities of the churches are mostly comprised of male members, with some token representations of women in some churches. Interestingly, women from the Christian community often form a significant percentage of highly educated professional women in India.

The mid-twentieth century saw the growing awareness of opening theological education for women and the inclusion of women in church ministry in the Western world. This awakening was obviously transplanted to the mission contexts around the world, observable in the admission of women for theological education and the ordained women ministers in some of the

Indian churches. Yet, the larger situation of women in the church poses unfinished mission tasks toward an inclusive community, wherein gender or other human construct categories do not hinder equality of all.

An example of an unfinished task of the Christian mission is demonstrated by a building at Leonard Theological College, Jabalpur in the central state of Madhya Pradesh. The Women's Hostel building in the College bears a plague with words inscribed into white marble stone, which reads, "[t]his Hostel is the Gift of the Methodist Women of America to the Women of India" dedicated on December 31, 1952. This building is one of the legacies of the American Methodist missions in the area. Today the building stands more as a symbol of mission societies' visions and Western churches' partnership with the nascent local Christian communities in infrastructure development, rather than to fulfill the vision of providing housing to a thriving number of women acquiring theological education to serve the churches. There are hardly half a dozen women in each academic year in the building that was built in the mid-twentieth century, envisaging a vision of growing number of Indian women in theological education. On the whole, in India the ratio of women pursuing theological education in comparison to men is dismal. The theological education scenario tells a lot about the churches' attitude and perception of women in the ministry of the church. I must hasten to add that women empowerment and inclusion is more complex and multiple factors, such as sociological, economic, cultural, and even theological reasons, contribute to the dismal participation of women in the church's ordained ministry.

Furthermore, a point to note is the fact that even in the recent writings of the history of Christianity in India, women and their participation find very little mention. For instance, in an otherwise excellent source of narrative history of Christianity in India, the book "Christianity in India" (2004) written by Leonard Fernando and G. Gispert-Sauch hardly mentions women from any perspective of mission.

## 3. Regional Case Study: Ao Naga Women in Northeast India

The region beyond West Bengal in eastern India, which borders Bangladesh, Burma, and China is known as "Northeast" in India. It comprises seven states, namely, Arunachal Pradesh, Assam, Manipur, Meghalaya, Mizoram, Nagaland, and Tripura.

The region has a distinct history, culture, and religion, largely different from mainland India. The region is home to numerous groups of indigenous people described as "Schedule Tribes" in the Indian Constitution. While there are general cultural traits shared by the people in the region, one of the fundamental differences is language. Almost every tribal group speaks a different language; therefore the lingua franca of the region is English. Northeast India is home to a high percentage of Christians in the country. States like Mizoram and Nagaland have almost 100 percent Christian populations.[27]

Beginning in the late nineteenth century, this region saw a large-scale response to Christianity, particularly in states like Mizoram, Nagaland, and to a certain extent in Meghalaya. Christianity is a prominent religion among the people today. The church, theological education, and mission activities are vibrant forces and demonstrate palpable influence upon the people. Women in the communities, however, have a complex role and status in both the church and the society at large. For instance, as noted earlier, in the Presbyterian Church in Mizoram, while there is no restriction for women to pursue theological education, they do not ordain women into the Eucharistic ministry. Mizo women, however, serve as theological teachers, evangelists, and missionaries. The salaries are unequal between men and women with the same theological education; a woman teaching in theological college is paid less than a man teaching in the same theological college under the same church structure—the difference being the ordination. While Mizo Christian women and their role and participation in the church is worth further exploring, the present study concentrates specifically on the Ao Naga Baptist Church, solely for the reasons of familiarity of the context and availability of sources.

To situate the case study, suffice it to narrate a brief survey of the people's culture and establishment of the church. The Naga people are categorized as indigenous people, also known as Schedule Tribe according to the Indian Constitution; they do not share the Indic (larger Hinduised) culture, religion, or language. For instance, some of the elements often identified as "Indian" in generalized perception of India, such as Hinduism, Buddhism, *bindi*,[28] Hindi language, caste practices, *saree*, the attire of Indian women, and social practices that were prevalent before modernization such as child marriage, dowry, and *sati* cannot be applied to the Naga people, or for that matter to other indigenous people of Northeast India. As indigenous people, the Naga people neither share the Sanskritic culture nor the many diverse linguistic cultures of the mainland India. This distinction has to be underscored because it bears on the understanding of women's role and status of the people in relation to Christian mission in the region, which has considerable differences from the role, status, cultural practices, and participation as observed in other parts of India.

Sharing a certain degree of similarity with other indigenous people, the Nagas were an oral culture living in close symphony with the natural world, self-contained and untouched by modern industrial ways of life. The British annexed the Naga inhabited areas on their way to Burma in the early nineteenth century. The American Baptist missionaries set up their mission in the late nineteenth century.[29]

As deduced from the oral traditions and cultural practices of the community, Ao Naga women's condition, role, and status before the encounter with Christian missions can be described as one of a complementary yet secondary position in relation to the men. There were no restrictions on their movements, they did not live in isolation but participated in community festivities and activities. The Ao women also enjoyed freedom to choose in marriage within the clan stipulated customary practices. Ao women also seemed to have religious freedom, since it is told that they could offer sacrifices and even serve as religious mediators, such as a *shaman* for the community. However, Ao Naga society is a patriarchal society, wherein, the male members have the power of all public decisions. Ao women had and still have no right for land inheritance and ownership, they were also excluded from the village governing council, which was a male-only council, comprising of clan representatives. Ao women had agency and voice only as much as the male-dominated culture permitted them. The argument of the case study is that these sociocultural positions of Ao women in a male-centric clan structure continue unchallenged even today in the Christian community. For instance, Ao women can neither inherit nor own clan's land even today.

Christian mission arrived in the late nineteenth century with the American Baptist missionaries in 1872, who had already established a mission center in the neighboring plains of Assam. Native Assamese Christians, Godhula Brown and his wife Lucy Brown were first sent for exploratory contact with the village of Molung. They were followed by the American Baptist missionary couple, Edward Winter Clark and Mary Mead Clark. Prior to this contact, there was an earlier mission effort undertaken among the Naga people, by Miles Bronson, which was cut short by ill health. The work of the Clarks with the assistance of the Browns soon resulted in the establishment of a Christian community by the year 1872 in the village of Molung.[30] From this village, Christianity spread rapidly to the neighboring villages and tribes. By the early twentieth century, most of the Ao villages were Christianized and Ao Naga Christians were serving as "native" missionaries to the other Naga tribes.

The Naga Baptist mission was an American Baptist mission enterprise until the political stirrings were awakened among the Naga people. This roused suspicion in India regarding the role of Western missionaries in the political aspirations of the Naga people. Consequently, the missionaries from America were forced to leave the mission field by mid-twentieth century. Since then Naga Baptist Churches, including the Ao Baptist Church have been self-governing, self-supporting, and self-propagating of the new religion embraced. Today the Ao Naga Baptist Christians compose a significant resource for mission enterprise and theological education in India. Nonetheless, the conversion to Christianity took place arguably with many of the traditional cultural practices intact or at most given new interpretations, for instance, practices of clan identity, marriage customs, and naming are strictly observed in the contemporary lived Christianity.

Within this larger scenario of the Ao Naga Christian community, women's role, status, and participation are explored in the present case study. Ao women are mentioned in the records as being responsive to the missionaries' activity, particularly at school. The first school started by Mary Mead Clark was composed of more female students than male.[31] A woman convert, Tongpangla, was among the first batch of Clark's school who was sent as an evangelist to a neighboring village. Unlike some communities in India, women were not secluded from the society so they converted to Christianity as individuals as well as daughters and wives of male members who espoused the new religion.

The Women's Association of the Ao Baptist was organized in the year 1943, incidentally, a male missionary played a significant role as Dr. C. Hunter exhorted women toward the formation of the association.[32] According to the report, "[t]he main objective of the women's society was to participate in Mission and Evangelism"[33] for which purposes a full-time worker, Mrs. Jepdakla was appointed.

Among the Ao Naga Churches, there exists a parallel women's fellowship within the main church. The services are held every Thursday, called *Tetsur Sentep* (women church or women gathering). *Tetsur Sentep* is organized by the women themselves in all areas pertaining to leadership, fund raising, and mission activities. However, it should be underlined that the male pastor and the male-only deacon board carry out the final approval for the appointments and mission activities. Finances are also managed by the main church.

Right from the beginning there were no restrictions on women accessing the Bible or theological education, hence, Ao women were trained alongside the men in the Bible school at Impur, which produced leaders for the nascent Christian community, such as pastors and women-leaders for the women fellowship. The term used for the women leaders was *tetsur tesayula*, meaning "teacher for women" and they were Bible school or seminary trained. Recently, some churches have replaced the term *tetsur tesayula* with the term "associate pastor" for the woman assigned to the women's department.

Ao women therefore, appear to have had access to education and other modern changes wrought by Christian mission, fairly early on without discrimination. This is evident in the literacy rate of females, which is almost on par with the male counterpart. Ao women are seen in all areas of modern professions. Right from the beginning theological education was opened to the Ao women, albeit, most of them serve as teachers in church-related schools, assigned to the education department of the church, such as Sunday school and youth work.

Two senior Ao women who had completed their theological training in the 1970s, were ordained in the mid-nineties. It is worth noting that the ordination of women was carried out without much controversies or passionate debates. Today, there are six ordained women among the many male-ordained pastors, theological teachers, and church leaders. They serve as independent evangelists and theological teachers but none of them as full-time pastor. It must be mentioned, that the understanding and practice of ordination itself, has a complex function in the Ao Baptist Church in general. Male graduates of theological seminaries are not necessarily ordained upon their induction into ministry. Ordination follows years of service and recognition from the local church. Therefore, ordination is akin to an honor given in recognition of service rendered rather than an initiatory rite into the ministry of the church.

Despite the apparent progressive status of Ao women in the Ao Naga society, behind the façade, there hides a conservatism that is revealed by scratching the surface. To be precise, Ao women are yet to be full-time pastors, even at the structural level. At the attitudinal level, the clutches of the male-centric, patriarchal culture has cast its net deep and firm. Ao women are not considered eligible to serve in the village council, which is the governing power of the community. The Ao Christian society is yet to see an Ao woman politician. Incidentally, a recent proposal by the state to allot reservation for women leaders in the municipal governing body was opposed vehemently by some section of the Ao public. The policy remains unimplemented and women are still excluded from participation in the political aspect of the society.[34]

This brief discussion presents the complicated and ambiguous role and status of Ao Naga women; a position and participation that seems to be at best a paradox and at its worst a hypocrisy. While Christian mission certainly mediated and enabled their modern agency, it also assigned the women a limited space and a restraint voice.

## 4. Analysis of Christian Mission from a Women's Perspective

The lack of gender analysis of mission as pointed out by Dana L. Robert not only ignores the significant contribution women have made in making Christianity into a world religion, it also results in a one-sided aspect of Christian mission as establishment of a religion in new contexts. To ignore gender dimension of mission is to miss a vital evaluation of Christian mission. Christian mission at its core is about transforming human cultures that are oppressive.

The case of Christianity among the Ao Naga points toward these lacunae of Christian mission. While Christian mission was most fruitful in introducing the gospel of Christ to the Ao Naga, it is found wanting in creating an equal Christian community. The above description of Ao women in the church as well as the larger society reveals a gendered position and participation that is not very different from the pre-Christian mission days for the Ao women despite education and Christianization. This reality bespeaks of a limited and unequal position of Ao women despite education and seeks explanations to some questions that arise from such a paradoxical position. Is Christian mission inclusive of gender empowerment? Historically, to what extent did Christian mission create structures and constructed theological foundations toward emancipation of Ao Naga women? Was Christian mission restraint in its liberative dimension of mission? What role might have been contributed by Christian mission in providing "women only" space versus giving equal space and authority in the newly converted community? Is Christianity too much conditioned by the cultures and traditions it encounters? Why has Christian mission left unchallenged cultural practices that are particularly discriminatory and excluding of women? Did Christian mission from the West reify gender roles in the nascent Christian community in transplanting their own cultural mores regarding gender roles? What role could Christian mission have played in order to ensure equal voice, status, and participation for both men and women?

The position of Ao Naga women is more complicated than the simplistic perception of unobstructed women because there is no written cultural code that limits or restricts their freedom. They participate in the modern economy and employment structures within the state. It is within the church and the political structures they are denied full recognition and participation. This reality seems to be a continuation of the traditional position mixed with the nineteenth and early twentieth century's Christian mission ethos toward women.[35] Women were given education as far as they could be equipped to serve in the modernizing society, as nurses, teachers, and office assistants. Women were theologically trained to serve in the women and education departments. Apart from these roles, Ao women can neither claim authority nor have the right to participate in the clan council. Further, theologically trained women are either denied or discouraged for the Eucharistic ministry in the church. The limited roles for women can be described as "mission of crumbs" wherein women receive partial, peripheral, and left-over roles that have left them in the margins, negated and excluded.[36]

These gender roles among the modern Christian Ao society are not any different from the pre-Christian women situation. While women were not excluded from participation in the larger community festivities, neither were they kept in sequester quarters, Ao women were mere complementary to the male members, they were not included in the clan-council, and they could not inherit clan lands. Herein the critique against Christian mission lies, that they were far too much children of their time, in that radical re-orientation of gender equality was still in its nascent stage. Narola Imchen affirms this attitude that concerns for women's rights were limited within the mission organization but not in the larger society.[37]

The by-products of evangelization, namely education and professionalization acquired by women, are the tools for modern society, which are only to supplement the male members, just as the missionary wives were to their husbands. The structure within the missionary communities that assigned single women missionaries to minister to the women and areas such as education and medical missions sowed the seed and left the pattern for the native Christian community to follow. Dana Robert writes about the constraints and limitations that women within the Protestant Christian mission community had to negotiate due to their gender. Hence, women who were motivated with the evangelical call for serving as missionaries in distant lands often fulfilled this urge for mission by way of marriage. To serve as missionary, a woman often had to become an assistant to the husband who was considered as the primary executor of the Christian tasks of evangelization.[38] This pattern of gender relationship, gender roles and status within the new religion, Christianity, was followed in the newly converted communities, wherein women were assigned as assistants and limited to the women fellowship. The existing cultural position of women within the pre-Christian community further added to the reification of this gender role, consequently the limitation imposed upon women and the continuing discrimination.

From such limitations traced to the mission practice of gender inequalities, it is important to heed to Katja Heidemann as she challenges Christian mission to undertake a critical process of "analysis of ecclesial-religious and socio-political structures of subordination and exclusion, and understands missiological reflection as a practice of resistance and transformation."[39]

## 5. Questions for Discussion

1. What are the criteria to differentiate between the gospel's values of liberation and freedom within human cultures, such as Ao Naga?

2. Was Christian mission limited in the area of recognizing women as equally capable for service in the church and society?

3. What are some resources within the Bible that make it imperative for an inclusive, equal community?

4. What are the features envisaged in a missiology that is inclusive and gender-sensitive?

5. Should ordination and ensuring women as leaders in the church be one of the goals for mission of the church?

6. How can we ensure participation of women in the church and the larger society? What are some practical steps to empower and include women?

7. Should Christian mission require gender equality, gender inclusive partnerships between global funding Christian organizations and local churches?

## 6. Recommendations

1. *Bible study*: initiate contextual Bible studies that include hermeneutic of suspicions and re-reading of traditional and well-known texts from a women's perspective.

2. *Resource sharing*: theological resources for gender inclusiveness, such as liturgies, women experiences and programs between both inter and intra churches. Create commissions to study and make recommendations pertaining to women's role and participation to the member churches.

3. *Partnering*: maintain a critical/prophetic stance, mutually critical and a deliberate involvement. Partnering should not be limited to funds but accompaniment. In partnering projects, it can be required that women are represented in consultations and ensure women's voices at the decision-making bodies.

4. *Allotment of money*: churches and Christian organizations can allot money for specific women programs and develop deliberate measures to equip women leaders.

5. *Celebrate women's day/month*: to create awareness, conscience and networks and encourage the community members toward an equal community of men and women.

6. *Organize regular history* lessons and writing workshops to rediscover the crucial role women missionaries and native women converts have played in the history of the transmission of the new faith.

7. *Conduct regular seminars* on issues such as domestic violence, rape, women and HIV/AIDS and women empowerment programs.

## 7. Mission Concerns

1. Nagaland can qualify as one of the vibrant Christian communities in the Global South with marked mission involvement and the churches having a vital role in the society. Nonetheless, it is also a highly patriarchal society where women have a very small role in the society.

2. The Ao Naga Church understanding of mission needs to be enlarged beyond the traditional definition of salvation and areas of empowerment and inclusion of those culturally excluded need to be embraced as mission addressees.

3. Social conservatism and indigenous cultures with deeply ingrained patriarchal structures are vehement barriers for women to be equal with men in participation in the society and the church.

4. Mission projects can include mentoring, training, and development of women leaders for the community.

5. Creating social awareness and raising critical consciousness among the Ao Naga women remains a mission challenge.

## 8. Conclusion

Christian mission among the Ao Naga people of Northeast India brought multiple changes not only limited to religious conversion but also to other social aspects, and initiated the people toward modernization. As the native culture presented a relatively receptive society and without overt cultural practices of extreme gender exploitation, the evangelical task of sharing the gospel of Christ was unhindered and undivided. Both men and women embraced the new religion together. Both men and women were enrolled in the education facilities provided by the Christian mission. When these changes and facilities were put into practice, however, gender differentiation was assigned and women were allotted "women only" roles. This gender roles set in motion in the mission days have continued unchallenged to this day. Today's task of Christian mission then should be one of correcting these lacunae and building an inclusive community, wherein women also participate with their gifts and abilities for a mutually affirming and dependent society.

## Further Reading

Narola Imchen, *Remembering Our Foremothers: The Influence of the American Women's Movement on American Baptist Women Missionaries in North East India* (Jorhat: Eastern Theological College, 2003).

Aphuno Chase-Roy, *Women in Transition: Angami Naga Women From 1878 to the Present* (Kohima, Nagaland: Aphuno Chase-Roy, 2004).

Lalrinawmi Ralte, *Feminist Hermeneutics: On the Occasion of Silver Jubilee of Ordination of Women in the Church of South India (CSI)* (New Delhi: ISPCK, 2002).

## Endnotes

1. Dana L. Robert, "Women in World Mission: Controversies and Challenges from a North American Perspective," in *International Review Mission*, vol. 93, No.368, January 2004 (Geneva: World Council of Churches, 2004): 52.

2. Cf. http://www.ophi.org.uk/news/in-media (September 9, 2010).

3. See, Martha C. Nussbaum, *The Clash Within: Democracy, Religious Violence and India's future* (Ranikhet: Permanent Black, 2007). This edition was reprinted in India by arrangement with Harvard University Press.

4. The five countries are: India, Pakistan, Afghanistan, Somalia, Democratic Republic of Congo, see, http://1click.indiatimes.com/article/0axj1yD8UQ8v5?q=London (October 22, 2011).

5. For instance the recent controversies and debates surrounding the Women Reservation Bill reflects the resistance against women participation and progress spread across diverse political parties and socioeconomic classes, notwithstanding the political agenda involved. Even a state like Kerala, which is one of the most progressive states and has the highest literacy rate is faulted of social conservatism when it comes to women's issues.

6. Martha C. Nussbaum, *The Clash Within*.

7. One that stands out among the many is, Stanley Samartha, *One Christ, Many Religions: Towards a revised Christology* (Maryknoll: Orbis Books, 1991).

8. For instance the Isabella Thoburn College, Lucknow, is one of the earliest women colleges in Asia, started in 1886. See Maina Chawla Singh, *Gender, Religion, and "Heathen Lands"* (New York: Garland Publishing, 2000), 245-273.

9. Along with the reasons of limited resources available from the chosen areas, the writer belongs to the Baptist church in the Northeast and works in central-North India in a Methodist theological college.

10. The existing maritime trade route between Asia and the Mediterranean commercial world would have provided the possibility of travel to Thomas. For more detailed discussion, see, Leonard Fernando and G. Gispert-Sauch, *Christianity in India: Two Thousand Years of Faith* (New Delhi: Viking/Penguin, 2004), 60-66. See also, Robert E. Frykenberg, *Christianity in India: From beginnings to the present* (Oxford: Oxford University Press, 2008).

11. Mention must be made of the women situation among these Christians, albeit not an elaborate description. Kerala is one of the most progressive states in India, with a 100 percent literacy rate. Women are highly educated and visible in the state social and economic structures. However, the situation in the church is quite different from the larger society and presents a complex scenario. Almost in all the denominations of the Christian church, there are no ordained women for the Eucharistic ministry and most of the theological teachers and church authority are composed of the male members. For more details, see, Rowena Robinson, *Christians of India* (New Delhi: Sage Publications, 2003).

12. Leonard Fernando and G. Gispert-Sauch, *Christianity in India*, 73.

13. Robert de Nobili was one of the Jesuits who worked in South India during the seventeenth century, whose approach to mission created controversy. De Nobili wanted to introduce Christianity to the Brahmins, who were, according to the Hindu religio-cultural practices placed as the high caste in the caste hierarchy. In order to establish this desired contact with the Brahmins, de Nobili identified himself as a Brahmin by espousing their dress, food habits, and dwelling place. This generated considerable controversies at different levels such as social and theological. See, Leonard Fernando and G. Gispert-Sauch, ibid., 97-102.

14. Akbar is known mostly for his interest and strategic tolerance of other religions different from Islam. This interest resulted in the creation of a syncretistic religion known as *Din-i-illahi*, during his rule. See for more details, Richard M. Eaton, ed., *India's Islamic Traditions, 711-1750* (New Delhi: Oxford University Press, 2003).

15. Bartholomaeus Ziegenbalg was student at the University of Halle, Germany, influenced by the Pietistic movement in the Lutheran Church. Ziegenbalg and Henry Pluetschau were commissioned by the King of Denmark to be missionaries to India. See, Brijraj Singh, *First Protestant Missionary in India: Bartholomaeus Ziegenbalg 1687-1719* (New Delhi: Oxford University Press, 1999).

16. For the complex relationship between Christian mission and colonialism, see Brian Stanley, *The Bible and the Flag: Protestant Missions and British Imperialism in the nineteenth and twentieth centuries* (Leicester: Apollos, 1990), Judith M. Brown and Robert Eric Frykenberg, eds., *Christians, Cultural Interactions, and India's Religious Traditions* (Grand Rapids: William B. Eerdmans Publishing Company, 2002).

17. Brian Stanley, *The History of the Baptist Missionary Society, 1972-1992* (Edinburgh: T & T Clark, 1992).

18. The historical developments in the West, such as the age of Discovery, and the Enlightenment added to the fervor of crossing the borders and seas taking the gospel and the perceived benefits of modern civilization of Europe and America. See, William R. Hutchison, *Errand to the World: American Protestant Thought and Foreign Mission* (Chicago: University of Chicago Press, 1987); Brian Stanley, ed., *Christian Missions and the Enlightenment* (Grand Rapids: William B. Eerdmans Publishing Company, 2001).

19. The relationship of social reforms and Christian mission is complex, because the British Colonial power also provided significant instruments, such as legal and social discourse that addressed issues of socio-cultural reforms in the country. Among the plethora of resources on the topic, one of the earliest books is David Kopf, *British Orientalism and Bengal Renaissance: The Dynamics of Indian Modernization 1772-1835* (Berkeley: University of California Press, 1969); see also, Leonard Fernando and G. Gispert-Sauch, *Christianity in India*, 163.

20. Missionary magazines such as the *Missionary Register* played an important role in dissemination of the evangelical zeal for the "heathens," see, Andrew F. Walls, *The Missionary Movement in Christian History: Studies in the Transmission of Faith* (Maryknoll: Orbis Books, 1997; Edinburgh: T&T Clark, 1997), 251-252.

21. See, Howard Clark Kee et al., eds., *Christianity: A Social and Cultural History* (New Jersey: Prentice Hall, 1998).

22. Andrew F. Walls, *The Missionary Movement*, 241-254.

23. There was the need of comity, and the need for co-operation and collaboration resulted in mission conferences such as Edinburgh 1910. See Brian Stanley, *World Missionary Conference: Edinburgh 1910* (Grand Rapids: William B. Eerdmans Publishing Company, 2010); Ian Eliis, *A Century of Mission and Unity* (Dublin: Columba Press, 2010); William Richey Hogg, *Ecumenical Foundations: A History of the International Missionary Conference and its nineteenth-century background* (New York: Harper & Bros, 1952).

24. There are excellent resources for the micro history of individual mission societies, which recount their arrival, establishment and mission activities; they are not duplicated here for reason of space limitation: Methodists, Lutherans, Anglicans, Baptists, Presbyterians, Pentecostals, and many others established Christian communities in the country. Later, by the mid-twentieth century, India also saw a number of indigenous mission societies that carried out evangelization. See, Samuel Hugh Moffett, *A History of Christianity in Asia, Vol. II: 1500-1900*, Indian edition (Bangalore: Theological Publications in India,

2005), 431ff; Robert Eric Frykenberg, ed., *Christians and Missionaries in India: Cross-Cultural Communication since 1500* (Grand Rapids: William B. Eerdmans Publishing Company, 2003).

25. The social practice derived from the seclusion of women from the main society the *Zenana* was the women-only space for social and cultural activities of women.

26. For a helpful discussion on the 'women question' such as education and modernization of their status in relation to the colonial and missionaries, see, Geraldine Forbes, *The New Cambridge History of India: Women in Modern India*, Indian Edition (New Delhi: Cambridge University Press, 1996).

27. While almost all the Christian traditions and denominations are present in the region—Roman Catholic, Pentecostal, Indigenous, Assembly of God, an so on—this paper will limit itself to the Baptist church in Nagaland. The rationale being that Baptist churches among the Naga people were among the first Christian communities established by missionaries in the late nineteenth century.

28. A red mark on the forehead, resembling a large dot, worn by many women in India that signifies their marital status.

29. It has to be emphasized here that written sources, which are limited, date from the modern period only, prior to that little is known apart from the oral traditions; albeit there might be written documents in the languages of the neighboring people such as Burmese, Assamese, and Manipuri. Therefore, the source of information of the pre-conversion period is mediated through the colonial and mission ethnography.

30. There are number of studies on the history of Christianity among the Naga people, see among others, Mary Mead Clark, *A Corner in India* (Philadelphia: American Baptist Publication Soceity, 1907); Victor Hugo Sword, *Baptists in Assam: A Century of Missionary Service 1836-1936* (Chicago: Conference Press, 1936); F.S. Downs, *History of Christianity in India Vol V. Part 5 NEI in the Nineteenth & Twentienth Centuries* (Bangalore: CHAI, 1992); Bendangyabang Ao, *History of Christianity in Nagaland: A Source Material* (Mokokchung: Shalom Ministry, 1998); Narola Rivenberg, *The Star of the Naga Hills* (Philadelphia: The Judson Press, 1941).

31. Their names were: Tongpangla, Noksangla, Jongmayangla, Punayula, Purla, and Taripisu. See A. Olem Kilep, *Laishir Mungchen* (Molung, Nagaland: Molungyimsen Baptist Church, 1976), 60.

32. Esterine Iralu, Arenla Longchar, K. Kapfo, eds., *A Brief History of NBCC Women Department* (Kohima: n. a: n.d), 39. NBCC stands for Nagaland Baptist Council of Churches. Dr. Hunter served as a missionary among the Ao people, from 1948 to 1950. He was associated with the introduction of a "born again" experience of Christianity, which was the seed for the growth of charismatic Christianity among the Ao people, resulting in revival meetings etc. See, Atola Longkumer, *Shamans, Tanula Akuter (Holy Spirit People) and Naga Christianity: A Study of Religio-cultural Transition among the Nagas*, unpublished dissertation, SATHRI, Bangalore, 2006.

33. Iralu, Longchar, Kapfo, *A Brief History*, 39.

34. This phenomenon of social conservatism and rigid traditionalism has been critiqued in an article by the present writer, see, Atola Longkumer, *"Not all is well in my ancestors' home: An Indigenous theology of Internal Critique,"* in *The Ecumenical Review*, 62.4 (2010): 399-410.

35. Many books are available on the topic both in its general manifestations and specific context variations, for more details, see, Susan Hill Lindley, *"You*

*have Stept (sic) out of your Place": A History of Women and Religion in America* (Louisville: Westminster John Knox Press, 1996); Dana L. Robert, *American Women in Mission: A Social History of their Thought and Practice* (Macon: Mercer University Press, 1997).

36. Fulata L. Moyo,"'Who is Not at the Table?': Women's Perspectives of Holistic Mission as Mutually Inclusive," in Daryl Balia and Kirsteen Kim, eds., Edinburgh 2010 Vol II: *Witnessing to Christ Today* (Oxford: Regnum Books International, 2010), 245-252.

37. Narola Imchen, *Remembering our Foremothers: The Influence of the American Women's Movement on American Baptist Women Missionaries in North East India* (Jorhat: Eastern Theological College, 2003), 154.

38. Robert, *American Women in Mission*, 32.

39. Katja Heidemann, "Missiology of Risk?: Explorations in Mission Theology from a German Feminist Perspective," in *International Review of Mission*, Vol. 95 No. 368, (2004), 107.

CHAPTER 8

# Christianity and Women in Contemporary China[1]

*Kwok Pui-lan*

## 1. Historical Setting

In May 2005, Chong Yi Church, the biggest church in China, which sits about 5,000 people, was completed and dedicated in Hangzhou in Zhejiang Province in China. The ceiling above the spacious choir loft of this impressive church soars to more than two hundred feet and the prominent white cross at the center measures sixty feet tall. During the dedication ceremony, Yang Lüfu, at 90, conducted the choir of several hundred members with joyfulness and gratitude. The widow of the Rev. Cai Wenhao, a prominent Christian leader in Hangzhou, Yang has lived through the ups and downs of the Chinese churches: the adaptation to the founding of the People's Republic of China, the closure of churches during the Cultural Revolution (1966–1976), the reopening of churches in the late 1970s; and the phenomenal growth of churches in recent years.

When the People's Republic of China was founded in 1949, there were about 2.7 million Catholics, 700,000 Protestants, and 300,000 Orthodox Christians.[2] In the 1950s, Chinese church leaders declared their independence from missionary imperialism and launched the China Christian Three-Self Patriotic Movement: self-governing, self-support, and self-propagation. The Three-Self Patriotic Movement of the Protestant churches was formed in 1954;[3] in 1957, the Chinese Catholic Patriotic Association was established and the Chinese Catholic Church began to elect and consecrate their own bishops. However, many Chinese Christians remain suspicious of the Three-Self Movement and fearful of government control in religious affairs.

Instead of joining the Three-Self churches, they meet privately in independent or house churches for worship, Bible studies, and fellowship.

During the Cultural Revolution, all religious activities were suspended in China and churches were closed down and church properties confiscated. Many Christians suffered persecution, church ministers were sent to prison camps, and religious sisters were forced to return to secular life. At the end of this turbulent period, China reopened to the outside world and adopted more liberal policies. Christian churches reopened in 1978, and the China Christian Council was founded in 1980 as an umbrella agency for all Protestant churches. The Chinese Protestant churches entered a post-denominational period, with Christians of different denominational and liturgical backgrounds worshiping together side by side. Since 1980, over 50 million Bibles were published and distributed throughout China; Chinese hymnals and Christian journals and literature were also published. The Chinese Catholic Church also reopened, though relationship with the Vatican remains strenuous, with informal talks about establishing diplomatic relationship between the Vatican and China taking place on an on-again, off-again basis.

Emerging out of the nightmares of the Cultural Revolution, both the Chinese Protestant and Catholic churches have enjoyed unprecedented church growth. According to the statistics in 2010, there were over 23 million Protestant Christians in China, more than thirty times the figure for 1949; 56,000 churches and meeting points; and twenty-one seminaries and Bible schools. In addition, a few hundred thousand house churches were unregistered, with anywhere between 50-55 million adherents, according to one estimate. The Catholic population was estimated to be more than 12 million, worshiping in 6,000 churches, and there were well over 3,000 priests and 5,000 religious sisters. Women make up more than 70 present of Chinese Christians, and an increasing number of women enter Protestant seminaries to be trained as pastors and lay leaders. In 2003, there were over 400 ordained female pastors in China, constituting about one-quarter of the total number of pastors, and most of them having been ordained after the Cultural Revolution. In addition, there are more than 7,000 women church workers, comprising about 45 percent of the total number of church workers. Over one-third of the faculties of the seminaries and Bible schools are made up of women.[4] Several women occupy distinguished positions in the church, the most notable being the Rev. Cao Shengjie, former President of the China Christian Council, and the Rev. Gao

Ying, Vice President of Yanjing Theological Seminary. In the Catholic Church, formation of religious women resumed in the 1980s, with women religious working in different social sectors, including clinics, social services, nursing homes, and kindergartens. A small number of religious women were sent to study abroad, and upon their return they were appointed to teach in seminaries, the novitiate, and pastoral programs.

As Christian women in mainland China were adjusting to these tremendous political changes and their new-found religious freedom, their counterparts in Hong Kong and Macao braced themselves for the reunification with China after a long period of colonization. In 1997 and 1999, Hong Kong and Macao were returned to China by the British and Portugese governments, respectively, to become Special Administrative Regions. In this chapter, I will discuss the development of feminist consciousness and theology in contemporary China and Hong Kong, focusing on Chinese Christian women's understanding of the relation between church and state, their interpretation of the Bible, and their conceptions about women's body and sexuality.

## 2. Development of Feminist Consciousness and Theology

Christianity has played positive roles in the development of modern Chinese women's consciousness and movement. In the nineteenth century, Christian missions worked to improve women's lives and raised their status by opposing the practice of foot-binding and by providing female education. Influenced by their Victorian ideals of womanhood, missionaries regarded enlightened mothers as the foundation of building a strong society. They had spoken out against female infanticide and the inhuman treatment of *mei zai*, female children bought as domestic helpers or concubines. In addition, they introduced Western medicine and hygiene to China, and the first Chinese medical doctors were all trained under the auspices of Christian mission.[5] But the most important contributions were the opening of schools for women and girls and the advocacy for women to raise their self-consciousness and social status.[6] In the first half of the twentieth century, many women professionals and leaders of the women's movement were graduates of these mission schools. They initiated various social reforms for improving women's livelihood, such as the temperance movement, literacy campaigns, and programs for factory workers.

Chinese Christian women's feminist consciousness became heightened during the May Fourth Movement in 1919, when Beijing students took to the street to protest against China's weak response to the Paris Peace Conference, which granted German rights over Shandong Province to Japan. These iconoclastic students blamed Chinese traditional culture and feudal practices for contributing to China's backwardness and her failure to stand up to the West. Many criticized Confucian culture and argued that China should learn from the West, especially democracy and science. Among their radical demands included the abolition of patriarchal family, in favor of individual freedom and women's liberation. In response to the public outcry, Christian women published women's journals and discussed women's status and roles, relationship between the sexes, and women's social issues and problems in such publications as *Nüduobao* (Woman's messenger), *Nüxing* (Woman's star), and *Nüqingnian biao* (Y.W.C.A. magazine).[7] Christian women leaders such as Ding Shujing, Cai Sujuan, and Zeng Baosun reflected on their religious experience and their understanding of Jesus's life and ministry.[8] In a memorable speech on the position of women in the church at the second national convention of the Y.W.C.A. in 1927, Ding Shujung argued that women should be treated as full participants in the body of Christ, since Jesus respected women and allowed them to participate in his ministry.[9]

The Chinese Communist Party has an ideological commitment to women's liberation; soon after the founding of the People's Republic China, the government adopted various measures to improve the status of women. The Chinese Constitution recognizes the equality of the sexes, and Mao Zedong famously declared that "women hold up half of the sky." In the 1950s, the government initiated family reform and changed the Marriage Law, which aimed to liberate women from patriarchal family structures, customs, and ideology. These reforms undercut the power of gentry and male heads of household and could not be fully implemented because of local resistance.[10] During the Cultural Revolution, gender difference was minimized, when the whole China was awashed in a sea of dark blue or gray, as women and men wore the same Mao jackets and cut their hair short. Women were told that they were on equal footing with men and could contribute to building up a strong and prosperous China in the same way. When the churches reopened, Christian women found it jarring to see that women were treated as subordinate to men in the churches and were not permitted to perform certain roles, such as distributing bread and wine during Eucharist, for fear of offending some traditional Christians. Gao Ying, for example, lamented, "The feudal belief of men's superiority over women is so deeply rooted in people's minds that it is hard to overcome, even within the church."[11]

As their feminist consciousness gradually develops, Chinese women demand greater participation and leadership in the church. The majority of worshipers are women; with rapid growth in church membership and because of severe shortage of pastors, they have taken on very active roles. A greater number of women have been theologically trained and serve as pastors and seminary professors. Chinese Christian women have had frequent contacts with the churches outside China and have learned about women's activities in other countries. Numerous delegations of Christian women, including feminist theologians, have visited local churches, seminaries, the YWCA, and Christian agencies.[12] Chinese Christian women leaders also were invited abroad to visit churches and organizations, and to speak about women's position and involvement in the church. A number of Christian women, such as Gao Ying and Zhang Jing, went abroad for graduate studies and learned about feminist hermeneutics and theology, and they introduced these ideas upon their return. Their publications can be found in *Nanjing Theological Review*, the *Chinese Theological Review*, and other ecumenical journals.

In Hong Kong, feminist theology was introduced with liberation theology and contextual theology during the 1970s. The pioneering work of Mary Daly and Rosemary Radford Ruether presented a radical critique of Christianity's androcentric symbols and the patriarchal and hierarchal church. Some of the female seminarians became aware of the ways male-dominated Christian values and patriarchal Confucian culture mutually reinforced one another. In the 1980s, courses on feminist theology and biblical interpretation were taught in some of the more progressive seminaries. When Asian feminist theology began as a grassroots movement in the early 1980s, feminist theologians in Hong Kong participated in it from the beginning. In 1987, a conference on Chinese feminist theology was held in Hong Kong, with fifty-two participants from Malaysia, Singapore, Sabah, and Korea. The proceedings were published as *Huaren funü shenxue chutan* (Towards a Chinese feminist theology).[13] Hong Kong Christian women have been exposed to new theological ideas from outside and to the ecumenical movement in Asia and worldwide, because the Asian Women's Resource Centre for Culture and Theology and the Christian Conference of Asia were stationed for some time in Hong Kong.[14]

In 1988, the Hong Kong Women Christian Council was established in response to the World Council of Churches' Ecumenical Decade for Churches in Solidarity with Women (1988–1998). Its objectives include: the establishment of gender equality in church and society; the reflection of Christian faith from the perspective of women, the raising of women's consciousness and the promotion of their social participation; and their networking with other women's groups, both local and overseas.[15] Its members include Catholics and Protestants, men and women, lay and ordained, expatriates and local Chinese. Through lectures and workshops, and its magazine *Shi* (Interpretation) and other publications, the Council promotes contextual feminist theology in Hong Kong. The Council also works frequently with other Christian and secular political organizations to address domestic violence, to work for social justice and women's rights, and to stand in solidarity with other marginalized groups

The Council first visited mainland China in 1994 and made connections with Christian and secular groups, such as the All-China Women's Federation and the YWCA. Since then study tours and exchanges with seminaries and other agencies have continued. In 2002, the Council joined with other Christian organizations to host an international conference on "Feminist Theology in Chinese Contexts," with fifty-nine women pastors, lay leaders, and scholars from Taiwan, Malaysia, Singapore, and Hong Kong. Participants discussed the development of feminist theology in the churches, academy, and religious communities in their various contexts.[16] The Council also organizes regular feminist Bible studies and has produced a short video on feminist theology and pastoral care.

## 3. Relation between Church and State

The relation between the church and state has been a sensitive issue because of the Communist Party's staunch atheist stance and its suspicion of religious activities. Although the Constitution provides for the freedom of religion, the government restricts religious practices to government-sanctioned organizations. The State Administration for Religious Affairs is responsible for monitoring religious activities and religious groups; places of worship must register with the government. The government's religious policies have often changed with the vicissitudes of political movements sweeping through China and with the fortunes of China's leaders. During the Anti-Rightist movement and the Cultural Revolution, Christian leaders had been denounced, criticized, and sent to be reeducated. In order to survive and function in such an environment, Christians had to demonstrate that they were patriotic, progressive, and supportive of the government. The Chinese Christian church emphasized that Christians should "love-country, love-church" and strive to be model citizens, workers, and peasants.

To make their situation more complex, religious freedom often has served as the barometer for political freedom and human rights by observers of China. Incidents of religious persecution have been widely reported and have captured the attention of many people. Many Christians outside China regard the Three-Self churches as controlled by the government, and that only the "underground" churches are authentic and bearing true witness to Jesus Christ. Not surprisingly, the Chinese government regards reports of religious persecution and negative criticism of Chinese policies as anti-Chinese propaganda. When the churches reopened, some foreign religious agencies attempted to smuggle Bibles into China and engage in evangelistic activities forbidden by the government. Christian leaders toed a fine line in the reconstruction of Christianity in socialist China and in reestablishing international relationships.

With the downfall of the ultra-leftist leaders of the Cultural Revolution, the policy of religious freedom was restored and confiscated church properties gradually returned. Bishop K. H. King, the most prominent leader of the Chinese Christian church, said that the government should "show respect for religious liberty and conscience, refrain from repressing religion, treat all religions with equality, look after the legitimate rights and interests of all religions."[17] He further argued that Church should seek common ground with the government:

> As long as there is common ground between communists and Christians as Chinese citizens, as long as there is space for us to maintain Christian worship and witness and church life, and as long as ways are open for useful dialogue on the implementation of the principle of religious freedom, we see no justification for thinking that atheists are our enemies and that belligerency is called for.[18]

The late evangelical female leader Jiang Peifen also rejected a knee-jerk reaction against the Communists. She recognized the contribution of the Communist Party to the eradication of habits of the old Chinese society, such as prostitution, opium-smoking, and gambling. She pointed out that just as God has used the hands of the gentile king, Cyrus, to release the Israelites from bondage, God also can use non-believers today.[19] She saw the importance of the Three-Self Movement and of the prerogative for the Chinese church to run her own business: "If the Church had not returned to the Chinese people, there would have been no future for the Gospel in New China. The Gospel which we preached could be accepted by the people only if we stayed with them, sharing common thoughts, common feelings, and a common language."[20]

In 1995 Cao Shengjie, who was the Vice-President of the China Christian Council and Vice-Chair of its Commission on Women's Work at the time, delivered an important speech at the Non-governmental Organization Forum during the United Nations Fourth World Conference of Women in Beijing. She affirmed that, since the founding of the New China, the government has brought about changes to women's conditions, such as the rights for women to own property, the abolition of arranged and forced marriages, and the provision of female education. She contrasted this with women's widespread illiteracy and their subordinate position in the Chinese traditional society. The All-China Women's Federation, active both at the national and local levels, has worked toward women's Four-Self: self-respect, self-confidence, self-reliance, and self-strengthening. For Cao, the New China has brought social advancement of women and the improvement of women's status in the church.[21]

The Chinese church has called upon Chinese Christians to be both "good Christians and good citizens." As a leader of the Christian church, Cao did not see Christianity as incompatible with the Communist government. While Western observers have criticized China's human rights records, Cao noted that the government has been doing a better job in implementing religious freedom in the past twenty years. She said, "Our government's goal is to unite people of different faiths and ethnic identities to build up our socialist country. We can unite with them politically in serving the Chinese people, while respecting each other's religious faiths."[22] She also said that rumors about "persecution" of Christian churches may have come from outdated information during the Cultural Revolution, anti-Chinese propaganda, reports of cases that concern illegal practices of foreigners or cult leaders, and exaggeration of individual cases in which certain officials did not handle the policy of religious freedom well.[23] She welcomed fellowship and collaboration with Christians and churches in other parts of the world, but this must be based on mutual understanding, obedience of the Chinese law, and according to the needs of the Chinese church.[24]

Having witnessed the fate of the Chinese churches during political upheavals, Christians in Hong Kong had reasons to doubt whether religious freedom, human rights, rule of the law, and democracy would be guaranteed after the return to China. After the 1989 violent suppression of students' demonstration at Tiananmen Square, a strong and vibrant pro-democracy movement was formed in Hong Kong.

The Christian feminist movement in Hong Kong has been an integral part of this pro-democracy movement. Rose Wu, former director of the Hong Kong Women Christian Council, has been very outspoken about democracy and human rights. She fought for women marginalized by church and society, such as prostitutes, lesbians, and divorced women. She criticized that some of the church leaders have sought to appease China in the hope that China will not interfere in the future religious affairs in Hong Kong. Instead of speaking out for the oppressed of society, they have remained silent in supporting the status quo, or, at best, slow and incremental changes in Hong Kong's political development. She argued that human beings are creations of God and that "a just society can only be achieved if people are free to participate in the decisions that affect their lives."[25] During the transitional period, the Hong Kong Women Christian Council worked to promote women's political consciousness, self-determination, and an inclusive and global community.

Since 1997, Hong Kong has entered the postcolonial period, and many people in Hong Kong want to maintain their distinct identity as "Hong Kongese" instead of just being "Chinese." Angela Wai Ching Wong and other feminists have explored a postcolonial feminist theology from Hong Kong's context. Wong criticizes the nationalist movements in Asia following the Second World War for failing to pay attention to the oppressive situation of women. She also challenges the rhetoric of Asian liberation theology of an earlier generation for constructing the East and the West as binary opposites. The construction of "the West and the rest," she argues, re-inscribes the superiority of the colonizers. Instead, she sees the culture of Hong Kong as a hybrid, with the fusion of both Chinese and Western elements. Instead of portraying Asian women either as victims of colonial or patriarchal domination or as national heroines, she seeks to portray their multiple and complex identities using the literary resources of Hong Kong novelists. She cautions against a fictional and romanticized postcolonial return to one's indigenous culture and heritage and calls attention to the multilayered history and identity among Hong Kong people.[26]

# 4. Biblical Interpretation from Women's Perspective

Feminist theological writings in China focus on biblical interpretation and the roles of women in the church. Since the majority of the Chinese Protestant churches are evangelical in their outlook, the Bible remains authoritative for guiding Christian behavior. Chinese women leaders are aware that the Bible can be interpreted in ways that reinforce male domination, making feminist biblical hermeneutics necessary. Cao Shengjie writes:

> If we proceed from a literal interpretation, then there are things in the Bible that are not helpful to women's position. [...] Feminist theology has always stressed hermeneutics, not only for passages that value women, but have called for close study of those passages that have been seen as belittling to women. [...] Reading the Bible from a woman's perspective frequently brings women new light.[27]

Chinese Christian women use different interpretive strategies to emphasize women's roles and ministries in the Bible. They note the presence of women among Jesus' followers and that these women remain faithful to Jesus even to the cross. Chen Kuanrong, a teacher in Anhui Theological Seminary, has written on the women disciples of Jesus in Mark's Gospel.[28] She notes that women were present in Jesus' ministry though they often are not named, or are mentioned only in conjunction with their menfolk—Simon's mother-in-law, Jairus' daughter, the widow who gives her two mites, the woman who suffers from hemorrhage, and the woman who brings the jar of costly ointment. But Mark did mention women by name in the passion narrative in chapter 15: Mary Magdalene, Mary the mother of James, and Salome, probably the mother of the sons of Zebedee. Chen argues that these women must be the core persons of the larger group of women followers, just as Peter, James, and John were the core of the disciples. The women disciples exercised their ministries, for they watched over Jesus, expressing women's care, concern, and grief for him. They followed Jesus, listened to his preaching and teaching, and provided for him when he was in Galilee. They were the ones who stood near him on the cross, anointed him after his death, and were the first to witness his resurrection. Chen praised the dedication of these women disciples and said they have won respect and admiration throughout the ages.

Although women make up more than half of the parishioners, Chinese women do not enjoy equal status in church leadership and community life. Gao Ying notes that the church in China is still ruled by an older generation of male leadership, who are not ready to accept women's full participation. There is a strong presence of fundamentalism in the church's membership. Many women have internalized that they are inferior to men and feminist consciousness has yet to take root.[29]

Wang Peng, an instructor at Nanjing Theological Seminary, takes on the difficult task of reinterpreting Paul's prohibitions against women in 1 Corinthians. She recalls that pioneering Chinese Christian women, such as Ding Shujing, have blazed a trail in women's biblical interpretation, church structure, and equality between the sexes. Yet even today, some Christians have continue to use a literal and simplified interpretation of Paul to reinforce women's subordinate status in the church. Wang adopts a two-pronged reading strategy in her interpretation of Paul's view that women should cover their heads when praying and prophesying, and that women should not speak in public. First, she uses historical criticism to unpack the *Sitz im Leben* of the morally lax Corinthian church and points out that Paul has taken caution to avoid criticism from those outside of the church. She goes on to argue that "Paul's strictures on women in the church at Corinth existed in the fixed conditions of the time, and are not an absolute and universal teaching for women regardless of time or place."[30] Second, she uses the hermeneutical lens of a theology of reconciliation developed by the Chinese leaders such as Bishop K. H. Ting and Chen Zemin. She argues that, after the Cultural Revolution, the Chinese church needed to stress the message of reconciliation, which includes reconciling the tension between the two sexes. She brings out a dialogical model of interpretation, saying that, while we can use the Bible to examine traditional Chinese culture, there are also liberating elements in Chinese culture to enrich our understanding of the Bible, such as the emphasis on the *yin* in Chinese Taoism.[31]

To strengthen work among women, the National Three-Self Movement and the China Christian Council have established a Commission on Women's Work. The Commission has sponsored women's training and literacy programs at the national and local levels. Today women make up half of all seminary students. But Chen Meilin, an executive of the China Christian Council, points out that some churches, citing the words of Paul, still refuse to ordain women. And even when women are ordained, some churches do not allow women to consecrate the Eucharist. There are few women in decision-making bodies at different levels. Women only made up about 26 percent of the participants of National Chinese Christian Conferences. The Chinese church still has a long way to go in terms of recognizing the full equality and potential of women.[32] Since 1998, the Chinese Christian Church has initiated a project of theological reconstruction, which seeks to elaborate basic Christian beliefs and ethical norms in the national situation and culture in China. The Chinese female leaders feel that the voices of women must be heard and their issues must be an integral part of such a theological reconstruction.

## 5. Women's Body and Sexuality

A noteworthy development in feminist writings in China and Hong Kong is that women have broken the taboo to speak about women's bodies, sexuality, and sexual orientation. Wu Jinzhen, Associate Dean of Yanjing Theological Seminary, writes about women's beauty and women's consciousness, issues seldom addressed in Christian writings in Communist China. She argues that women's hairstyles and dresses have changed during the different periods of modern Chinese history. For example, women dressed almost the same as men did during the Cultural Revolution. Since China embarked on the journey of reform and openness, fashion and beauty have been re-introduced in the national discourse. Because of economic growth and a rising standard of living, middle-class women can afford to adorn themselves and to dress up. Wu notes that, within the churches, some people think that a woman who wears cosmetics or dresses up in a certain way is not spiritual. Wu notes that the quest of young urban women for fashion is not simply a quest for beauty, but the emergence of the individual. It may signify an intensification of women's consciousness as an individual subject, as opposed to the rigid gender roles defined during an earlier generation.[33]

Economic reform and openness to the outside also brought new challenges, as ideas such as sexual revolution, individualism, consumerism, and hedonism were introduced. Today, in the urban Chinese cities, trial marriage, cohabitation, and extramarital sex are no longer something to be marveled at. These new sexual behaviors challenge both traditional Chinese family values and the sexual ethics of the evangelical Chinese churches. Meng Yanling, who teaches at Nanjing Theological Seminary, argues that the church must develop a healthy teaching on sexuality and marriage that values women as equal to men. She cites the creation story in Genesis to argue that women and men are created as equal, mutually helping and complementary. She also says that Paul's teaching on gender relations is sometimes contradictory, as he tried to accommodate the Christian ideals to the culture of his time. For Meng, economic growth and women's participation in the labor market do not solve all women's problems, but they bring new tensions to family life. The instability of modern marriage means that women cannot rely on their husbands forever and must be strong and independent, seeking their own worth.[34]

Female leaders in China and Hong Kong have also paid attention to women who are marginalized because of their sexuality. Wu Jinzhen writes about the "gray women," a term that covers sex workers who serve as mistresses, escorts, and prostitutes. They are called "gray women" because they make their living on the margins of society, often hidden and secretive. Instead of condemning these women, Wu points to the societal structures that have driven them into prostitution and illicit liaisons. She says that the church can help by promoting women's economic equality and women's self-consciousness.[35]

In Hong Kong, gay and lesbian Christians have become more vocal and formed the Blessed Minority Christian Fellowship and demanded their rights. Rose Wu, a heterosexual woman who has worked in solidarity with the sexual minorities, has traced the development of lesbian and gay relationships in China and developed a liberation theology of right relationship. Based on the work of Carter Heyward and Beverly Harrison, she argues that we should embrace sexual minorities as equal members of our family. Although she knows that many churches in Hong Kong do not support her position, she supports same-sex marriages as having the same rights of heterosexual marriages.[36]

As we can see from the above discussion, feminist leaders in the Christian churches in China and Hong Kong are struggling with issues similar to those facing Christian women in Asia and other parts of the world: a long tradition of male dominance in church and society; rapid modernization and social changes; increased participation of women in the public sector; and women's rising consciousness. Modernization and economic growth may afford women more opportunities, which in turn have changed deep-seated attitudes regarding gender relations. Yet such changes also bring new issues not faced before, such as higher rate of divorce, domestic abuse, and the reappearance of the sex industry. Although Western feminist hermeneutics have been introduced to China and feminist theology is now being taught in several seminaries, Chinese feminist leaders caution that they cannot accept this wholesale, but must develop their own feminist theology based on China's political and social conditions. It is encouraging to see that women leaders are writing more frequently on feminist theology and breaking their silence on taboo subjects. As Gao Ying says: "doing feminist theology within the Chinese church and Chinese society is an important and significant part of the historical and worldwide movement for women's equality and liberation. . . . It will enable humanity to be a much better co-creator with God."[37]

## Further Reading

Kwok, Pui-lan, *Chinese Women and Christianity, 1860–1927* (Atlanta, GA: Scholars Press, 1992).
Wong, Angela Wai Ching, *The Poor Woman: A Critical Analysis of Asian Theology and Contemporary Chinese Fiction by Women* (New York: Peter Lang, 2002).

## Endnotes

1. This article is a slightly revised version of the article of Kwok Pui-lan, "Christianity and Women in Contemporary China," *Journal of World Christianity*, Vol 3, No 1 (2009), 1-17.
2. Zhuo Xinping, "China" *Cambridge Dictionary of Christianity* (Cambridge: Cambridge University Press, 2010), 206.
3. See Wallace C. Merwin and Francis P. Jones, eds., *Documents of the Three-Self Movement: Source Materials for the Study of the Protestant Church in Communist China* (New York: National Council of the Churches of Christ in the U.S.A., 1963).
4. Chen Meilin, "The Status and Role of Women in the Growing Church of China," *Chinese Theological Review* 17 (2003): 99.
5. Zhang Yan, "Christianity and the Modern Chinese Women's Movement," *Chinese Theological Review* 11, no. 1 (1996): 76-87.
6. Wang Lixin, *Meiguo chuanjiaoshi yu wan Qing Zhongguo xiandaihua* (American missionaries and modernization of China in late Qing) (Tianjin: Tianjin People's Press, 1997), 225-35.
7. Ma Changlin and Yang Hong, "Zongjiao, jiating, shehu—mianxiang nü Jidutu de xuanjiao—yi *Nüduo, Nuxing, Nüqingnian bao, Funü* wei zhongxin," (Religion, family, society—evangelism toward female Christians—focusing on the *Woman's messenger, the Woman's Star,* the YWCA *Magazine,* and *Women*), *Xingbie yu lishi: Jindai Zhongguo funü yu Jidujiao* (Gender and history: modern Chinese women and Christianity), ed. Tao Feiya (Shanghai: Renmin chuban she, 2006), 22-67.
8. Kwok Pui-lan, *Chinese Women and Christianity, 1860–1927* (Atlanta: Scholars Press, 1992), 167-78.
9. Ding Shujing, "Funü zai jiaohui de diwei" (The position of women in the church), *Nüqingnian* (Y.W.C.A. Magazine) 7, no. 2 (March 1928): 21-25.
10. Kay Ann Johnson, *Women, the Family and Peasant Revolution in China* (Chicago: University of Chicago Press, 1983).

11. Gao Ying, "Women, Feminist Theology, and the Church in China," *Church & Society* 86, no. 5 (May-June 1996): 71.

12. Cao Shengjie, "Feminist Theology and the Chinese Church," *Chinese Theological Review* 15 (2001): 64.

13. Ho Xiaoxin, ed., *Huaren funü shenxue chutan* (Towards a Chinese feminist theology) (Hong Kong: Lutheran Theological Seminary, 1988).

14. The Asian Women's Resource Centre for Culture and Theology published an Asian women's theological journal *In God's Image*, and the Christian Conference of Asia had a women's desk.

15. See the website of the Hong Kong Women Christian Council, http://www.hkwcc.org.hk/public/content.aspx?c=47 (October 5, 2011).

16. Hong Kong Women Christian Council, ed., *Funü muyang yu shifeng* (Ministering women, women in ministry: A conference report on feminist theology in Chinese contexts) (Hong Kong: Hong Kong Women Christian Council, 2005).

17. K. H. Ting, "Religious Liberty in China: My Perspective," in *God Is Love: Collected Writings of Bishop K. H. Ting* (Colorado Springs: Cook Communications Ministries International, 2004), 560.

18. Ting, "A Wide Door for Effective Work Has Opened, and There Are Many Adversaries," in *God Is Love*, 473. See also Philip L. Wickeri, *Seeking the Common Ground: Protestant Christianity, the Three-Self Movment, and China's United Front* (Maryknoll: Orbis Books, 1988).

19. Jiang Peifen, "China," in *A New Beginning: An International Dialogue with the Chinese Church*, ed. Theresa Chu and Christopher Lind (Toronto: Canada China Programme of the Canadian Council of Churches, 1983), 85. Jiang gave this speech in 1981, and unfortunately some of these vices have come back.

20. Ibid., 87.

21. Cao Shengjie, "Chinese Christian Women in Education and Development: Understanding the Compatibility of Faith and Action for Women in a Changing Society," *Church & Society* 86, no. 5 (May-June 1996): 76-81.

22. Cao Shengjie, "The Current Situation in the Chinese Church," *Chinese Theological Review* 16 (2002): 57.

23. Ibid., 57-58.

24. Ibid., 61-62.

25. Rose Wu, "1997 and the Destiny of the Hong Kong People," *In God's Image* 16, no. 2 (1997): 10.

26. Angela Wai Ching Wong, *The Poor Woman: A Critical Analysis of Asian Theology and Contemporary Chinese Fiction by Women* (New York: Peter Lang, 2002).

27. Cao Shengjie, "Feminist Theology and the Chinese Church," *Chinese Theological Review* 15 (2001): 70.

28. Chen Kuanrong, "Women Disciples of Jesus," *Chinese Theological Review* 17 (2003): 76-84.

29. Gao Ying, "Women, Feminist Theology," 69-75.

30. Wang Peng, "On Paul's Prohibitions of Women in 1 Corinthians," *Chinese Theological Review* 15 (2001): 91.

31. Ibid., 99-100.

32. Chen Meilin, "The Status and Role of Women," 98-103.

33. Wu Jinzhen, "Looking for Meaning Beyond Mere Existence—Women and Church Development in China," *Chinese Theological Review* 15 (2001): 82-83.

34. Meng Yanling, "Women, Faith, Marriage: A Feminist Look at the Challenges for Women," *Chinese Theological Review* 18 (2004): 85-100.

35. Wu, "Looking for Meaning," 79-81.

36. Rose Wu, "A Story of Their Own Name: Hong Kong's Tongzhi Culture and Movement," in *Off the Menu: Asian and Asian North American Women's Religion and Theology*, ed. Rita Nakashima Brock et al. (Louisville: Westminster John Knox Press, 2007), 275-92.

37. Gao, "Women, Feminist Theology," 73.

CHAPTER 9

# Mission and Gender Justice from a Korean Protestant Perspective[1]

*Meehyun Chung*

## 1. Introduction

The call to mission is closely related to the act of receiving.[2] The word "mission" derives from the Latin term *mittere*, which means "to (be) sent." More than that, however, the call to mission involves "testifying to the Good News," and certainly not spreading mechanisms of fear and bondage. In order to testify about the Good News it should be primarily received like two Marys did: Mary, the mother of Jesus, received the message of liberation from an angel (Luke 1:25-56). She made it her self-determination to follow the Good News and showed her readiness to believe God. The other Mary, the female disciple of Jesus, received the message of the resurrection from the risen Jesus (John 20:10-18). Proclaiming and missioning are resulting acts of receiving. Proclaiming the Good News is combined with healing actions, which include efforts to reduce the suffering and trauma of those poor in material goods, to free those constrained by hostile power structures, and to cure those obsessed with the fear of not being rich and strong.

The song of Mary and the Easter message as the call to mission through receiving are not only present at the turning points "from death to life," "from anxiety to boldness," "from desperation to hope," and "from sadness to joy," they also represent the empowerment of the voices of the marginalized who, be it due to gender or any other reason, are ignored and shunned. God's call to mission enabled two women with no special institutional power to witness the miracle of Christmas and Easter. Through their calling they were liberated from silence and hidden oppression.

"Mission" is a concept with a thick history and many meanings. In such circumstances, it is inappropriate to either negate or glorify the conflicts that have risen among these meanings. While many Western Europeans now hesitate to use the terms "mission" or "Jesus Christ" people, in the so-called former mission countries, especially in Korea, do not necessarily share this attitude, and live and work positively with such terms on a daily life. While it is important to take seriously the negative impacts of missions, and to reach an understanding and revealing of their "dark sides" within our evaluation of the past, it is also important to underline, and not to diminish positive aspects. The Korean case is also similar. For instance, Christianity brought deliverance for women but with limitations. After the establishment of churches women's work became invisible and new types of bondage were created within church structures.

The goal of this article is not to investigate the problem or strength of Western mission movements in general[3] or in Korea in particular. Rather I would like to articulate the limitation and weakness of women's movements within Korean missions. Thus Korean women could be self-critical and develop new perceptions for women in mission.

## 2. Historical Setting: Beginnings of the Transmission and Appropriation of Protestant Christianity in Korea

Korea is often called "the land of morning calm." It rarely, however, enjoys quiet mornings, and is a fiercely contested country with deep social and political divisions. Japanese colonial rule (1910–1945) and the subsequent partition of the country (1945) have had fundamental and unsettling effects on its society. After the Russian-Japanese war (1904–1905) the USA, Great Britain, Germany, and France agreed on a secret treaty with Japan that legitimized Japanese colonial interests in Korea. Subsequently, in 1910, Japan formally annexed Korea, thus beginning the tragedy that has led to the present divided state of the country.

Protestant Christian mission was initiated in 1884 in Solnae, presently in North Korea, by a Korean named S. Y. Suh. After that followed a wave of missionary initiatives by Protestants from outside the country, paralleling somewhat the path of the foreign Roman Catholic missions during the eighteenth century. First the Presbyterians and the Methodists came, soon followed by Baptists, Anglicans, and other denominations. The first Presbyterian missionary in the country was Horace Grant Underwood (1859–1916), originally from Great Britain, but a resident of the United States prior to his arrival in Korea on April 5, 1885. He arrived with his Methodist friend and fellow missionary, Henry G. Appenzeller (1858–1902), originally from Switzerland.

There are many reasons why the Presbyterian Church grew more vigorously than the Methodist, or the church of any other denomination, but they fall outside the scope of this article. Generally speaking, however, Presbyterians, who now form the majority of Protestants in Korea, emphasized the growth of churches and church structures rather than the social work of hospitals or schools. As a result of these priorities—priorities established and guided from abroad, effectively "made in the USA"—a puritan and fundamentalist Presbyterianism spread throughout Korean society, carrying the imprint of Calvin's theology, however changed or perverted, as it had made its way from Switzerland to Scotland, thence to the USA, and from there to Korea.

Throughout Korean history, women have played a variety of roles in the hierarchies of society and their role was not restricted in the public place; but to summarize quickly, since the thirteenth century, when Confucianism was introduced as the ordering principle, the role of women has been restricted to family and private circles. During the Chosun dynasty (1392–1910), lasting roughly 500 years, Confucianism was both state philosophy and dominant social ideology. During this period women were systematically subordinated to men, losing all the public functions which they had practiced before the introduction of Confucianism.[4]

The arrival of Christianity in Korea led to fundamental changes within the Confucian order. On the positive side, women discovered that according to the gospel they were equal with men before God. Christian missionaries are significant agents in education and health care throughout the world. As well, Christianity contributed considerably to their education: schools for women were established and, by reading the Bible, they learned Korean script. Yet Christianity did not lead to the complete emancipation of women from male domination. Rather, elements of Confucian thought, which continue as a national philosophy and serve as traditional religious ethics, have now been reinforced by a conservative Protestant fundamentalism, and this powerful dynamic is imbedded within the hierarchical, male-dominated practices and constitution of the Presbyterian

Church in Korea. Despite the biblical teachings that emphasize equality among people (cf. Gal 3:28), it must be noted that the mainstream churches are not at all very keen in propagating this liberating element of the gospel. Foreign missionary work has in fact reinforced the traditional dichotomy between female and male domains. The Western patriarchal system of Christianity is combined with local cultural patriarchy.

The first female missionary, Mary F. Scranton (1832–1909), a North-American Methodist, came to Korea in the year 1885. While accompanying her son, who worked as a missionary doctor in Korea, she saw the suffering majority of women and decided to dedicate herself to them. Having a special interest in educating women, she opened a girls' school in 1886, which evolved into Ewha Womans University.[5] She founded it with the help of the last Korean Empress, Queen Min (1851–1895), who was later on brutally assassinated by the Japanese mob.[6] Female missionaries were mainly active in educating women and providing medical services. The efforts of female missionaries to raise the standard of living of all Koreans, both male and female, should not be forgotten or minimized. Many of them dedicated their lives to such work, and some among them, with or without their children, suffered personally due to difficult living conditions, lack of suitable education facilities, and so on.[7] These women sacrificed themselves and the quality of their family life to free Korean women from the restrictions of traditional ways of thinking and acting.

However, there were other missionaries of both genders who lived in luxury and cared primarily for their own interests. They behaved like foreign diplomats and ruling officials, claiming the absolute truth of Christianity and its expression in Western culture. They never intended a gospel indigenous to Korea. Western middle-class Christian lifestyle and culture became the standard of ideal life. As a result, Korean Christians under their influence attached little value to their own culture, and quickly oriented "westerly." Sometimes the role of foreign missionaries, consciously and unconsciously, was and is developing and strengthening the elite groups who worked closely with the missionaries in propagating and strengthening their foreign culture. The majority of poor Koreans at this early period of Korean Christianity were deeply longing for Western affluence and style (clothes, hairstyle, household goods, and so on). Due to the spreading influence and material attractions of Western culture, early Christian Koreans turned into representatives of the Western bourgeoisie.[8] However, the socialist ideal, which had brought some Korean Christian women together to work for social equality and Korean independence, struggled and failed during the 1930s against the ruthless repression of a determined Japanese occupation.

While Korean women have played a decisive role in constructing the church, after its establishment they lost their public functions within it, as also happened within early Christianity in general. After the institutionalization of churches, women lost their official status in the church hierarchy. As soon as the Korean churches became better established, women were marginalized. As it had happened so often in church history, women did the diaconal work while men took over the leading functions. Women found themselves expelled from leading positions and only men retained executive power.

The commitment of "Bible women" in the churches in Korea was more important to the spread of Christianity than the success of the so-called "Nevius method."[9] Due to the cultural convention of separating women and men in public, it was impossible for foreign male missionaries to visit Korean women at private domains and distribute Bibles, or to tell them the Good News.[10] Thus, it was the efforts of the many nameless Korean women evangelists, reaching out to other women that proved to be effective. Or, to grasp the historical dynamic more accurately, it was the women evangelists who built the foundation upon which the Nevius method could succeed. The Nevius method was no longer liberating for women but, critically examining, a new version of confinement and bondage. Thus the Korean church became, and remains, male dominated. In case of the process for female ordination, it took more than fifty years in the major denominations of Protestant churches to ordain. Even though female ordination is possible now, it is still not practiced generally.

The beginning and the growth of the Korean Pentecostal churches must be viewed in this context as well.[11] Pentecostal churches in general recognize and underline women's leadership because they believe the charisma of the Holy Spirit does not exclude women. Jashil Choi,[12] the mother-in-law of Yonggi Cho, and Yonggi Cho,[13] the former pastor of Yoido Full Gospel Church, attended a Bible School before they were planting the church. A first church service was celebrated in Choi's flat and in the year that followed a so-called tent community was established. It was a very simple and cheap form making the tent a place of worship. From the beginning both of them stressed the importance of healing the body. Then the congregation grew so rapidly, that it counted over 100,000 members after a few decades and had to move to other quarters. In 1973 it moved into the present building. Today it is the largest Pentecostal church in Korea with 750,000 registered members.[14] While Jashil Choi, as a woman, worked really hard in general, her influence on church structure was small. Her son-in-law, Yongi Cho, was much more recognized officially and anchored structurally in the church. In other words, Jashil Choi did a lot of preparatory work that was never acknowledged enough. Her experience was similar to that of the first missionary in the Gospel of John, Mary. She had been ordered by Jesus himself to pass on the Good News of Easter. But only after male followers began to carry out this assignment, the matter became official. This continues unto this day, and thus even in Pentecostal churches and many other denominations the majority of clericals are men, while you find women mainly as leaders of Prayer Mountains. In these prayer houses[15] you find a few conventionally or structurally firmly anchored forms. Flexibility is much more common than in other denominations. While women were not successful in finding their position in established congregations and in an urban environment they succeeded better in becoming leaders of prayer houses in rural areas and on mountains. There is a certain affinity between prayer houses and shamanist rituals concerning the form of appearance and the kind of leadership.

Korea was not colonized by European or American forces, but rather by the non-Christian country of Japan. Therefore, one does not find the same resentment against Christian colonial power as one does elsewhere. Trust in the Christian God was not initially related to submissiveness to a great worldly power. Yet, as a result of the widespread success of the American missions, in my opinion Christian submission to God has become linked with submission to the dominant ruling power. Christian power and the fear of and trust in God have become associated with the fear of and trust in the USA. Fundamentalist and closed-minded conservative Christians in both Korea and America support this tendency, although it is destructive of Korean self-determination and impedes Korean political independence.

Most foreign missionaries during Japanese colonial rule, reflecting fundamentalist leanings, opposed Korean national political awareness and those movements which aimed at the political independence of Korea. They stressed political abstinence and subordination to governmental authorities, in effect encouraging the acceptance of Japanese colonial rule. In this way, the strength of Korean native opposition to occupation was directly weakened through the spread of the Protestant missions. Politics is certainly not the primary task of church and mission. Yet in emulation of the prophetic tradition, and in a sense of advocacy, mission can—for the sake of worldwide peace—contribute to a deepening awareness of the nature of sociopolitical questions, and proclaim statements that support social justice.

## 3. Case Study on a Shadow Side of Women in Mission: the Case of Helen K. Kim[16]

A serious public debate broke out in Korea in 1999, when Ewha University controversially, and unsuccessfully, attempted to endow a prize named after Helen K. Kim. During the twentieth century, Kim (1899–1970) was the most prominent Korean woman both within her own country and on the international stage. She was a true pioneer of the women's movement,[17] the first to earn a doctorate and the first Korean president of what was then Ewha College, now the world's largest women's university. She was also first woman who has been chosen outside of the United States to write the order of worship for the World Day of Prayer in 1930. She garnered international attention through her many activities and works, one example being her participation at the International Mission Council in Jerusalem in 1928. According to the report of a German participant, she was immediately recognized for her engagement and demeanor.[18] Due to an early education with American missionaries and further studies in the USA, her English was excellent, allowing her to eloquently share her passion for women's issues. Among the few representatives from Asia she quickly won attention for her commitment to the women's emancipation. In the plenary, speaking as a representative of Korean women, she said:

> The secular system of life in Korea, influenced largely by the teachings of Confucius, fully recognizes the instrumental value of women in the maintenance of home and society. But only when the life and message of Christ were brought to Korea did the women find themselves to have intrinsic values. Christ has shown clearly both in His life and in His teachings that to God one human personality, whether it be man's or woman's, bond or freeman's, is just as valuable as any other. Christian young women, and men as well, of Korea have learned this lesson and are diligently seeking to apply this teaching consistently to their lives. . . . I think Christ would pity us women, if we still are timid

and hesitate about bearing witness to Him in all the walks of life, not only in domestic life, but also in the industrial, commercial, political and international life of humanity. I think He would say to us: "Women, have I not freed you? Why are you still so timid? Go forth courageously with my message into all the phases of human life. They need you there, and there you have a distinct contribution to make at this stage of human society."[19]

With perfect clarity she pleaded for the emancipation and deliverance of women: "Christ showed clearly in his life as in his teachings that, before God any human personality is as valuable as any other, whether man or woman, whether servant or free. . . . While Christ never forbids any woman to witness to him, nowadays women are not allowed in many of the churches to preach from the pulpit, not because they lack faith or fervor, but just because they are women."[20] Beyond that, she showed courage when she contradicted the Japanese bishop who had denied racism in Japan:

> Then Miss Kim asked the bishop, whether he did not know that from the eight ministries in the Korean government only one was directed by a Korean subject, and even this but nominally. Whether he did not know, that among the 18,458 members of the police force in Korea only 7,337 were Korean and all of them in low ranks only, and that the situation was similar in the railways. Whether he did not know that, when Korea suffered an earthquake, Japan did not even utter one word of compassion. Wilson's fourteen points were not abided by. To the day there was no justice for suppressed peoples. This speech took a few minutes only but it caused us so much to think about! How deep was the insight into the plight of a nation yearning for freedom and independence, of a Christendom fighting for the highest values![21]

While Helen K. Kim opposed Japanese politics in Jerusalem, her reputation today is tarnished due to public statements she made in Korea during the 1930s and 1940s; statements allegedly made before young men and women that have been interpreted as willfully supporting Japanese imperial ambitions and recruiting young soldiers and so-called "comfort women" for the cause.[22] During the Asian-Pacific war (1937–1945), Japan repeatedly violated international laws while initiating brutal violence against both men and women. Among these egregious violations was sex slavery: approximately 200,000 Asian women from the Philippines, Taiwan, China, Thailand, Indonesia, and Malaysia, but mostly from Korea, baited with false promises of work, were transported to military centers where they "served" the Japanese soldiers. This enforced prostitution was systematically organized as a conscious policy by the Japanese government.[23]

Kim's reputation is in dispute because her stand against the Japanese colonial power was not clear. In fact, her stand was clearly ambivalent. Some charge her with collaboration, the main evidence being her support for Japanese military policy. It can be assumed, however, that she was under immense pressure from the Japanese government and that her actions had, as their main aim, the protection of Ewha College. Perhaps Kim believed that her influence in getting women into positions of power within Korean society justified her political position regarding Japanese occupation. Modernization and enlightenment were more important to her than national integrity, and her priority was the education of elite women. The question whether she sufficiently considered the importance of class differences in her feminist work is germane. In her position as a leading member of various bodies she pleaded for the integration of Korean society within Japanese society, and showed a clear pro-Japan tendency in many of her statements.[24] After being elected president of Ewha College in 1939, a time of increasing brutality as the Japanese military attempted to recruit soldiers, laborers, and sex slaves to further war ends, her mindset became yet more fixed.[25]

After the national deliverance from Japanese occupation in 1945, Helen K. Kim became strongly anti-Communist, this time in order to win the support of the American provisional government to help her change Ewha College into Ewha University. Kim's relations with the USA, however, at least as represented by its churches, had always been excellent. This was especially true of the Methodist Church, which had been of direct personal assistance to her since its early years of mission, and which had founded Ewha—an institution central to Kim's life, which did, indeed, become a center of feminism.

The privileged and influential Korean elite under anti-Communist American rule, post–1945, was the same, more or less, as the privileged elite under Japanese rule.[26] This partially reflected educational opportunities abroad, mainly in the USA. These social elite, under both regimes, did not oppose dictatorial rule, but rather benefitted from it. Only at the end of a long process of democratization was the reality of this social history publicly acknowledged in South Korea. Only since the achievement of a truly civil, non-military government during the late 1980s has such a critique been allowed to publicly flourish.

This parallels, more or less, the evolution of feminist discourse, as the average woman in the early feminist movement in Korea was located in the upper middle class. The aims of these women were freedom from the limitations of traditional thought and the modernization of society. The problems of the common people, which can only be addressed through genuine grassroots justice in a community oriented society, were neglected. To advance an elite minority, the powerless majority suffered. This was the result of one-dimensional thinking and a top-down approach toward social change.

To sum up, it must be stressed that Western missionary activities did indeed help with the emancipation of Korean women and the modernization of the country in a Western direction, yet this was an incomplete initiative, without the full recognition and empowerment of all women in the whole society as well as of other marginalized groups.

By my case study I not merely intend to criticize Helen Kim's glorious achievement, but my concern is to find out in a constructive way what and how we can learn from her case. Helen Kim and her career were not limited only to domestic space; she took the public space as a woman. In that point Korean women gained dignity through the American mission's work because they got a chance for education and found self-value. However, it depends on the interpretation of how she used her power on this public space. She also took over the presidency of the college as the first Korean woman from an American woman. Self-determination as a Korean was guaranteed in this area, in comparison to many other mission activities, where the hegemonic power still remained in mission's donor churches and agencies.

Feminist liberation ideas and practices shouldn't be limited to a certain elite group. Powerless groups should be empowered by feminist groups too. Otherwise the feminist movement could remain an unbalanced movement just for a minor elite group.

## 4. Conclusions and Recommendations

What kind of aspects in mission should be underlined from women and gender perspective? What then is the task of Korean Christian mission in the twenty-first century? Below, I try to find ways to answer these questions and to pursue new perceptions on them.[27]

### 4.1 Gender and Mission

Gender justice is still an important agenda to develop. However, feminism and gender justice without cross class

fertilization are one-dimensional and are an unbalanced movement for liberation. Traditional mission work is an example
of gender discrimination and segregation. While "inner" mission—diaconal works and nursing—were considered mainly
female responsibilities during the nineteenth and twentieth centuries, "external" mission and *oikumene* were considered male
responsibilities. Everything related to "inner" was considered
passive, female, and mundane, in stark contrast to everything
related to "external," considered active, male, and something
special. As a matter of fact, in established Christian traditions,
mission was a task for men while lesser yet important tasks
were declared women's duties. Women's work was not considered, in itself, independent.[28] It was considered self-evident that
mission was a male responsibility, while necessary and related
"minor" labors were women's responsibilities.[29] Women were
not treated as self-reliant personalities, nor officially involved
in decision making, although at the same time it was taken for
granted that they would assume great responsibility and perform demanding jobs, for example, running schools, medical
centers, and orphanages. Needless to say, women were and are
to a large extent the backbone of church and mission.[30]

Since the beginning of the twentieth century, single Western
women have been sent out to the so-called mission fields with
distinct autonomous responsibilities. They no longer only traveled as wedded companions ("mission brides"[31]) and they
attained positions they would not have achieved in Western
society at that time. However, traditional missionary work
supported obedient and diligent women rather than a feminist movement. A quote from the director of Basel Mission,
Karl Hartenstein (1894–1952), emphasized this aspect, "In any
case the woman mission work may not be connected with the
emancipation movement of the woman. The independence and
development of the gifts of the women must be established in
the welfare and social work, but not in the feminist movement,
which has an anti-religious root."[32] He identified emancipation
with anti-Christianity.

In the case of Korean it is almost the same: Western patriarchy
traveled with the missions and was allowed to entwine with traditional Confucian patriarchy, wherein both were strengthened.[33]
Thus, in the so-called mission areas, two patriarchal traditions
exist, mutually self-reinforcing. While some Western missionary
women gained an agency and task within the mission field, who
were still denied to practice in their own countries, this was
not the case for women of color. The ethnocentricity of Western

Christian mission created an environment where white mission women, as representatives of a superior Christian culture, were symbols of emancipation, while women of color, along with their respective cultures, were devalued and demeaned.

Because emancipation through mission was most often effective within the middle class or the elite, the pressing problems of the common people were neglected. Thus, the small elitist groups of native women actively supported by women missionaries were usually incapable of practicing solidarity with the yet more marginalized.[34] Women's movement shouldn't be based on the vulnerability of others. The discussion of women and gender in mission should not be limited to a discussion of sexual justice; a broader, more formative discussion is required, correlating gender to all aspects of social, economic, cultural and political life.[35] Conceptual categories such as ethnicity, class, sexual orientation, age, religion and so on, along with gender, have inclusive as well as exclusive functions, and effective analysis of any of them can only be undertaken within a thorough and encompassing critique of power structures.

Today Korea is the second largest country sending missionaries to different parts of the world. Now Korean patriarchy is also exported through these activities. Women still play a role as traveling wedded companion wives. Potentiality of women, independency and capability of women are not asked. Nevertheless, mission should contribute to reduce international stereotyping masculinity and femininity, to evaluate a value system to find invisible potential goodness and to share different gifts between men and women. The desired approach to gender in mission is context based and inclusive of color, not simply a white ideology or Korean ideology that is influenced by a white ideology exported to the other continents. To strengthen such awareness is to strengthen self-esteem, critical thinking, and self-determination. In order to achieve it, we need to read and interpret the Bible with new eyes and bodies.

## 4.2 *Redressing the World: The Economic Justice And Mission*

In the twenty-first century, where women play a significant role for decision making and leadership, mission should be considered in the world's economic systems. It could be achieved through reflecting on solidarity with marginalized people. In about 1882 the USA, Germany, Russia, and France urged Korea to open its harbors to limited trade. During the period of this enforced opening, missionaries—both male and female—began entering the country. It was, in the early years, difficult for Koreans to differentiate between mission, cannon, and warships. But in spite of popular reservations about the constellation of world politics, Christianity spread quickly. Many missionaries served with devotion in very humble circumstances, but it is necessary to recognize and critically evaluate the prestige and profit of the majority of missionaries who lived in luxurious circumstances, perhaps the most famous being H. G. Underwood (1859–1916), the so-called "missionary millionaire."[36] Many among them possessed and managed mines, and the God of Western Christianity was strongly associated with material blessings. For this reason it was difficult to recognize structural sin; affluence was glorified and poverty cursed. The yearning for Western wealth, as represented by these missionaries, proved strong, and native cultural values waned.

In the twenty-first century, it is mission's responsibility to play a meaningful role in the development of an alternative globalization. Missions have, in the past, played an active part in creating the presently unjust worldwide economic system, and their reorientation is more than important. Even partial restoration for what was destroyed during colonial rule and system can be a significant sign of responsibility. The Kenyan theologian Jesse N.K. Mugambi raised critical question:

> Some Christians, as individuals, have participated in and lobbied for the "polishing" of global capitalism, not for its "abolition." As institutions, churches in the North Atlantic are an integral part of the system, not separate from it. How then, can Christians in the North Atlantic, as beneficiaries of this system, share a common faith in Christ with their destitute counterparts in Africa, Asia and southern America?[37]

The regeneration of the original wealth with which God blessed the Global South is paramount. Poverty caused by the capitalist system must be reduced. In the global grip of neo-liberalism, only few profit while the majority suffers one crisis after another. Unfortunately, Korean mission methods support this system instead of supporting a healing process.

Needless to say there are many missionaries who are dedicating their life for serving people under difficult life conditions. But the problem of Korean mission is described as pure imitation and repetition of European and American mission methods and styles in the previous century due to ignoring the local cultures and religious backgrounds. Korean churches are also doing many charity works in different parts of the world. However, there is a huge lack of cooperation with the local churches and theological seminaries. In other areas where Islam or Buddhism as major religions dominate and Christian mission is officially prohibited, it is common for Koreans to organize short-term mission projects in a provocative way, which is not helpful for sustainable development of church and theology. Ecumenical cooperation is more than urgent in order to use finances more justly, transparently, and efficiently.

The millennium development goals[38] are not merely a catchphrase. Poverty reduction was always one of concerns of mission. A healthy mission, then, would promote a worldwide ecumenical Christian community as an instrument of advocacy for the voiceless, the marginalized and the dispossessed, and would commit to sustainable development, rather than act primarily as an agency of charity.[39] Mission would offer a new framework in which to promote the "caring" economy, quite distinct from "Cowboy" capitalism.[40]

## 4.3 Unity Through a Reconciliation of Pluralities: Peacemaking as New Perception of Mission

Cold War ideology and anti-Communism still remain strongly in Korean Christianity. But mission in Korea should focus on peacemaking. The partitioning of the mission field, executed with blind enthusiasm and zeal,[41] resulted in a splintered Korean church rampant with competing denominations. Denominationalism, tribalism, family centrism, and salvation egoism are all factors that separate people from one another. Thus, the Korean church has become a paradigmatic example of the fragmentation of Protestantism. The denominational division of the Korean Protestant churches is not only a domestic problem within Korea, but also a problem in the so-called mission field. Rivalry among churches and Christians work out as cannibalism. Moreover, due to lack of an ecumenical mindset there is also a lack of cooperation among different denominations. Interreligious cooperation is beyond concern. It remains only a zeal and diligence for gaining "unreached people" or believers of other faiths. The others are just treated as targets and objects, as unreached people for conversion.

One of the most important challenges faced by a holistic mission in Korea, as elsewhere in the world, is the spreading of Christian ethics, especially to overcome dualism and community within a vibrant ethos of the common good. Mission didn't only bring the message of liberation, but also the mechanics of fear. The blind claims for a Christian "absolute truth" have strengthened a dualistic mode of thinking, allowing unrestrained dualistic imaginations of blessing and curse, friend or enemy. Whoever lives in fear of hell is not easily healed from feelings of guilt or fears of punishment. This religious intimidation, which hinders the integration of both individual and society, must be critically evaluated: it encourages blind acceptance of unjust social political systems, and prepares its believers to make villains of others both within and outside the church. Thus, it becomes extremely difficult to withstand the lies and misrepresentations of destructive and deadly powers. It has become more important than ever to overcome a culture of death and dissociation, and to promote a culture of reconciliation, on the side of life. Our historical memory of the negative aspects of mission should be investigated and confessed, in order to avoid idealizing one extreme within a dualistic pattern of thought, but similarly, we must investigate the transformative energy that is clear within the heritage of Christian mission.[42] By overcoming an obsession with proselytizing to capture souls, by seeking to create unity within an active pluralism, mission can discover a new integrity within a new vision.[43]

The scar of the Second World War and Japanese colonialism still remain in the Korean peninsula in many different ways.[44] Mission is an act for healing and a delivering sign of hope, encouraging people for life. Enthusiasm of mission shouldn't be misused neither as manipulative instrument for church quantity growth, nor drawing attention to escape domestic problems. Blind anti-Communism combined with colonial heritage and a triumphalist idea of Christianity in South Korea should be corrected.

In our century, mission can serve to free us from a power-obsessed, rapacious ideology, and release the affluent from their fear of losing hegemonic supremacy, while strengthening the benefits of integrative thought and holistic action. In the case of the Korean peninsula, reunification and peace are the most necessary priorities of an urgent mission. It shouldn't be understood merely as absorption of North Korea from South Korea through capitalism. Frequently, reunification means to surrender their socialist vision and status. Since the Korean War, the Korean peninsula is rocked by the hostility between the governments of both Koreas.[45] The Korean War was even a substitute war for super powers during the Cold War era. Conflicts, tension, and military provocation remain among people. The tragic experiences, devastating effects of war and its impact on people's mind and society shouldn't be repeated. The 1953 Armistice Agreement should be replaced with a Peace Treaty[46] which will ensure security and peace not only in the Korean Peninsula, but also in the North East Asia region and furthermore the whole world.

In many other parts of the world in the twenty-first century, one of the greatest problems is islamophobia, while the Korean peninsula still suffers from ideological conflicts of the Cold War. The commonality of the two phenomena is the fear of others and dualism to demonize others. However, the message of Jesus allows us to listen to one another with compassion, creating larger spaces in which others may find the freedom to speak, so that we will no longer be repelled by difference, and fear of the other no longer delays peaceful coexistence.

## 4.4 Final Remarks

Since Korea experienced colonialism, war, military dictatorship, and democratization processes, Korean people could understand other people in the Global South where people have similar experiences. Moreover, Korean culture is based on agriculture, which is also very similar to the cultural backgrounds of other majority countries of the Global South. On the other hand, through technical development and modernization it is easy to relate to developed countries. A high educational level, culture of preservation like *Kimchi*, which are Korean fermented pickled vegetables and *Ondol*, which is a Korean system of under floor heating are helping to prepare for the future. Coldness through north continental influences and hotness from the Pacific Ocean let people adjust to both climates. Script culture, which is related to the Global North in general as well as oral culture, which is related to the Global South are combined with Korean cultural heritage. So Korea has had these both aspects and can make connections between cultures. Due to geographical conditions Korea suffered in history. But for the same reason Korea could play a role as a bridge maker between the North and the South.[47]

Frequently ecumenism in Korea is understood as a pro-Communist ideology or liberal ideology, as if mission and evangelism were not a matter of ecumenism. Usually mission is only emphasized in evangelical denominations as legitimate strategy for Christianity. Of course it depends on the perception of mission. If it is only understood as proselytism, there is no future oriented dimension. To transform our understanding and to find a new perception of mission is very important. In fact there are weaknesses and strengths of the ecumenical line and the evangelical line as well. The ecumenical denominations underlined mostly social activities and the desire of individual faith but matters of spirituality were ignored. In order to pursue a new perception of mission it is important to remember the combination of these two streams of individual salvation and social salvation. Issues of social justice are not exclusive concerns of ecumenical line, as individual evangelism is not the monopoly of evangelical line.[48] Evangelical line and ecumenical line should learn mutually and listen to each other toward pursuing new perceptions of mission in changing landscapes and moving together toward life.

Mission can play a positive, integrating role in public life, helping people to live together harmoniously during a period of cultural and religious pluralism. While, in the recent past, the quantitative growth of Christianity was a primary concern, to find profound definition of mission and awareness of a new role in neo-colonialist period, is demanded. It can help to perform more mature Christianity. To me, personally, this maturity would reflect, and be rooted within, mutual learning aimed at the sharing of benevolence and goodness among the peoples of all continents. It is important to deeply grasp the relations of mutuality and interdependence. Mission must no longer mean expansion and conquest; rather its task must be justice, peace, and the integrity of creation. It is an empowerment among people and between creatures with the aim of preserving life together. Gender justice means to recognize the value of others and to build up new value systems. It could be applied for mission.

To acknowledge former mistakes does not reflect a loss of trust in the gospel. Rather, we need to discover, or invent, a variety of postcolonial approaches; new methods of thinking that multiply, and do not reduce, encounters between diverse subjects, each with agency. This implies that all cultural, philosophic, and religious ideas must be weighed and interpreted from within their own cognitive perspectives. To change our value system—to create new attitudes toward one another, and to the other creatures with which we share the earth, and to the earth itself—is demanding. In applying postcolonial insight we can—in the East as in the West, in the South as in the North—develop

Christianity in new ways.[49] In this sense, mission is both possible and necessary!

"Awake, O north wind; and come thou south; blow upon my garden, that the spices thereof may flow out. Let my beloved come into his garden and eat his precious fruits." (Song of Sol. 4:16 KJV)

## 5. Questions for Discussion

1. What are the implications of women's movements for the future, if also women themselves are not free from power struggle and failed empowering other marginalized groups? How do we evaluate power and how can power be used differently without imitating patriarchal patterns?

2. What kind of impact on women's empowerment can you find in your community? What kind of impact and activities of mission could be used globally and locally for urgent social economic justice issues?

3. Is Christianity a vehicle for political liberation and transformation or does it still create other bondages of oppression? How could mission and evangelization be used not as triumphalistic ideology, but as a tool for peacemaking?

## Further Reading

Jesse N. K. Mugambi, "The Modern Christian Missionary Movement as an Antecedent of Globalization," in *Theologies and Cultures. Ecumenism: Towards a Prophetic Reconstruction.* Formosa Christianity and culture research centre, M. P. Joseph, ed., Vol. VII, No.1, (June 2010): 107-125.

## Endnotes

1. This article is a revised and enlarged version of the article of Meehyun Chung: "Mission possible! Toward a new perception of mission," *Madang. International Journal of Contextual Theology in East Asia* Nr. 13 (2010).

2. It is important, and necessary, for those sharing the reformed Protestant perspective to re-evaluate mission, and in particular the value of "receiving." Both the Catholic mission since the sixteenth century and the Protestant mission since the nineteenth have proceeded with the same mentality: North American and European Christian churches send material help to non-European people whose role it is to thankfully receive. This is not a conversation among equals, but a hierarchical relationship rooted in dependency, most obviously so within the economic sphere. Thus, Euro-American Christian culture presents itself as high value while non-Euro-American culture is systematically devalued. Instead of true exchange, we have a mechanical dualism of greater and lesser. The theology within *Missio Dei* helps to correct this attitude, as God is both the cause and the subject of the mission, helping to

minimize the arrogance and pride inherent within a hierarchical paradigm of mission. All Christians are called to contribute as instruments of God to God's mission, and all humans equally receive God's grace. Before any missionary ever thought of mission, God was present, sending out the good news. Recognizing this allows one to overcome the systemic injustice that flows from subject-object relationships among people. Receiving is an action that must go both ways, subject to subject, to remain positive. We can see, too, that giving is related to hospitality, an important value received by the giver, and an important action within the reality of population migration. In the changing landscape of global Christianity, it is appropriate to emphasize values of receiving that go far beyond material goods, and would include the nonmaterial values, such as spiritual solidarity and shared prayer.

3. For instance, how the middle-class white feminism in the nineteenth century influenced British missionary work, cf. Susan Thorne, "Missionary-Imperial Feminism," in *Gendered Missions. Women and Men in Missionary Discourse and Practice*, ed. Mary T. Huber and Nancy C. Lutkenhaus (Ann Arbor: The University of Michigan Press, 1999), 39-65.

4. The only public practice left to women was Shamanism. Although shamans lacked social recognition and were among the lowest social class, they could, at least, execute their duties in public. Yet this does not mean that they were emancipated. The shamans lived with the people, solving everyday problems and giving comfort in their own way. They played an important role, mainly among women, but their effects were not all positive. Shamanism, as it is actually practiced, is closely connected to family centrism, private domain and material blessing, lacking developed social ethics, although this was at its beginning one of its aims.

5. Ewha Womans University is one of the world's most successful mission histories. Compared to other mission schools and universities, it is a well-developed and mature institution which currently educates 20,000 female students in a broad range of faculties; http://www.ewha.ac.kr/english/ (July 23, 2011).

6. Queen Min wanted to open Korea to Western culture and modernism, and communicated to that end with the foreign missionaries and diplomats of her time. She named the school Ewha, referring to the flower of the pear, as many blossomed in the area of the first building.

7. A building and cemetery were established during the centennial of the Korean Protestant Church to honor the lives and work of foreign missionaries; http://www.yanghwajin.net/ (July 23, 2011).

8. See Soonkyung Park, "The Korean Nation and the Problem of Mission," therein: *Re-unification and Christianity* (Seoul: Hangil, 1986), 159.

9. See ibid., 99. This method, named after the American Presbyterian missionary John Livingston Nevius (1829–1893), aimed, from the very beginning, at the active participation of native Christians in evangelizing their compatriots. New proselytes were normally admitted to baptism only if they brought at least their wife but, wherever possible, even more candidates. Nevius "emphasized especially the importance of self-propagating, self-governing and self-supporting churches. Bible study, strict discipline of believers, cooperation with other Christian groups and 'general helpfulness where possible in the economic life of the people' [...]. His principles so shaped the Protestant Church in Korea, that much missionary work as well as local church leadership and organization follow his original design to this day." (From an article about Nevius in G. Anderson, ed., *Biographical Dictionary of Christian Mission*,

(Grand Rapids: William B. Eerdmans Publishing Company, 1998), 490. It should be noted though that while independence was encouraged in matters of spreading the gospel and financial support, it was suppressed in matters of Church leadership.

10. With the same pattern Catholic mission happened through nuns instead of priests. Cf. "The History of Olivetan Benedictine Sisters of Busan," which was started in Manju 1931; http://www.osboliv.or.kr/ (July 23, 2011).

11. Cf. Meehyun Chung, Pneumatology: Can the Holy Spirit be manipulated? (unpublished)

12. S. Jashil Choi, *Wunder in Korea* (Karlsruhe: Verlag Missionswerk Der Weg zur Freude, 1981).

13. http://davidcho.fgtv.com/ (August 15, 2010).

14. S. Edinburgh 2010. Witnessing to Christ Today. Vol. II, ed. Daryl Balia and Kirsteen Kim, (London: Regnum, 2010), 233f. For a more detailed historical development of this church see: Younghoon Lee, *The Holy Spirit Movement in Korea. It's Historical and Theological Development* (Oxford: Regnum, 2009) 91-117.

15. Usually it is located on mountains, so the houses are called Prayer Mountains.

16. Cf. Meehyun Chung, "Mission Impossible!? Zwischen Evangelisation und Emanzipation in Südkorea," in *Zeitschrift für Mission* Jg. 1-2 (2006): 147-153.

17. Helen K. Kim was, literally, a pioneer in many ways, but especially in what concerned the new role of women. A nice photo of her, taken in Marseille in 1928 on her way to Jerusalem, shows how quickly she adjusted to modernization. She dressed the modern Korean way and wore short hair, which, at the same time, reflected the Western style of the twenties. Other Korean women, and even pious European Christian women, had long hair bound in a chignon. In later years, however she changed her style, wore long hair and dressed in traditional Korean clothes with the aim of strengthening Korean national identity.

18. Cf. Martin Schlunk, ed., *Von den Höhen des Ölberges* (Basel: Ev. Missionsverlag, 1929), 62.

19. Reports of the Meeting of the International Missionary Council at Jerusalem, Easter 1928, Bd.I., 372, quoted by Karl-Fritz Daiber, "Begegnung mit einer Unbekannten. Helen Kim auf der Tagung des Internationalen Missionsrates 1928 in Jerusalem, Reports 1," in *Zeitschrift für Mission* Jg. 1-2 (2006), 144.

20. Ibid., 78f. (translated into English by Ernst Schmid).

21. Ibid., 81f.

22. She followed the Japanese colonial policy of the time and renamed herself Yamagi Kasran. Some of her articles display a very strong pro-Japanese attitude, supporting participation in the Japanese holy war and imperialism; cf. Yamagi Kasran, "We Provide so that Others Might Work," in *Chokwang*, Dec., 1943, 56; Yamagi Kasran, "Conscription and the Determination of Korean women," in *Shinsidae*, Dec., 1942, 28-29.

23. At first this subject was never publicly mentioned in Korea, as the loss of virginity among unmarried young women was considered shameful and unmentionable. There is even a very coarse swear word, used against women, which had originally been coined for women returning from the Mongolian Empire in the twelfth century, and then used again in the seventeenth century against women returning from China, who, it was considered, had offended

the honor of their families and the nation. Although innocent of any guilt, the abused women were forced into silence, unable to express their suffering or to bring the historical truth to public attention. It was only during the 1980s that women, mainly Christian women, began to openly address this subject. In 1992, the Korean Council for Women Recruited by Japan for Military Sex Slavery—a non-denominational, interreligious and ecumenical initiative—was established. It now unites thirty-seven women's groups; www.womenandwar.net (July 22, 2011). During the following year, at the Conference on Human Rights in Vienna, the problem of Japan's military sex slavery was brought to world attention for the first time. And every Wednesday since 1992 there has been a peaceful demonstration in front of the Japanese embassy in Seoul, South Korea's capital, expressing the Council's demands that the Japanese government should admit and apologize for its crime of military sex slavery; that the full dimension of military sex slavery shall be made public; that the victims be recognized through commemorative plaques; that the victims and their families be paid indemnity; that the historical reality of military sex slavery be included in school books to inform the younger generations; and that the responsible criminals should be held to account and punished. In 2005, in connection with the 60th anniversary of the end of the war, a major campaign was initiated in Korea appealing to the Japanese government to address this historical wrong. The United Nations and the International Labour Organization were urged to summon the Japanese government and asked that it officially apologizes and offers compensation to the victims. The UN and ILO were asked not to accept Japan as a member of the UN Security Council as long as it refused to confront its past. Until this day the Japanese government has not officially apologized, nor has it recompensed the victims. Hush money has been offered to the "Asian Women's Fund," but the majority of the victims of forced military prostitution did not agree to such an inappropriate solution and rejected it.

24. In her autobiography she recognized her pro-Japanese actions during this period, even though they may have been forced upon her. Suffering from sore eyes, she seems to have viewed this as punishment. Cf. Helen K. Kim, *The Small Life in the Light* (Seoul: Ewha University Press 1999), 163f., 174f.

25. Her name is included in *The Dictionary of Collaborators*, compiled by a group of scholars (Research on Collaborationist Activists), released in November 2009. Cf. *The Dictionary of Collaborators* (Seoul: Institute for Research in Collaborationist Activists, 2009).

26. These phenomena happened in many other countries, including Germany and South Africa. Those who participated in oppositional movements, and frequently their children, missed out on better educational opportunities. The activities were an impediment to advancing within society. Promotion across social classes is difficult in any society, and although Truth Committees have been established in many countries to move toward greater openness and justice, it is extremely difficult to offset the lasting effect of an established hegemonic elite, that seeks to benefit from the new situation. Cf. Karl Rössel, "Die Fahne hoch...!" Die faschistische "Internationale" von Buenos Aires bis Shanghai, in; Iz3w, May/June 2009, 21.

27. Cf. Meehyun Chung, "Vertrauen auf das Evangelium unter den Bedingungen des Neukolonialismus," in *Mission Erfüllt? Edinburgh 1910 – 100 Jahre Weltmission* (Hamburg: Missionshilfe Verlag, 2009), 103-110.

28. A quote from inspector J. F. Josenhans of Basel Mission in the nineteenty century confirms this, "Women are but an impediment to mission."

Waltraud Ch. Haas, *Erlitten und erstritten. Der Befreiungsweg von Frauen in der Basler Mission 1816–1966* (Basel: Basileia, 1994), 31.

29. Cf. Christine Keim, "Mission und Menschenbild—eine weibliche Perspektive," in *Zeitschrift für Mission* Jg. 1-2 (2006), 51ff.

30. Cf. Dana L. Robert, *Christian Mission: How Christianity Became a World Religion*. (Malden/ Oxford: Wiley-Blackwell, 2009).

31. Cf. Dagmar Konrad, *Missionsbräute. Pietistinnen des 19. Jahrhunderts in der Basler Mission* (Berlin: Waxmann, 2001).

32. Christine Keim, *Frauenmission und Frauenemanzipation: eine Diskussion in der Basler Mission im Kontext der frühen ökumenischen Bewegung (1901–1928)* (Münster: Lit, 2005), 97.

33. Patriarchy does not merely mean biological male dominance, but includes, more generally, the ideology of rule and attitudes of dominance.

34. One clear example is the case of Helen K. Kim, mentioned above.

35. In the World Missionary Conference, which was held in 2010 in Edinburgh, the number of female delegates has increased significantly compared to 1910. There was a transversal theme on Women in Mission and Gender. Nevertheless, in my opinion, the women of color and indigenous women did not have sufficient space and time in the plenary sections to let their voices be heard. In that sense, the issue of "mission and power" should be developed more intensely. Cf. Edinburgh 2010, *Witnessing to Christ today*, Vol. II, ed. Daryl Balia (et.al) (Oxford: Regnum Books International, 2009–2010), 86-102.

36. See Dukju Rhie, *Die Spuren der Frauen in der 100 jährigen koreanischen Kirchengeschichte* (Seoul: The Christian Literature Society, 1985), 27.

37. Jesse N. K. Mugambi, "The Modern Christian Missionary Movement as an Antecedent of Globalization," in *Theologies and Cultures. Ecumenism: Towards a Prophetic Reconstruction*. Formosa Christianity and Culture Research Centre, ed. M.P. Joseph, Vol. VII, No.1, (June 2010): 117.

38. http://www.un.org/millenniumgoals/ (July 22, 2011). See also Mugambi, ibid., 117:

"Global Capitalism has evolved from exploitative social structures dating from the colonial period. Most churches in the North Atlantic are contented with sending donations to the destitute individuals and communities in Africa. As a matter of policy, no church would be prepared to condemn global capitalism as an unjust system."

39. "Owing to the asymmetrical relationship between the North Atlantic older churches and their offspring in Africa, it is difficult for African churches to be critical of their powerful and wealthy 'Brothers and Sisters in Christ' abroad. Yet it is unnecessary for such criticism to be articulated. Rather, the responsibility is on the churches of the North Atlantic to be self-critical within their own national and regional contexts, and to give account of their faith in critical response to their ecclesiastical offspring in Africa and elsewhere, and also in relation to the principalities and powers under which they live, move and have their being [...] Taking responsibility each in our own contexts is the Christian way for our present and future." Mugambi, ibid., 120.

40. "Thus the ideology of global missionary expansion was given biblical legitimacy by appealing to that verse in which Jesus is reported to have challenged his disciples to 'go into all the world' and spread the Good News of God's deliverance of the oppressed from bondage (Luke 4:16-22; Isa. 61:1-2). Ironically, the collaboration of the modern missionary enterprise with imperial regimes, both directly and indirectly, negated the same biblical citation through which missionary expansion was justified," Mugambi, ibid., 113.

41. After Christianity became a powerful and dominant religion, it lost the prophetic voice it had before it was institutionalized. As a ruling ideology, Christianity took on a triumphant aspect, achieving hegemonic status as it spread throughout the world. Christianity promoted and consolidated dualistic thinking, and maintained itself as the final measure of goodness. Mission, within this ideology, is understood merely as the tool that captures souls. From the beginning of its history in the sixteenth century, institutionalized mission has been used to distract European society from recognizing and addressing major problems within its borders by diverting attention to the problems beyond.

42. To idealize is to hinder our discovery of historical truth, and the work to avoid the idealization of Christianity is, in itself, salutary and necessary.

43. In saying this, I do not simply mean to suggest interreligious cooperation, but interdenominational cooperation within Christianity as well. Justice, peace, and a profound recognition of the wholeness of creation is the necessary goal, creating tolerance toward diverse beliefs among diverse peoples from different ideologies, lands, and cultures. While such tolerance can be misinterpreted as ignorance or indifference, it has nothing to do with passive sufferance: it is, rather, a positive and active step toward creating an enhanced awareness of and empathy toward others.

44. Usually people know the problem of Hiroshima and remember peace. But it is not indicated what happened beyond Hiroshima. It is true that many noncombatants perished in the bombardment of Hiroshima. But it is also true that this bombardment had a prologue. Therefore the sequence of events should be noted, who was "innocent," without trying to justify the action of the Americans. The victims of this violence in Hiroshima were part of a nation that inflicted untold misery, aggression, and death upon other nations. That is why Auschwitz and Hiroshima can not be mentioned in the same breath, although both atrocities were equally awful. Japan went very quickly from being a perpetrator to a victim in the world community through the bombardment of Hiroshima and was able to downplay relatively easy its unjust deeds. Beyond that it is unfortunately little known that very many Koreans died during the dropping of the atomic bomb on the war factories in Hiroshima and Nagasaki. These Koreans had been smuggled into Japan as enforced laborers during the annexation. Their medical treatment was not covered after the radiation because the Korean people in Japan were discriminated as third-class. The health complications, from which many continue to suffer to this day, are not treated because Koreans are treated as a social underclass in Japan. Cf. Meehyun Chung, "Dem Schweigen ein Ende setzen. Koreanische Trostfrauen kämpfen für Gerechtigkeit," in *Schlangenbrut. Zeitschrift für feministisch und religiös interessierte Frauen* (Nr. 111, 2010), 43f.

45. For instance, the Journal *Mission and Theology* of The Presbyterian College and Theological Seminary Press, ed. Kwang Soon Lee, deals with issue of Korean war; The 60th Anniversary of Korean War and Church: War, Disaster, Peace. *Mission and Theology*, Vol. 26, (2010). Unification of the South and North Korea and mission. Vol. 15, (2005). North Korea is still treated as object for hostility. There is a lack of perspectives for encountering between North and South Korea. North Korea is the birthplace of Korean Christianity. Merely Christian capitalist triumphalistic ideas remain instead of self-critical efforts.

46. Cf. Signature campaign for a Peace Treaty in the Korean Peninsula, which is launched by the The Presbyterian Church in the Republic of Korea (PROK) on Dec. 1, 2010. The Peace Treaty should substantiate the June 15, 2000

and the October 4, 2007 North-South Joint Declarations signed by the leaders of the two Koreas.

47. "It tends to be assumed that the people of the OECD have everything to give and teach, but nothing to learn or receive from the rest of the world. Despite the fact that a large proportion of the essential primary commodities used in the OECD originate in the rest of the world—particularly in Africa, the nations of tropical Africa are portrayed as beggars destined for destitution, at the mercy of the affluent." Mugambi, "Globalization", 121.

48. It is already indicated in the "Lausanne covenant" (1974) as following: "5. CHRISTIAN SOCIAL RESPONSIBILITY. We affirm that God is both the Creator and the Judge of all people. We therefore should share his concern for justice and reconciliation throughout human society and for the liberation of men and women from every kind of oppression. Because men and women are made in the image of God, every person, regardless of race, religion, color, culture, class, sex or age, has an intrinsic dignity because of which he or she should be respected and served, not exploited. Here too we express penitence both for our neglect and for having sometimes regarded evangelism and social concern as mutually exclusive. Although reconciliation with other people is not reconciliation with God, nor is social action evangelism, nor is political liberation salvation, nevertheless we affirm that evangelism and sociopolitical involvement are both part of our Christian duty."

49. "Christians as individuals and churches as social institutions are challenged to discern new ways of relating between peoples, cultures and nations in accordance with the ethical principle of Leadership, not Lordship." Mugambi, "Globalization," 125.

CHAPTER 10

# Naitō Julia and Women Catechists in the Jesuit Mission in Japan and the Philippines

*Haruko Nawata Ward*

## 1. Historical Setting

The Society of Jesus was founded in Rome in 1540 during Catholic Reform.[1] One of the Jesuit primary marks was mission both in Europe and around the globe. Another mark of the Society was that it was intended only for priests and men. The Jesuits developed a complicated relationship with women. While their *Constitutions* prohibit women's membership, women adopted Jesuit apostolic ministries in their own contexts. In the historical records, one finds in almost every Jesuit mission, women catechists who acted as effective missionaries.[2] The Jesuit concept of mission is summarized in their expression, "to help souls." A soul in this case represents the whole person. Thus to help souls goes beyond guiding persons to accept the Christian faith, and involves serving both the spiritual and material needs of anyone who comes under the Jesuit care.

Francis Xavier began the Jesuit mission in Japan in 1549 under the conditions of Portuguese patronage.[3] This was a transitional period in Japanese history. The emperor's power had declined and the lords of sixty-six "kingdoms" fought feudal wars. Three military strongmen arose as unifiers: Oda Nobunaga, Toyotomi Hideyoshi, and Tokugawa Ieyasu. After Xavier left in 1551, the Jesuit mission grew steadily without competition for the first fifty years. The diocese of Funai was established in 1588. Nobunaga and Hideyoshi favored trade with Portugal and suppressed militant Buddhists. Hideyoshi bore colonial ambitions toward other Asian countries. He invaded Korea and China between 1592 and 1597. He was also keenly aware of Spanish colonization of the Philippines and was ever suspicious about the foreign missionaries in Japan. He issued the *Edict of Expulsion of the Padres* in 1587, and executed twenty-six men in 1597. Ieyasu established the Tokugawa government in 1603. The Christian population had grown to 300,000. The Franciscans, Dominicans, and Augustinians from Spanish Manila arrived while the Protestant Dutch and English began trading with Japan. The Tokugawa adopted Confucianism as its state ideology in 1607, and consolidated its power in 1615. It banned Christianity in 1612, deported missionaries in 1614, and exiled and exterminated Christians by 1650 at least on the surface. It closed Japan to all foreign communications between 1641 and 1868 when the Meiji government took over. The ban of Christianity was finally lifted in 1870.

The Jesuits in the Japan mission stretched the idea of cultural accommodation beyond the simple adaptation of local dress, food, and courtesy. They learned the Japanese language, classic literature, and Buddhist teachings and practices. They published Christian literature and engaged in interreligious disputations. They developed a special class of Japanese male catechists called *dōjuku* and *kanbō*, and bent its rule to work closely with women catechists. The church began ordaining Japanese priests in 1601. Despite the myth that the Jesuits took a top down approach for their conversion enterprise, these Jesuits and their Japanese companions reached all strata of the society. They developed many layers of lay leadership and their lay confraternities would survive underground for two hundred years of suppression.

## 2. Case Study: Naitō Julia and her "Women's Society" (Miyako no bikuni) in Japan's Christian Century

### 2.1 Biographical Notes on Naitō Julia

Naitō Julia was born around 1566 to a higher samurai family in Tango.[4] Her brother Naitō Tokuan became the Lord of the Kameyama and Yagi Castles. He was baptized as João in Kyoto in 1565, and supported the Jesuit mission in Tango. One does not know where Julia grew up, but perhaps she experienced the Christian evangelization of the Yagi Castle by a woman cat-echist, Catharina of Tanba. At the defeat of Shogun Ashikaga Yoshiaki by Unifier Nobunaga in 1578, Tokuan João lost his feudal possessions. Around 1588, he went to serve Konishi Yukinaga Agostino in Higo. By then Julia had been married and was already a widow. She became a *bikuni* (nun) and eventually an abbess of a Jōdo Buddhist monastery in Kyoto. She was a well-respected teacher and preacher of Jōdo Buddhism to the noble lords and ladies, including the wife of Hideyoshi. In 1596, she heard a sermon by a Jesuit brother, and became converted to Christianity. After studying catechism, she was baptized and shortly afterward confirmed by the bishop. As a new convert, in order to prove the legitimacy of her new beliefs, she staged a religious disputation between herself and her former Buddhist master priest. She was also outspoken against Buddhist wor-ship of the idols. The angry Buddhist leaders appealed to Ieyasu to order her arrest in 1601. They tried to ambush her in 1603, but she escaped to Nagasaki and Arima.

## 2.2 A "Female Branch" of Jesuits' Society

Around 1600, Julia founded a woman's society called Miyako no bikuni in Kyoto. This society followed the Jesuit model of active apostolate. She and several other women took three monastic vows under Jesuit Fathers Gnecchi-Soldo Organtino and Pedro Morejón. Dressed in black and with a shaven head, these Christian *bikuni* lived according to Julia's rule. Their house, which stood next to the Jesuit church, provided retreat for other women. From this house, women catechists, such as Iga Maria and Nagashima Madalena, went out to preach, engage in pri-vate conversations or public religious disputations, and teach Christian literature. They were able to visit noblewomen in con-finement whom the Jesuits or male catechists could not visit. Naitō Julia and her Miyako no bikuni worked in the network of many other women catechists. Together with another notable leader Kyōgoku Maria with her women disciples, Naitō Julia and her catechists converted thousands of women and men to Christianity, from the aristocracy to the poor, between 1601 and 1610.[5] Because of such successful proselytization, the Jesuits called Julia and Maria "Fathers' Apostles." These women cat-echists baptized, educated, counseled, and in the absence of the priests heard confessions of the converts.

Women's activism and networking across social classes were diametrically opposed to Tokugawa's Confucian principles.

The Confucian society places women in their proper families. This new Christian women's movement was perhaps one of the reasons for the strong hostility the Tokugawa government held against Christianity. In fact, the government felt such a threat that it persecuted Naitō Julia and her Miyako no bikuni. In what is now known as the Great Expulsion of 1614, the government expelled clergy and major Christian leaders from Japan. Julia and the fourteen women of the Miyako no bikuni were deported from Nagasaki to Spanish Manila along with fifteen Jesuits including Pedro Morejón, as well as the families of Takayama Ukon Justo and Naitō Tokuan João. The exiles resettled in the village of San Miguel outside Manila in early 1615.

## 2.3 Religious Vocation of the Women Catechists

There are several venues in which Naitō Julia and the Miyako no bikuni pursued their mission in Japan. The most obvious is the work of religious conversion. How did the women catechists engage in this work? First, they learned the basic teachings of Japanese religions. Most late medieval Japanese practiced one of the twelve schools of Buddhism. Pure Land (Jōdoshū), True Pure Land (Jōdo-Shinshō), Nichirenshū, and Zen were popular among the feudal and merchant families. Each school had absorbed elements of Ancient Shinto to different degrees. Shinto received the patronage of the imperial and aristocratic houses. Confucian teachings had a few scholarly elite followers. The women catechists were ready to explain the differences among these various religions. The Jesuits in Kyoto recognized the advantage of entrusting much of this work to Naitō Julia, who was already a renowned teacher of Buddhism before her conversion to Christianity.

Second, the women catechists knew the basic Christian teachings and were able to communicate these in familiar terms comparable to those in the existing religions. Women needed to answer such questions as: How does the Christian paradise differ from Buddhist Jōdo (Pure Land)? Is the Christian soul (*anima*) the same as the Buddhist soul (*kon*)? Where does the soul go after the body dies? Is there a reincarnation and what is the incarnation? Because this was the first time that Christianity was introduced in Japan, there were not always equivalent concepts or expressions. The Jesuits in Japan experimented with Latin, Portuguese, and Buddhist expressions in "translating" the Christian message into Japanese. Later this translation problem would develop as the name of God controversy in the Jesuit

China mission, which eventually adopted the name Tianzhu (Lord of Heaven) for the Christian God. But at this early phase, the translation projects gave more creative space for communication. Instead of calling God *kami* (Shinto gods or goddesses) or *hotoke* (Buddha), the Japanese Christians chose the more neutral Latin *Deus* as God's name. Christians were commonly called Kirishitan derived from Portuguese *christão*. While there was a Japanese word for neighbor, Portuguese *proximo*, which expressed more intimacy, was used. There was no Japanese equivalent for the concept of Christian love, and the word *otaisetsu* (to regard someone as most precious) was invented. In order to say, "Love your neighbor as God loves you," would contain multilingual and multicultural boundary crossing. Not only the missionaries, but also Japanese Jesuit priests, brothers, *dōjuku*, and women catechists daily engaged in such "translating" activities.

## 2.4 Written Records of Women's Impact in Mission in Japan

Results of such efforts are evident in the published and manuscript works prepared by the Jesuit Press. The genre of the published materials is called Kirishitanban. It uses the character style called *kanamajiri*, intended for women readers. In 1605, Jesuit brother Fucan Fabian published *Myōtei mondō*.[6] Although it bears his name as the single author, I argued elsewhere that *Myōtei mondō* was probably based on the work of Naitō Julia and the Miyako no bikuni. In his preface Fabian states that he composed it to be read by noblewomen in confinement, and that it is a standard manual for women catechists who would guide their reading. The entire book in three parts is written as a dialogue between two women. Myōshū, a Jōdoshū nun, poses questions about the different schools of Buddhism, Shinto, Taoism, Confucian teachings, and Christianity, and Yūtei, a Christian catechist, answers these questions guiding Myōshū eventually to desire Christian baptism. Fabian must have taken Naitō Julia and the women of Miyako no bikuni as the model for Myōshū as a war widow and Yūtei as the daughter of a Confucian scholar. He was in fact one of the Jesuits who worked very closely with the women of Miyako no bikuni. He eventually married one, left the Society, and became a famous apostate writer of *Deus Destroyed*. Yet what he composed in *Myōtei mondō* fairly reflects the religious dialogue, education, preaching, and translation work of women catechists and their contribution to the Jesuit mission in the early 1600s.

## 2.5 Social Concerns Addressed by Women Catechists

One of the reasons for the success of women catechists in helping women convert was the prevalent misogyny in Japanese Buddhism. All late medieval Buddhists, even the most egalitarian Pure Land and True Pure Land schools, adopted and popularized an extra canonical sutra called Ketsubonkyō (Blood-bowl sutra).[7] It teaches that women are inherently unclean and sinful, destined to sufferings in a blood lake after death, because of their menstrual and childbirth bleeding. There was very little that women could do to save themselves from this eternal doom. This teaching caused much heartache for women who expected death at any moment in the age of wars and violence. Because women catechists understood this pain, they were able to persuade Buddhist women to embrace a lesser misogynist doctrine of Christian sin and salvation. Reversely, some women who belonged to a minor school of Shinto-Buddhism that affirmed stronger female religious agency rejected Christianity.

The Japanese feudal system treated women only as objects of familial strategy, and was often unjust to women. Family patriarchs arranged marriages and concubinages of their female members in their extended *ie* (household) for political alliances. In these alliances, age differences or personal wishes did not matter. The alliances shifted often according to the changes of the ruling lords. The Japanese laws allowed men to have multiple wives for pleasure as well as to produce sons. The laws also gave men the right of easy divorce while women did not have such rights. The physical and sexual abuse of women was accepted as good discipline. Many women found solace in becoming Buddhist nuns; however, most of the nunneries were connected to families, and at times, even the nuns were forced to marry according to their families' conveniences. Naitō Julia and women catechists spoke against such injustices. They helped women escape from abusive situations, and provided them safe houses. Women catechists also established a new type of collegial relationship with special class of men, namely Japanese Jesuits. These included a famed preacher Brother Tōin Vicente, in the early years in Kyoto, and Brother Thadeu, a painter, who became a fellow exile to Manila. While the Japanese society became xenophobic, women catechists maintained their collegial relationship also with foreign-missionary Jesuits. There were also non-Japanese members in Julia's society. Korean-born Park Marina was a war hostage in Hideyoshi's invasions, and became a vital part of the Miyako no bikuni. Naitō Julia's mission then was also to create this new alternative spiritual family structure for social religious outcasts in an increasingly hostile environment.

## 2.6 Naitō Julia's Leadership Ministry

In addition to her work of conversion, Naitō Julia's mission as a Christian abbess should not be ignored. While she abandoned some elements of her Buddhist past, she carried on other usable elements into her new Christian abbess-hood. Both Buddhism and Christianity are monastic religions. Like a Christian monastery, a Buddhist nunnery gave safe haven for nuns where they could receive education and develop spiritual gifts. Some nuns eventually gained recognition and authority, and were ordained and became abbesses as Julia did. As a Buddhist abbess Julia was already used to studying and interpreting scripture, and teaching and expounding on it to her temple congregants and community of nuns. She was already maintaining the life devoted to prayers for deceased souls. She provided liturgical leadership and spiritual discipline for the nuns in her community. She exercised her administrative skills to run its institutions. Most of the Buddhist nunneries were under the supervision of male priests. As a very new Christian abbess, Julia also overcame an extra hurdle. Even though the Jesuit *Constitutions* did not endorse a women's society, she persuaded the two Jesuit priests (Organtino and Morejón) to help her formalize the Miyako no bikuni. These Jesuits heard their confessions regularly. The Jesuit annual letters and reports did not shy away from describing the activities of Julia and her community as if they belonged to their Society but cautiously left their affiliations vague. The fact that they were exiled to Manila together proves that both the Miyako no bikuni and the Jesuits, as well as the authorities in Japan regarded them(selves) as companions in mission.

## 2.7 Christian Witness Through Martyrdom

The ultimate mission of Naitō Julia and the Miyako no bikuni was martyrdom: to testify to their faith under penalty of death. In 1613, the governor of Kyoto arrested Julia and her women. First, the officials threatened to expose their naked bodies in public and sell them to brothels. They knew that such shaming was vexing to these women who had taken a vow of chastity. However, the women were not afraid because they believed that they were following Christ who was also stripped before his crucifixion. Then the officials tortured women in the method called *tawarazume*. They stuffed each woman into an empty burlap bag except her head. They tied the bag tightly with a rope, and piled all the bags on the frozen ground of the execution site in snow. They thought that the pain of prickly straw on bare skin, hunger, cold, immobility and humiliation would cause the women to renounce their Christian faith. Yet these women sang choruses in praise of God. When a relative of Lucia de la Cruz forcefully carried her away to her father's house, she shouted "I am a Christian, I am a Christian" all the way. As soon as she was untied, she ran back with the sack in her hand to be with her companions. When a Buddhist priest tried to persuade a woman to recant, she laughed and spat on his face. When the judge tried to release the women, they refused saying, "We are Christians, and we will not leave here, unless you make a public announcement that we do not want to abandon our holy faith. Otherwise, leave us here until we die." By these words, songs, and actions, Naitō Julia and the Miyako no bikuni demonstrated their allegiance to Christ. The women were not able to achieve their desired martyrdom, but were deported from Japan as dangerous criminals.

## 2.8 A Change of Calling in Manila

While the Jesuit exiles in Manila continued to seek ways to go back to Japan or go on to another mission, there were no longer any need for women catechists for a small Japanese exile community in Manila. Naitō Julia and her women drastically changed the course of their mission there. Not being able to communicate in Spanish and assimilate into the new culture, these fatigued confessors (survivors of torture) became strictly enclosed. They did not accept new recruits although because of their fame, there were many applicants. They did not appear in public any longer except to visit the Jesuit church next door for the Mass. Instead they chose a deeply contemplative life and maintained a close relationship with their Jesuit confessors (priests who heard their confessions). The women spent their hours in intercessory prayers, receiving visions, keeping private spiritual diaries, and observing spiritual discipline. Naitō Julia died in 1627, and Nakashima Magdalena became the second superior. The last members Luzia de la Cruz and Tecla Ignatius (third superior) died in 1656. The Jesuits celebrated solemn Masses and buried them in their church as if they were their own members of the order.

The Jesuit reports of Naitō Julia and the Miyako no bikuni were read by their contemporary Catholic communities in Portugal, Spain, Italy, France, and other European places, including English exiles on the European continent, as well as New Spain (Mexico), and gave inspiration and encouragement to them.[8] Which of their contemporary women catechists in other global Jesuit missions had access to these stories needs further investigation.

## 3. Questions for Discussion

1. In what unique historical context did Naitō Julia's mission emerge? Do you think that studying each historical context is significant to understand what "mission" might have meant in that particular context?

2. What types of mission did Naitō Julia engage in? What restrictions and dangers did Julia face because she was a woman? What elements of creativity and resilience do you find in her mission? How important was networking with others to her? What biblical and theological meaning do you find in her mission?

3. After reading this case study, how would you define Christian evangelism, proselytization, conversion, and mission? What examples of interreligious resources did Naitō Julia have for her mission?

4. What does your church history textbooks say about Catholic Reform, Catholic mission, monastic women, and the Jesuit missionary movement in the early modern period? What negative myths do you find? How does this case study demonstrate their inaccuracies in historical memory? Do the textbook writers have denominational or national biases which deform truthful representation of the "Other"? Do these textbooks provide any women examples? What theological significance does rethinking church history and mission history bring?

5. How did your images of early modern Japanese and Korean-born women change or did not change after reading this case study? What adjectives do you give to Naitō Julia and other women catechists? Does the study of a historical example help us combat social stereotypes and our own internalized pictures of passive and powerless Asian women and/or Catholic nuns?

6. Do you think that obtaining official recognition from the authorities in church hierarchy empowers women missionaries? Do women missionaries, like women ministers, need full financial support, title recognition, and a kind of ordination from their endorsing bodies?

# Further Reading

## *Foundational Principles and Early History of the Society of Jesus*

William V. Bangert, *A History of the Society of Jesus*, 2nd ed. (St. Louis: The Institute of Jesuit Sources, 1986).

Luke Clossey, *Salvation and Globalization in the Early Jesuit Missions* (New York: Cambridge University Press, 2008).

John Patrick Donnelly, "New Religious Orders 1517-1648," in *Handbook of European History, 1400-1600: Late Middle Ages, Renaissance, and Reformation*, ed. Thomas A. Brady, Jr., Heiko A. Oberman, and James D. Tracy. 2 vols. (Grand Rapids: W.B. Eerdmans, 1996).

John W. O'Malley, *The First Jesuits* (Cambridge: Harvard University Press, 1993).

John W. O'Malley, Gauvin Alexander Bailey, Steven J. Harris, and T. Frank Kennedy, eds., *The Jesuits: Cultures, Sciences, and the Arts, 1540-1773* (Toronto: University of Toronto Press, 1999).

John W. O'Malley, Gauvin Alexander Bailey, Steven J. Harris, and T. Frank Kennedy, eds., *The Jesuits II, Cultures, Sciences, and the Arts, 1540-1773* (Toronto: University of Toronto Press, 2006).

Saint Ignatius of Loyola, *The Constitutions of the Society of Jesus* (trans. and ed.), George E. Ganss (St. Louis: The Institute of Jesuit Sources, 1970).

Saint Ignatius of Loyola, *Ignatius of Loyola: Spiritual Exercises and Selected Works* (trans. and ed.), George E. Ganss (New York: Paulist Press, 1991).

John W. Witek, "From India to Japan: European Missionary Expansion, 1500-1650," in *Catholicism in Early Modern History: a Guide to Research*, ed. John W. O'Malley (St. Louis: Center for Reformation Research, 1988), 193-210.

## *Early Modern Jesuit Japan Mission*

Charles Ralph Boxer, *The Christian Century in Japan, 1549-1650* (Berkeley: University of California Press, 1951).

Michael Cooper, "A Mission Interrupted: Japan," in *A Companion to the Reformation World*, ed. R. Po-chia Hsia (Malden: Blackwell, 2004), 393-407.

Michael Cooper, ed., *The Southern Barbarians: the First Europeans in Japan* (Tokyo: Kodansha International in cooperation with Sophia University, 1971).

George Elison, *Deus Destroyed: the Image of Christianity in Early Modern Japan* (Cambridge: Harvard University Press, 1973).

Neil S. Fujita, *Japan's Encounter with Christianity: The Catholic Mission in Pre-Modern Japan* (Mahwah: Paulist Press, 1991).

Ikuo Higashibaba, *Christianity in Early Modern Japan: Kirishitan Belief and Practice* (Leiden; Boston: Brill, 2001).

J. F. Moran, *The Japanese and the Jesuits: Alessandro Valignano in Sixteenth-Century Japan* (London; New York: Routledge, 1993).

Andrew C. Ross, *A Vision Betrayed: the Jesuits in Japan and China, 1542-1742* (Maryknoll: Orbis Books, 1994).

Georg Schurhammer, *Francis Xavier, His Life, His Times*, trans. M. Joseph Costeloe (Rome: Jesuit Historical Institute. Vol. 4 [1984]: Japan and China, 1549-1552).

Josef Franz Schütte, *Valignano's Mission Principles for Japan,* trans. John J. Coyne, 2 vols. (St. Louis: The Institute of Jesuit Sources, 1980, 1985).

M. Antoni, J. Üçeler, "The Jesuit Enterprise in Sixteenth- and Seventeenth-Century Japan," in *The Cambridge Companion to the Jesuits,* ed. Thomas Worcester (Cambridge: Cambridge University Press, 2008), 153-168.

Haruko Nawata Ward, *Women Religious Leaders in Japan's Christian Century, 1549–1650* Series Women and Gender in Early Modern World (Aldershot, England; Burlington, VT: Ashgate, 2009).

## Women and the Jesuit Global Missions

Alicia Franschina, "A Jesuit Beata at the Time of Suppression in the Viceroyalty of the Río de la Plata: María Antonia de Paz e Figueroa, 1730-99," in *Jesuits II* (2006): 758-771.

Allan Greer, *Mohawk Saint: Catherine Tekakwitha and the Jesuits* (New York: Oxford University Press, 2005).

Gail King, "Candida Xu and the Growth of Christianity in China in the Seventeenth Century," in *Monumenta Serica: Journal of Oriental Studies* 47 (1998): 49-66.

Jean Lacouture, *Jesuits: a Multibiography* (Washington, DC: Counterpoint, 1995).

Jessie Gregory Lutz, ed., *Pioneer Chinese Christian Women: Gender, Christianity, and Social Mobility* Studies in Missionaries and Christianity in China. (Bethlehem, PA: Lehigh University Press, 2010).

Laurence Lux-Sterrite, *Redefining Female Religious Life* (Aldershot, England and Burlington: Ashgate, 2005).

Karl Rahner, ed., *Saint Ignatius Loyola: Letters to Women* (New York: Herder and Herder, 1960).

Elizabeth Rapley, *The Dévotes: Women and Church in Seventeenth-Century Convent* (New York: Doubleday, 1994).

Elizabeth Rhodes, "Join the Jesuits, See the World: Early Modern Women in Spain and the Society of Jesus," in *Jesuits II* (2006): 33-49.

Elizabeth Rhodes (trans. and ed.), *This Tight Embrace: Luisa de Carvajal y Mendoza* (Milwaukee: Marquette University Press, 2000).

Gemma Simmons, "Women Jesuits?" in *The Cambridge Companion to the Jesuits* (2008): 120-135.

Haruko Nawata Ward, "Jesuits, Too: Jesuits, Women Catechists, and Jezebels in Christian-Century Japan," in *The Jesuits II* (2006): 638-657.

Haruko Nawata Ward, "Women and the Confraternity of Misericórdia in the Early Modern Portuguese Seaborne Empire: Goa, Salvador da Bahia, Nagasaki," in *Neue Zeitschrift für Missionswissenschaft* 58, no. 4 (2002): 241–60.

## Endnotes

1. For literature on the foundational principles and early history of the Society of Jesus, see section 4.1 (Further Reading) at the end of this chapter.

2. For literature on the women catechists in the Jesuit global missions, see 4.3.

3. For literature on the early modern Jesuit Japan mission, see 4.2.

4. The primary sources on Naitō Julia and the Miyako no bikuni are found in John Hay, *De Rebvs Iaponicis, Indicis, et Pervanis Epistolae* (Antwerp: Martini Nutij, 1605); Fernão Guerreiro, *Relação Anual das Coisas que Fizeram os Padres da Companhia de Jesus nas suas Missões do Japão, China* [...] *nos anos de 1600 a 1609*, 3 vols (Lisbon and Evora: 1603–11); Pedro Morejón, *Relacion de la Persecucion que vvo en l'a Yglesia de Iapon* [...], *el año de 1614; y 1615* (Mexico: Ioan Ruyz, 1616); idem, *A Brief Relation of the Persecution Lately Made Against the Catholike Christians, in the Kingdome of Iaponia, 1619*, trans. William Wright (St. Omer: The English Jesuit College of Saint Omer, 1619; London: The Scolar Press, 1974); idem, *Nihon junkyōshi*, trans. Sakuma Tadashi (Tokyo: Kirishitan Bunka Kenkyūkai, 1964); Gabriel de Matos, *Lettera annua del Giappone del M.DCXIV* [...] *de la Compagnia di Giesu* (Rome: Zanneti, 1617); Francisco Colín, *Labor Evangélica, ministerios apostolicos de los obreros de la Compañía de Jesús, fundacion, y progressos de su providencia en las Islas Filipinas* (Madrid, 1663; ed. Pablo Pastells, Barcelona: Henrich, 1904), vol. 3, 500-562. The major secondary studies include: Kataoka Rumiko, *Kirishitan jidai no joshi shōdōkai: Miyako no bikunitachi* (Tokyo: Kirishitan Bunka Kenkyūkai, 1976); Haruko Nawata Ward, *Women Religious Leaders in Japan's Christian Century, 1549-1650* (Aldershot, England; Burlington: Ashgate, 2009), 61-104.

5. See Shibuya Mieko, *Kyōgoku Maria* (Toyooka: Tajima Bunka Kenkyūkai, 1983).

6. Modern critical edition of Fucan Fabian, *Myōtei mondō* is available in *Kirishitan kyōrisho*, ed. Ebisawa Arimichi et al. (Tokyo: Kyōbunkan, 1993). See also Haruko Nawata Ward, "Jesuit Encounters with Confucianism in Early Modern Japan," *Sixteenth Century Journal*, 40-4 (2009): 1047-1069.

7. On misogyny of medieval Japanese Buddhism, see Barbara Ruch, ed. *Engendering Faith: Women and Buddhism in Premodern Japan* (Ann Arbor: Center for Japanese Studies, University of Michigan, 2002); and Motoko Takemi, "'Menstruation Sutra' Belief in Japan," *Japanese Journal of Religious Studies* 10/2–3 (1983): 229-46.

8. Early modern Catholic women who modified the active apostolate and spirituality similar to the Jesuits' for women include Angela Merici (1474-1540); Catherina de Ferão in Goa (1556-77); Mary Ward (1585-1645) and the English Ladies (f. 1615); Luisa de Carvajal y Mendoza (1566–1614) in England; Jeanne de Chantal (1572-1641) and the Visitation (f.1610); Marie de l'Incarnation (1599-1672) in Quebec; Candida Xu (1607–80) in China; Kateri Tekakwitha (1656-80) in Mouhawk; and Sor Juana de la Cruz (1651-95) in Mexico to name a few.

CHAPTER 11
# Women's Society and Deaconesses' Mission in the Philippines

*Chita Rebollido-Millan*

## 1. Introduction

The Philippines is known as Asia's only predominantly Christian country. Of its population of 97 million, more than 90 percent are Christians and among the Christians about 80 percent belong to the Roman Catholic Church.[1] Catholicism was brought by the Spaniards when they colonized the country for three centuries (1565-1898). The country entered a new era when Ferdinand Marcos was elected as president in 1965. In November 1969, Marcos won an unparalleled reelection but the election was accompanied by violence and charges of fraud, so civil disorder grew. Using the rising wave of lawlessness and the threat of a communist insurgency as justification, Marcos declared martial law on September 21, 1972 and remained in force until 1981. Marcos ruled by decree, curtailed press freedom and other civil liberties, and ordered the arrest of opposition leaders and militant activists. After the presidential election in February 1986, both Marcos and his opponent, Corazon Aquino, declared themselves the winner, and charges of massive fraud and violence were leveled against the Marcos faction.[2]

The church, especially the Roman Catholic Church, was very visible during the dictatorship regime. Cardinal Jaime Sin was a vocal critic of Marcos. His help was sought particularly during the People Power days in February 1986 for the people to go to Epifanio Delos Santos Avenue, the revolution venue, to support the military rebels. And indeed, hundreds of thousands of Filipinos went, including nuns, priests, students, workers, businessmen, housewives, and others. They were armed with nothing but rosaries, crucifixes, and religious images; they knelt in front of loyalist tanks praying and singing religious hymns, and men and women linked arms together to block the troops. And the peaceful civilian-military uprising forced Marcos into exile and installed Corazon Aquino as president on February 25, 1986.[3]

## 2. The Place of Women in the Early Beginnings of the Methodist Church in the Philippines

The official beginning of Methodist missionary work and Methodism in the Philippines is claimed to have started on March 5, 1899 when Bishop James Thoburn delivered his first sermon in a worship service held at Teatro Filipino in Manila. There were about seventy American soldiers and fifty Filipinos in attendance.[4] In 1900, the Woman's Foreign Missionary Society (WFMS) sent its representatives to begin their work in the Philippine Islands. The first four missionaries who began mission work in Manila were: Mary A. Cody, kindergarten teacher; Cornelia Moots, evangelistic worker; Anna J. Norton, medical doctor; and Julia F. Wisner, teacher from the Girl's School in Rangoon, Burma. In that year and years following, there were more male missionaries, around eight of them, who arrived in the Philippines together with their wives.

The Woman's Foreign Missionary Society organized themselves into an official body called "Woman's Conference," which met separately from the Clergy District Conference. In 1902, Anna Norton, a medical doctor, began a Bible class for women, an Epworth League for the youth, and a Sabbath school for children, while Dora Taggart Brown organized a junior league. But these missionaries encountered difficulties in communications, so they wished to train women to teach the hundreds of Filipino children.

Not long after, the Philippine Islands District Conference, with Presiding Elder Homer Stuntz, approved the immediate opening of a deaconess training school in Manila. The deaconess program was intended for training of competent women committed to serve the church and community under the authority of the Methodist Church. On July 1, 1903, Ms. Winifred Spaulding, a deaconess and director of the Kansas City Deaconess Training School, opened the deaconess home and training school with four girl enrollees. She was followed in 1905 by Ms. Marguerite Martha Decker, a deaconess-nurse, who spent thirty-three years of her life as principal of Harris Memorial Training School. Today, The United Methodist Church (UMC) in the Philippines has an official membership of about 600,000, but it serves a much larger community of close to 1 million. From six annual conferences in 1968, it has grown to nineteen annual conferences, and in its 2008 Central Conference, three more annual conferences were created to bring to a total of twenty-two annual conferences.

# 3. Philippine Women's Experience

## 3.1 Women's Society of Christian Service (WSCS)

**Mission** is an often-used word that means different things to different people. But for this particular paper, I am borrowing the Irish Methodist Church's definition: "mission involves the building up of the church, helping people to find a faith for living, the nature of our relationship with God and others, and the enabling of leadership in the church."[5] In simpler terms, mission involves both relationship with God and with people, with willingness of heart and mind to express one's faith in creative and meaningful means, be they in small or immense ways. Filipino church women, since the inception of Christianity in the country, have been engaged in mission work. In the earlier centuries, women were found taking part in church mission through menial work like: cleaning the church for Sunday worship services, altar flowers arrangers, setting up the lectern/altar for the Sunday worship service, preparing snacks or meals during church meetings or conferences, raising funds for church projects and programs, teaching in Sunday schools, singing in the choir, and so on. Seldom were women found at the center stage of mission work, such as being the evangelist/preacher during revivals or evangelistic nights, as a clergy who delivered Sunday sermons, or one who took the lead in organizing a team to respond to an urgent community need. In short, women were meant for small mission while men carried out the big mission.

The Women's Society of Christian Service (WSCS) is an official lay organization within the UMC structure. It is composed of United Methodist women from forty years old and above. During annual regular sessions reports are given about the work done by the women. Reports of annual conference women presidents and the Board of Women's Work, the umbrella organization of all church women's groups, will be largely used in this paper to document the mission involvement of church women.

In 1975, women actively participated not only in church services but also in community projects by involving in green revolution (planting of trees) and home and community beautification drives, according to Villamil.[6] They held the "Recognition of Outstanding Women" from the local to the district levels, and on to the annual conference level. It is worth noting that women also engaged in mission work outside their place or country. In 1977, each woman member shared her one least coin or 5 centavos monthly or P.60 centavos annually. The amount collected, humble it may be, was given for the repair of the Philippine Mission House in Okinawa. Cac[7] concluded in her report: "The women of the church are a potent force for action in the church and in the community." Soon the "small" ones became "bigger." In the 1980s the women dreamed and they dreamed big. They envisioned owning a seminar house or development center for women where they could house their conferences and meetings. So every annual conference had to find ways to produce money toward this big project. A Yamaha Concert was sponsored by the women where they raised a substantial amount, according to Lopez.[8]

A different type of mission was performed by the women in the mid-1990s. Millan reported of the loans they gave to their "less fortunate" sisters, made possible by their monetary gains from their Souvenir Program Project '94. They also passed two resolutions: (1) an appeal for government disapproval of the proposed cement plant in Bolinao, Pangasinan, and (2) a call for sustained and dynamic church involvement in women's issues and concerns as propelled by the Flor Contemplacion tragedy (a Filipino domestic helper abroad who killed her employer as self-defense, but was sentenced by the court).[9] It is noticeable how women's mission has expanded from their families and churches to the bigger society. Another woman president reported that women distributed love gifts to church workers in cash and in kinds. *Saranay* (help/support) were organized in some districts where a certain amount is given to the bereaved families of members who died. They also helped in the needs of the local and district parsonages. Student deaconesses and students pastors were given gifts while some women were sponsors to these students. "The women are like Deborah in the Bible," added Galazo.[10]

In the later decades of the twentieth century, church women embarked on bigger mission than what they previously did. To be more relevant to the times, they expanded their work through a Medical/Optical/Dental/Evangelistic (MODE) Mission in far flung *barrios* (villages) or places. A team of medical doctors, dentists, nurses, deaconesses, clergy, and laywomen would go to a *barangay* (rural community) to give free physical consultations to patients, accompanied by free medicines, free dental check-up and extractions. Others also distributed Bible tracts or conducted brief Bible studies while they were waiting for their turn to be checked by the doctors. Indeed, both the physical and spiritual needs of the people were met by MODE mission. Expanding their mission, women ventured into mini-finance mission. Gatmen reported about giving financial help for the completion of the district parsonage's main gate and the improvement of its comfort room.[11] Women's resourcefulness was evident also if only to be able to push through with their services and projects. Navata's report mentioned of livelihood projects they undertook, such as pig dispersal, *May Pera Sa Basura* (There is Cash in Trash), food processing, candle making and flower arrangement. Navata also reported that one of their two outstanding accomplishments was the conduct of an ecumenical World Day of Prayer and International Women's Day Celebration, with the UMC women spearheading the activity.[12] This shows how Methodist women cross traditional boundaries and spread out their wings to reach out those in other denominations, as well as those outside the church.

## 3.2 Deaconesses in the Philippines

The deaconess ministry is a unique and effective church ministry whereby women are active in mission through the church. Harris Memorial College of the Philippines, the only school in Southeast Asia that trains young women for service in the church and community, has provided the foundational missional work of equipping female students to serve persons of all ages within and outside the church through religious education and kindergarten education. Started in the year 1903, then as deaconess home and training center by Ms. Spaulding, it grew up to become Harris Memorial Training School under Ms. Margeurite Decker in 1903; then as Harris Memorial School in 1951 under Dr. Prudencia L. Fabro; and later as Harris Memorial College Development Center for Women in 1975, which offers training and education not only for the Philippines but also for Southeast Asia.

In the earlier years of Harris existence, deaconesses were trained in medical work for women and children with Dr. Rebecca Parrish, a medical doctor from Indiana, USA. Selected Harris girls received practical training in the care of patients, in the art of visiting the sick, and offering spiritual support. Then eventually, senior students had to spend one semester at

Mary Johnston Hospital as part of the curriculum. Dr. Parrish expressed, "They asked me point blank, can a woman know enough to be a doctor?"[13] Harris pioneered kindergarten education in the Philippines with Brigida Garcia Fernando, a graduate of Columbia University Teacher's College in the USA, opening the first kindergarten class in the Philippines at Hugh Wilson Hall in 1922. The Kindergarten Teacher Training Program was launched as the first of its kind in the country, hence, making Harris the pioneer in kindergarten education in the country. Then in 1940 efforts were exerted toward application for recognition and permit from the Bureau of Education to offer a Junior Teacher's Certificate to graduates of the kindergarten curriculum, and fortunately, it got its full recognition in 1948.

Since then, there were a lot of young women graduates in this specialized field of early childhood education. They are usually appointed by the bishop to churches with kindergarten schools or to open kindergartens if none yet. Harris graduates who major in kindergarten education are often sought after by parents in the community because of the excellent training they have. Not only that, there are few college graduates in early childhood education so this multiplies the demand for Harris graduates. The kindergarten classes/schools are put up by churches as their service project in reaching out to the community. As a matter of fact, pupils from different religious backgrounds outnumber the Methodists. To date there are many UMC related schools offering not only preschool education but also elementary and secondary education. And women dominate the teaching force in every school, mainly because of their nurturing and caring instinct or nature.

In 1928, twenty-five years after its founding, Harris has graduated 210 young women who went out to serve the local churches in various roles as "evangelists, Junior League and Sunday School teachers, Bible teachers, workers with mothers and women in general, home visitors, and teacher in Bible institutes. On many occasions, they filled the position of pastor/preacher in the absence of the clergy. Some served as assistants to missionaries."[14] Then the succeeding years saw Harris moving from training its young women students as evangelists, to preparing them to serve in a variety of ministries. Some were assigned to found girls' dormitories or to manage them.[15] It also came to a period when American missionaries relegated roles and responsibilities to Filipino deaconesses. In 1951, the baton of Harris leadership was passed on from an American missionary to Prudencia L. Fabro, the first Filipino director. "For many in the church, handing the directorship to a Filipino affirmed and recognized Filipino women leadership."[16]

It is claimed that the church grew because of Harris graduates who actively contributed their talents and skills, and worked as hard as the clergy. Its quality of graduates was attributed to the biblical and spiritual grounding instilled upon them by an institution whose mission was to shape young women for Christian service.[17] This was affirmed by Robledo that deaconess work from 1903 to 1978 contributed significantly to the growth and expansion of Philippine Methodism, and played a distinct role in the development of a visible female leadership in church and society whereby they transformed the traditional concept regarding the subservient role of women. The deaconesses' visible religious activities in towns and *barrios* eroded the customary image of native women as shy, weak, and indecisive. With their courage to fulfill a task in the church and in the community, that of uplifting women to a better quality of life, deaconesses have demonstrated that they, too, were freed from the crippling constraints of their communities and were empowered and equipped to transform others.[18]

Unlike clergy who are ordained, deaconesses are commissioned by the bishop and are usually assigned to local churches as coworkers of clergy, or in church-related institutions. To date, data shows that there is a total of 1, 244 male clergy while women workers, including deaconesses, total 844. In sum, male clergy make up about two-thirds of the workforce of the Philippine UMC, while one-third are women pastors and deaconesses. The large number of women church workers is probably due to the fact that a training institution for deaconesses is established in the country, and also because women pastors are warmly accepted by the church, and it is no longer an issue as it used to be.

## 3.3 Women Making a Difference

Filipino women are told to have made history especially during the American era. Unlike women in other parts of Asia, Latin America, and Europe, they enjoyed greater rights. They were free to work in an office, study with men in co-ed schools, and date without chaperones. Women became doctors, lawyers, and scientists. The first Asian women to vote and hold public office were the Filipinos (1937).[19] In the same vein, women in the Methodist church started to be more active, even aggressive, in their involvement in the life and ministry of the church in the 1980s. If in the earlier years they contend themselves to prepare snacks or meals for their male counterparts, the time has changed, women thought. They soon started to accept positions in church councils, boards, or committees. They were beginning to realize that decisions for the life of the church largely take place in these structures of councils, boards, and committees so they wanted to be in. That realization opened their minds and hearts to participate more fully in the church through the decision-making bodies.

But the journey for the women was not easy, nor was it fast. Very often, women found themselves elected as secretaries or chairpersons of committees and boards. There seemed to be "feminization" of positions such that chairpersonship of councils or boards could hardly be given to women. But today, by the concerted efforts of women they have penetrated the "glass ceiling" in the church structure. They now occupy positions that used to be held only by men before. Deaconesses made history in the Philippine UMC when they walked out during their Philippines Annual Conference session in 1983. As practiced in the earlier years, deaconesses were seated to equalize clergy and lay representation. Of the conference composition of ninety-four ministers and eighty lay delegates, the sixty-one deaconesses were only asking for eleven seats. But in spite of their appeals to consider them in filling up the disparity in membership in the conference, these fell on deaf ears of the clergy and laypeople. So the deaconesses walked out of the conference on May 25, 1983. They "bewailed the fact that their presence was required but their vote did not count; they were expected to implement programs and decisions but they were not part of the decision making."[20]

To the knowledge of most church people, some deaconesses were/are activists in their own rights. They either took the form of social mission to the underprivileged, oppressed, and marginalized of the society as a form of response to the signs of time. To them it is a fulfillment of a calling as stated in the Book of Discipline (which contains the laws, plans, polity, and process by which United Methodists govern themselves): the ministries of deaconesses and home missionaries reflect the commitment to "function through diverse forms of service directed toward the world to make Jesus Christ known in the fullness of his ministry and mission, which mandate that his followers alleviate suffering; eradicate causes of injustice and all that robs life of dignity and worth; facilitate the development of full human potential; and share in building global community through the church universal."[21] A few are believed to have joined the revolution during the martial law regime because of their strong conviction on social holiness. One of them, Filomena Asuncion, is duly recognized as one of the Philippine heroes. Her name is listed at *Bantayog ng mga Bayani* (Heroes Monument) along with other contemporary heroes. Others continue with their struggle for liberation from poverty and systems that justify and validate oppression both inside and outside the church.

It is also important to mention the Women's Issues Committee's vision of election of a woman bishop. The National WSCS endorsed Dr. Elizabeth Tapia for the Episcopal leadership in 2000 because they felt that it was ripe for the Philippine UMC to have a woman bishop. But the central conference electorate did not see the way women foresaw so their vision was not realized then. But having tried is far much better than never to have tried at all. After all, the delegates saw for themselves how united the women were for this cause that others sighed, "women are somebody to wrestle with." The attendance and participation of women to empowerment and enablement seminars and reading the Bible from a women's perspective must have paved the way for women's development that soon they clamored to be part of the decision-making bodies of the church hierarchy, not only in the local level but also up to the district, annual, and national levels, and where possible, even at the international level.

Church records (see Tables 1 and 2) show women's participation in the decision-making bodies of the UMC, namely, the Philippines Central Conference (PCC), Coordinating Council, and the General Conference.

## Table 1. Delegates to the Philippines Central Conference (PCC) and Coordinating Council By Year and Gender

|  | Male | Female | Total |
|---|---|---|---|
| Delegates to the Philippines Central Conference 1996 | 335 | 143 [30%] | 478 |
| Delegates to the Philippines Central Conference 2000 | 314 | 170 [35%] | 484 |
| Delegates to the Philippines Central Conference 2008 | 326 | 170 [34%] | 496 |
| Delegates to the Coordinating Council Q 1996–2000 | 28 | 15 [33%] | 43 |

Sources: *Board of Women's Work*
*Millan's Research*
*CLPAC Official Journal, 2000*

# Table 2. Delegates to the General Conference By Year and Gender

|  | Male | Female | Total |
|---|---|---|---|
| Delegates to the General Conference 2000 | 21 | 5 [19%] | 26 |
| Delegates to the General Conference 2008 | 26 | 10 [28%] | 36 |

Source: *Daily Christian Advocate 2000*
        *Daily Christian Advocate 2008*

Table 1 shows the delegates at the 1996, 2000, and 2008 Philippines Central Conferences (PCC), the highest legislative body in the country, and at the Coordinating Council (quadrennial 1996–2000, 2008–2012), the legislative body that meets in between Central Conference sessions. Out of the 478 PCC delegates in 1996, there were 143 women or thirty percent (30%), while that in 2000, out of 484 delegates there were 170 women or thirty-five percent (35%); and that in 2008, out of 496 delegates there were 170 women delegates or thirty-four percent (34%). This shows an increase of 27 women delegates or four percent (4%) in 2000, and a slight decrease percentage wise (1%) of women delegates in 2008. As to delegates to the Coordinating Council, in 1996 there was a total of 43, fifteen (15) or thirty-three percent (33%) of whom were women; and in 2008 there was a total of sixty (60), twenty-two (22) or thirty-six percent (36%) of whom were women. This shows an increase of seven (7) women or 3 percent (3%) after 12 years. The above data tell that increase of women's participation through the highest church legislative bodies in the country, is rather little or slow with just one percent every quadrennial.

Table 2 shows the Filipino delegates to the General Conference in 2000 held at Ohio and in 2008 at Texas, USA. Out of 21 delegates in 2000, 5 were women or 19 percent; and out of 36 delegates in 2008, 10 were women or 28 percent. There was an increase of 5 women or 9 percent within the span of two quadrennial. The increase of women delegates to the General Conference within two quadrennials is higher than the increase of women delegates to the Philippines Central Conference or the Coordinating Council. It is safe to conclude that the change in women's involvement in leadership and mission is due to their exposures to more seminars and trainings, particularly the "Women's Empowerment" seminars spearheaded by the

Board of Women's Work. This women's board accounted its strength on education and advocacy programs. It highlighted the "Bible-in-Context" seminars for women leaders and some church workers designed to develop deeper biblico-theological foundation and sharpen tools in social analysis, and "Women's Formation Courses," which were tools for women's empowerment.[22]

The program of the Board of Women's Work on "Violence Against Women" (VAW) started in 1996 as an awareness-raising campaign, but through the years, it evolved into a regular program of education and empowerment with development and establishment of networks for referral of victims. In 2008 it offered direct service assistance to victims of violence. The VAW program was also strengthened by the inclusion of advocacy on "Violence Against Children." The women's board conducted an intensive trainers' training that specifically targeted church women who were psychologists, social workers, deaconesses, clergywomen, lawyers, and young people—who will embrace the call of serving as service providers to VAWC.[23]

A "Women in Social Advocacy" program was also held aimed at promoting the UMC's Social Principles among women through study and analysis of societal and church issues. It is worth noting that a Basic Paralegal Training was held upon the request of one annual conference. Out of the context of that annual conference, which had a large number of recorded human rights violations, the training zeroed in on biblico-theological reflection, human rights framework as an international instrumentality of the United Nations, documentation of incidences, conducting fact-finding missions and formation of quick reaction teams. The Board of Women's Work also facilitated a one-week exposure program for women and youth to experience living with the marginalized people of some sectors of the Philippine society.

The women also have its ministry to indigent students and retired Bible women workers. The report stated: "Despite our financial limitations, one glaring testimony of our life and ministry is our effort to help young and indigent students who are in need of assistance for them to finish their studies. Since the birth of the women's board, this has been a regular part of our service and ministry. Perhaps, it is our natural connection with the young that motivated us to pursue this service despite our many limitations."[24] Its programs include financial assistance to poor but deserving female students and a pension for retired Bible women.

In the international arena, Filipino United Methodist women have proven their skills, knowledge, values, and attitude to mission through holding the highest helm of leadership in women's organizations. The late Dr. Patrocinio Ocampo, a deaconess, was the first Filipino who became World President of the World Federation of Methodist Women serving from 1966 to 1971, and later became Vice President of the Philippine Christian University in Manila, followed after forty years by Dr. Chita R. Millan, also a deaconess, who was elected as World President in 2006 to serve until 2011 at the same Federation. Another deaconess, Ms. Chita R. Framo, also became the President of DIAKONIA, a World Federation of Sisterhoods and Diaconal Associations, from 1992 to 2002. Other deaconesses are Dr. Elizabeth Tapia, professor at the Bossey Ecumenical Institute of the World Council of Churches in Switzerland for three years and center director of Drew University Theological School for four years, and Rebecca Asedillo and Emma Cantor-Orate as missionaries of the General Board of Global Ministries of the UMC. These are just to name a few. It can be observed from above that women's involvement in mission indeed, has taken wider and deeper forms. It is hoped that women will continue to engage in mission in everyway possible as what John Wesley, the founder of Methodism, advised: "Do all the good you can, by all the means you can, in all the ways you can, in all the places you can, at all the times you can, to all the people you can, as long as ever you can."

## 4. Analysis/Critique from Women's Perspective

History would tell us that Filipino women are almost always engaged in mission. It may be the "humble" or "small" forms of mission starting with their families, taking care of their own husbands and children for twenty-four hours each day, spreading out to their neighborhood when they offer their help to a sick neighbor or share their food to a hungry person, then they do mission right in their workplace by trying to listen to a colleague who is in distress if only to make a difference. But these forms of mission are not that acknowledged by the church, much less, documented. They seem to be taken for granted, forgetting Jesus' rebuke, "whatever you did to the least of these my brethren you did it to me." Attention is focused more on big mission projects that call for huge sums of money to be able to implement the mission plan, such as construction of a church building or multi-purpose center, establishment of a school, putting up a cooperative, and so on. And since the men are the bread winners in the family, they become major players in the mission plan and in the mission kick-off until completion.

Given the scenario where women seem to be at the tail rather than at the head or at the background rather than on focus, women should not be disappointed but rather, they should all the more be challenged to do mission together and they can do it with love and compassion as exemplified by our Lord Jesus Christ. Women should affirm one another's strengths, gifts, talents, resources, skills, expertise, and even differences. Affirmation is a very positive way of strengthening oneself and lifting up one's self-esteem. When that affirmation is internalized, then it allows one to be more self-confident and doing mission would be easier, faster, and lighter.

After all, Filipino women must have long practiced the theology of struggle as popularized by Fr. Edicio dela Torre. Such theology acknowledges that struggle for freedom and human dignity, for transformation of persons and communities, requires a great amount of faith because a struggle without an element of faith will never last long. This struggle has been inspiring and guiding the people in their fight against the enslaving forces of domination and exploitation. Dela Torre continued: "A theology of struggle, like a theology of liberation, has to start with a prior theme—suffering—the conditions from which people need liberation against which they struggle, e.g., poverty, oppression, exploitation, etc."[25]

There is a great need for women to make themselves available for improvement or development by grasping every opportunity that comes their way. Attendance to empowerment seminars, gender awareness trainings and the like, can help much from shunning away from the concept "in a box" about women, which are often detrimental or impede women's progress and development. And when one woman is empowered, she should also empower other women so the cycle goes on and on. When there are more empowered women, their number will get bigger and their force will be stronger. There is the saying "there is power in numbers."

## 5. Questions for Discussion

1. Where were Filipino women situated during their earlier years in mission engagement? Were they at par with men? Why or why not?

2. Why are women usually described as "unnamed" or "unsung" heroines? Who wrote their stories/history?

3. What are women's strengths in mission? How could they complement with men's strengths to make mission more effective and relevant?

4. What developments in mission occurred among Filipino women in the last two or three decades? What could be the factors that paved the way for such improvements?

5. What can the church do to ensure that women enjoy complete acceptance and leadership on equal footing with their male counterparts?

## 6. Recommendations

I strongly believe that out there in the vast fields the "harvest is ripe but the laborers are few." From the past, we have seen how church women engaged in mission. Then at present, we see how their forms of mission and ministries have retained those of the past and introduced some changes to fit into the present. And into the future, that mission will continue to evolve. Time and again, mission fields will always turn up and missionaries will always be called for. How will Filipino church women respond to the call?

Let me list some of the challenges and concerns women are confronted with in terms of "missioning" and how they can be addressed.

1. *Prioritization of missions.* Undoubtedly women participate in mission. But seemingly, they have so many forms of ministries yet small in nature. Within a region there are women's groups involved in several small ministries instead of focusing on major concern collectively. I believe that if women come together in groups and look intently on the needs of the church and community, then prioritize their missions, the results may be much better and its impact may be greater. I am afraid that the women are "spreading thinly their butter."

2. *Multiple tasking.* Women these days find themselves playing multiple roles with their corresponding tasks: as a wife, mother, cook, laundry woman, cleaner, employee outside the house, church leader, community worker, and so on. All these works are usually done by the woman, which makes her not an ordinary woman but a "super" woman. It is the home and her family that takes most of a woman's time so there is hardly time for the other tasks. Women's roles need to be assisted by democratization in the family. That includes tasking in domestic

chores, family processes of decision making or consensus, and the promotion of collective action as a family. The church could also be a strong agency to promote family responsibilities that could be taken up in several venues like Sunday schools, Bible studies, pastor's sermons, or seminars/trainings.

3. *Lack of support from the church.* The women's society is claimed to be the most active lay organization of the church. Women are said to be pillars and live wires of the church. But these come often as verbal acknowledgment from church leaders; I wonder if they are documented. Yet, behind those beautiful words expressed are hollow spaces, so to speak, in support of women's mission work. The Board of Women's Work, which is the national umbrella of all church women's organizations (women's society, deaconesses, women clergy, clergy spouses), has for so many years been requesting a slice on the central conference budget for its programs. But to her dismay, the only help the church could give is the free space of its room at the headquarters building in Manila. The women's board has to raise its own money in order to fund its own programs.

4. *Pervasive concepts of women.* We are now in the twenty-first century with many changes and developments, especially the use of computers and the Internet. Alongside these developments we see openness to new ideas and concepts, such as "women's empowerment." Although it should be remembered that even long before, sometime in the 1800s, the working women had long risen to demand their rights. It just comes now with a new name, "women's empowerment" though its intention is very similar to the agenda of women in the past. A review of women as creatures in God's image, together with their rights and responsibilities, are spearheaded by women or feminist groups so now there is such a biblico-theological reflection using "women's perspective" or "women's lens" and seminars/trainings on women's empowerment. Much has been done along this area of increasing the level of awareness of women but there needs to be a continuing education on women—their rights, gifts/abilities, responsibilities, both by women and men. This will help wipe away, slowly it may be, the pervasive or traditional concepts of women shaped and handed down by culture that are detrimental to their progress and advancement, for example, women are good for nothing, women are meant only for the home, women have no power or identity of their own but are dependent on the male/s in the household, wives are exclusive properties of their husband so they should submit to them, women are sex objects, women have no legal rights, and so on.

5. *Continuing male leadership dominance.* Patriarchal practices may have lessened to a certain degree in the Philippines. This could be vouched, as obvious as that, by the two extraordinary women who held the highest position in the country, the late President Corazon Aquino and President Gloria Macapagal-Arroyo. But even with two women as presidents of the country, there is no doubt that male dominance and elitism are still practiced in many spheres of public or church life. Indeed, the church is not exempt from it. The data itself on women's election as delegates to the Philippine Central Conference and General Conference, the highest decision-making bodies both in the country and worldwide, point to the fact that it is far yet for women to be in equal representation with their male counterparts. Realizing this, the Board of Women's Work came up with its recommendation in 2000: "the need for an equal and fair representation of youth, women and men in the decision making positions at all levels of church life."[26] But this equal and fair representation can be achieved if and only when women themselves commit for this cause. They should come together to strategize how to get the number. Some male sympathizers for women's causes may be found, but they are rare. So initiative should be borne by women, cultivation should also be done by women, and together, efforts should be exhausted to make this possible.

# 7. Conclusion

Filipino women tend to be more liberated compared to other Asian women. They are fortunate that their families love them and did not abort them solely on the basis of their gender. They are encouraged to go to school; in fact, there are more females who complete secondary level (61.87 percent girls, 48.39 percent boys), and more females (54.48 percent) in higher education enrollment in 2005-2006 than males (45.52 percent).[27] Women also hold the purse of the house and have power to decide how to spend the money. But these few things being enjoyed do not affirm the general perception that gender discrimination does not exist in the country. Indeed, gender discrimination is still evident in different sectors of the society.

There subsists to these days a deeper problem: "violence," which comes in various forms against Filipino women. A lot of women are now coming out to share their sad stories of violence/abuses, breaking the silence that they held for long. Apparent are incidences of abuses: physical, psychological, sexual, and even economic. Statistics on VAW shows that in 2001 there were 9,132 VAW cases, and then in 2008 the number of VAW cases reported to the police rose by 21 percent from the 2007 report. Physical injuries and/or wife battering are the most prevalent cases nationwide, followed by rape and acts of lasciviousness.[28] These alarming cases are being addressed by church women, especially the women's board and the women's society, and other non-governmental organizations, if only to be relevant to the present time.

Women, in all levels of church structure, are immersed into its life and ministry. You would find them doing the menial things, such as: being altar flower arrangers, church cleaners, kitchen staff, choir gowns laundry women, or dipping into the church programs and ministries such as: being Sunday school/Bible study teachers, choir members, organists, preachers, money counters, or functioning within the church structure, such as: being chairpersons of boards or committees, delegates to conferences, participants/facilitators to trainings/seminars, and so on. But in spite of all the tangible and observable contributions of women, the church has not come to the point of according women what are due to women. Proverbs 31:31 says, "Give her credit for all she does, she deserves the respect of everyone" (GNT); but this is not observed in its strictest sense.

There are reasons for women to jubilate: (1) the ordination of women clergy in The United Methodist Church, which used to be taboo in earlier years; (2) the granting of voice and vote to deaconesses by the General Conference 1996 action; (3) the increasing involvement and participation of women in the highest decision-making bodies of the church, the Philippines Central Conference and General Conference; (4) the election of women to key or high positions in the international community. Much has been done by the Filipino women in mission but much yet remains to be done!

## Further Reading

Alberto S. Abeleda Jr., *The Nation in Focus. Philippine History and Government* (Quezon City: Saint Bernadette Publications, Inc., 2005).

Nonie S. Aviso, B. Asedillo, L. Garibay, eds., *Currents in Philippine Theology* (Quezon City: Kalinangan Book Series II. Institute of Religion and Culture, 1992).

J. M. Bunyi et al., eds., *Celebrating a Century of God's Faithfulness: Harris Memorial College and the Deaconess* (Rizal: Plus Sign Enterprises, 2003).

Chita R. Millan, *Spirituality: At the Core of Leadership Among Successful United Methodist Women Educational Leaders* (Dissertation. De La Salle University, Manila, 2008).

Liwliwa T. Robledo, *Gender, Religion and Social Change. A Study of Philippine Methodist Deaconesses, 1903-1978* (Dissertation. The Iliff School of Theology and University of Denver, Colorado, USA, 1996).

# Endnotes

1. http://en.wikipedia.org/wiki/Philippines, February 7, 2011.

2. www.philippinecountry.com, February 7, 2011.

3. Alberto S. Abeleda Jr., *The Nation in Focus. Philippine History and Government* (Quezon City: Saint Bernadette Publications, 2005).

4. J. M. Bunyi, et al., *Celebrating a Century of God's Faithfulness. Harris Memorial College and the Deaconess* (Rizal: Plus Sign Enterprises, 2003), 6.

5. http://www.irishmethodist.org/mission/what_is_mission.php, February 12, 2011.

6. *Official Journal of the Northwest Philippines Annual Conference*, 1975.

7. Ibid., 1977.

8. Ibid., 1985.

9. Ibid., 1995.

10. Ibid., 1999.

11. Ibid., 2002.

12. Ibid., 2004.

13. Bunyi, *Celebrating*, 15.

14. Ibid., 26.

15. Ibid., 49.

16. Ibid., 62.

17. Ibid., 29.

18. Liwliwa T. Robledo, *Gender, Religion and Social Change: A Study of Philippine Methodist Deaconesses, 1903-1978* (PhD diss., The Iliff School of Theology and University of Denver. Colorado, 1996), 231-232.

19. Gregorio F. Zaide, *Philippine History and Government* (Quezon City: All Nations Publishing, 62004), 146.

20. Bunyi, et al., *Celebrating*, 114.

21. Par 1314.1, *The Book of Discipline of The United Methodist Church* (Nashville: The United Methodist Publishing House, 2008).

22. Darlene Caramanzana and Chita Framo, Board of Women's Work Quadrennial Report to Annual Conferences, 2006.

23. Darlene Caramanzana, Board of Women's Work Executive Secretary's Report, 2008.

24. Ibid.

25. Edicio de la Torre, quoted in Nonie S. Aviso, B. Asedillo, L. Garibay, eds., *Currents in Philippine Theology* (Quezon City: Kalinangan Book Series II. Institute of Religion and Culture, 1992), 58, 62.

26. Official Journal of the Central Luzon Philippines Annual Conference, 2000.

27. http://www.ncrfw.gov.ph/index.php/statistics-on-filipino-women, (February 18, 2011).

28. Ibid.

CHAPTER 12

# More than Wives: Rediscovering the Little "m" in our Mission History

## A Case Study of Four Missionary Wives in Early Aotearoa/New Zealand

*Cathy Ross*

## 1. Introduction

It was the little "m" that got me going. When I discovered that the early Church Missionary Society (CMS) missionary wives to New Zealand were expressed as an anonymous little "m" next to their husbands' names in the *CMS Register*, I felt that this was deeply unjust. This form of description continued well into the twentieth century! John V. Taylor, former General Secretary of CMS wrote in his Newsletter of April, 1968: "Such appendages to a husband's name were until 1950 the only form in which wives appeared in the list of missionaries in the CMS Pocket Book."[1] These women accompanied their husbands to a distant land, learned the language of the local people, suffered real hardships and made their own contribution to the cause of the CMS mission and yet were unnamed and unacknowledged by the mission society that sent them. Further exploration was called for and so I began a fascinating journey of research, delving into the lives of four of these women—reading their letters and diaries, which detailed their daily concerns and their mission engagement. I also discovered that their disappearance was a common theme in the historical records elsewhere. As I read through church and mission history, I asked myself: "where are the women and what were they doing?" Surely all these married male missionaries had wives! It is as though a camera lens has been trained through the ages of the church and women are missing. As Patricia Hill commented, "The women have simply disappeared."[2] However, it is not that women were absent from church and mission history—women have always been there—but rather that history has been written from a particular standpoint from which women were often excluded. This was apparently the case with *The CMS Register.* Only husbands' names were thought worthy of recording and remembering. In fact, we still see a hangover of this attitude in twenty-first century United Kingdom—letters addressed to Mrs. Stephen Ross for example. Again, this nomenclature makes the wife virtually invisible.

## 2. Historical Background

Church history has focussed on the great, public events where women were usually on the periphery. Life outside these great events was not considered worthy of attention and so women's experience was discounted and devalued. A sharp distinction was made between the public world of men and the private domain of women. Women were seen as incapable of causing events to happen and so their experience was either ignored or marginalised. They were believed to be inferior beings, both physiologically and morally, and so were seen as passive objects rather than active agents of history. Male experience was considered to be normative and this is what was recorded. Information about women was far less abundant and accessible than information about men and so until relatively recently, women have been virtually invisible from history, both sacred and secular. The task of restoring women to history and history to women is a necessary and important one to gain a more fully orbed appreciation of human history.[3]

## 3. Case Study

This is also the case in the relatively more recent church history of Australia and Aotearoa/New Zealand. Patricia Grimshaw, in an article on the history of Australian women, lamented:

> It would be difficult to point to a national historical tradition which more clearly represented a celebration of white male achievement. . . . Women as a whole (unlike rabbits, sheep and horses) were not discussed, except by virtue of the social effects of their absence: the distorted sex ratio of the colonies, for example, and its effect on population increase.[4]

A similar lament has gone up about the history of women in Aotearoa/New Zealand:

> As the story of the European settlement of Aotearoa has been told, golddiggers, missionaries, pastoralists, soldiers, adventurers, and agricultural labourers have been brought into view. It is the men who settle the country and break in the land. Women are viewed only in terms of their relationship to men: "the pioneers and their wives." They are mute appendages, unnamed and therefore unidentified.[5]

Because women have been seen as adjuncts to men, "women have been systematically written out of historical and anthropological records."[6] In effect, women's experience was subsumed under that of men's. As a result of feminist scholarship, increasing attention is now being paid to the specific experiences and lives of women missionaries and settlers as revealed through their letters and diaries. This allows the researcher and reader "insight into both the practical and spiritual lives of these women as well as the gendered dimensions of their lives as missionaries."[7]

Women and their activities have been missed because history has been considered in male-centered terms. Now women are beginning to ask what would history be like if it were seen through they eyes of women and reordered by women's values and definitions? The context in which women lived was studied—her relationships, her social networks, her power, her position in society. The camera lens began to focus on female experience as different from that of men but which could provide an equally important part of the story. As Gerda Lerner affirmed, "[the] record of female experience [was] an essential first step towards writing a new history."[8] This refocusing of the lens on women's experience is in itself a feminist act. History is no longer seen from an objective, uninvolved standpoint but rather becomes the subject of personal engagement as women seek to draw out new stories, new values, and definitions from the lives of women. The experience of women, their daily lives and involvements have become subjects of research seen as valid and important to gain a clearer picture.

The issues of who is retelling the story and which sources are accessed and interpreted are significant. Feminist historians are vitally involved as they research and interpret history. They refute the possibility of recording an objective history and indeed claim that objectivity has often been a mask for hiding personal agendas or for concealing women. This is where the imagery of "refocusing the camera" is helpful. Feminist historians claim that, in the past, historians have tried to be the camera themselves, giving an unbiased, objective snapshot of history. However, feminist historians maintain that the photographer interprets history and that by refocusing the camera, new understandings and interpretations can emerge. This also has the advantage of not excluding what has already come into focus as this approach is able "to recast an old familiar photograph in a provocative new light, rich with telling detail, harmonizing background and subjects into a coherent whole."[9]

This case study is an attempt to refocus the camera, to train the lens on certain women in the history of Aotearoa/New Zealand, to bring their lives and experiences into focus, out from behind the shirttails and to ask certain questions of and about them.

## 3.1 Angel in the House

The four women from our history, Charlotte Brown (1795–1855), Anne Wilson (1802–1838), Elizabeth Colenso (1821–1904), and Catherine Hadfield (1831–1902) were all Church Missionary Society (CMS) missionary wives. Charlotte and Anne came to New Zealand with their husbands; Elizabeth and Catherine grew up in missionary families in New Zealand and married CMS missionaries already serving here. Their husbands were missionaries with the CMS and were recorded in the CMS Register as such. Their wives were not as they were not considered to be missionaries. "Missionary work . . . was clearly perceived as a task performed by men that women merely supplemented. Missionary was a male noun; it denoted a male actor, male action, male spheres of service."[10] However, Jocelyn Murray has made clear in her research on the CMS that long before any women were officially accepted, unmarried women as well as wives were serving overseas.[11] From the beginning, the CMS encouraged its men to go as married men with families in order to be able to model pious domesticity and the ideal Christian family. It was often exactly this Victorian ideology, which worked for and against women.

The "the angel in the house" phenomenon, led to some ambiguity in the working out of women's role and identity within an evangelical worldview.[12] It was clear that women were supposed to be subordinate and that home and children were their sphere, yet they still had influence. In fact many women argued that if they were the upholders of Christian values they should be able to use their influence outside the home in philanthropic activities and in social reform. It was a small step from the love of family to the love of the larger human family and this step was made easier by Christian teaching. Female reformers hailed Christianity as an emancipating influence which could give enormous scope to woman as wife and mother and by extension, to society. This philanthropic impulse was readily linked with an evangelistic motive. Others such as Sarah Lewis, in her book *Woman's Mission* (London, 1839) extolled woman's missionary spirit as "the flow of maternal love."[13] She also stated that women were God's instruments "for the regeneration of the world."[14]

So while this ideology of domesticity was at one level deeply conservative, at another, it held within it the seeds of its own subversion. Within the home women could exercise a certain amount of power. As Davidoff and Hall comment: "If the moral world was theirs, who needed the public world of business and politics?"[15] It was believed that women were the moral regenerators of the home and the nation and this could have wider ramifications as women became involved in philanthropic activities and engaged in mission service. Although evangelical theology was conservative and limiting in terms of a woman's role, it also provided an effective justification for women's involvement in social reform and philanthropy in the public arena as an extension of their moral and spiritual activities in the home. Another interesting outcome was the founding of women's organisations. Women began to reach out to other women in sisterhood, in solidarity, on the common ground of domesticity. They would create friendships with other women and within this lay the beginnings of many women's organizations which over time developed and flourished in a more formalized way.[16]

Women's involvement in charitable endeavors grew remarkably during the course of the nineteenth century. This has been referred to as the "angel out of the house" phenomenon, which recognized women's role in a wider context.[17] Anglican social campaigner Josephine Butler, in 1869, also claimed that "the extension beyond our homes of the home influence" would regenerate society and thereby serve to enhance family life.[18] Anne Summers described women's philanthropic work as a "home from home."[19] Women were involved in a wide variety of charitable activities.[20] Some of the most notable were: Sunday school teaching, Girls' Friendly Societies, missionary auxiliary societies seeking to raise funds for overseas mission work, the temperance movement, a network of penitentiaries and houses of refuge for prostitutes and parish visiting where spiritual and physical needs were ascertained and met.[21]

And so "the angel in the house" becomes "the angel out of the house." On the one hand, women were accorded a special role as civilizers within the home, which gave them a status morally superior to men. On the other hand, it was this role within the home intimately tied up with domestic and childcare responsibilities, which often limited their availability for mission work outside the home. For the CMS, rooted in evangelical theology and piety, personal vocation and calling could transcend gender and therefore work in the wives' favor at times.

In order to bring these women's lives into focus in a historical context constructed by both men and women, new analytical questions are needed. What kind of work were these wives doing? To what extent did they serve as active missionaries in their own right? How did the women themselves understand their role and calling? Did they believe they had a vocation for missionary service, which they could fulfill as a missionary wife? What did these women contribute to the outworking of mission and how did they go about it? Finally, how different would the mission of the CMS in Aotearoa/New Zealand have been without the work and involvement of these wives?

These are some of the questions that a feminist historian would want to address to these women in order to adjust the focus and train the lens on them. In the main, these questions will not be answered by reading traditional histories and biographies. As Charlotte Macdonald has highlighted, the rediscovery of our pioneer women has tended to view them as either women-as-victims or as women-as-glorious-heroines. "The immortalised image of the pioneer woman is an ideal one."[22] I have read about these four women as well as reading their diaries, journals, letters to family and friends to try to present a realistic picture of them. Universalist stances and grand overarching themes have proven to be unsatisfactory and unreal representations of the stuff of people's lives. We know from our own experiences, that these women fashioned and created their experiences as they recorded them so that the account of their experiences is already just that—an account with layers of meanings; shades and shadows of what is told and what is not. Just as we also know that we, as historians, are not simply revealing a single history that is waiting to be uncovered but rather are shaping and creating a quilt or a narrative out of a selected set of materials.

## 3.2 *Vocation and Marriage*

Most missionary wives were helpmeets to their husbands, enlisted to join in their husbands' work and to support their

husbands in their high calling. They were primarily to be providers of conjugal comfort and homemakers so their husbands
could be the missionaries. As Dana Robert has observed, in
her research on missionary wives from New England at the
same period: "Regardless of their personal qualifications, most
women in New England could live out a missionary vocation
only if they married male missionaries."[23]

Each of these women had a quite clear vocation to mission as
they stated in their diaries and letters. Charlotte Brown shared
the firm, evangelical conviction of her husband that this was
her calling, which God had mapped out for her. Although she
dreaded the separation from family and friends, she was convinced of her calling and wrote in a letter to a friend:

> My heart sometimes sinks at the thought of parting with so many
> beloved friends but my way has been so clearly marked out and
> so many various obstacles have been removed that I cannot but
> confidently hope that I have not presumptuously undertaken the
> task that is to engage my future life. . . . If our Heavenly Father
> (as I trust He has) has indeed pointed my way He will support
> under every trial.[24]

Anne Wilson also experienced a definite missionary calling and
it was under her "gentle influence" that her husband John came
to this vocation also.[25] There are many journal entries, which
express her quite explicit sense of vocation and her awareness
that God has given her a task to fulfill. Her journal entries on
the boat en route for New Zealand show that she took this
vocation very seriously. "Many things have lately combined
to make one feel more desirous to go to the poor heathen. The
more I hear of them the more my heart seems drawn to them."[26]
However, her belief in this strong vocation to make Christ
known mingled with inner feelings of personal inadequacy and
spiritual frailty plagued Anne all her life. She could cry out to
God: "Oh when shall Jesus be truly known in the world?"[27] and
two weeks later be in despair about her missionary fervor: "The
low state of missionary spirit at this house is truly grievous."[28]
Anne endears herself to the reader by so freely writing of her
struggles to fulfill her vocation. She used the Maori word *pouri*
(gloomy, dark, miserable) in her letters to her husband several
times to describe her state of mind. Yet she was not overcome by
these feelings as she counted it such an honor to serve God and
to make Christ known. Her vocation and commitment to Christ
was the foundation, which kept her in New Zealand, serving
alongside her husband. "My beloved husband, should we not

rather rejoice that we are called to suffer for one Gospel. . . . Oh may we ever walk with Him and nothing know beside nothing desire, nothing esteem but Jesus crucified."[29] It was sentiments such as these that kept Anne serving to the end, despite her painful illness and excruciating death one day before her thirty-sixth birthday, probably of breast cancer.

For Elizabeth Colenso it is quite clear that their marriage was not a love match. William, her husband, explained that for him Christ was primary and that because he had devoted himself to Christ's cause, his need was for "a helpmeet for me being also devoted, or willing, to devote herself, to the same blessed Service."[30] It appears that both of them were fully aware that initially there was little love but William recorded that, "I fully firmly believed that mutual affection would surely follow, for all I wanted was a suitable partner, particularly in mission work—this was ever uppermost."[31] For William, his mission work was his priority and for Elizabeth it may well have been a means to fulfill her missionary vocation and be useful. Robert has stated that the desire for usefulness was a major motivating factor for women in mission at this period.[32]

## 3.3 Work

In the history of mission, missionary wives were generally seen as helpmeets to their husbands. Their primary role was to provide a stable home, offer gracious hospitality and to run well-ordered households reflecting Victorian piety, morality, and domesticity. Each of these women, however, was heavily involved in teaching Maori women and children in schools. They taught domestic skills as well as literacy. Charlotte's husband, Alfred noted in his journal: "Mrs. B. commenced a school for girls, 60 of whom attended. The next day there were 70 and the day after 50 pupils. A week later Charlotte started a morning infant School."[33] It was not easy for her because she had to labor alone without the help of any other missionary wives and by September 11, 1835 Alfred was writing to Henry Williams: "Mrs. B. has now been labouring alone for 15 weeks with a large infant school in the morning and a girls' school in the afternoon, and I quite fear that one of the schools must shortly come to a stand, unless she gets assistance."[34] Later at Te Papa, despite ill health, Charlotte commenced another school. Her school was obviously well known and respected as once, during the war with Rotorua, one of the chiefs told Alfred that "he only went to "fight" to seize some female slaves to attend Mother Brown's school!"[35]

Elizabeth Colenso, who had been brought up on a CMS mission station, ran her own school, with its own curriculum and program from the age of nineteen. In 1842, her father wrote to the CMS bitterly complaining of the faithful teaching Elizabeth had provided with neither recognition nor remuneration from the CMS: "My eldest daughter who has been labouring in the most indefatigable and successful manner amongst the native females and children for the last four and a half years has never had any remuneration for her services with the exception of ten pounds which was given to her by the Committee two years ago."[36]

It seems that Elizabeth was a vital part of the CMS establishment but was neither recognized nor valued by them. After her marriage to William, Elizabeth ran an infants' school at St John's College, Waimate so successfully that William believed his ordination was postponed because Elizabeth's work was more valuable to the Bishop's than his. "It was doubtful if I should emerge at all as an Ordained Missionary. My thoughts were *not* theirs. And Mrs. Colenso was wanted more and more every day."[37] On arriving at Ahuriri, a remote and inhospitable place for a mission station, Elizabeth worked tirelessly, both within the home and without. Her husband wrote: "She too had a heart for her Station work in the Girls' and Infants' schools in which she did good service and was always an excellent mother to her children."[38] Sadly, nine years after arriving at Ahuriri, Elizabeth left William after discovering that he was the father of her house help's child. She lived briefly in Auckland with her two children before spending seven years working with the Ashwells at Taupiri. Benjamin Ashwell was grateful for her assistance and praised her highly. He described her work and contribution as follows:

> We were greatly strengthened, in 1854, by the arrival of Mrs. Colenso to assist my wife; it was impossible for anyone to take a greater interest in missionary work; her knowledge of native language could not be surpassed, and her influence with the native children was very great in season and out of season. She was sedulously at work, not only for the school but for the natives generally.[39]

She then took her children to England for five years where she was deeply involved in social work and overseeing Bible translation. Thankfully, her Bible translation work has been acknowledged. Carleton, in his biography on Henry Williams, wrote: "The Old Testament was put through the press in England by the Rev George Maunsell . . . the Rev. W. T. Mellor, and Mrs.

Colenso, daughter of Mr. Fairburn, an able and intelligent scholar."[40] After returning briefly to New Zealand, she agreed to go and help out at the Melanesian Mission in Norfolk Island for four months where she remained for twenty-two years. Elizabeth is an intriguing case because she served both as a missionary wife and as a "single" missionary. There is no evidence that she was ever recompensed by the CMS for her service after she left her husband.[41]

Catherine (Kate) Hadfield was also brought up on a mission station at Paihia as she was a daughter of Henry and Marianne Williams. Before her marriage to Octavius she lived with her brother and his wife at Otaki and taught in the mission school. She wrote to her parents: "There were 80 children today when I counted. Then there are two rooms and the schoolmaster has the big room, and Mary and I, the Native schoolmaster each have a class in the next room."[42] Kate continued teaching in the school after her marriage, as well as educating her own daughters.[43] She accompanied her husband on numerous journeys around the region and she was the first white woman to make the overland journey from Auckland to Otaki, (with their small baby son), such was her eagerness to return to their mission work together. A biographer of Octavius noted: "Not only was Kate the first Pakeha woman to make this journey, together with nine-months-old Henry—but she appears to have done so in the face of some male opposition."[44] She also accompanied Octavius on two journeys to England. On their first journey she gave birth to their third child on the boat. After moving to Wellington and now finding herself the wife of Bishop Hadfield she was fully involved in parish work and in fund raising through church bazaars. It appears that the bazaars were organized and run entirely by women and that Kate was a keen patron of them. She also took an interest in the disadvantaged and marginalized. According to her daughter, "People who were 'down and out' turned at times to the Bishop's wife and told her their difficulties."[45] She served as the first Vice-President of the Girls' Friendly Society (GFS) in Wellington. The GFS was founded in England in 1875 with the object of uniting "women and girls in a fellowship of prayer, service and purity of life."[46] This was work that Kate undertook independently of her husband as it seems that this was definitely women's work only for women. The daughters of both Lady Jervois and Kate were also serving on the Committee with their mothers. Lady Jervois' daughter was a Council member and Kate's daughter was the librarian.[47] Kate's daughter seemed to be following in her mother's footsteps in engaging in mission and community service. The GFS was a large part of Kate's life and work while she resided in Wellington.[48] Even in their retirement to Marton, Kate remained involved in church life and affairs. She became the first President of the Marton Parochial District Guild. Kate worked diligently alongside her husband all her married life.

## 3.4 Family Life

Certainly it was the missionary wives who were responsible for running the home and modeling pious Victorian domesticity. Although these women were involved in much missionary work, husbands and wives inhabited different spheres. Anne Wilson commented soon after her arrival in New Zealand: "We have thus begun housekeeping in this savage land. I have schools to attend to and girls under my charge, besides my own children."[49] Anne was involved in teaching at the native schools and training and domesticating local Maori girls which was seen as an important task for missionary women. The first mission school was established in Paihia in 1823 and its first pupils were Maori women and girls. By 1833, when Anne arrived this sort of education was well established and Anne fell into the expected pattern, modeled especially by the Williams' families. The accepted pattern seemed to be that the male missionaries would teach school early in the morning to leave the rest of their day free for other tasks. For their wives however, the early morning was an extremely busy time with household chores when they needed their Maori girls to help. So it was decided that Maori girls would be instructed at a different time of day.[50] The local Maori women, Nga Puhi, were considered corrupted and ignorant. The CMS view was that Christian family life was to be modeled and their society to be "civilized" by the introduction of Christianity.[51] As Fitzgerald observed, English family values predominated. "Salvation was predicated on the adoption of Christian values and practices that involved amongst other things, the external elements of English culture; clothing, language and gender appropriate behaviour."[52] Local Maori women would imbibe these values by emulating missionary wives and their homes. "Within the mission family home, Nga Puhi women would come into contact with ideal Christian women who would offer an example of domesticity and teach them how to become good wives and mothers."[53] This certainly seemed to be the pattern, which Anne and the other wives followed during her years in New Zealand.

At times, when their husbands were away traveling, which was often the case, these wives were sometimes the only European left on the mission station and were left responsible for running it. For example, in 1850 and 1851 William Colenso was away from the mission station 118 and 131 days respectively.[54] This meant the wives had to deal alone with all sorts of issues ranging from the pastoral and unexpected visitors, to managing recalcitrant workmen, facing marauding war parties and dealing with disasters. Charlotte was without Alfred on the occasion of the devastating fire, which delayed their removal into their home by many months. Kate was without Octavius when a party of rebel Kingite Maori were in the district and it was she, ever resourceful, who organized the making and hoisting of a Union Jack to deter their entering the mission station. She encouraged Octavius in his battle against the flagrant injustice of the Taranaki land sales. She made extra copies of his first pamphlet for the Chief Justice. She openly sided with the Maori and helped them formulate a petition to the Minister of Native Affairs.[55] In the face of injustice, neither she nor her husband eschewed political involvement.

These women were often called on to exhibit bravery and resilience in ways more private than their husbands but no less demanding.[56] Regular childbirths, often in remote locations with no medical assistance, frequent absences of their husbands, assuming prime responsibility for the education of their children, offering hospitality in sometimes trying conditions, tiredness, language difficulties and illness were just some of the issues to be faced with fortitude. There is little doubt that these women played an essential role in mission endeavor. Their labor was essential to the work of the mission. They performed and directed the practical tasks such as teaching, nursing, cooking, and other tasks normally assigned to the women's sphere as well as providing a role model of Christian family life. Theirs was hardly a shirttail experience. Gillett comments that while women have always been involved in mission:

> Their role might come under the category of "Best Supporting Actress" at an Academy Awards Ceremony because female involvement in the mission field has usually been seen as a corollary to the work of their male counterparts. Women's involvement in mission originated through the work of missionary wives who have always been expected to accompany and aid their husband in his endeavours."[57]

This is certainly how missionary wives have been regarded over the centuries—as adjuncts to their husbands. However, the role of these women was far more than providing hearth and home for husband and children. All these women experienced and lived out a vocation in mission. They ran the mission station while their husbands were away, taught at the mission schools as well as teaching their own children, provided hospitality for visitors, nurtured the spiritual lives of their family and domestics, learned the language, translated texts into Maori, and provided the focus for family life. Certainly the mission work of the CMS in Aotearoa/New Zealand would have been very different without the involvement and engagement of the missionary wives.

## 4. Questions for Discussion

1. How and where do we need to refocus the camera in our context so that we can tell the stories of our foremothers?

2. How do we encourage women to express and work out their vocation in mission?

3. What is the place of women's work for women? Is this still valid and helpful or does it create an unhelpful binary distinction?

4. The place of the family—what is the role of women in your particular context?

## 5. Recommendations

1. Become aware of the mission history of our own contexts and especially the role women played.

2. Explore and celebrate the holistic approach to mission that women practice.

3. The gender issue is a justice issue—make people aware of this and ensure that women's voices and perspectives are heard.

## 6. Mission Concerns

1. Visibility of women is a concern. Women need to be role models so that others can imagine possible forms of involvement and ministry.

2. Women's engagement may bring about a more holistic understanding of mission which may challenge more traditional approaches to mission.

3. Women's work for women—does this need to be recaptured and encouraged or is it outdated?

# 7. Conclusion

How different is it for women in mission today? Having marginalized and often ignored women's contribution to mission in the nineteenth century, how are we now going to recognize and affirm women's role in mission in the twenty-first century?

Currently, it is estimated that there are two to three times more women mission partners working cross-culturally than men.[58] However, in the Western evangelical world of mission, that may be the only good news for women. There are very few women running either denominational or interdenominational mission agencies. Women are woefully under-represented at the levels of determining policy and of decision making. It is a far cry from 1900 when there were forty-eight mission societies in North America fully supported and staffed by women.[59] These women were involved in Bible teaching, medical programs, higher education, orphanages, ministries of compassion and much more. Women supported and publicized this work.[60] These women's mission societies developed because women became impatient with male-dominated mission boards. However, they were eventually pressured to merge with the mainline boards and so by the 1950s few were left and even fewer women were in positions of leadership. Sadly, this is still the case for women in mission in the twenty-first century.

Even more tragic is the downgrading of women's ministries as a reaction to secular feminism. Dana Robert writes: "As I have gone around interviewing women mission activists in conservative churches, I have heard the same sad refrain: there is less room for women's mission today than there was twenty or thirty years ago."[61] She continues that stories of gender bias and dismissal of women's gifts would "break your heart." Dana Robert issues a pertinent warning within the North American context: "Recent information indicates that Southern Baptist women are beginning to turn away from missions. If history is any indicator, with the women muzzled, it will only be a matter of time before the mission program in the entire denomination begins to decline."[62]

Thankfully, this is only part of the picture. We know, from the research of Andrew Walls and others, that the heartlands of Christianity have moved and the center of gravity has shifted south. There are now more Christians in the Majority World than in the West and probably more missionaries from the Majority World also.[63] This has heartening implications for women in the church and in mission. According to Robert, 70 percent of

Christians in African Indigenous Churches are women, 80 percent of house church members in China are women, in Korea cell groups are mainly led by women, and in Latin America Protestant women join churches to encourage better family life while Roman Catholic women are active in the Base Christian Communities to improve social conditions for their families and communities. Robert claims that while vocations for Roman Catholic sisters are on the decline in the Western church, non-Western sisters are discovering their own vocations. In Africa, she maintains that "women in both African Initiated Churches and historic denominations are at the cutting edge of their missionary expansion during a period of explosive growth in African Christianity."[64]

She suggests that, "In the evangelistic leadership of non-Western women, we can see the continued relevance of the supposedly old-fashioned, gender-based women's missionary movement."[65] For many of these women in the Majority World, most of whom are married, their concern is home and family. Robert cites research done in Colombia that shows that Pentecostalism and evangelical Christianity raises the status of women and strengthens family life by encouraging the men to give up drinking, smoking, and affairs and therefore rehabilitating family life.[66] Life in the Majority World is generally characterized by a holistic approach. As Mercy Oduyoye has written: "Women have transformed the traditional church, hospital, school into mission as relationships."[67] Women are involved in mission and in outreach for the betterment of communities and families—their approach to mission is holistic. Women's approaches to mission have reflected, what Robert has called, a "messy alliance" between evangelism and grassroots concerns for home, family and community.[68]

What are the implications of all this for the future of Christianity in the West? These CMS missionary wives of the nineteenth century who were able to juggle family life with a wider concern for society may well hold the key for the future of women's involvement in mission. The future of mission, both within the West and beyond, depends on taking seriously the place of women in mission.

## Further Reading

Bowie, Fiona, Deborah Kirkwood, and Shirley Ardener, eds., *Women and Missions: Past and Present Anthropological and Historical Perspectives* (Oxford: Berg, 1993).

Jones, Serene, *Feminist Theory and Christian Theology, Cartographies of Grace* (Augsburg: Fortress, 2000).

Robert, Dana, ed., *Gospel Bearers, Gender Barriers* (Maryknoll: Orbis, 2002).

Ross, Cathy, *Women with a Mission, Rediscovering Missionary Wives in Early New Zealand* (Auckland: Penguin, 2006).

Stinton, Diane, *Jesus of Africa, Voices of Contemporary African Christology* (Maryknoll: Orbis, 2004).

# Endnotes

1. John V. Taylor, *CMS Newsletter* (April 1968): 1.

2. Quoted in Janet Crawford, "Church History," in *An A to Z of Feminist Theology*, ed. Lisa Isherwood and Dorothea McEwan (Sheffield: Sheffield University Press, 1996), 27-30.

3. Joan Kelly has stated that this is the dual goal of women's history. She goes on to state, "In seeking to add women to the fund of historical knowledge, women's history has revitalised theory, for it has shaken the conceptual foundations of historical study." Quoted in Elisabeth Schüssler Fiorenza, "The 'Quilting' of Women's History: Phoebe of Cenchreae," in *Embodied Love Sensuality and Relationship as Feminist Values*, eds. Paula M. Cooey, Sharon A. Farmer, and Mary Ellen Ross (San Francisco: Harper and Row, 1987), 38.

4. Patricia Grimshaw, "Writing the History of Australian Women," in *Writing Women's History International Perspectives*, eds. Karen Offen, Ruth Roach Pierson, and Jane Rendall (Bloomington: University of Indiana Press, 1991), 154-55.

5. Bronwyn Labrum, *Women's History, A Short Guide to Researching and Writing Women's History in New Zealand* (Wellington: Bridget Williams Books, 1993), 9-10.

6. Fiona Bowie, "Introduction: Reclaiming Women's Presence," in *Women and Missions: Past and Present Anthropological and Historical Perspectives*, eds. Fiona Bowie, Deborah Kirkwood, and Shirley Ardener (Oxford: Berg, 1993), 1.

7. Mary Taylor Huber and Nancy C Lutkehaus, "Introduction: Gendered Missions at Home and Abroad," in *Gendered Missions: Women and Men in Missionary Discourse and Practice*, eds. Mary Taylor Huber and Nancy C Lutkehaus (Ann Arbor: University of Michigan Press, 1999), 7.

8. Quoted in Frances Porter, Charlotte MacDonald, and Tui MacDonald, eds., *"My Hand will write what my Heart Dictates": The unsettled lives in nineteenth century NZ as revealed to sisters, family and friends* (Auckland: Auckland University Press, 1996), 10.

9. Margaret Lamberts Bendroth, "Men, Women and God: Some Historiographical Issues," in *History and the Christian Historian*, ed. Ronald Wells (Grand Rapids: Eerdmans, 1998), 91.

10. Quoted in Bowie, "Introduction: Reclaiming Women's Presence," in *Women and Missions*, 1.

11. See Jocelyn Murray, "Anglican and Protestant Missionary Societies in Great Britain: Their Use of Women as Missionaries from the late 18th century to the late 19th century," in *Exchange* 21, no. 1 (April 1992), 1-28; and Jocelyn Murray, "The Role of Women in the CMS 1799-1917," in *The CMS and World Christianity 1799–1999*, eds. Kevin Ward and Brian Stanley (Grand Rapids: Eerdmans, 2000), 66-90.

12. This is the title of a Victorian poem by Coventry Patmore where the woman is extolled as having traditionally feminine virtues such as love,

intuition, virtue, and beauty. "As Patmore's title suggests, the angel brings a more than moral purity to the home that she at once creates and sanctifies, for which her mate consequently regards her with a sentimental, essentially religious reverence." Carol Christ, "Victorian Masculinity and the Angel in the House," in *A Widening Sphere: Changing Roles of Victorian Women*, ed. Martha Vicinus (Indiana: Indiana University Press, 1977), 146.

13. Quoted in Frank K. Prochaska, *Women and Philanthropy in Nineteenth Century England* (Oxford: Clarendon Press, 1980), 7.

14. Ibid., 13.

15. Leonore Davidoff and Catherine Hall, eds., *Family Fortunes: Men and Women of the English Middle Class* (London: Hutchinson, 1987), 183.

16. Note, for example, the growth of women's mission boards in the USA during the nineteenth century, so that by the end of that century nearly half of the mission boards in the USA were Women's Boards. Over 3 million women were involved, and by the early twentieth century this had become the largest Women's Movement in the USA. Unfortunately, their existence was relatively short-lived and by the 1920s their demise was complete.

17. Elizabeth K. Helsinger, Robin Lauterbach Sheets, and William Veeder, "Sarah Lewis and Woman's Mission," in *The Woman Question, Society and Literature in Britain and America 1837–1883 Volume One: Defining Voices*, ed. Elizabeth K Helsinger, Robin Lauterbach Sheets, and William Veeder (Chicago: The University of Chicago Press, 1983), xi-xvii.

18. Ibid., 131.

19. Quoted in Anne Summers, "A Home from Home: Women's Philanthropic Work in the Nineteenth Century," in *Fit Work for Women*, ed. Sandra Burman (London: Croom Helm, 1979), 33.

20. See Linda Wilson, "'Constrained by Zeal:' Women in Mid-Nineteenth Century Conformist Churches," in *Journal of Religious History* 23, no. 2 (1999), 190.

21. Kate Hadfield became a founding Vice-President of the Girls' Friendly Society in Wellington in 1883.

22. Bronwyn Labrum, *Women's History*, 19.

23. Dana Robert, *American Women in Mission: A Social History of their Thought and Practice*, (Macon: Mercer University Press, 1996), 18.

24. Letter to Mary Beams, quoted in *'My Hand will write what my Heart Dictates': The unsettled lives in nineteenth century NZ as revealed to sisters, family and friend*, eds. Frances Porter, Charlotte MacDonald, and Tui MacDonald (Auckland: Auckland University Press, 1996), 60.

25. At the time of her death, John wrote of his great loss to the Society in England, "and when I tell you that 'the desire of mine eyes,' my beloved wife, under whose gentle influence the Lord first led me to a knowledge of myself and of my Saviour, is taken from me, you will perceive that my loss is great indeed." in "Obituary of Mrs Wilson, Wife of Mr J. A. Wilson, Catechist of the Church Missionary Society in New Zealand," *Church Missionary Record*, vol 10, no 8 (Aug 1839), 170.

26. Anne Catherine Wilson, "Letters and Journal of Anne Catherine Wilson/collected," ed. and trans. M. G. Armstrong (Alexander Turnbull Library, hereafter WTU: MS-Papers-3943, 1832-38), 29 August 1832.

27. Ibid., 22 May 1836.

28. Ibid., 5 June 1836.

29. Ibid., letter to John, Puriri, Monday 27 June 1836.

30. William Colenso, "Letters qMS-0491-0492," (WTU, 1834–1853). Letter from William Colenso to Robert Maunsell, Paihia, 4 April 1842. Underlining in original.

31. William Colenso, "Autobiography - typescript 88-103-1/01," in *Further Papers*, ed. A. G. Bagnall (WTU), 28.

32. Robert, *American Women*, 33.

33. Joan C. Stanley, "'Giving Honour unto the Wife'," *Journal of the New Zealand Federation of Historical Societies* 1, no. 11 (June 1981), 8.

34. Quoted in William H. Gifford and H. Bradney Williams, *A Centennial History of Tauranga* (Dunedin: A. H. & A. W. Reed, 1940), 78.

35. C. W. Vennell, *Brown and the Elms* (Tauranga: The Elms Trust, 1984), 74.

36. Letter from W. Fairburn to the CMS, Maraetai, 10 February 1841, William Fairburn, "Church Missionary Society Archives. Letters and papers of Individual Missionaries and Others, Australian Joint Copying Project M223," (Kinder Library MIC 014, 1820-1879).

37. William Colenso, "Autobiography," 31. Underlining in original.

38. Ibid., 38.

39. B. Ashwell, "Recollections of a Waikato Missionary," (Auckland: 1878), 19.

40. Hugh Carleton, *The Life of Henry Williams Archdeacon of Waimate*, ed. James Elliott (Wellington: A. H & A. W. Reed, 1948), 186.

41. She had been gifted some land by her father on the occasion of her marriage which provided her with a small income.

42. Octavius Hadfield, "Octavius Hadfield Papers Vol 5," (WTU: qMS-0901, 1839-1902), letter to parents, Otaki 24 June 1851.

43. All these women were responsible for the education of their own children; usually their daughters only as their sons went to the school for missionaries' children at Paihia.

44. Christopher Lethbridge, *The Wounded Lion Octavius Hadfield 1814-1904 Pioneer Missionary, Friend of the Maori and Primate of New Zealand* (Christchurch: The Caxton Press, 1993), 159.

45. Amelia Caroline Hadfield, "A Short Account of the Life of Catherine Hadfield," (WTU: qMS-0893, 1952), 9.

46. Fiona McKergow, "Girls Friendly Society," in *Women Together*, ed. Anne Else (Wellington: Department of Internal Affairs/Daphne Brasell Associates, 1993), 129.

47. President: Lady Jervois; Vice-President: Mrs. Hadfield; Council: Miss Jervois, Mrs. Coffey, Mrs. Thorp, Mrs. Stock, Mrs. Rolleston, Miss Stock, Miss Greenwood, Mrs. Atkinson; Librarian: Miss Hadfield; Treasurer: Mrs. Harcourt; Secretary: Miss Battersbee. Mollie Gambrill in "Girls' Friendly Society in New Zealand, 1882-1983," (Wellington: [Girls' Friendly Society], 1983), 3-4.

48. Today the GFS functions in Wellington Diocese alone and has refocused its welfare work on disadvantaged women. "In 1991 GFS Wellington gave individual help to 396 women; most were referred by local women's refugees and other agencies, including the Department of Social Welfare," in McKergow, "Girls Friendly Society," 131.

49. Wilson/Armstrong, "Letters and Journal," 29 September 1833.

50. See Valerie Carson, "Submitting to Great Inconveniences: Early Missionary Education for Maori Women and Girls," in *Mission and Moko Aspects of the Work of the Church Missionary Society in New Zealand 1814-1882*, ed. Robert Glen (Christchurch: Latimer Fellowship, 1992), 56-72.

51. The Grace family followed a similar pattern in the 1850s, "We have thought it our duty to give our domestics English in place of Native food, together with the use of knives and forks, plates, cups and saucers, etc..." Letter to Henry Venn from Thomas Grace, Turanga 2 December 1850. S. J. Brittan et al., eds., *A Pioneer Missionary among the Maoris 1850-1879 Being Letters and Journals of Thomas Samuel Grace* (Palmerston North: G. H. Bennett and Co. Ltd., n d).

52. Tanya Fitzgerald, "Unfamiliar Voices: Women's Participation in Missionary Work in NZ 1818-1841," (Auckland: Auckland Institute and Museum Public Lecture, October 1999), 14.

53. Ibid., 15.

54. Colenso, "Letters." "Annual Report for 11 months ending Nov 30th 1850." And "Report for 12 months ending December 1st 1851."

55. According to her daughter, "Kate assisted them [the Maori] with a petition to the Hon. J. C. Richmond, Minister for Native Affairs. She helped with the forming of it and put it into English. Mr. Richmond read it and realizing the unseen hand remarked 'the voice is the voice of Jacob, but the hand is the hand of Esau.'" in A. Hadfield, *A Short Account*, 7.

56. Myra Rutherdale, in her study of CMS women in Northern Canada at the same period, comments similarly, "Women missionaries were described as brave heroines, although these representations of bravery or heroism differed from those of men," in Myra Rutherdale, *Women and the White Man's God: Gender and Race in the Canadian Mission Field* (Vancouver: UBC Press, 2002), 115.

57. Rachel Gillett, "Helpmeets and Handmaidens: The Role of Women in Mission Discourse," (BA Honours, University of Otago, 1998), 1.

58. Unfortunately, David Barrett decided to omit gender statistics from the *World Christian Encyclopaedia*. However, anecdotal evidence and a brief survey of NZ based mission agencies bears out this statement.

59. Virginia Patterson, "Women in missions: facing the 21st Century," in *Evangelical Missions Quarterly* (January 1989): 62.

60. See R. Pierce Beaver, *American Protestant Women in World Mission, A History of the First Feminist Movement in North America* (Grand Rapids: Eerdmans, 1980).

61. Dana Robert, "Women and Missions: Historical Themes and Current Realities," in *Twentieth Century Missions and Gender Conference* (Boston University: Unpublished, March, 2000), 12.

62. Ibid., 12.

63. See Patrick Johnstone and Jason Mandryk, eds., *Operation World 21st Century Edition*, (Carlisle: Paternoster, 2001), Appendix 4, The World's Missionary Force, 747.

64. Dana L. Robert, "Introduction" in *Gospel Bearers, Gender Barriers*, ed. Dana L. Robert (Maryknoll: Orbis, 2002), 25.

65. Ibid., 13.

66. Ibid., 15.

67. Quoted in Kirsteen Kim, "Mission in Feminist Perspective" in *CMS Bulletin* (Winter Issue, 1995), 25.

68. Robert, "Introduction" in *Gospel Bearers*, 21.

# CHAPTER 13

# Missionaries' Commitment in Mexico: Women's Education and Resistance to Violence

## A Reflection from the Feminist Theology of Liberation

*Marilú Rojas Salazar (mstl)*

## 1. Introduction

The theology and the missionary work carried out by women in Latin America "was born in the framework of an option that was not only the woman's but of all oppressed categories, for whom the church made a preferential option."[1] The participation of the poor as subjects of their own processes of liberation has constituted one of the most important elements of ecclesial renovation, especially in what refers to the Roman Catholic Church, to which I belong, and in which I place the present paper as member of a religious congregation (born and) living in Mexico.

## 2. Historical Background

Interculturality is one of the main characteristics of Latin America. Its historical roots trace back to the European conquest and colonial Christian mission, the enslavement and exploitation of the indigenous peoples, and the African peoples brought to the new continent. In 1493, Pope Alexander VI gave the discovered territories to the kingdom of Castilla (Alexandrian Bulla). In Spain, as a consequence, a system of castes was imposed, which placed the woman in the lower strata of society. This element will have a strong influence on the way the indigenous women were treated during the colonial times.

In Mexico and Peru, for example, the conquest generated immensurable violence against indigenous women. One of the reasons for that was the fact that military conquering men violated them and used them as currency and lovers, as it is mentioned by Marisa Navarro and Virginia Sánchez Korrol: "The indigenous women were violated, murdered and enslaved, branded with iron, requested or delivered as presents or as tokens of friendship, and were parts of the war booty gained by the Conquistadores."[2]

Some women, however, as it was the case of Malintzin (Doña Marina), served as translators and collaborators in the process of conquest. Malintzin was an extraordinary woman of Mexico, the first person representing interculturality during colonial occupation of Mexico, negotiating and interpreting between Hernán Cortés and Moctezuma.[3] Some others, as it was the case of the Guaraní women, fought against the conquistadores. Indigenous and black women also kept a resistance against the conquest and against the evangelizing mission not only because they were associated to violence but also in order to keep alive the religious, indigenous and African traditions.

In the framework of this colonial Christian inheritance women were made invisible and disappeared from the books, and therefore from historiography. With the exception of some, such as Sister Juana Inés de la Cruz (1651–1695), who found in the convent an alternative space for the intellectual development of the woman in the Colonial times and who not only developed her literary career but also a recognized theological career,[4] the majority disappeared or remained anonymous. The situation of European women who lived in the new continent did not differ much from that of other women since they were equal to European men only in terms of race. For the rest, European women were subordinated to their men: married women to their husbands, single women to their fathers, and widows to their sons. They could not exercise roles of authority, study, or have a public seat. In that regard, they were equal to indigenous and slaves. European women, however, enjoyed a higher stratum than indigenous and black women, since the latter worked as cook, seamstresses, and servants of their white mistresses. Indigenous and black women were exploited, then, and even exposed to the sexual abuse of their masters.

In its majority, the Catholic Church, associated to the Crown, carried out the Christian mission in the new continent including Mexico (1504-1620).[5] Soon, several religious groups and orders, such as Dominicans, Franciscans,[6] and Jesuits arrived. With them, female religious orders also came, such as Dominicans, Augustinians, Clarisses, Franciscans, and Carmelites. Curiously, religious women did not come as missionaries to the indigenous and black women, nor as collaborators of the male missionaries, but with the main goal of educating the daughters of Spanish families. Only later on, permission was granted to *mestizas* and *criollas*,[7] who could prove their "purity of blood" (not descendants of black slaves or indigenous people), to enter the convents.[8] In this way, the Christian mission rested on the leading roles of religious men, while religious women played a secondary role: education of daughters of Spaniards and criollos in the Christian manners and the traditional roles assigned by men to women, wives and mothers.

At the beginning of the processes of independence in the entire continent, toward the nineteenth century, women had a great participation in Mexico, Venezuela, Colombia, Puerto Rico, and Cuba. Even though they fought as well as the men in order to achieve the desired independence of their countries, however, the laws of the new independent states contradictorily denied the emancipation and the right to vote to women. "In countries where a strict separation of sexes in public matters was the custom, governments were not prepared to set in place mixed and lay school systems. The need to educate women was, in the opinion of some, a frivolity, and others feared that movement as a first step towards future demands on equality."[9] For example, in Mexico, it was only until 1869 when the first schools for girls was established, and later on, Brazil and Argentina opened this possibility. Education of women was considered to be progressive at that time. Several of those education centers were in charge of female religious orders. In this way, the sense of the Christian mission was slowly changing.

In the decade from 1960 to 1970, following the Vatican Council II (1962–1965), Latin America suffered important changes, since besides being submerged in poverty, it was also dominated by dictatorial systems. In this way, revolutionary political movements of liberation spread in the entire continent. In spite of women's participation in those liberation movements, the "feminization of poverty," and the triple marginalization of the woman on the account of their sex, economic resources and race, prevailed throughout history.

In this framework, feminist theology of liberation in Latin America emerged in the decade of the 1970s, amidst three concrete contexts. First, feminist theology of liberation in Latin America is located in the contextual framework of revolutionary political movements of liberation that spread through the continent, and in which women had an important participation. Second, it emerged in the context of liberation theology, in which women started to get involved actively in the lives of the Comunidades Eclesiales de Base (CEBs), Christian base communities, making a clear option for the poor in the popular movements and associations. Third and finally, it emerged amidst the wave and strength of feminism from the first world, especially that coming from North America.

## 3. Commitments of Women Missionaries

### 3.1 Women Educators

After the independence and revolutionary movements in nineteenth-century Latin America and in front of the lack of ability of the new governments to answer the demands on education, health, and social welfare, a strong missionary movement started in the female religious life in the Catholic Church. Convents of contemplative life started to shift toward centers offering missionary services such as schools, hospitals, orphanages, and asylums, in which they tended the needs of the poor. That shift was emphasized, however, only as a result of the so-called Cristero movement in Mexico, an armed conflict that lasted from 1926 until 1929, between the government of Plutarco Elías Calles and the Catholic lay militias led by priests. The Cristero movement resisted the legislation and public polices oriented to restrict the autonomy of religions in general and the Catholic Church in particular.

Catholic religious and missionary congregations were in charge of the education of girls during that period, and the one that followed. Female orders exercised an important leadership in the education of the woman in cultural, social and religious levels not only in Mexico but throughout the whole continent. That was the case of congregations such as The Company of Mary, Sacred Heart, Carmelites, Dominicans, Franciscans, and many others. We have to remember that it was only until 1888 when, for the first time, women in Latin America got access to a university education in Mexico.[10]

The mission of female religious orders in the Catholic Church was centered on education during a period of almost fifty years (1920-1970). Girls were taught to read and write,[11] catechism and manual arts. Education in Mexico at the beginning of twentieth century changed since a group of liberal politicians approved the secular education of women, not only as a means of progress for women but also as a way to limit the control of the Catholic Church over women and the family. Catholic religious women, however, kept their leadership in the education of women, which was seen as a special mission: "educated women must support their husbands and be efficient housewives, cultivated mothers of strong, active and determined children. Widows and other single women, heads of families, also need the skills gained via education in order to gain an income for themselves and their families."[12] There were some religious congregations that founded some schools in indigenous zones and among rural populations where it was almost impossible to have access to education.

Later on, the Christian mission of religious women was reduced to groups of middle and upper classes, distancing themselves more and more from the poor, who continued to be deprived of education. Nevertheless, without the educative labor of the schools of female religious orders, women would be in greater disadvantage and with a higher level of ignorance than men. On the one hand, the contribution to the process of improvement of the woman and her social development in the public sphere by religious women as educators has been fundamental. On the other hand, the Christian mission in the education of women did not change at all the patriarchal roles assigned to women as good wives, excellent mothers and "good Christians." An example of that is the fact that in today's Mexican society, and in the majority of the countries in Latin America, society is based upon the undisputed and supreme authority of the father, and the absolute sacrifice and abnegation of the mother.[13]

## 3.2 *Women Resisting Violence*

Latin America is one of the continents in which violence has been the best weapon that the patriarchate has employed against women. An example of that is the female homicides that have been committed in Ciudad Juarez since 1993, in the state of Chihuahua, a border area with United States. "The dead women of Juárez," as they are commonly referred to, show the horrors of violence against women.

To be a woman in Ciudad Juárez is more dangerous than in other places in the country; there, more than 400 women have been assassinated in the past ten years; 600 more are disappeared. Disposable bodies, dispensable bodies, erasable bodies. Some were just girls, adolescents. The stories of injustice, complicity of the powerful, we know them all. The crimes continued to be unsolved. And since impunity generates more impunity, more corpses continue to appear. With an average of two murders per month, misogyny, taken to the most terrifying level of cruelty, continues to feed on the bodies of women at the border.[14]

The violent reality that women suffer, not only in Mexico but also in other parts of the continent, is ever present since domestic violence is more common than what one would think: "home for millions of women has become in a place more dangerous than the streets."[15] Some women have said that this violence is a slow, humiliating, and continuous death that plants a seed in the formation of male children and that it becomes part of an common educational system that predominates in the minds and attitudes of future generations.

In Mexico, it is common to hear women who suffer from this violence say, "it is my cross." It is very frequent to find in Sunday sermons and homilies in many churches preachers exhorting women "to carry their crosses." Some pastors and clergymen encourage women to bear with the patience of Christ the physical abuse as a expiating sacrifice for the forgiveness of their husbands' sins in order to "save" and "convert" them from sin.

Some women share in the groups of biblical reflection and in the Christian base communities how in many occasions when looking for a word of advice they have talked to their pastors about the situation of violence they are exposed to live in their families. Those pastors or priests have advised them to remain at home and review their "behavior" in regard to their husbands. They are exhorted to obey and to be faithful for the sake of a sacrificial love that it is able "to give all" for love as Christ did. What those pastors and priests are not able to understand is that such imposed "love" is violently killing women.

In some mountainous zones in Veracruz and Chiapas (Mexico), girls of twelve and thirteen years of age are exchanged for goods by their fathers. The father, before the exchange takes place, sexually abuses the girl. In other cases, when a girl is raped, instead of asking for a penal punishment for the aggressor, the father demands that the rapist marries the girl as the only way to "wash her honor."

Challenged by this reality, the concept and the way to exercise the Christian mission for a large group of female religious congregations in the Catholic Church has been changing toward other forms of commitment such as social transformation, the defense of human rights, the pastoral work with immigrants, a variety of medical and pastoral services in indigenous communities of

Peru, Guatemala, Mexico, and Ecuador, the pastoral work with women and girls on the streets, popular committees in search for better living conditions in the *favelas* (Brazil), in the barrios and poor suburbs surrounding big cities (Mexico), the creation and maintenance of centers for biblical reflection, and Christian base communities at the South of the continent.

This form of Christian mission of a large group of lay and religious missionaries emerged with greater strength from the post era of Vatican II, and to this date it is still in transformation with women as new social actors. Women are fighting more and more in order to eradicate the systems and codes of violence against the woman that are instituted throughout the continent. The work of Catholic missionaries, lay and religious, has taken another perspective: to dignify and reintegrate into the community those without a face, following the example of Jesus' love for the poor.

It is important to mention, however, that from the beginning of the colonization, the missionary tales tell us that after the children, native women, center of the domestic life and religiosity, were the ones who progressively incorporated to their traditions the new religious proposal and who established the basis for the so rooted popular Catholicism, enriched in some regions by the religiosity of the enslaved population. According to the data provided by Ana Maria Bidegain, white European women were responsible to transmit the Christian faith in their new homes, and were also the ones who transmitted the faith to the indigenous and black women who worked for them.

Later on, toward 1932, with the foundation of the women's branch of the Catholic Action, in charge of Christine de Hemptinne in Brazil, and Teresa Oddeson in Chile, this movement was extended to Montevideo, Buenos Aires, Santiago, Lima, Bogota, Caracas, and one could say that since then, lay and religious Catholic women started to participate more actively in the missionary work and social commitment in Latin America.[16] This was only the preamble to a movement of catechist, missionary and parish leading women that gained strength in the post Vatican II Council period, and that started since 1965 until 1985 with an emphasized option for the poor in the framework of the liberation theology that characterized Latin America.

In order to achieve that goal, missionaries have associated themselves to humanitarian groups, non-governmental organizations, and diverse associations that promote the dignity of the woman and that defend her rights. Without these associations, missionary work would be almost impossible since the structure of violence is socially and politically accepted. The Latin American Conference of Religious Women and Men (CLAR), and the diverse national conferences of Catholic religious men and women have added their efforts to this new form of mission. This implies a commitment to transform social realities, a more ethical character in the defense of human rights, and a line of evangelical-prophetic cut to denounce the evil in society. Such is the case of the Maryknoll sisters in Peru and Bolivia.

Not all missionaries, religious, lay, pastoral agents and theologians, agree with this form of mission, however, nor do they agree with the line of liberation, the defense of the rights of the woman and with feminist theology. Not all women who study or do theology in Latin America are feminist either. One could say that there is a large group of women at the interior of the churches who declare themselves as "feminine" rather than "feminist" and who continue to keep the hierarchical patriarchal roles. I have to clarify, however, that the term feminist is "the radical concept that women are persons" according the theologian Elisabeth Schüssler Fiorenza, and "this definition emphasizes that feminism is a radical concept, and at the same time, ironically emphasizes that in the XX century, feminism is a concept of common sense. Women are not ladies, wives, servants, seductresses, or labor beasts but are fully citizens."[17] The feminine, on the other hand, is the social, cultural, political, and religious construction that men have made about the roles that according to their interests women should have.

These leaderships of women have gained strength. Women have entered many fields such as sciences, arts, politics and economics. This, however, does not mean that the recognition of the woman as equal to the man has been achieved in every area of private, professional, religious and social life. The leadership of women in the church has been that of catechists, and that of being responsible for the life and dynamism of communities where pastors and presbyters are not present. Women are committed with popular movements and with organizations of women who fight for the recognition of their rights and the rights of their children. They are also responsible for and coordinators of communities where the bible is being reflected upon, the liturgy is celebrated, and concrete commitments are generated in order to give solution to the needs of the lives of their members. However, because women leaders do not expect to get "official" recognition by the Roman Catholic Church women continue to perform a double duty: at work and at home or at home and at church. In the churches they do not receive monetary recognition for their work either. They continue to be "objects of reflection" of the ecclesiastic patriarchate, even though there is a long way walked by women who search to constitute themselves as subjects of reflection. This process of subjectivity is being realized at the margins of the Catholic Church.

## 4. Analysis

In the abovementioned cases of study we find two concrete ways in which lay and religious women exercise the Christian mission in the context of the Catholic tradition: education and resistance to violence. The question is: why do we put together two subjects that seem to be disconnected? In my opinion, these are two of the "weapons" that the patriarchate has employed in order to subordinate and oppress women in society, culture and religion. Women, lay and religious, however, have decided to follow the path of evangelization via a missionary commitment that is able to give answer to the historical realities in which they live, and which demand from them a concrete evangelical posture.

First, one of the most important critiques that liberation theology has received, and that is also applicable to the missionary work in Latin America, is the omission of the missionary leadership of women. Just as traditional patriarchal theology, the androcentric history and ecclesial documents, liberation theology, and the Catholic Church in general, "included" women as further members of the poor. Latin American women, however, as Elina Vuola rightly says, are not satisfied with "a simple addition of women to the poor."[18] It is necessary that the work and leadership of women in the "official" church have an "official" recognition and canonically approved rights.

Second, if the missionary leaderships of women do not count on an "official" recognition in terms of salaried offices from the Roman Catholic Church, so that women have to continue to perform a double duty, then, women will remain "objects of reflection" despite their efforts to constitute themselves as subjects of reflection. The process of subjectivity is being done at the margins of the "official church" precisely because the latter has not opened the path to the recognition, remuneration, and space that women need. Missionary religious and lay women, on the other hand, have made an option for the poor and the woman as a constitutive element of the Christian mission, thus constructing their own identity. They have not found this identity inside the patriarchal structure of orthodox tendency in the Catholic Church since inside this structure the woman is seen as an "object" of the mission and not as an active "subject" of it.

Third, from the perspective of feminist theology and the critical hermeneutics of gender, emancipatory education was and continues to be one of the most important feminist causes since the majority of the poor in the world are women. "Two-thirds of the 876 millions of illiterate people in the world are women; when they are 18 years old, girls have an average of 4.4 years of less education than men of their same age; out of the 121 million of non-schooled children in the world, 65 millions are girls."[19] The lack of academic formation of women is an element that shows what Latin American theologians have called "the feminization of poverty."[20] It is an element that shows the injustice, the exclusion and marginalization of women, especially indigenous who suffer a triple exclusion: for being women, for being poor, and for being indigenous.[21] Education is until today an element to which they have difficult access, since this possibility is easier for women in the first world.

Fourth, the reality that missionary women are facing in Latin America is important to mention. Not only that they have to overcome the patriarchalism and machismo reigning in society in general but they also have to constantly face the clericalism in the church, as well as the control of the theological thought and the ministerial exercise in the hands of men.

Fifth, the experience of being indigenous, *mestiza* and *mulata* women; in other words, Latin Americans are the result of the mixture of three races: indigenous, black and white peoples. This fact gave us a character of interculturality, pluralism, and diversity that allows us to value differences.[22] However, it is a double-edged sword. On the one hand, we have the values already mentioned; on the other hand, it is not the same to be a white woman, educated, of middle class and with more opportunities of development than to be an indigenous woman, poor and with less or no opportunities.

Sixth, missionary religious and lay Catholic women, who committed themselves to work with the poor and excluded women in the decades of between 1970 and 1990, did not continue their academic formation and, thus, became part of the women lacking almost completely theological and academic formation. It is true that the option for the poor implied a total and demanding commitment, and to abandon their formation was seen by many as a consequence of that option. This, however, became a detriment to the theological reflection and the missionary leadership of women, leaving these competences in the hands of men.

In both cases of study we could see that there are clear limitations. On the one hand, missionary educators forgot that part of their mission was to provide a more critical and liberating education, and that part of their mission was a commitment with the realities of poverty. On the other hand, the women who have defended the rights of women against violence, and who have made a clear option for the poor, forgot their own academic and theological formation, becoming, thus, similar to those who they sought to assist.

Seventh, it is necessary more than ever to deconstruct the codes of education in which women were formed. Those codes of education are perpetuating violent thinking and behavior, historiography, for example, are always shaped from the point of view of wars, battles, murders and betrayals. Men are depicted as avid warriors and liberators, while women are relegated as simple collaborators or not even mentioned.

Violence has behind it a great supporter: educational systems. Learning and educative processes of "daily life," conforming culture are seen as a hermeneutical place of feminist theology of liberation in which a critical analysis from the perspective of gender is needed. Daily life as the departing point of reflection of the feminist theology of liberation implies to unveil all forms of violence occurring such as: codes of language sustaining violent behavior, thought, traditions, and attitudes. Laura Segato affirms that the system of communication that is established in the body of women who are murdered or raped has a deeper language:

> If the violent act is understood as a message and the crimes are perceived as orchestrated in a clear responsorial style, we find ourselves with a scene where the acts of violence behave as a language that is able to function efficiently to those who understand it, those warned, those who speak it, even if they do not participate directly in the enunciating action. For this reason, when a system of communication as the violent alphabet is installed, it is very difficult to uninstall it, eliminate it. Constituted and crystallized violence as a system of communication becomes a stable language and comes to behave with the quasi-automatism of any language.[23]

This analysis is not only applicable to violent acts such as murder, rape and sexual abuse of women, but it is also applicable to the economic, political, social and religious aspects in which norms, schemes and attitudes of domination, control and subordination are handled. In our cases, from the religious discourses until the very moral and ethical norms are all exposed to those codes of violence. "The problem of violence as a language becomes even more grave if we consider the fact that there are certain languages that, in determined historical conditions, tend to become lingua franca and to generalize beyond the ethnic or national frontiers that served as their original niche."[24] This is the case in the religious sphere, in which the image of God as man is overemphasized; a monocentric image of God as one, whose Son is a begotten male, and whose followers and heirs of his power and authority are only men hierarchically organized.

Eighth, the risk of renouncing to deconstructive process of these elements could generate an anachronistic, romantic and idealist vision, of the Christian mission, or generate a theology of victims and victimizers where it is necessary to uphold the idea of the "scapegoat". In a sacrificial religion such as Christianity there is the risk that women become the "scapegoats" or the "victims." This would engender, as R. Girard says, "a mimetic process" of violence.[25]

The critical proposal of the Latin American feminist theology of liberation in face of this mimetic process of violence, understanding the term *mimêsis* as *imitation*,[26] is centered in the line of Ricoeur's proposal, who affirms that, "mimêsis is the restoration of the human, not only in the essential, but also in an order more elevated and more noble. The proper tension of the mimêsis is double: on the one hand, the imitation is at the same time a picture of the human and an original composition; on the other hand, it consists in a restoration and a shift towards the high. This feature, together with the former, takes us to the metaphor."[27] Following this idea, in the case of violence as an imitation process that is transmitted in a society with schemes and codes of language and education that are violent, we could say that it would remain as a "picture of the human and an original composition" which makes us think that of the impossibility of breaking the chain since culture, codes of language, discourses and forms of education are inside this "picture of the human" of misogynist and violent character.

The Latin American feminist theology of liberation, however, proposes a "restoration and a shift" in which the woman ceases to be a victim and becomes autonomous, free and with power of decision and resistance to the codes of violence that keep her oppressed. The idea is not to become a victimizer but to achieve that is called a *theology of empowerment*. While the attitude of victim is maintained, it is impossible to have a dialogue between women and men as equals. The Latin American feminist theology of liberation searches to overcome the tendency of a theological victimize and to shift to the high since the empowerment is understood as

> a process by which the oppressed achieve a measure of control over their lives when taking part with others in the development of activities and structures that allow people to participate in the matters that affect them directly. In its course, people become able to self-govern effectively. This process requires the use of power, but not of the "power over" others or the power of domination as it is the traditional case. It is the power of "power of being able" or the power as a skill that it is generated and shared amidst the dispossessed while they begin to give form to the content and the structure of their daily life and, thus, to participate in a movement for social change.[28]

This "power of being able" is the attitude and the level of relationship that we find in Jesus with women (John 4:4-42), and, in my opinion, it is one of the ways in which the Christian mission, the woman and the theological reflection need to reorient themselves in order to overcome the violence and patriarchal domination.

## 5. Questions for Discussion

1. Can you starting from your own knowledge and experience, contribute to a process of "reading women into Latin American mission history," giving to them names and faces?

2. What are the new missionary paradigms that women should recreate from the Gospel in order to answer adequately to the concrete reality of violence against women?

3. Could we say that there is a certain "genetic" charge of violence inherited from the West into Latin America? How could the Christian mission from the feminist theology overcome the destructive legacy and transform it into a constructive present?

4. What is the commitment of the churches in front of the violation of the human rights of women? How could the churches be *good news* when at their interior the rights of women are many times violated, neglected or omitted? What new missionary paradigms would help to resist and transform the concrete realities of violence against women?

# 6. Recommendations

First, we, missionary women, need urgently to decode and dialogue critically with the existent system of significations in the multiplicity of cultures where violence against women is generated; as well as in the educational, theological and missionary processes in which the new generations of women and men are being formed.

Second, we, feminist theologians who come from continents where codes of violence are installed and educated directly or indirectly, need to denounce before the civil and religious instances these situations. The best way to fight against institutionalized violence is to unmask it and make it public.

Third, we, theologians and missionary women from different religions, need to articulate the intercultural, interreligious, and ecumenical dialogue that is able to give answer to the situations of women who demand with urgency an ethical commitment of justice and defense of their rights in face of oppression, violence, and disregard that women suffer for being women, for being of a certain ethnic group or for thinking differently.

Fourth, we need to generate new ways of knowledge and learning in the spheres where we work as catechists, pastors, or coordinators of groups of biblical and theological reflection. The religious, biblical, and theological formation from the critical feminist perspective should be a tool that would lead us to the liberation from multiple and multiplying forms of oppression in which we live. Only in this way the gospel preached by Jesus would be good news for women.

Fifth, it is necessary to re-establish the wisdom of our indigenous peoples and our ancestors' cultures so that they can become a different way of "knowing"; a new epistemological field whose codes of knowledge are not patriarchal nor are hierarchically structured or founded on exclusion or violence. This is the meaning of ecosophy. The proposal of an ecosophy or ecotheo-sophia from the perspective of the ecofeminist theology is founded not only on the change of violent relationships toward harmonious relationships, but also on the forms of wisdom and relationship with the divinity of the indigenous peoples. This form of wisdom should be considered as a theology that integrates the experience of the masculine and the feminine in the metaphors of the divinity, without considering them as mere traditions and not proper theology. The indigenous wisdoms as theologies are being a way to propose the cosmic harmony and the *práxica* in the relationships of all the beings that form the cosmos.

Finally, we need to reconstruct the self-esteem of women by facilitating them the access to the epistemological knowledge of a theology of empowerment that is able to create in women the self-conscience, valorization, and the recovery of the body, words and actions. This implies a change in the content and forms of education, as well as the access of women to emancipatory and liberating education. Religions and churches need to rethink their theological discourses that have served consciously or unconsciously to keep a misogynist education, especially when the majority of their members are women.

# 7. Conclusion

The Western cultures of the sixteenth century that invaded Latin America were a carrier of three vices: alcoholism, violence, and machismo as forms of control, power over and domination of the conquered territory. "The ethnohistory of gender revealed that Colonialism, Eurocentrism and capitalism had been crucial in the transformation of the position of women for the worse."[29]

The cultural ideas of gender are closely linked to the roles and social relationships, as well as to gender typologies determining how human beings live, think and act. A reason behind the violence against women and the control of them is that patriarchal-minded males fear to lose their territory and domination. This fear of losing the power of control leads them to take extreme actions including violence in all its forms and install violence as cultural elements that holds society, religion, politics and economy together. In this way a structure that intertwines all levels of social life is created.

When studying the codes of language and violence against the body of the woman, we find that violence is not only a weapon of the patriarchate to control but that it is also a language and a system of communication that seeks to transmit itself and that it has addressees. What do men want to communicate when beating, raping, sexually, physically or verbally abusing or even killing many women?

The violated body of the woman can be taken as a symbol of territoriality. Let us remember that according to Segato: "it has been constitutive of the language of tribal and modern wars, that the body of the woman be attached as a part of the conquered country. The sexuality versed upon itself expresses the domesticating, appropriating act by inseminating the territory-body of the woman."[30] This has also been the case of indigenous women violated by European conquistadores in Latin America.

Sexual violation of the body of the woman aims at achieving physical and moral control over the victim. "The moral reduction is a requirement for the domination to be consumed, and the sexuality, in the world as we know it, is impregnated of morality."[31]

If we add to all that the moralizing discourses and the emphasis given in our patriarchal churches on "taking care" the morality of women in order to keep the "family and reproductive values," then, we could suspect that behind these codes of ethic there is a strongly institutionalized religious violence against the body and sexuality of women that has to do with control, territory and domination.

The present challenge of women and of the Christian mission is to give answer to the historical realities that society demands nowadays. We need new missionary paradigms to bring the good news to a new society, with new and diverse realities.

## Further Reading

María Pilar Aquino, *Our Cry for Life. Feminist Theology from Latin America* (New York: Orbis Books, 1993).

María Pilar Aquino, Daisy L. Machado and Jeanette Rodriguez, *A Reader in Latina Feminist Theology. Religion and Justice* (Austin: University Texas Press, 2002).

Alirio Cacéres Aguirre, "Ecotheology: Epistemological Approaches," in *Concilium, International Review of Theology 3*, ed. Elaine Wainwright, Luiz Carlos Susin and Felix Wilfred (London: SCM, 2009).

Marysa Navarro and Virginia Sánchez Korrol, *Women in Latin American and the Caribbean* (Indiana: Indiana University Press, 1999).

Elina Vuola, *Limits of Liberation Praxis as Method in Latin American Liberation Theology and Feminist Theology* (Helsinki: Suoma Lainentie Deakatemia, 1997).

## Endnotes

1. María Pilar Aquino, Nuestro Clamor por la vida. Teología Latinoamericana desde la perspectiva de la mujer (San José: DEI, 1992), 17. "Nació en el marco de una opción que era no solamente de la mujer, sino de todas las categorías oprimidas, por las cuales hacía un opción preferencial toda la iglesia." All translations from Spanish to English by M. Rojas Salazar.

2. Marysa Navarro and Virginia Sánchez Korrol, Mujeres en América Latina y el Caribe (Madrid: Narcea, 2004), 83. "Las mujeres indias fueron violadas, asesinadas y esclavizadas, marcadas a hierro, pedidas o entregadas como regalo o en señal de amistad, y fueron parte de los botines de guerra obtenidos por los conquistadores."

3. Sandra Messinger Cypess, *La Malinche in Mexican Literature: from History to Myth* (Austin: University of Texas Press, 1991).

4. Ana María Bidegain, *Participación y Protagonismo de las Mujeres en la Historia del Catolicismo Latinoamericano* (Buenos Aires: San Benito, 2009), 16.

5. According to Enrique Dussel this is the period in which an Indian church is trying to be implemented.

6. Bernardino de Sahagún (1499-1950) was one of the Franciscan religious brothers who was prominent because of his interreligious dialogue with the Aztecs.

7. The term *Mestiza* is used to designate a person whose father or mother is of European or white origins and the other parent is of indigenous origins.The term *Creole* is used to designate a person whose parents are European or white but whose birthplace is in the Spanish conquered places in America.

8. Aquino, *Nuestro Clamor por la vida*, 116.

9. Ibid., 143. "En países donde la estricta separación de los sexos en los asuntos públicos era lo acostumbrado, los gobiernos no estaban preparados para poner en marcha sistemas escolares mixtos y laicos. La necesidad de educar a las mujeres era, en opinión de algunos, una frivolidad, pero otros temían ese movimiento como un primer paso hacia futuras demandas de igualdad."

10. Navarro and Sánchez Korrol, *Mujeres*, 146.

11. Ibid., 146.

12. Ibid., "las mujeres educadas debían apoyar siempre a sus esposos y ser eficientes amas de casa y cultas madres de hijos fuertes, activos y decididos. Las viudas y otras mujeres solteras, cabezas de familia también necesitaban de las capacidades adquiridas con la educación a fin de ganar el sustento para ellas mismas y para sus familias."

13. Ibid., 173.

14. Rita Laura Segato, "La escritura en el cuerpo de las mujeres asesinadas en Ciudad Juárez: territorio, soberanía y crímenes de segundo estado," in *Cuerpos sufrientes. Debate feminista*. Vol. 37 (México: METIS, 2008), 78. "Ser mujer en Ciudad Juárez es más peligroso que en otros lugares del país; allí han sido asesinadas más de 400 mujeres en los últimos diez años; 600 más están desaparecidas. Cuerpos desechables, cuerpos prescindibles, cuerpos borrables. Algunas eran apenas niñas, adolescentes. Las historias de injusticia, de complicidad por parte de los poderosos, las conocemos todos. Los crímenes siguen sin aclararse. Y como la impunidad genera más impunidad, continúan apareciendo cadáveres. A un promedio de dos asesinadas al mes, la misoginia llevada al más aterrador nivel de la crueldad sigue alimentándose de cuerpos de mujeres en la frontera."

15. Marifé Ramos, "Prevenir la violencia a través de la educación," in *10 palabras clave sobre Violencia de Género*, ed. Esperanza Bautista (Navarra:Verbo Divino 2004), 387; "el hogar para millones de mujeres se ha convertido en un lugar más peligroso que la calle."

16. Ana María Bidegain, *Participación y Protagonismo de las Mujeres en la Historia del Catolicismo Latinoamericano*, 53-152.

17. Elisabeth Schüssler Fiorenza, *En la Senda de Sofía. Hermenéutica Crítica feminista para la liberación* (Buenos Aires:Lumen-Isedet, 2003), 12.

18. Elina Vuola, *Teología Feminista. Teología de la liberación. La praxis como método de la Teología Latinoamericana de la Liberación y de la Teología Feminista* (Madrid: IEPALA, 2000), 113. "un simple añadir las mujeres a los pobres."

19. Datos aportados por "La Primera Jornada de Cooperación educativa sobre género y educación," in *Educación de mujeres y niñas en Iberoamerica* http://www.oei.es/genero/documentos/Educacion_de_mujeres.pdf (December 23, 2009). "Dos terceras partes de los 876 millones de personas analfabetas del mundo son mujeres. De acuerdo a los datos de esta organización, dos terceras partes de los 876 millones de personas analfabetas del mundo son mujeres; al cumplir 18 años, las chicas tienen una media de 4.4 años menos de educación que los hombres de su misma edad; de los 121 millones de niños no escolarizados en el mundo, 65 millones son niñas."

20. Margot Bremer, "La mujer en la Iglesia Latinoamericana," in *10 palabras clave sobre la Iglesia Latinoamericana,* ed. Pablo Richard (Navarra: Verbo Divino, 2003), 265-67; "la feminización de la pobreza"

21. Elisa Estévez, "Iglesia," in *10 mujeres escriben teología*, ed. Mercedes Navarro (Navarra: Verbo Divino 1998), 191.

22. Barbara E. Reid, *Reconsiderar la cruz. Interpretación latinoamericana y feminista del Nuevo Testamento* (Navarra: Verbo Divino, 2009), 30.

23. Segato, *"escritura,"* 91. "Si el acto violento es entendido como mensaje y los crímenes se perciben orquestados en claro estilo responsorial, nos encontramos con una escena donde los actos de violencia se comportan como una lengua capaz de funcionar eficazmente para los entendidos, avisados, los que la hablan, aun cuando no participen directamente en la acción enunciativa. Es por eso que, cuando un sistema de comunicación con alfabeto violento se instala, es muy difícil desinstalarlo, eliminarlo. La violencia constituida y cristalizada en forma de sistema de comunicación se transforma en un lenguaje estable y pasa a comportarse con el cuasi-automatismo de cualquier idioma."

24. Ibid., 91. "El problema de la violencia como lenguaje se agrava aún más si consideramos que existen ciertas lenguas que, en determinadas condiciones históricas, tienden a convertirse en *lingua franca* y a generalizarse más allá de las fronteras étnicas o nacionales que le sirvieron de nicho originario."

25. René Girard, *El chivo expiatorio* (Buenos Aires: Anagrama, 1986); René Girard, *La violence et le sacré* (París: Grasset, 1972).

26. Paul Ricoeur, *La metáfora viva* (Madrid: ediciones Cristiandad, 2001), 61; Paul Ricoeur, *La Méthapore Vive* (París: Du Seuil, 1975).

27. Ibid. 61. "La mimêsis es restauración de lo humano, no solo en lo esencial, sino en un orden más elevado y más noble. La tensión propia de la mimêsis es doble: por una parte, la imitación es a la vez un cuadro de lo humano y una composición original; por otra, consiste en una restauración y en un desplazamiento hacia lo alto. Este rasgo unido a lo anterior nos lleva a la metáfora."

28. Ann Ferguson, *¿Puede el desarrollo propiciar el empoderamiento y la liberación de las mujeres?* http://www.globaljusticecenter.org/ponencias/ferguson_esp.htm (December 7, 2009). "un proceso por el cual los oprimidos logran una medida de control sobre sus vidas al tomar parte con otros en el desarrollo de actividades y estructuras que permiten que la gente participe en los asuntos que les toca directamente. En su curso la gente se habilita para autogobernarse efectivamente. Este proceso requiere el uso del poder, pero no del 'poder sobre' otros o el poder del dominio como es el caso tradicionalmente. Sino el poder es 'el poder de poder' o el poder como una capacidad que se genera y se comparte entre los desposeídos mientras empiezan a dar forma al contenido y a la estructura de su vida cotidiana y así participar en un movimiento para el cambio social."

29. Ma. Soledad Vieitez Cerdeño, "Miradas antropológicas de género," in

*Miradas desde la perspectiva de género. Estudios de las mujeres,* ed. Isabel de Torres Ramírez (Madrid: Narcea, 2005), 69. "La etnohistoria del género revelaba que el colonialismo, eurocentrismo y capitalismo habían sido cruciales en la transformación de la posición de las mujeres para peor."

30. Segato, "escritura," 93. "Ha sido constitutivo del lenguaje de las guerras tribales o modernas, que el cuerpo de la mujer se anexe como parte del país conquistado. La sexualidad vertida sobre el mismo expresa el acto domesticador, apropiador, cuando insemina el territorio-cuerpo de la mujer."

31. Ibid., 93. "La reducción moral es un requisito para que la dominación se consume y la sexualidad, en el mundo que conocemos, está impregnada de moralidad."

# CHAPTER 14

# Churches and Social Service: Presbyterian Women in Mission in Guatemala

*Karla Ann Koll*

## 1. Introduction

Guatemala, the Central American republic known as "the land of eternal spring" with its majestic volcanoes and beautiful lakes, lies just south of Mexico. Though organized Protestant mission work did not begin until 1882, Guatemala today has the highest percentage of people who identify themselves as Protestants in its population of any Latin American country. Though an excellent history of Protestantism in Guatemala exists, written by Virginia Garrard-Burnett, no one has looked at this history from the perspective of women.[1]

This case study looks briefly at the women who served with the Presbyterian Mission in Guatemala during the first one hundred years of organized Protestant presence in the country.[2] Of the 108 mission workers sent by the Board of Foreign Missions (1882–1958) of the Presbyterian Church in the United States of America (PCUSA), and its successor board, the Commission on Ecumenical Mission and Relations (COEMAR) (1958–1982) of the United Presbyterian Church in the United States of America (UPCUSA), sixty-eight were women. Of these, thirty-one served as single women. Yet the denomination established by the Presbyterian Mission, the National Evangelical Presbyterian Church of Guatemala (*Iglesia Evangélica Nacional Presbiteriana de Guatemala – IENPG*) has been very slow to recognize and affirm the leadership gifts of women.[3] An examination of the roles the women assumed in the work of the Presbyterian Mission within

Guatemala allows us to ask questions about the relationship between church planting efforts and mission-founded social service institutions in terms of empowering or disempowering the leadership of local women.

## 2. Historical Background

Roman Catholicism was brought to the country we know today as Guatemala by the invading Spanish in the early sixteenth century. The papal bulls that authorized the conquest charged the Spanish crown with Christianizing the peoples Europeans did not even know existed before the voyages of Christopher Columbus. Guatemala was inhabited by the Maya, divided into at least twenty-two language groups. While Christendom was dividing in Europe, the Spanish firmly established Christendom in the New World, imposing the institutions of the Roman Catholic Church on the indigenous populations who survived the military conquest as well as European colonists and the mixed-race mestizo population as it emerged.

Guatemala, together with the rest of Central America, gained independence from Spain in 1821. The Roman Catholic Church remained the official state religion. The Liberal party came to power in 1871 and Justo Rufino Barrios seized the presidency in 1873. Like Liberal administrations elsewhere in Latin America, the Liberals of Guatemala embraced an ideology of progress as they sought to modernize the country. A lay government was established, as well as a civil registry and public cemeteries. The Liberals confiscated church properties and sought to limit the social power of the Roman Catholic Church, especially in the area of education where the church enjoyed a near monopoly. Barrios declared freedom of worship in 1873 to encourage immigrants from Europe and North America to bring their Protestant churches with them along with their technical knowledge, skilled labor, and capital to aid in the modernization of the country.

Jose Miguez Bonino has described the relationship between the Liberal political project in Latin America and historic Protestant mission efforts as a convergence of interests. The mission boards took advantage of the openings created by Liberal reforms to launch mission efforts in the continent, convinced that their religious vision was more compatible with modernization than traditional Roman Catholicism. The Liberals sought allies as in their struggle to restrain the influence of the Roman Catholic Church.[4] In the case of Guatemala, Barrios and those surrounding him drew on a variety of intellectual and religious movements for their political project.[5] When Barrios was asked in 1882 by the Board of Foreign Missions of the Presbyterian Church if he would consider allowing Protestant missionaries to work in Guatemala, the president made one demand. The mission was to start a school.[6]

In 1882, Presbyterians from the United States were already working in mission in Argentina (1823), Colombia (1856), Chile (1873), Brazil (1859), and Mexico (1876). When the opportunity presented itself to undertake mission work in Guatemala, the Board of Foreign Missions jumped at the chance and rerouted a missionary couple who were candidates for service in China. In many ways, the Presbyterian Mission in Guatemala was typical of historic Protestant missions in Latin America. The mission sought to establish a Presbyterian church, evangelizing among people disaffected from the Roman Catholic Church. In addition to church planting, the mission sought to disseminate Protestant values beyond the congregations they formed, especially through schools. The mission also ran a printing press, publishing tracts, magazines, and books. As on other historic Protestant mission fields, women outnumbered men as mission workers. And like other historic Protestant missions in Latin America, the Presbyterian mission in Guatemala did not develop a consistent focus on women.

## 3. Presbyterian Women Serving in Guatemala

The roles assumed by Presbyterian women sent from the United States to work in mission in Guatemala were determined in part by the particular historical moment in which they served. In general, single women missionaries arrived with particular assignments, while married women responded to the needs of the Mission and their particular interests. The first thirty years were a time of trial and error as missionaries sought to define the goals of the mission and the population to be reached. In the second decade of the twentieth century, the work of the mission consolidated in growing congregations and social service institutions. After Guatemalan Presbyterians established a national church structure in 1950, control of both the church and the mission-founded institutions was passed to the national leadership as the number of missionaries serving in the country, both men and women, declined. In the 1960s and 1970s, while Guatemala suffered under military dictatorships and an expanding civil war, mission workers explored new directions in service.

## 3.1 Pioneer Period 1882–1912

The first woman missionary sent by the Presbyterians to Guatemala was Sallie A. Hart Hill (1882–1886), the wife of Reverend John Clark Hill.[7] Rev. Hill began holding services in English immediately upon his arrival in Guatemala City in late 1882. Sallie Hill arrived a couple of months later and seems to have dedicated herself to meeting the challenges of running a household in a foreign country. A preacher from Mexico helped Rev. Hill organize the first Spanish-speaking congregation in December of 1884 with nine members, none of whom were women.[8] It appears that reaching out to Guatemalan women was not part of the vision of the Presbyterian Mission at the beginning.

The opening of the school requested by President Barrios had to wait for the arrival of Mary Lizzie Hammond (1883–1893) and Annie E. Ottoway (1884–1888), teachers sent by the Board.[9] The *Colegio Americano*, using English as the language of instruction, opened its doors in early 1884 with twenty-five students.[10] Barrios sent his own children to the co-educational primary school and told his cabinet members to do the same. When problems with creditors forced the Hills to abandon the country in 1886, Hammond and Ottoway kept the Mission going by maintaining a Sunday school while they ran the *Colegio Americano*.[11]

In September of 1887, the Board sent Rev. Edward Haymaker and Esther Jane "Belle" McClelland Haymaker (1887–1903, 1920–1928) to Guatemala to take over the church work. Rev. Haymaker reorganized the work in the capital and began evangelistic work in other communities to develop Presbyterian congregations. His wife tended a family that eventually grew to include nine children plus a set of Guatemalan twins. The Haymakers were in Guatemala until they withdrew in 1903 because of Edward's health, though they returned later.

Imogene Stivers (1888–1891), who replaced Annie Ottoway, expanded the work of the school by opening a kindergarten. But the *Colegio Americano* soon closed. The parents who sent their children to the *Colegio* were liberal-minded Catholics of the political elite who did not mind the Presbyterian Mission subsidizing their children's education, yet they had no intention of becoming Protestant.[12] The Mission's next venture in education, under Rev. Haymaker's direction, was a school for poor boys with a local teacher, which opened in early 1893.

The Haymakers began work in Quetzaltenango, Guatemala's second largest city located in the western highlands. Another couple, William Gates and Clara Fitch Gates (1893–1902) first worked in Guatemala City before they transferred to Quetzaltenango in 1898 to establish a permanent mission station there. Though Clara Gates was a gifted musician, she does not appear to have had the emotional stability to withstand the rigors of missionary life. They finally withdrew from Guatemala shortly after Quetzaltenango suffered a major earthquake.[13]

In 1903, the Board decided to send new mission personnel to revitalize the work in Guatemala. At this time, missionary women begin to show concern for working with women within the church. Corinna Hedges Allison (1903–1922) was the first of the married missionary women to take an activist role in the work. While her husband ran the Mission's printing press, Corinna Allison promoted groups of "Bible women." Unlike other contexts where Bible women were trained primarily as evangelists to reach out to women, Corinna Allison's work seems to have focused on training women to lead Bible studies for women within the context of the church.[14]

Corinna Allison was also a physician's daughter who pushed the Board to begin medical work in Guatemala. Not only was there little medical care available for the majority of the population, Protestant believers were at times denied treatment by the nuns who served as nurses in the public hospital. In 1906, the Board sent Dr. Mary Gregg (1906–1916) to Guatemala. As a foreigner, a woman, a Protestant missionary and a homeopathic physician, Dr. Gregg was unable to be licensed to practice medicine in the country, but the medical establishment as it existed at the time did not interfere with her practice. She tended to patients in her office and also did extensive visitation.[15]

Anne Halloway, formerly a missionary with the Central American Mission, joined the Presbyterian Mission in 1906 when she married Rev. Walter Eugene McBath, the missionary the Board had sent to Quetzaltenango in 1904. Anne McBath is credited with helping to start the first women's society in a Presbyterian church in Guatemala. The McBaths were interested in beginning work among the Quiché, the largest Mayan group around Quetzaltenango, but the Board was reluctant to start work with the Indians. The Board shared the belief with the Liberal government that progress required the assimilation of the indigenous population. The Board advocated doing evangelistic work in Spanish and teaching people to read the Bible in Spanish as quickly as possible. The McBaths resigned from the Board in 1913.[16]

## 3.2 Mission Institutions and a Growing Church, 1912–1950

After thirty years of work in Guatemala, the Presbyterian Mission embarked on the building and consolidation of several institutions that provided new opportunities for both foreign women and Guatemalan women. The number of mission workers assigned to the Guatemala Mission increased steadily over the next four decades. Single women continued to serve in, and many times lead, the social service institutions, while the married women worked primarily in the church in a variety of support capacities. After years of encouragement from mission workers on the ground, the Board embraced work in Mayan languages. Women missionaries made significant contributions in this area. The Presbyterian congregations grew steadily during these decades. The process of creating women's organizations within the church structures, not a priority for the mission or for Guatemala Presbyterians, went very slowly.

Through the fundraising efforts of Corinna Allison, the *Hospital Americano* was opened with twelve beds in 1913. Scientific nursing was as yet unknown in Guatemala at the time. The Board appointed Henrietta York (1913–1918), a registered nurse who, together with Dr. Gregg, opened a school for nurses in late 1913. Dr. Gregg, the only woman doctor assigned by the Board to work in Guatemala, left for health reasons in 1916. The first three nurses graduated in 1917, shortly before a major earthquake destroyed the hospital building and most of Guatemala City.[17]

The Allisons closed the boys' school and pushed for the Board to open a school that would, like the *Colegio Americano*, reach a wealthier stratum of Guatemalan society. The new girls' primary school opened in 1912 with Grace Stevens (1912–1914) and Beulah A. Love (1912–1916) as teachers. Eleanor Morrison (1915–1942, 1946–1953) arrived in 1915 to work at the school and stayed for many years. After the earthquake, the school was moved to Quetzaltenango where it opened in 1918 with fifteen students. The Mission decided to keep running a school in Quetzaltenango after the school in Guatemala City was rebuilt.[18]

The rebuilt institutions and the growing church brought an influx of new mission workers. Single women missionaries continued to direct and serve on the teaching staff of the two schools, often moving between the two schools as needed.

Some served for only two or three years while others dedicated a lifetime to education in Guatemala. One of the later was Elsie Weeks (1933–1962), who worked at both schools as well as with the network of rural schools the Mission ran after the 1944 revolution. She was the director of the school in Guatemala City for fourteen years. Married missionary women joined in teaching in the 1940s. It should be noted that in Guatemala married women were prohibited from teaching in public schools until after the 1944 revolution.

Ruth McConnell Ainslie (1922–1957) directed the newly reopened nursing school while her husband, Dr. Charles Ainslie, directed the hospital. Mrs. Bessie M. Nurminger (1922–1957) came to be head nurse and for a time she also directed the nursing school. The hospital and nursing school attracted a number of women missionaries. In over four decades approximately 250 Guatemalan women graduated from the school. Some worked at the mission hospital, but most found jobs elsewhere.[19] Women were also responsible for the expansion of the Mission's medical work outside of Guatemala City, serving as nurses in rural clinics. An example was Ruth Esther Wardell (1949–1979), founder of the Mam Clinic near San Juan Ostuncalco which she directed for three decades.

While single women missionaries worked in the institutions of the Mission, married women missionaries tended to work in the church alongside their husbands. They worked with women, children, and youth in the churches. Those with musical skills contributed to worship life of the congregations. When the Mission began a seminary in Guatemala City in 1935, several of the married missionary women taught there together with their husbands.

The 1920s marked an important shift in mission policy toward the use of indigenous languages. When missionaries began arriving in Guatemala, they found that they were in a country with a majority Mayan population who spoke about twenty-two different languages and most of whom were illiterate. Early on the missionaries advocated for mission work in Mayan languages and after forty years of work in the country the Board was finally willing to listen. Three missionary women made pioneering contributions in linguistics, but the work of the two married women was overshadowed by that of their ordained husbands.

Dora McLaughlin Burgess (1913–1957) and Paul Burgess began learning Quiché as soon as they arrived in Quetzaltenango in 1913, but Dora soon became the better translator.[20] They worked with Mayan evangelists and advocated for interdenominational work in Mayan languages. In 1941, the Burgesses, together with missionaries from the Primitive Methodist Church, founded the Maya Quiché Bible Institute to teach men to read and write in Quiché at a time when it was still illegal to teach in an indigenous language in public schools in Guatemala. In 1945, single women were welcomed into the student body of the Institute. In 1947, the Quiché translation of the New Testament prepared by Dora Burgess and Patricio Xec was published.[21]

The first missionaries sent by the Board to work exclusively in a Mayan language were Rev. Horace Dudley Peck and Dorothy Miller Peck (1922–1963/1963–1970). Dorothy had studied Greek at Wellesley College in Massachusetts. The Pecks established themselves in the area west of Quetzaltenango and began reducing the Mam language to writing. Dorothy identified with Mam women by wearing traditional Mam dress, even preaching in the markets in full Mam dress. Dorothy was also a musician and she published the first Mam hymnal in 1927. The Pecks used their furloughs for linguistic studies at Harvard University (1927–1928) and the University of Chicago (1935). The Pecks published their translation of the New Testament in Mam in 1940. That same year the Pecks established the Mam Center near San Juan Ostuncalco. The holistic vision of the center focused on literacy training in Mam, study of the Bible, agricultural training, evangelism, and medical care.[22]

In 1947, Gail Maynard (1947–1978) joined the work in Quiché at the Bible Institute. In 1954, she and Patricio Xec produced a preliminary Quiché Spanish dictionary.[23] She also wrote educational materials in Quiché that were published by the Ministry of Education.[24] Upon her retirement from mission service with the UPCUSA, she continued in Guatemala as a volunteer with Wycliffe Bible Translators.

After forty years of work in Guatemala, Mission began to organize presbyteries in the early 1920s, an important step in the process of sharing authority with local pastors. It would be more than twenty years before women in the Presbyterian church in Guatemala had their own organization beyond the local church level. Presbyterian women in Guatemala adopted the same structure as their sisters in the United States, creating organizations that parallel the structure of the denomination. The Central Presbyterial was organized in 1948 and the Occidente Presbyterial was formed in 1950. Missionary women, both married and single, were active in these organizations.[25]

## 3.3  A National Church and the Dissolution of the Mission, 1950–1962

In the context of Guatemala's first democratic government, elected after the 1944 revolution, Guatemalan Presbyterians pushed to have their own national church. Mission policy was also changing as historic Protestant mission boards confronted the paternalism of their past mission efforts. The Synod of the National Evangelical Presbyterian Church of Guatemala (IENPG) was organized in May of 1950. The number of Presbyterian mission workers had peaked in Guatemala in the decade of the 1940s. Over the next twelve years, most of the institutions founded by the Mission were passed into the hands of the national church. The process of dissolving the Mission as a legal structure and placing the work under national control, known as integration in Presbyterian circles, was completed in 1962. The new working relationship between the two churches meant that missionaries, known as fraternal workers after integration, would serve at the invitation of and under the supervision of national leaders. As integration approached, the Board sent two couples to support the Guatemalan church in pastoral ministry, but the opportunities for service by single women were greatly reduced.

Now that a national church structure existed, the Guatemalan Presbyterian women organized as well on a national level. The *Sinodica*, as the national organization of Presbyterian women is known, was founded in 1952. Marjorie Morrison (1951–1958) seems to be the only mission worker assigned to work primarily with the women of the church, though she also served as interim director of the school in Quetzaltenango. Many of the married missionary women gave their active support to the women's organizations in the church.

Both schools were led by single women missionaries until the early 1950s, except for a brief period of three years in the 1930s when men from the Mission directed the school in Guatemala City. At that point the school became a boys' school and later coeducational. By the 1950s, both schools were coeducational and offered secondary as well as primary grades. The first Guatemalan director of the school in Guatemala City was Sara Ortiz, one of the twins who had been raised by the Haymakers, who became director in 1952.[26] In 1950, William Ross (1950–1982) was appointed by the Board to the administration of the school in Quetzaltenango. His wife, Irene Jones Ross (1950–1981) also served in the administration and as a teacher in the school in Quetzaltenango.

During the 1950s, the *Hospital Americano* continued to provide health care with the support of the Board of Foreign Missions and mission personnel. But the institution proved unsustainable. New laws imposed after the 1954 coup d'état forced the closing of the nursing school. As integration approached, the mission board decided to sell the hospital to a group of local doctors rather than burden the national church with an institution incurring high operating costs.[27]

## 3.4 New Directions in Mission in a Context of Growing Violence, 1962–1982

For the UPCUSA, integration meant a move away from church-centered mission, in part because the Guatemalan Presbyterian Church was now responsible for its own internal life. There was also a growing recognition in historic Protestant mission circles that the social inequalities in Latin America were not being addressed by either the Protestant churches or by mission schools catering to the small middle class. Most of the new generation of mission workers, assigned starting in the late 1950s, shared these concerns, though many Guatemalan Presbyterians did not. In Guatemala, the resistance of the ruling elite to allow structural changes to come about through peaceful means fed a growing guerrilla movement. In turn, the existence of an armed movement seeking revolutionary change was used by the army to justify massacres of entire villages. While many Latin American countries suffered under military dictatorships during the 1960s and 1970s, Guatemala experienced genocidal repression aimed primarily at Mayan communities that eventually left 200,000 dead. Growing political polarization within Guatemala and divergent understandings of Christian faithfulness led to tensions within the IENPG as well as between the UPCUSA and the IENPG.

Now that mission workers served at the invitation of the national church, the IENPG requested missionary couples to work with the different presbyteries in specific tasks. The UPCUSA sent a rural sociologist, Donald Sibley, to work in development in the western highlands. Anna Grant Sibley (1956–1978) taught in the program to train agricultural promoters and she also wrote for a journal dedicated to expanding understandings of mission. Grace Allen Gyori (1962–1980) and Thomas Gyori worked primarily in the North Presbytery. Among other tasks, Grace served with Pro-Salud, the program in preventative healthcare the IENPG started after the sale of the *Hospital Americano*. The Mam Center was one institution that remained under the leadership of missionary couples, where nurse Roberta Helm Winter (1957–1966) emphasized preventive healthcare and Sara Jane Scotchmer (1969–1982) used her artistic talents to produce educational materials. Long-term mission workers, both married couples and single women, were not replaced when they retired and withdrew from service.

The Evangelical Presbyterian Seminary in Guatemala was the birthplace of Theological Education by Extension (TEE), a movement to expand access to theological studies by taking classes and materials to where church members live.[28] Missionaries and leaders in the Guatemalan church struggled with how to provide relevant theological education across multiple cultural contexts. In the early 1960s, the seminary headquarters was moved to a rural location and extension classes were started in many communities. The inductive method of teaching the Bible encouraged participants to articulate theological understandings out of their own cultural context and in response to the needs of their communities. Not surprisingly, rural Maya living in poverty came to different conclusions from people in the capital city. Extension classes allowed married women in the Guatemalan church access to theological education for the first time. Though missionary men—Ralph Winter, Jim Emery, and Ross Kinsler—are usually given the credit for starting theological education by extension, married missionary women like Gennet Emery (1952–1966) and Gloria Gibson Kinsler (1963–1977) also taught classes. Gennet Emery, a trained anthropologist, also wrote one of the first academic studies of Protestantism in Guatemala which was published in 1970 after she left mission service.[29] As the civil war intensified, sending professors out to teach in communities became too dangerous and the program was curtailed.

In preparation for the celebration of the centennial of Presbyterian presence in the country, the IENPG requested personnel from the Latin American Center for Pastoral Studies (CELEP) to help the church with contextualized evangelism by relating the gospel to community needs and strengthening the witness of local churches. Gloria Salazar (1979–1982) and Andres Garcia arrived in Guatemala in 1979 with salaries provided by the UPCUSA. As an Ecuadorean, Gloria was the first Latin American woman to serve as a missionary of the UPCUSA in Guatemala. Gloria, who had helped to start CELEP's women's ministry program, focused part of her work on women.

The Maya Quiché Presbytery requested a mission worker to help them produce Christian educational materials in Quiché. The UPCUSA sent Rev. Cynthia Pattishall-Pleasant (1979–1981), the first ordained woman pastor to serve as a mission worker in Guatemala and the first single woman appointed after integration. As Pattishall-Pleasant became acquainted with the situation of women in the presbytery, she began to address the role of women in the church. She worked with the seminary to open seven extension centers for women. She wrote two books on women in the Bible that were translated into Quiché. When she and some of the students began to advocate for women's ordination in the IENPG, the presbytery took away her vote. In 1981, as the army's brutal counterinsurgency program focused in the department of El Quiché, Pattishall-Pleasant returned to California.[30] It would be another fifteen years before the IENPG would consider the question of women's ordination.

In 1982, during one of the most violent periods of the civil war, the National Evangelical Presbyterian Church of Guatemala led the centennial celebration of the coming of Protestantism to the country. By the end of that year, all Presbyterian mission workers from the United States had withdrawn from the country, bringing to a close a century of missionary presence.

## 4. Analysis

In the history of the IENPG that was published for the centennial celebration of the church in 1982, the chapter on Presbyterian women and their ministry begins with the following statement: "In spite of the fact that the Presbyterian Church of Guatemala is a church eminently directed by men, we recognize that the role of women has been decisive within the church."[31] The text goes on to delineate the areas in which Presbyterian women were active: Sunday school teaching, music, as deaconesses, in the women's societies, and in the home.[32] How did a mission with so many strong and highly competent women produce a national church so conservative and closed to the gifts of women? Many factors, some of which were completely out of control of the women missionaries, contributed to this situation.

Patriarchal relationships existed in Guatemala long before Protestant missionaries arrived. The Maya worldview celebrated complementarity between the genders. Though women shared in political and spiritual leadership in many of the Maya city-states, this complementarity remained asymmetrical as most power was held by men.[33] The invading Spanish armies used rape as a tool to subjugate indigenous populations. The Spanish imported their own forms of patriarchy as they built a colonial society. Interethnic relationships over four centuries tended to reinforce patriarchy, leaving women, particularly Maya women, with little space for autonomous action.

The historic Protestant mission approach to Latin America rarely included a specific focus on evangelization of women or women's advancement. Protestant missions in Latin America made their primary appeal to "the rational nature of man" and strove to present their religious vision as the thinking man's alternative to Roman Catholicism.[34] The women who made up the Commission on Women's Work of the Congress on Christian Work in Latin America held in Panama in 1916 lamented that they could not find much bibliography on situation of women in the continent.[35] They also noted that the women's missionary movement had first organized to reach out to the "prisoners of the harem and zenana," women living in the Orient where social conditions dictated that only women missionaries would be able to reach women.[36] In Latin America, women were perceived as being more integrated into society and work with women was seen as part of general efforts to improve social conditions. For this reason, the report of the regional conferences that were held in various cities after the Panama Congress did not include a section on women's work.[37] As noted above, the first Spanish-speaking congregation organized in Guatemala City had a reported membership of nine men and no women.

Although transcultural agents such as missionaries are involved in the transmission of particular forms of Christianity, appropriation depends on local agents. The process of appropriation tends to reinforce certain dynamics within the local cultural context while challenging others. In the case of Guatemala, the first Protestants were working-class men who were willing to risk the social stigma involved in breaking with Roman Catholicism, but they did not challenge traditional gender roles.

Though Presbyterians were the first organized Protestant group in Guatemala, in the early twentieth century the dispensationalist fundamentalism of the Central American Mission because the dominant theological vision among Guatemalan Protestants, including Presbyterians. This faith mission founded by Cyrus Scofield established a permanent presence in Guatemala City in 1899. As Thomas Bogenschild notes in his study of the origins of fundamentalism in Western Guatemala, the clear moral rules offered by fundamentalism proved attractive to many in communities undergoing social changes brought on by modernization. The more sophisticated herme-neutic offered by the Presbyterian missionaries proved less appealing.[38] Literal readings of the Bible, especially the texts that demand wives be submissive to their husbands and order women to remain silent in church, are seldom good news for women. According to this conservative theological vision, the only legitimate role for the church is evangelism, therefore the social service institutions in which single women missionaries played such an important role are not seen as legitimate forms of mission.

While women missionaries, particularly the single women, had leadership roles within the social institutions founded by the Mission, the ordained men were clearly in charge of the church work. The wives of these men, even when they were doing other work in the Mission, were perceived as pastors' wives within the church. There was another model of wom-en's church leadership present in Guatemala. Ruth Esther Smith, a recorded minister in the Society of Friends, served as the superintendent of the Friends Mission in Guatemala from 1907 to 1947. She planted and pastored several churches, riding between communities on a mule in the early days. The Friends Bible institute in Chiquimula received and prepared female stu-dents for pastoral ministry from the time of its founding.[39]

While women in the churches in the United States organized to support the mission work of the church, the women's societ-ies in the Guatemalan church served to reinforce domesticity.[40] Missionary discourse on Christian marriage, in writings by both men and women, undoubtedly contributed to this focus.[41] The missionaries viewed the high numbers of illegitimate births as evidence of immortality and the failure of the Roman Catholic Church. They promoted marriage as the path to moral reform of the society. They also believed that marriage would improve the status of women. Married missionary women who ran Christian homes and supported the work of the local church were lifted up as models to be emulated. The nascent women's organizations in the Guatemalan Presbyterian church assumed this discourse on Christian marriage as their own as they created a space for women in the church.

It is interesting to note that the single Protestant missionary women assumed roles, at least initially, in which Roman Catholic nuns had served, teaching children and caring for the sick. The Protestants, however, had science on their side, pedagogy and modern medicine. The missionaries trained Guatemalan women to be teachers and nurses, but the Guatemalan women lacked the support of a religious order or mission board as they sought to live out their vocations. Work remains to be done to recover the histories of the Guatemalan women who graduated from the schools run by the Presbyterian Mission.

The women missionaries and the Guatemalan women who became Presbyterian did not create any mechanisms within the church for women's involvement beyond the women's societies. The situation was different in Mexico just to the north, where Bible schools were organized for Mexican women to train them to work as missionaries in the church. Just as foreign women missionaries had done in the past, the Mexican Presbyterian women who graduated from these schools took on many teaching and pastoral responsibilities in the church, but without the authority, recognition, or economic remuneration given to male pastors.[42]

The same factors that limited women's participation in the churches have also contributed to the lack of attention to women in the historiography of Protestantism in Guatemala and elsewhere in Latin America. As noted, the historic Protestant missions in Latin America did not focus specifically on women. Most histories written to date have emphasized the development of church structures where women have had little power. Only recently have women gained access to theological education that provides them with tools for recovering and telling the story of women in their churches.

## 5. Questions for Discussion

1. To what extent did Protestant missionary women stand outside the gender expectations of the local communities where they served? Did this limit their ability to serve as role models for local women?

2. Is the growth of Protestantism in Latin America (and elsewhere) empowering or disempowering for women?

3. Under what conditions does the arrival of Protestantism add another layer to existing patriarchal structures and under what conditions can a new religious vision challenge patriarchy?

## 6. Recommendations

1. Oral histories need to focus on recovering the experience of local women to discover how they appropriated the message and example of foreign missionary women.

2. Archival materials from foreign women missionaries need to be made available to those researching women's history in the countries where they served.

3. Training resources for mission need to be developed that place marriage and family issues within the framework of God's mission rather than as ends in themselves.

## 7. Conclusion

Though the majority of Presbyterian missionaries from the United States who served in Guatemala from 1882 to 1982 were women, the Presbyterian Mission did not focus consistently on working for women. The Mission's educational work was directed first at boys and girls of the ruling elite, then at poor boys, then at girls from the nascent middle class. The Mission passed into the hands of the national church two co-educational schools located in the two largest cities in the country. The medical work of the Mission required skilled nurses, an effort that incidentally provided professional training and opportunities for employment and service to Guatemalan women. Eventually women were allowed into the institutions that had been created to provide theological education for Guatemalan men, but the only space for women in the church remained the women's societies. Much more research needs to be done to explore how local women may have been empowered through their interactions with foreign women missionaries even though they received little or no recognition from the national church that resulted from Presbyterian mission efforts.

## Further Reading

Lois A. Boyd and R. Douglas Brackenridge, *Presbyterian Women in America: Two Centuries of a Quest for Status*. 2nd ed. (Westport, CT: Greenwood Press, 1996).

Virginia Garrard-Burnett, *Protestantism in Guatemala: Living in the New Jerusalem* (Austin: University of Texas, 1998).

F. Ross Kinsler, ed., *Ministry by the People: Theological Education by Extension* (Maryknoll, NY: Orbis Books, 1983).

## Endnotes

1. Virginia Garrard-Burnett, *Protestantism in Guatemala: Living in the New Jerusalem* (Austin: Univ. of Texas, 1998).

2. The primary source for this case study is the official history of the National Evangelical Presbyterian Church of Guatemala that was published

on the occasion of the centennial celebration of Presbyterian (and Protestant) presence in Guatemala. Iglesia Evangélica Nacional Presbiteriana de Guatemala (IENPG), *Apuntes para la historia* (Guatemala: IENPG, 1982). Many primary sources, such as letters and newsletters written by the missionaries, are housed in archives in the United States and not readily available to researchers in Guatemala.

3. The IENPG approved the ordination of women as pastors and ruling elders in 1998.

4. José Míguez Bonino, *Faces of Latin American Protestantism* (Grand Rapids: Eerdmans, 1995), 4-5.

5. Thomas E. Bogenschild, "The Roots of Fundamentalism in Liberal Guatemala: Missionary Ideologies and Local Response, 1882–1944" (Ph.D. diss., Univ. of California, Berkeley, 1992), 24-68.

6. Edward M. Haymaker, "Footnotes on the Beginnings of the Evangelical Movement in Guatemala, 1946," TMs, 16.

7. Unless otherwise noted, the dates of service and activities of the women missionaries listed is taken from "Apéndice C: Actividades misioneros," in IENPG, *Apuntes*, 493-504.

8. "La obra misionera," in IENPG, *Apuntes*, 73.

9. Haymaker, 16.

10. "La obra misionera," 73.

11. Haymaker, 17-19; "La obra misionera," 74-76.

12. Haymaker, 18-19.

13. "La obra misionera," 83-85; Haymaker, 39-40.

14. "La obra misionera," 90-91.

15. Haymaker, 58-60.

16. "La obra misionera," 89; Haymaker, 40.

17. "El Sínodo y las instituciones," in IENPG, *Apuntes*, 163.

18. Ibid., 189.

19. Ibid., 164.

20. Anne Marie Dahlquist, *Trailblazers for Translators* (Pasadena: William Carey Library 1995), 91-94.

21. "La obra misionera," 101-104.

22. "La obra misionera," 103; "El Sínodo y las instituciones," 172-75.

23. Patricio Xec and Gail Maynard, "Diccionario quiché preliminar: Quiché-español, español-quiché," Mimeographed. Quetzaltenango, Guatemala, 1954.

24. For example, Gail Maynard, *Chatakej uwowuj* (Guatemala: Ministerio de Educación, 1966).

25. "La mujer presbiteriana y su ministerio," in IENPG, *Apuntes*, 346-47.

26. "El Sínodo y las instituciones," 186.

27. Ibid., 164-66.

28. Kenneth B. Mulholland and Nelly de Jacobs, "Presbyterian Seminary of Guatemala: A Modest Experiment Becomes a Model for Change," in *Ministry by the People: Theological Education by Extension*, ed. F. Ross Kinsler (Maryknoll, NY: Orbis Books, 1983), 33-41.

29. Gennet Maxon Emery, *Protestantism in Guatemala: it's influence on the bicultural situation with reference to the Roman Catholic background, Sondeo* no. 65. (Cuernavaca, Mexico: Centro Intercultural de Documentacion, 1970).

30. Cynthia Patishall-Baker, letter to author, 14 Aug. 2001.

31. "La mujer presbiteriana," 345.

32. Ibid.

33. Traci Ardren, "Women and Gender in the Ancient Maya World," in *Ancient Maya Women*, ed. Traci Ardren (Walnut Creek, CA: Altamira Press, 2002), 1-12.

34. Robert E. Speer, *South American Problems* (New York: Student Volunteer Movement, 1912), 147.

35. "Report of Commission Five on Women's Work," in Committee on Cooperation in Latin America, *Christian Work in Latin America: Report of the Congress on Christian Work in Latin America Held in Panama, February, 1916, vol. II* (New York: Missionary Education Movement, 1917), 111-112, 122.

36. Ibid., 113-14.

37. Committee on Cooperation in Latin America, *Regional Conferences in Latin America* (New York: Missionary Education Movement, 1917), xiv.

38. Bogenschild, "The Roots of Fundamentalism."

39. Ron Stansell, *Missions by the Spirit: Learning from Quaker Examples* (Newberg, OR: Barclay Press, 2010), 85-135.

40. On Presbyterian women in the United States, see Lois A. Boyd and R. Douglas Brackenridge, *Presbyterian Women in America: Two Centuries of a Quest for Status*. 2nd ed. (Westport, CT: Greenwood Press, 1996).

41. For an example of this missionary discourse, see Edward Haymaker, "Editorial: The Christian Home," *Guatemala News* 23:4 (April 1932): 1-4.

42. For a testimony from a graduate of one of the Bible schools, see Eva Domíguez Sosa, "En la Escuela Bíblica Central las preparan para ser pastoras," in *Tiempos de hablar: reflexiones en torno a los ministerios femininos*, ed. Laura Taylor de Palomino (México, DF: Ediciones STPM, 1997), 209-13.

CHAPTER 15

# Swiss-German Protestant Women in Mission: The Basel Mission (Nineteenth to Twenty-first Century)

*Heike Walz*

## 1. Introduction[1]

Pietism,[2] a movement of spiritual awakening within the Reformed churches in German-speaking Switzerland, and the Lutheran churches in Germany,[3] profoundly shaped the work of Protestant missionaries' from the Basel Mission.[4] Many years ago, as I undertook vigorous youth work in my home village in Southern Germany, I too found the spirit of Pietism attractive. Later, as I studied theology and became acquainted with the negative aspects of European colonial mission history, I began to ask critical questions: why was the spread of the gospel combined with the imposition of European civilization, its cultural, political, and economic power?

This view too was later challenged. When I was involved in "mission in solidarity"[5] between the global North and South, I served as a young pastor at the Presbyterian Women's Centre Abokobi in Ghana. The late Rev. Rose Akua Ampofo delivered a sermon, the contents of which surprised me: She gave thanks to my grandmothers and grandfathers who had come to Ghana as missionaries to spread the gospel! Ghanaian Christians had experienced God's mission through the ambivalent European mission. "Women's work for women," a concept of women in mission, is one of the seeds to have germinated in God's mission. During the past years, as I served the Evangelical Mission Society in Basel (*mission 21*) by teaching theology in Buenos Aires in Argentina,[6] I worked within the tensions created by the persistence of old mission methods and development of new models such as "partnership in mission." In truth, however, my experience of living side by side with the people often extended beyond such formal patterns. For me, ambivalence itself provides a hermeneutic key for reflecting on the experiences of the Swiss-German women engaged in foreign mission treated in this essay. In short: my own story mirrors the various approaches to mission held in German-speaking Europe today.

While the fields of business, politics, astronautics, the military and even football teams have a particular "mission" today, in the church life of German speaking Christians and—most of all—in foreign mission, there exists a widespread hesitancy to use the term "mission" at all.[7] Sometimes, even pastors are reluctant to have any association with mission due to the perception that mission is a movement of manipulation and the imposition of an ideology.[8] Instead, they argue: "Do not bother others with your faith; respect personal beliefs as everybody's private affair." In Germany, this attitude results from secularization, the privatization of religion, and the pluralist society. It has also to do with the shameful history of the propaganda and manipulation that occurred during Nazism and the Holocaust. Furthermore, some sectors of the society disguise xenophobia with the language of a "Christian leading culture" in an effort to curtail the development of a multireligious society. Hopefully, reluctant attitudes toward the imposition upon others of one's own world view and belief system will help avoid a repetition of the violent history of European colonial mission and political and economic "missions" to peoples in the South.

The Evangelical and Pentecostal wings of the Christian church, both in Germany and abroad, focus especially on church growth and expansionist forms of mission to call individuals to a radical "born again" conversion experience. Yet, "mission," in the sense of the communication of the good news of the gospel, has in recent years become important for the Evangelical Church in Germany,[9] not only because of the significant decline in church membership, but also because Christian institutions, Christian culture and language have become remote to people particularly in East Germany.[10] Unfortunately, the rich ecumenical resources drawn from Global Christianity have not been directed to the question of "mission" in Europe. Nor has the agency of women in mission been considered pivotal. But new concepts of mission have emerged, such as "mission as hermeneutics of the Other," which includes respect and empathy toward religion and culture of the Other, "mission as living together,"[11] "mission as interreligious dialogue,"[12] "mission in a pluralist society,"[13] and "doxological mission."[14]

The history of women missionaries has attracted attention since the 1990s,[15] with the implementation of gender policies in both Swiss and German mission societies. Gender studies in mission[16] are less frequent, and studies on masculinities in mission[17] almost do not exist at all. In the perspective of German speaking feminist theology, "mission" is perceived as connected with an authoritarian, triumphant, violent, overall powerful and patriarchal understanding of God and Christianity. Of course, feminist theologies themselves show a "missionary drive" as far as the spread of emancipation, liberation, and gender equality is concerned. Few theologies of mission from women's and feminist angles have emerged so far.[18]

My approach has partly been influenced by discussions with the feminist postcolonial criticisms of mission developed by Musa W. Dube, Kwok Pui-lan, and Mrinalini Sebastian,[19] but I am aware that theologians in non-English speaking contexts (especially in Latin America) largely resist the application of Anglophone postcolonial theories to their distinct contexts.[20] Their critique is, rather, focused on "Empire" and "neoliberal globalization." While migration studies, politics of migration and asylum,[21] and gender studies in theology have assumed feminist postcolonial perspectives, these insights have had little to no impact on German-speaking mission studies. Thus I am not sure if I am able to fully resist explicit or implicit images of "the Third-World-Woman"[22] in this essay. I am challenged to practice self-criticism with regard to privileges, whiteness, power relations, socio-economic hierarchies and binary symbolic oppositions between "European" and "non-Western" people.

Therefore, I will look for contradictions between "European mission ideals" promoted officially and the concrete actions of missionaries from Europe and their interlocutors. European women's mission would have been impossible without encounters, co-operations, theological, and linguistic discussions and negotiations with African, Asian, Latin American, and Pacific women and men. The latter were missionaries themselves and made a greater contribution to the mission enterprise than the foreigner did.

The case study will focus mainly, but not exclusively, on the Basel Mission from the ninrteenth until the twenty-first century, that is, to *mission 21* today. This is one of the most important mission societies in German-speaking parts of Europe.[23] Drawing on the rich documents and photographs available in the Basel

Mission Archive, good research exists that deals with women sent by the Basel Mission.[24]

## 2. Historical Background in Switzerland and Germany in the Nineteenth Century

Four aspects shape the historical background of women in mission in Germany and Switzerland in the nineteenth century: the Protestant mission movement, gender perceptions of women and men in society and church, women's emancipation movements, and colonialism. A new epoch of the Protestant mission history started in the nineteenth century. There was such an incredible boom of the mission movement across all Protestant denominations that the famous founder of mission studies, Gustav Warneck (1834–1910), described it as the "century of mission."[25]

The "Inner Mission" or "Home Mission," developed by Johann Heinrich Wichern (1808–1881) in 1848, addressed the poor and sick people at home. It aimed at a rebirth or awakening of Christianity by setting up Sunday schools and Christian education, as well as homes for uncared children, rescue missions for prostitutes and drunkards, nurseries, asylums for strangers and social work with prison inmates. Inner Mission was a Protestant response to the social problems and the pauperization caused by rapid industrialization.[26] Women played an important role as deaconesses. They stepped in the "Inner Mission" as social workers among poor, sick, and elderly people and women in childbirth. Bible reading and spiritual support was part of their mission.[27]

The "Inner Mission" was connected with the "External Mission" to spread "the good news of the Gospel" to the people in Asia and Africa. Some women had already been sent abroad by the Moravians in the eighteenth century, but only in the nineteenth century was a "women's mission movement" initiated. At the beginning, missionaries' wives were sent abroad. Educated, unmarried women missionaries were included in the missionary project by the 1840s. This developed to its height between 1880 and 1920.[28]

The women's mission movement was rooted in the concept of two separated *gender* characters for women and men in the bourgeois society and the church. Women were considered as passive and emotional, and men as active and rational. Women had to dedicate their lives to the private sphere of the house, the family and motherhood, while men worked in the public spheres of politics and industrial work.[29] Yet within this binary opposition of the private and public sphere, women, especially when they were unmarried or widows, were increasingly expected to accomplish tasks as mothers and caretakers outside the house, the task of "mothering within the extended family."[30] Socioeconomic changes caused by industrialization and women's emancipation movements provoked the establishment of female professions such as teachers, nurses, secretaries, or accountants. The bourgeois liberal movement called for higher education, access to universities and the right for women to vote. Confessional Protestant and Catholic women's organizations participated as well, though their profile was more conservative.[31]

The German-speaking mission movement had begun before the rise of colonial empires, but, with the rise of these empires, the mission enterprise soon shared in the colonial and imperial spirit and became stamped by the European feeling of superiority.[32] Women participated actively in colonialism by supporting their husbands who were serving as colonial officers, missionaries, and as active members of colonial associations at home. Nevertheless, white European women fulfilled complex and contradictory roles, being perpetrators, victims, and critics in German colonies.[33] Their relationships with African and Asian women were also contradictory and ambivalent.[34]

## 3. Case Study: Contradictions within Women's Missionary Work of Basel Mission

Two concrete examples will be presented as case studies: the stories of women who, in serving as missionary wives or unmarried missionaries, struggled with contradictions inherent in their mandate. To situate them in their historical context, I will give a rough overview on five periods and models of understanding women's missionary work within the Basel Mission.

### 3.1 Five Periods and Models of Understanding Woman's Role in Mission

Founded in 1815, the Basel Mission originated as a Protestant interdenominational mission society, supported by the Lutheran Church of Württemberg in Southern Germany and the Reformed Churches in Switzerland. Mission work was constantly promoted by the journal "Protestant Heathen Messenger," by annual reports and mission feasts, and by supporting groups.[35] In Basel,

wealthy citizens were involved in transnational trade and interested in expanding commerce. In 1956, more than about 2500
male missionaries had been trained in theology and handicraft
work (printing, textile manufacturing, weaving) in order to create employment opportunities for the local people abroad. At the
beginning of the First World War (1914–1918), the Basel Mission
had become the largest mission society in German speaking
Europe.[36] The Reformed Church and the Pietistic movement were
closely collaborating in Basel.

During the first period until the 1840s, the Basel Mission
sent out only men as missionaries. For the Committee of the
Basel Mission (the direction), the problem was that these men
wanted to get married or were already engaged. So Inspektor
Christoph Gottfried Blumhardt (1779–1838) formulated the
"principles of marriage" in 1837. According to these, male missionaries could marry with the permission of the Committee.
Missionaries' wives were considered helpers, but rarely called
"missionaries."[37] Usually, the missionary brides knew their
future husband only by photographs and the exchange of letters.[38] Many women hoped to break out of the limited space of
their homes, to explore foreign countries and to realize themselves by working for the Kingdom of God. Missionary wives
were housewives and enablers of their husband's work. They
represented the mission house in their respective mission stations in Africa or Asia. They were to exemplify high standards
of housekeeping and the European Christian ideals of monog-
amous marriage, the family and womanhood. Normally they
employed African or Asian women, who assisted them in managing the household.

As "helpers" they usually filled gaps, teaching "female"
skills,[39] without either remuneration or an official status within
the missionary society.[40] The impact of missionaries' wives was
immense, however, because only women were allowed to meet
local women in their living spheres inside the houses, e.g. *zenanas* in India. This presented an opportunity for missionaries'
wives to introduce local women to the Bible outside of male
control.

The second period is marked by the controversial decision to
send out unmarried female missionaries. North American and
British mission societies served as a model for other European
mission societies.[41] The Anglo-Saxon concept of women´s mission for women became introduced to the European continent.
In 1841, Inspektor Ludwig Friedrich Wilhelm Hoffmann (1808–
1873) published his programmatic text "The education of the

female sex in India. A call for Christian women in Germany and Switzerland."[42] He argued that the Christian faith had contributed to the advancement of the status of women in the West. He considered "heathendom" and "superstition" as the main reasons for the "slavery of the female sex"[43] in other parts of the world. "White women saving brown women from brown men," as postcolonial feminist theorist Gayatri Chakravorty Spivak (*1942) later described it.[44]

The Women's Association of the Basel Mission was founded in 1841. While the Women's Mission Committee consisted of thirteen women, men remained in charge, as was typical in other women associations of the Inner Mission. In 1842, the first two female teachers were sent to India.[45] Women in Basel were engaged with policy making, fundraising, public speaking, and supporting one or several women missionaries. The Basel Women's Mission Committee connected with other women mission associations in England, Geneva, Berlin and "female mission friends" in Germany and Switzerland.[46] But, in the following years, the Women's Mission Committee, became increasingly powerless. It was only in 1901 that Women's Mission was re-established as a separate organization, now under the leadership of the women themselves.[47]

Some unmarried women were active as teachers, especially from the 1850s to the beginning of the nineteenth century, but missionaries' wives were the main actors during that time.[48] Records show that even some missionaries' wives and widows did not agree with sending out unmarried women.[49] Thus, the Basel Mission hesitated to send unmarried women abroad until the beginning of the twentieth century. This was also the case in the Netherlands[50] and in Norway.[51] However, the "woman missionary" was transformed into a profession with salary, old-age pension, a regular theological training and medical formation by the end of the nineteenth century.

The International Mission Conference in Edinburgh 1910 marks the beginning of the third period. The two women delegates, Elise Raaflaub (1878–1944) and Johanna Metzger (1876–1956) from the Basel Mission, were impressed by the agency and theological contributions of English female missionaries to the Conference. Johanna wrote a forty-page record in which she recommended that a sisters' institute for the preparation of female missionaries be founded. The Edinburgh conference provoked a radical change of mind in Basel: in 1911, the Sisters' Institute was founded and more women received solid training to become missionaries.[52] While the Basel Mission's women's missionary work was stagnant during the First World War, it flourished again in the years 1920–1940. A secretary for women's mission was established in 1928 and occupied by Dorothee Sarasin (1894–1968) until 1964.[53] Various German missionary societies amplified their co-operation, for example, by establishing a working group of German Evangelical women in mission in 1925 that formed part of the German Evangelical Mission Council.[54]

Because of the Second World War, during the fourth period, the women's missionary movement suffered a decline in its activities. In 1966, the Basel Mission renewed its regulation, which meant dissolving the Basel Women's Association and integrating it into the Basel Mission as the Commission for Women's Work. The idea was to create a "partnership between man and woman in the direction" of the Basel Mission.[55]

The fifth period since the 1990s shows a paradigm shift from women's issues to gender mainstreaming in development organizations, fostered by the legislation of the European Union. Mission 21, like other German missionary societies, established the Women's and Gender Desk in 2001.[56] Basel Mission and *mission 21* underwent a process of structural transformation toward "partnership at eye-level" with their partners abroad.[57] Efforts were made to foster a mutual exchange of historical views, theological perspectives, and visions between women from the South and North as "sisters from two worlds,"[58] but also via South-South networking between women from Africa, Asia, and Latin America.

## 3.2 The Ideal of European "Christian Motherhood" While sending Children Back to Europe

Missionaries' wives had to embody the "Christian" ideal of good motherhood, which included the comprehensive and "ordered Christian education" of their children. Coincidentally, they often had to send their children back home as early as age five or six. If the children could not live in the household of some family members or friends in Europe, the mission society took care of them via "missionaries' sons' boarding schools" or the "missionaries' daughters' institutions." This was a common practice at the Basel Mission[59] and in other missionary societies like the Rhenish Mission[60] and the Northern German Mission.[61]

The Basel Mission released a "children's regulation" in 1853 only after Inspector Josef Josenhans (1812–1884) sent a twenty-six-page paper to the missionaries abroad outlining arguments in favor and against two options: It would either be necessary to build boarding schools in India for all missionaries' children, or to develop girls and boys institutes in Basel. Most of the missionaries agreed with the second option, which was also the favored option of the home base in Basel.[62]

The children's regulation reflects the dualistic division between "pagan" education and the "Christian spirit." Schooling had to be based on German-Swiss culture and language and in correspondence with the missionary tradition. The Basel Mission argued against bringing up the children in schools on the mission fields due to the potential of being "poisoned" by the "bad influence" of "pagan" customs or even being sexually seduced by "pagans."[63]

Gender divisions are obvious as well. Missionaries' wives were not allowed to educate their sons. Neither, however, could the male missionaries do it because they had to dedicate themselves to mission full-time. Femininity was constructed as being a good wife and mother. By contrast, the focus of the male missionary's masculinity rested not in being a good husband and father, but in being a missionary.[64] Similar gender divisions applied to the education of girls and boys. Only boys were given a higher level of education at the middle of the nineteenth century. Girls were educated for their future life as wives in the household. As such, a basic knowledge in reading, writing, calculating, history, and geography was sufficient.[65]

Sending their children back to Europe was painful for both mother and father. Some missionaries' wives wrote in their "diary of the children" about the trauma of letting their children go. In Johanna Ritter's (1884–1970) words: "We as mission people could only be something for our children for a short time."[66] She could neither experience how her children were growing up, nor influence their education. She could only expect seeing them during furlough in Europe after some years.[67]

"Mission children" often suffered from a cultural shock when they came back "home."[68] But was it their home? Often they had difficulties adapting themselves to the rigid system of the Swiss and German children's homes, nor was their "mother tongue" German. Sometimes they dreamed of free adventures in the bush under African's hot sun.[69] Separation and alienation between parents and children were but one of the sacrifices the missionaries assumed "for the mission."[70] Missionaries' wives were "relieved" from the care for the elder children. Their life was expected to belong entirely to the mission.[71] Today we would say that mission children had to live in "patchwork families."

Today, this separation of the family seems to be contradictory to the "Christian ideal of family," because living together in the extended family was self-evident in Germany and Switzerland—as it was also the case among African and Asian peoples.[72] Maybe the mothers of mission children at that time did not always interpret the separation as a contradiction, but as an unquestionable sacrifice.[73] However, while "brotherhood and sisterhood" were promoted in mission, children turned out to be an obstacle. Missionaries' wives had to represent the model of "Christian motherhood," but had to renounce being mothers for their own children.

The last generation of these "children of mission" is, today, about seventy years old. In the main, they have felt traumatized by the separation from their parents and by their experiences of being outlandish and strange during their whole life. Until today, many of them keep in touch with other "children of mission" and come together in workshops held for "mission children" at *mission 21* to exchange experiences. Some of them travel to the country of their childhood, to retrace the footsteps of their forebears and to meet descendants of their indigenous caretakers.[74]

## 3.3 The Ideal of European Whiteness and Black African Women Missionaries as Key Actors

The Basel Mission considered white European women as key actors in the mission task, but engaged black Africans from the Caribbean because many European missionaries had died on the Gold Coast. African American Christians founded a Black Atlantic Missionary Movement, arguing that Christianity and modernity had come to Africa also through an "African" movement searching for a "black African" Christianity.[75] However, the "universal Christian community" of the Basel Mission did not promote a full communion between whites and blacks, and especially not interracial marriage, as we will explore now using the example of Catherine Mulgrave (1827–1891).

Catherine Mulgrave was a Moravian returnee and the Basel Mission's first women teacher at the Gold Coast.[76] Her interesting biography shows the intertwinement of gender, race, and class questions, but also her pioneer work and key role as a female missionary. As it is possible to trace her own voice only in few letters written by herself, scholars must rely on the letters and reports from others, mainly male missionaries.

Catherine was born in Angola as a daughter of a Christian family, but kidnapped by slave traders at the age of six. During a storm, the ship overturned off the coast of Jamaica where slaves had already been declared free. The Governor of Jamaica, the Earl of Mulgrave, took care of Catherine and his wife educated her. After the couple had left for England, Catherine was educated in a boarding school run by Moravian missionaries, received training as a schoolteacher and worked in her profession.

When George Thompson (1819–1889), originally from Liberia and the first black African missionary of the Basel Mission, came to Jamaica searching for Christianized blacks in the Caribbean, Catherine and George came to know each other. After their marriage, Catherine moved to Christiansborg (today Accra) in Ghana. They had two children, but in 1849 Catherine divorced George due to his extramarital relationships. While George went back to Liberia, Catherine remained at the mission station and worked as a schoolteacher. Her reflections about her future, but also her devotion and faithfulness to her vocation are expressed in a letter to Inspektor Josenhans in 1850: "I know that I ought not to consult my own ease, the question should be, how can I be useful in the world? I hope I shall be directed by the Lord. Oh that God would use me as an instrument whether it be in the domestic circle or in arduous teaching of the young."[77]

Conflict developed between Catherine and the Basel Mission when she married Johannes Zimmermann (1825–1876), a white missionary, in 1851. Amongst other aspects, this marriage afforded a solution for her economic problems and the difficulties in maintaining herself and her children on her small salary as missionary teacher. Mulgrave and Zimmermann affronted the marriage rules because they married without permission of Basel Committee and because interracial sexual contact and marriage were prohibited. "Policy in the mission at that time discouraged even casual social interaction between Africans and Europeans, if it appeared 'too familiar'."[78] Surprisingly, the Basel Mission did not dismiss Johannes Zimmermann despite this "willful breach of the rules." They did, however, stipulate that he "was no longer to consider himself a European citizen and that he must never expect to bring Catherine or their children to Europe."[79] Johannes Zimmermann had prior knowledge of this potential consequence. In his letter to the Basel Mission Committee, he declared that Africa was "his new home." He even named his marriage with Catherine as a "marriage with Africa."[80] Apparently his wish "to be to the Africans like an

African" had to do with his experience of a life-threatening illness and his healing by an African healer, while Basel Mission had not given him permission to return to Europe for treatment. Though the case of Catherine and Johannes Zimmermann is an exception, it demonstrates that European missionaries did occasionally cross over racial barriers.

During this period, racist discourses were reinforced in the Basel Mission due to the "scientific racism" that drew on theories of social evolution. Some scholars argue that anthropologists reinforced the already existing theory of the "curse of Ham"[81] by supporting scientific racism. Interpretations of Catherine's marriage to Johannes illustrate how race issues (her 'scandalous' interracial marriage) intersect with gender issues (remarriage is better for her as compared to remaining a divorced woman) and with class issues (she is not considered a "simple village girl," but a Christian European "civilized" and educated woman).[82] Catherine's mission work in Ghana shows that she "represented a template for an 'African' Christian womanhood in the Basel Mission."[83] Furthermore, she developed a self-contained conceptualization of women's missionary work. On several occasions, mission records regard her as a key person for the mission work in Ghana. Local missionary brothers in Ghana supported Catherine's marriage with Johannes Zimmermann because they feared losing her to a rival Methodist Mission.

In fact, Catherine developed a wide range of women's missionary activities as a married, divorced, remarried, and finally widowed female missionary. Catherine was mother of two children from her first marriage, a daughter (Rosina, born 1844) and a son (George born 1846).[84] As a mother and missionary's wife, Catherine also served as a missionary. She founded a girls' school in Christiansborg in 1843. Records concerning her school were all-over positive and it was acknowledged by the Basel Women's Association in 1847. Moreover, Catherine was an evangelist among women as she formed regular meetings of women's groups. Most likely Catherine adopted the Moravian model of women's classes independent of men. Already in 1848, she was familiar with the local language Ga and with Ghanaian customs. After her marriage with Johannes Zimmermann in 1851, Catherine was not only in charge of her girl's school, but also assisted him in his linguistic work. In 1852, she became the housemother of the new boarding school of the catechist-teacher training seminary established by her husband. In 1854, she established a prayer meeting for women. During the following years, Catherine continued these activities in Christiansborg, Abokobi, and Odumase. Catherine also had five more children with Johannes Zimmermann.[85]

Though Johannes Zimmermann was not permitted to travel to Europe, in 1872 the couple received the order to travel to Basel because the Basel Mission thought that Johannes Zimmerman had to be "resocialized." Supposedly, he had become "too African." In 1876, Catherine's husband died during another visit to Germany. Catherine came back to Christiansborg as a missionary widow. Records refer to her as "our spiritual mother" because of her engagement in classes and house visits. She also had assisted in the deathbed conversion and baptism of a former male servant of the missionary Andreas Riis (1804–1854).[86]

Catherine Mulgrave served as a schoolteacher and transmitter of civilizing mission of Christian middle-class womanhood, and as an evangelist, linguist, housemother, mistress of the domestic sphere, manager of the mission household, a precursor of today's "women's fellowships" in Ghana, and as a spiritual mother, maybe in some way anticipating the future female pastor's service. Most of her woman's missionary work took place within the context of her intercultural marriage. Today we would say she was a migrant, a bridge builder, or an "in-between" person linking European white and African black settings. Being shaped by European Moravian piety and the "Basel Mission's order," she engaged with (what we would call today) "contextualization" and "inculturation" of European Christianity in Africa, namely within a tri-continental dialogue between her origins, the Caribbean, and the local customs in Ghana.

In some ways, the missionary work of Catherine and Johannes did not maintain the clear distance between "heathen" African settings and European "Christian" spaces, for example, with respect to the mission station and clothing. It would be interesting to know the ways in which Catherine brought European Christian ideas and cultural traditions into dialogue with religious traditions from Angola, Jamaica, or Ghana. Speculation on this point, however, is difficult, as the sources do not provide much information. After Catherine's death in 1891, her daughter Auguste also served the Basel Mission in Ghana. But there was a good deal of confusion over how she should be classified: was she a Ghanaian teacher or a European missionary? Catherine and Auguste seem to be early examples of what we call "transculturation" today. Their lives represent an encounter of cultures, and clear differences between them are difficult to discern.[87]

# 4. Critical Analysis of the Case Study from Women's Perspective and Conclusions

A critical analysis of the case study shows a contradiction between the ideal of European women's emancipation and its reality. Salvation, liberation, and emancipation from the "slavery of the female sex" (Johannes Hoffmann) in the South was the aim, but the "civilizing women's mission" was countered by obvious gender barriers within the Basel Mission, the Swiss-German society, and the churches themselves at that time. The ideal of opposite gender characters between women and men led to gender hierarchies so that men even became leaders of the Women's Mission Association in Basel. While Basel women missionaries wanted to bring "good news" of women's education and emancipation to women in Africa and Asia, their own gender barriers and limits within a more or less "masculinized" concept of mission remained invisible. The question has to be left open to what extent European female missionaries were themselves aware of these ambivalences.

Contradictions and gaps between "the ideal and the reality" have been identified with regard to motherhood and fatherhood as well. While promoting feminine ideals of "good Christian motherhood," missionaries' wives had to send their own children back to Europe. Ideals of Christian masculinity did not encompass "good fatherhood." However, this joint venture between "maleness" and "mission" was also thwarted by the urgent need of women missionaries to share their faith with African or Asian women, and thus with their families. One can even talk about a gendered "two classes" missionary agency: Female missionaries had to follow men in the mission field, without competing with them regarding a similarly qualified preparation for their dedication in the mission field (for example, knowledge of local languages), without leadership in worship and the administration of sacraments. They and the local women had to stay "feminine" in order not to transform themselves and the locals into "half-men."[88] Male missionaries were supposed to live their family life in correspondence to their calling. Women missionaries were expected to subordinate their missionary calling to their marriage since marriage was esteemed as the highest and final calling in a woman's life. Independent women's missionary work was limited to single women.

The idea of the "European female missionaries' whiteness" was sidelined by the urgent need of black African women who could cope much better with the climate in Ghana than the missionaries from Europe. This is another example for the co-operation with locals or "repatriates" to communicate more persuasively that Christianity is black and African. Even if interracial marriages and officially excepted love relationships remained an exception, such deviations from the norm pointed to the vision of Christian community between blacks and whites beyond ethnic and race barriers. The distance and the gaps between the mission society in Basel and the "lived mission" with its appropriators, for example, in Ghana, could sometimes break off the rigid Pietistic order and open up new ways of intercultural encounters.

My critical analysis also includes a German-speaking historiography of women in mission. I discovered four approaches that can reflect in which way hermeneutical approaches to historiography of women in mission have changed during the last decades.[89] The first approach focuses on narratives and biographies of European women in mission abroad. Since women in mission are still marginal in standard works on European mission history,[90] these authors see their main duty as making visible daily life stories of European women in mission. However, a critical analysis of the concepts of women's missionary work and the interactions with local people is mostly omitted.[91] An overall positive view of female missionaries (as "heroines") has been overcome, but the authors hover on the edge between appreciating European womens' mission as "gospel bearers" in spite of "gender barriers"[92] and criticizing the dark sides of their agency.

The second approach interprets European women missionaries' history as a feminist emancipation story.[93] Emphasis is laid on the chances foreign mission offered to European female missionaries to develop their talents, to serve as pioneers, to "empower" women in Africa or Asia, and sometimes even to fulfill tasks in the mission country, which would have been impossible for a woman in Switzerland or Germany at that time. However, this approach sometimes tends to overlook the asymmetry in power relations and negotiations between European women missionaries and women in Africa and Asia.

Here the third approach comes in. It explores intercultural encounters between European women and the women appropriators of Christian faith.[94] It assumes that non-European women were not merely receiving or responding, but rather "actors" of mission, contributing, resisting, and negotiating with their European counterparts about religion, Christianity, femininity and masculinity, womanhood and manhood, and so forth.

Thus, it becomes a question of how to explore these intercultural encounters, negotiations, co-operations and conflicts took place and the results.

The fourth approach presents an explicit gender approach in order to analyze the intertwinement of women's and men's gendered lives and relationships in mission, though men's studies in mission remain rare.[95]

Each approach is still necessary. It is difficult, and sometimes impossible, to include each of the four approaches in one research work. However, future German-speaking research work on women in mission should place special emphasis on the third and fourth approaches. It remains a future challenge to deal with the tension between the invisibility of the *her*story[96] of European women doing mission and a self-critical, postcolonial and gendered view on the intercultural encounters between European and non-European women missionaries.

## 5. Questions for Discussion

1. How do you perceive the interactions and relationships between Swiss-German women in mission with the local people, especially women?

2. What can be learned, in your opinion, from the positive and negative aspects and the contradictions of the Basel women's missionary work for women engaged in mission today?

## 6. Recommendations

The contradiction between the European understanding of mission as "sending emancipation" to African and Asian women, and the simultaneous ignorance regarding gender, race, and class barriers, along with the incomplete emancipation of women in their own context, has served to exploit women's emancipation for "civilizing mission." Therefore I will give two examples of German-speaking feminist missiology willing to change this paradigm.

Katja Heidemanns questions the sending model of mission and prefers a concept of mission as listening and receiving. Thus, mission is interpreted in relational dimensions, not, however, in a romanticizing sense. Relationship and connectedness also include a local and global responsibility for structural injustice: "participation in God's mission requires identifying what is death healing."[97] God's mission is understood as the active presence of the Holy Spirit, the *ruah*, who gives strength to the "exhausted, burnt out and breathless". Heidemanns calls this a "missiology of risk."[98]

For Marion Grau[99] "rethinking mission in the postcolony" also means moving "toward a reciprocal resolute articulation and practice of Christian faith." That is why she uses a "poly-dox" methodology for missiology: missionaries and their interlocutors create "theological friction" as they negotiate religious, cultural, sexual, and socioeconomic aspects of their faith, which are embedded in power and gender.[100]

Thus, contemporary feminist missiologists explore the epistemological questions of missiology. They look carefully at the baggage we carry with us. My recommendation for a feminist missiology in Europe is to continue this exploration of how to overcome a missiology of control over people, land, resources, and gender relations, which has been dominant in European mission history.

## 7. Conclusion

This essay emphasized the contradictions and ambivalences between the proclaimed ideals of European women's mission and the lived reality on site. In today's ecumenical encounters of European women with women in Africa, Asia, Latin America, and the Pacific, it is important to deal with one's own gender, class, and race barriers in Europe. However, it remains fascinating to see how God's spirit *ruah* blows, especially when our foremothers and forefathers in mission subverted official policies of gender, race, and class by living their faith, their joys and afflictions together. May this spirit always renew intercultural encounters between North-South and South-South in the future.

## Further Reading

Waltraud Ch. Haas and Ken Phin Pang, *Mission's History from the Woman's Point of View* (Basel: Basel Mission, 1989).

Mary Taylor Huber and Nancy C. Lutkehaus, eds., *Gendered Missions: Women and Men in Missionary Practice and Discourse* (Ann Arbor: The University of Michigan Press, 1999).

Dagmar Konrad, *Missionsbräute, Pietistinnen des 19. Jahrhunderts in der Basler Mission* (Münster, New York, München, Berlin: Waxmann, 2001).

Ulrike Sill, *Encounters in Quest of Christian Womanhood: The Basel Mission in Pre- and Early Colonial Ghana* (Leiden, Boston: Brill, 2009).

Heike Walz, Christine Lienemann-Perrin and Doris Strahm, eds., *Als hätten sie uns neu erfunden. Beobachtungen zu Fremdheit und Geschlecht* (Luzern: Edition Exodus, 2003).

Christoph Schnyder, *Macht teilen. Die Auseinandersetzung zwischen der Basler Mission und ihren Partnern um Strukturen und Visionen* (Frankfurt a.M.: Lembeck, 2009).

# Endnotes

1. I am grateful to Christine Lienemann-Perrin, Dagmar Konrad, and Henning Wrogemann for their most valuable comments to earlier drafts of this article. I owe special thanks to my colleague John Flett for editing the article with regard to English style.

2. Pietism is a religious reform movement within Lutheranism, which combines the Reformed emphasis on personal faith and heartfelt devotion ("heart religion" against "head religion," as the founder Philipp Jakob Spener said in the seventeenth century). Later it became concerned with education and social work. The Moravian Church is connected with Methodism and profoundly influenced by Pietism. Pietism has persisted until the twenty-first century. Today the term is often used for religious expressions of inward devotion and moral purity, see Ulrich Gäbler, ed. *Der Pietismus im neunzehnten und zwanzigsten Jahrhundert: Geschichte des Pietismus Bd. 3* (Göttingen: Vandenhoeck & Ruprecht, 2000).

3. The term "Swiss-German women" encompasses both Swiss-German women from Switzerland and German women from Germany.

4. In 2001, the Basel Mission joined four other missionary societies, which formed together the Evangelical Missionary Society Basel (mission 21). Since 2007, the Basel Mission, the Evangelical Mission in the Kwango area, the Moravian Mission and the South-Africa Mission have combined to support the associations of mission 21, see www.mission-21.org (August 05, 2011); see Christoph Schnyer, Macht teilen: *Die Auseinandersetzung zwischen der Basler Mission und ihren Partnern um Strukturen und Visionen* (Frankfurt a. M.: Lembeck, 2009).

5. This is an allusion to the new name "Evangelical Mission in Solidarity (ems)," which the former "Association of Churches and Missions in the South-western of Germany (ems)" adopted in June 2010, see http://www.doam.org/archiv/textea/ems/2010_zeichen_en.pdf/ (August 05, 2011).

6. I was teaching Systematic Theology at *Instituto Universitario ISEDET* in Buenos Aires from 2005 until 2009, see www.isedet.edu.ar (August 05, 2011).

7. See Henning Wrogemann, *Den Glanz widerspiegeln. Vom Sinn der christlichen Mission, ihren Kraftquellen und Ausdrucksgestalten* (Frankfurt a. M.: Lembeck, 2009), 20-29.

8. During the formation of *mission 21* there was a controversial discussion concerning whether the term "mission" should be part of the name of the new missionary society.

9. The *Evangelische Kirche in Deutschland (EKD)* is, in English, the "Evangelical Church of Germany." "Evangelical" church means that these are Protestant regional churches. The EKD is a federal union of twenty-two Lutheran, Reformed, and united regional churches and carries out joint tasks with which its members have entrusted it, see http://www.ekd.de/english/about_ekd.html (August 05, 2011).

10. Less than 20 percent of the German population belong to the regional protestant church in Saxony and Thüringen *(Evangelische Kirche in Mitteldeutschland)*. Not-practicing church members citizens are often the "normal" case, see Evangelische Kirche in Mitteldeutschland, *Kirchliches Leben*

*in Zahlen. Statistische Übersichten 2008* (Magdeburg: Landeskirchenamt der EKM), 2009, 7, in http://www.ekmd.de/attachment/aa234c91bdabf36adbf2 27d333e5305b/3d1549f64c5e11dfa501ad2640f166a866a8/Kirchliches_Leben_ in_Zahlen_EKM_2008.pdf (August 05, 2011).

11. See Theo Sundermeier, *Den Fremden verstehen: Eine praktische Hermeneutik* (Göttingen: Vandenhoeck & Ruprecht, 1996).

12. See Christine Lienemann-Perrin, *Mission und interreligiöser Dialog* (Göttingen: Vandenhoeck & Ruprecht, 1999).

13. See Andreas Feldtkeller (ed.), *Mission in pluralistischer Gesellschaft* (Frankfurt am Main: Lembeck, 1999).

14. See Wrogemann, *Den Glanz widerspiegeln.*

15. There is quite a wide range of investigations in German, but I restrict myself to mention some works written in English, see Ulrike Sill, *Encounters in Quest of Christian Womanhood: The Basel Mission in Pre- and Early Colonial Ghana* (Leiden, Boston: Brill, 2009); Julia Besten, et al., eds., *Sisters from Two Worlds: The Impact of the Missionary Work on the Role and Life of Women in Namibian Church and Society* (Köln: Rüdiger Koppe, 2008).

16. See Mary Taylor Huber and Nancy C. Lutkehaus, eds., Gendered Missions: Women and Men in Missionary Practice and Discourse (Ann Arbor: The University of Michigan Press, 1999); Heike Walz, Christine Lienemann-Perrin, and Doris Strahm, eds., *Als hätten sie uns neu erfunden. Beobachtungen zu Fremdheit und Geschlecht* (Luzern: Edition Exodus, 2003).

17. See Michael Weidert, «*Solche Männer erobern die Welt*»: *Konstruktionen von Geschlecht und Ethnizität in den katholischen Missionen in Deutsch-Ostafrika 1884–1918* (Trier: Dissertation Universität Trier, 2007), in http://ubt.opus. hbz-nrw.de/volltexte/2007/439/pdf/Dissertation_Michael_Weidert_FB_III_ Solche_Männer_erobern_die_Welt.pdf (August 5, 2011).

18. See section 6.

19. See Laura E. Donaldson and Pui-lan Kwok, *Postcolonialism, Feminism, and Religious Discourse* (New York: Routledge, 2002); Musa W. Dube, "Go therefore and make Disciples of All Nations (Matt. 28:19a). A Postcolonial Perspective on Biblical Criticism and Pedagogy," in *Teaching the Bible: The Discourses and Politics of Biblical Pedagogy,* ed. Fernando Segovia and Mary Ann Tolbert (Maryknoll: New York, 1998); Mrinalini Sebastian, "Reading Archives from a Postcolonial Feminist Perspective: Native Bible Women and the Missionary Ideal," Journal of Feminist Studies in Religion, vol. 19, no. 1 (2003); Heike Walz, "Die Dritte-Welt-Frau? Geschlechterdifferenz im Scheinwerfer der Kritik postkolonialer Denkerinnen," in *Als hätten sie uns neu erfunden. Beobachtungen zu Fremdheit und Geschlecht,* ed. Heike Walz, Christine Lienemann-Perrin, and Doris Strahm (Luzern: Edition Exodus, 2003).

20. Often Latin American theologians working on (feminist) postcolonial critique live as migrants in the USA, see, for example, Nancy E. Bedford, "Making Spaces: Latin Amercian and Latina Feminist Theologies on the Cusp of Interculturality," in *Feminist Intercultural Theology: Latina Explorations for a Just World,* ed. Maria Pilar Aquino and Maria José Rosado-Nunes (Maryknoll/ New York: Orbis Books, 2007).

21. See, for example, Maria do Mar Castro Varela and Nikita Dhawan, *Postkoloniale Theorie: Eine kritische Einführung* (Bielefeld: Transcript, 2005).

22. See Chandra Talpade Mohanty, "Under Western Eyes: Feminist Scholarship and Colonial Discourses," in *Third World Women and the Politics of Feminism,* ed. Chandra Talpade Mohanty, Ann Russo, and Lourdes Torres (Bloomington: Indianapolis, 1991).

23. Because of lack of space it will be scarcely possible to indicate similar tendencies in other German-speaking or European missionary societies. A broader view on women in mission in Eastern, Middle-Eastern, and Southern Europe remains a future project. I need also to omit reference to Roman Catholic women in mission.

24. See the digitized photographs in www.bmpix.org (August 05, 2011).

25. See Michael Sievernich, *Die christliche Mission. Geschichte und Gegenwart* (Darmstadt: WBG, 2009), 91.

26. See Ursula Röper, ed., *Die Macht der Nächstenliebe. Einhundertfünfzig Jahre Innere Mission und Diakonie (1848–1998)* (Stuttgart: Kohlhammer, 2007).

27. See Christa Diemel and Eva Hurst, "Gehilfinnen und Gefährtinnen: Basler Frauen in Wohltätigkeit und Mission," in *Mit Geld, Geist und Geduld. Frauen und ihre Geschichte zwischen Helvetik und Bundesstaat*, ed. Yvonne Brütsch, et al. (Bern: eFeF-Verlag, 1998), 102-105.

28. See Eulenhöfer-Mann, *Frauen mit Mission. Deutsche Missionarinnen in China (1891–1914)* (Leipzig: Evangelische Verlagsanstalt, 2010), 60-62, 97-98.

29. See Karen Hausen, "Die Polarisierung der 'Geschlechtscharaktere': Eine Spiegelung der Dissoziation von Erwerbs- und Familienleben," in *Sozialgeschichte der Familie in der Neuzeit Europas. Neue Forschungen*, ed. Werner Conze (Stuttgart: Ernst Klett, 1976).

30. See Diemel and Hurst, "Gehilfinnen und Gefährtinnen," ibid., 105.

31. See Ute Gerhard, *Frauenbewegung und Feminismus. Eine Geschichte seit 1789* (München: Beck, 2009).

32. See Sievernich, *Die christliche Mission. Geschichte und Gegenwart*, 91-92.

33. See Mariann Bechhaus-Gerst and Mechthild Leutner, eds., *Frauen in den deutschen Kolonien* (Berlin: Ch. Links, 2009).

34. See Martha Mamozai, "Einheimische und 'koloniale' Frauen," in *Frauen in deutschen Kolonien*.

35. Since 1828, male missionaries of the Basel Mission were sent to the Gold Coast (Ghana), to India (since 1834), to Hong Kong and Southern China (since 1846), to the German colonies in Cameroon (since 1886) and to Northern Togo (since 1912) (see Rennstich 2000, 309). In 1972, it started missionary work in Latin America and in 1973 in Sudan.

36. Karl Rennstich, "Mission—Geschichte der protestantischen Mission in Deutschland," in *Der Pietismus im neunzehnten und zwanzigsten Jahrhundert. Geschichte des Pietismus Bd. 3*, ed. Uwe Gäbler (Göttingen: Vanderhoeck & Ruprecht, 2000), 309. More than half of the missionaries were originally from Southern parts of Germany, but the central office was in Switzerland (see ibid., 311). During the period of Nazism in Germany, the Basel Mission was part of the Confessing Church, which resisted Nazism. After the Second World War (1939–1945), the German wing of Basel Mission was founded in 1954 (ibid., 309).

37. See Waltraud Ch. Haas, *Erlitten und erstritten. Der Befreiungsweg in der Basler Mission 1816–1966* (Basel: Basileia, 1994), 21-26.

38. See Dagmar Konrad, *Missionsbräut: Pietistinnen des 19. Jahrhunderts in der Basler Mission* (Münster, New York, München, Berlin: Waxmann, 2001).

39. For "Gehülfin" in German, see Annemarie Toepperwien, *Seine "Gehülfin": Wirken und Bewährung deutscher Missionarsfrauen in Indonesien 1865–1930* (Köln: Rüdiger Köppe, 2004).

40. With regard to the Dutch Missionary Society, see Rita Smith Kipp, "Why Can't a Woman Be More like a Man? Bureaucratic Contradictions in the Dutch Missionary Society," in Gendered Missions, 153.

41. See Vera Boetzinger, *"Den Chinesen ein Chinese werden"*: *Die deutsche protestantische Frauenmission in China 1842–1952* (Wiesbaden: Franz Steiner, 2004), 90.

42. Ludwig Wilhelm Friedrich Hoffmann, *Die Erziehung des weiblichen Geschlechts in Indien* (Stuttgart: Liesching, 1841).

43. Ibid., 4.

44. Gayatri Chakravorty Spivak, "Can the Subaltern Women Speak?" in Colonial Discourse and Postcolonial Theory: A Reader, ed. Patrick Williams and Laura Chrisman (New York: Columbia University Press, 1994), 93.

45. See Haas, *Erlitten und erstritten*,30. Eleven unmarried women women missionaries and 151 missionaries' wives served for the Basel Mission in 1900, see ibid., 44 and 200.

46. See Diemel and Husrt, "Gehilfinnen und Gefährtinnen, " 105-109.

47. Haas, *Erlitten und erstritten*, 42, 46, 58, and 200.

48. See Sill, *Encounters in Quest of Christian Womanhood*, 35-73.

49. See Haas, *Erlitten und erstritten*, 28-29.

50. See Kipp, "Why Can't a Woman Be More like a Man?" 153-55.

51. See Line Nyhagen Predelli and Jon Miller, "Piety and Patriarch: Contested Gender Regimes in Nineteenth-Century Evangelical Missions," in Huber and Lutkehaus, eds., *Gendered Missions*.

52. See Christine Keim, "Aufbruch der Frauen in Edinburgh 1910,"*Interkulturelle Theologie. Zeitschrift für Missionswissenschaft*, vol. 36, no. 1 (2010): especially 57-63.

53. See Christine Keim, *Frauenmission und Frauenemanzipation: Eine Diskussion in der Basler Mission im Kontext der frühen ökumenischen Bewegung (1901–1928)* (Münster: LIT, 2005), 71-73. Afterward, Dr. Béatrice Jenni, Ruth Epting, Marie Claire Barth, and Johanna Eggimann held this office.

54. "Arbeitsgemeinschaft der deutschen evangelischen Frauenmission," see Keim, "Aufbruch der Frauen in Edinburgh 1910," 64.

55. See Haas, *Erlitten und erstrtten*, 74.

56. See http://www.mission-21.org/de/mission-21/unser-missionswerk/frauen-und-gender/ (accessed 05.08.2011). Rev. Rose Akua Ampofo from Ghana was in charge of the Women's and Gender Desk from 2002 until 2003. It became vacant after her fatal accident in Peru. Since 2005, Dr. Meehyun Chung has served as Director.

57. Other examples are the Council for World Mission (CWM), the United Evangelical Mission (UEM), the Association of Churches and Missions in South Western Germany and even earlier since the 1960/70s the *Communauté Évangélique d'Action Apostolique* (CEVAA).

58. See Besten, et al., eds., *Sisters from Two Worlds*.

59. See Konrad, *Missionsbräute*, 315-21. Currently, Dr. Dagmar Konrad works on a research project about childhood in the context of Basel Mission (nineteenth to twentieth century) from a cultural studies' perspective, as she told me personally. The research project is supported by the Department of European Ethnology of Basel University and financed by the Swiss National Science Foundation (SNF).

60. See Annemarie Töpperwien, *Heimgeschickt. Ein Bericht über Kinder von Missionaren der Rheinischen Mission* (Köln: Rüdiger Köppe, 2008).

61. See Eulenhöfer-Mann, *Frauen mit Mission: Deutsche Missionarinnen in China (1891–1914)*, 110-12; Kipp, "Why Can't a Woman Be More like a Man?" 153.

62. See Konrad, *Missionsbräute*,315-16.

63. See ibid., 316; Töpperwien, *Heimgeschickt*, 16.

64. See Konrad, *Missionsbräute*, 317.

65. See Töpperwien, *Heimgeschickt*, 19-42.

66. Konrad, *Missionsbräute*, 320 (translation HW).

67. See ibid., 316; Ilse Theil, Reise in das Land des Todesschattens: *Lebensläufe von Frauen der Missionare der Norddeutschen Mission in Togo/ Westafrika (von 1849 bis 1899)—eine Analyse als Beitrag zur pädagogischen Erinnerungsarbeit* (Berlin: LIT, 2008), 112.

68. Contemporary migration studies have established research on "third culture kids," see David C. Pollock and Ruth E. van Reken, *Third Culture Kids: The Experience of Growing up among Worlds* (Yarmouth, ME, London: Intercultural Press, 2001). Further research is necessary to investigate whether there are similarities between them and the mission children in the past centuries.

69. See Töpperwien, *Heimgeschickt*, 43-62.

70. See ibid., 108.

71. See ibid., 128. During the Nazi Regime in Germany, the directors of the children's homes attempted to keep the missionaries' children away from the Nazi propaganda, at least in the region of the Mission House in Barmen (see ibid., 88). Since 1933, the Mission Society had to cope with financial problems. During the Second World War (1939–1945), it was difficult for the children and their parents to maintain communication. After the war, in 1948, the last missionaries' children's home was closed (see ibid., 41-42).

72. Theil, *Reise in das Land des Todesschatten*, 112.

73. Dagmar Konrad investigates about this issue in her research project as she told me in an email contact.

74. With respect to contemporary "mission children," see Klaus Hampe, "Zuhause—was ist das? Missionarskind zu sein, ist ein Schicksal mit ausserg-wöhnlichen Herausforderungen und Chancen," *Auftrag*, no. 2 (2011).

75. See Sill, *Encounters in Quest of Christian Womanhood*, 110.

76. The following section about Catherine Mulgrave draws on the research works of Predelli and Mill, "Piety and Patriarchy," 83-87; Konrad, *Missionsbräute*,235-52; Sill, *Encounters in Quest of Christian Womanhood*, 110-33. Page references will be indicated only when direct citations from these texts are used.

77. Sill, *Encounters in Quest of Christian Womanhood*, 242; Konrad, *Missionsbräute*, 78.

78. Predelli and Miller, "Piety and Patriarchy,84.

79. Ibid.

80. See Konrad, *Missionsbräute*, 248-49.

81. The "curse of Ham" refers to a story told in Genesis 9:20-27. Ham's father Noah places a curse on Ham's son Canaan because he had seen Noah naked when the latter was drunk in the tent. The "curse of Ham" has been used to justify racism and enslavement of black African people (especially in North America), who were believed to be descendants of Ham.

82. See Predelli and Miller, "Piety and Patriarchy," 86-87.

83. See Sill, *Encounters in Quest of Christian Womanhood*, 111.

84. See ibid., 116-18.

85. Johanna was born in 1852, Johannes in 1854, Auguste Amalia in 1858, Gottfried in 1861, and Christoph in 1866; see the picture of the family in ibid., 130.

86. See ibid., 131.

87. "Transculturation refers to processes of translation, adaptation, redefinition and appropriation engendered by the encounter between people of different cultural and religious backgrounds," see Klaus Hock, "Religion als transkulturelles Phänomen: Implikationen eines kulturwissenschaftlichen Paradigmas für die Religionsforschung," *BThZ*, vol. 19, no. 1 (2002), 82.

88. See Kipp, "Why Can't a Woman Be More like a Man?" 154-55.

89. My aim is to highlight the strengths (and sometimes weaknesses) of each approach, but not to establish a sort of hierarchical "ranking list." Certainly this is a rough pattern, some authors combine two approaches.

90. See Andreas Eckl, "Grundzüge einer feministischen Missionsgeschichtsschreibung: Missionarsgattinnen, Diakonissen und Missionsschwestern in der deutschen kolonialen Frauenmission," in *Frauen in deutschen Kolonien*, ed. Marianne Bechhaus-Gerst and Mechthild Leutner (Berlin: Ch. Links, 2009), 132.

91. See, for example, Theil, *Reise in das Land des Todesschatten*; Töpperwien, *Seine "Gehülfin"*; Haas, *Erlitten und erstritten*.

92. Dana L. Robert, *Gospel Bearers, Gender Barriers: Missionary Women in the Twentieth Century* (Maryknoll, NY: Orbis Books, 2002).

93. See, for example, Keim, *Frauenmission und Frauenemanzipation*; Doris Kaufmann, *Frauen zwischen Aufbruch und Reaktion: Protestantische Frauenbewegung in der ersten Hälfte des 20. Jahrhunderts* (München, Zürich: Piper, 1988); Haas, *Erlitten und erstritten*.

94. See, for example, Konrad, *Missionsbräute*; Besten, et al., eds., Sisters from Two Worlds; Sill, Encounters in Quest of Christian Womenhood; Boetzinger, "*Den Chinesen ein Chinese werden*"; Mirjam Freytag, *Frauenmission in China: Die interkulturelle und pädagogische Bedeutung der Missionarinnen untersucht anhand ihrer Berichte von 1900 bis 1930* (Münster, New York: Waxmann, 1994); Huber and Lutkehaus, eds., *Gendered Missions*; Kaufmann, *Frauen zwischen Aufbruch und Reaktion*.

95. See, for example, Huber and Lutkehaus, eds. *Gendered Missions*. I have partly tried to implement the fourth approach in the case study about Catherine Mulgrave and Johannes Zimmermann. As scholars from Asia, Africa and Latin America write their history of women in mission in this study book, we agreed that I would not implement the third approach.

96. The term *"her*story" (instead of *"hi*story) is used here (like women's studies do) as an alternative form of historiography which emphasises particular experiences of women.

97. See Katja Heidemanns, "Missiology of Risk? Explorations in Mission Theology from a German Feminist Perspective," *IRM*, vol. 93, no. 368 (2004), 108.

98. See ibid., 111.

99. Marion Grau comes originally from Southern Germany. She is Associate Professor of Theology at the Church Divinity School of the Pacific in Berkeley, USA.

100. Marion Grau, *Rethinking Mission in the Postcolony: Salvation, Society, and Subversion* (New York: T&T Clark International, 2011), 38-45, 288.

# PART III

# *CONSEQUENCES FOR THEOLOGICAL REFLECTION ON MISSION*

# "Without Faces": Women's Perspectives on Contextual Missiology[1]

*Cathy Ross*

## 1. Introduction

In 2006, Dana Robert asked the following question, "What would the study of Christianity in Africa, Asia, and Latin America look like if scholars put women into the centre of their research?"[2] She argues that the current demographic shift in world Christianity should be analyzed as a women's movement as women form the majority of active participants. In this volume Philomena Mwaura and Damaris Parsitau Seleina argue that the church in Kenya has a feminine face and that it owes much of its growth to the work of local women who spread the gospel. We hear a similar story in Korea where Meehyun Chung claims that the work of the Bible women was vital to the spread of Christianity. So what is missiology and what would it look like if considered from a woman's perspective?

Various definitions of missiology[3] claim that it means the ongoing, intentional reflection on the practice of mission with the purpose of effecting change in the way mission is carried out. Kirk writes that its task "is to validate, correct and establish on better foundations the entire practice of mission."[4] Mwaura makes a plea for missiology to empower and transform. So the discipline begs for application and praxis—its aim is to bring about change. Therefore missiology calls not only for study, research, and reflection but also for self–evaluation and engagement. It needs to be self-critical and light on its feet so that change can be embraced and effected. This means that missiology as a discipline is always contingent on new discoveries, always tentative as it tries new approaches, always humble as it learns from elsewhere.

What does it mean then to engage in a contextual missiology? This is a current discussion in theology as theologians debate the place and role of context in theologizing. Bevans maintains that there is only contextual theology "that is specific to a particular place, a particular time, a particular culture."[5] He argues that the role of present human experience is vital in working out our theology, the understanding of our faith. Human experience is not an optional add-on; it is a God-given part of who we are—our social location (where we live), our family and background, our community, our culture—all have an impact on how we do our theology. Bevans affirms that theology *"must* be contextual; but it must also be in dialogue, open to the other, ready to change, ready to challenge, ready to enrich and be enriched."[6] As Paul Matheny writes in a recent book on contextual theology, "Interpretations of the meaning of Christ for faithful living can be and are often meaningful beyond the particularity of the local theology that gave it birth."[7] And so it is for missiology also—for the study of mission, its purpose and methods, its motivation and its goal. If we keep this in mind—if we are ready to dialogue and to listen and learn—then our missiology will be not only contextual but also humble. This volume is an attempt to be part of this dialogue, presenting experiences and reflections on mission from a variety of different contexts.

If women do indeed form the majority of active participants in the world church, what might women's perspectives contribute to the discipline of missiology? Would the practice of the discipline be very different? Would the issues and ideas under consideration be new? How might the approach be fresh? Might there be an element of surprise as unexpected approaches may emerge?

Historians have discovered that reading history from the viewpoint of women has brought fresh insights and new questions. New and different sources have been brought to light. Women's names and experiences have not often appeared on the great documents or as part of the great events of history but women have been there thinking, reflecting, writing journals, diaries, letters within their own families and networks. It has been this more personal, more "ordinary" history that feminist historians have tried to being into focus—history that deals with everyday life and relationships in the social context of the time. Perhaps women's perspectives on missiology can offer a missiology "from below," a more ordinary, a more personal, a more modest missiology.

Women's perspectives certainly offer a participatory approach. When I presented the first draft of this paper surrounded by the women who have written for this book, I was flooded with ideas, comments, new and challenging insights, which has meant a not only significant rewriting of the original draft but also personal growth as I have heard how some of my ideas need nuancing, developing, editing or just forgetting in various contexts. Their thoughts and input were rich and diverse and have enlarged and corrected my small world. Their input confirmed for me that missiology can only be contingent and must be contextual. There can be no grand theories, no totalising statements—we come from such diverse and different contexts—the contrasts are legion. It is a privilege to hear the stories and to be gently challenged to try to think outside my context, and incorporate the insights of others into my few thoughts. I suspect this is a particular challenge for Western scholars and raises all sorts of questions regarding intellectual property, publishing rights and indeed even how scholarship is carried out and evaluated.

Finally, before proposing some ideas from women all over the world that might lead us in this direction, let me offer you a brief and delightful definition of missiology that breathes fresh life into this search, "Missiology therefore is the study of the Church as surprise."[8]

## 2. A Missiology of Emptiness and Hiddenness

A missiology of emptiness was first suggested by Korean woman missiologist, Chun Chae Ok in 2004.[9] I believe that this resonates with much of women's engagement in and experience of mission. A missiology of emptiness is about emptying self to the point of self-sacrifice. It is about *kenosis* as expressed in Philippians 2:5-11. Scholars debate two possible meanings here: Jesus' taking on the form of a servant by becoming human (the incarnation) and Jesus' self-surrender and the giving of his life on the Cross (self-sacrifice).[10]

For women, their involvement in mission is often experienced from this point of weakness, sacrifice, and invisibility. Historically, we know that women have been deeply engaged in the work of mission, but because women were seen as adjuncts to men, they were "systematically written out of historical and anthropological records."[11] In fact, *missionary* was a male noun— "it denoted a male actor, male action, male spheres of service."[12]

Throughout the history of mission, women have often been nameless and faceless. The early records of the Church Mission Society (CMS) sometimes did not even note the name of the wife—merely according her a little "m" to denote that the male missionary was married. Young Lee Hertig entitled her article on nineteenty-century Bible women and twentieth-century evangelists in Korea, "Without a Face" because they remained "invisible and faceless."[13] Yet despite this, they "carried the gospel from house to house and were sacrificially devoted to their labour of love."[14] She claims that once the church began to become institutionalized, "masculinization of the Korean church took place, and the hard labour of the Bible women remained invisible and faceless. Patriarchal leadership took over and continued to harvest the Bible women's work with women's labour credited to male leadership."[15] Meehyun Chung also confirms this claiming that the new Christian movement became "a new version of confinement and bondage" as women were once again marginalized and so the "Korean church became, and remains, male dominated."[16] The male dominance within the church is a refrain throughout this book. From Ethiopia to the Philippines, as we read in this volume, it seems that pervasive concepts of womanhood, which demean women's dignity, personhood and identity, are rife. Male leadership continues to dominate so women must take the initiative and continue to move forward. According to Belaynesh Bekele Abiyo from Ethiopia, women take courage and hope from Jesus as "the boundary breaker" who enables transformation of their situation.[17] Although male leadership is still prevalent in Pentecostal churches in Kenya, Philomena Mwaura and Damaris Parsitau Seleina offer a fascinating study of three women in leadership who challenge the gender stereotypes in African cultures. These women provide role models of women in leadership so that it is possible to imagine a different way and this begins to undermine and undo the patriarchal public culture and worldview.

The kind of work often performed by women—hospitality, visiting, counseling, ministries of compassion and children's work—has tended to be seen as secondary to the primary tasks performed by men. As Chita Rebollido-Millan expressed it in her article on women in The United Methodist Church in the Philippines, "women were meant for small mission while men carried out the big mission."[18] The women cooked or handed out tracts while the men preached and led the services. Often Christian women's roles in church and mission have not been recorded nor sufficiently recognized.

"Women evangelists, women deacons, mothers and daughters are the ones who most of the time, give their total service for the faith community and its neighbors in visiting, in prayers, in counseling and in a variety of aids. Women's witness with the gospel to the world is carried out in weakness and selflessness."[19] Women are familiar with approaches that are hidden, less recognized and rarely celebrated. We need to recover these perspectives in our missiology. After all, this was the approach of Jesus in his ministry where he emptied himself for the sake of others, where he sometimes even asked people to keep his healing miracles secret, where he declared that the first would be last, and told his disciples that we all need to take up our cross to follow him.

There is, however, another side to this story. Feminists would claim that a missiology of emptiness and a missiology of hiddenness are not healthy approaches for women. They say that women are already socialized into self-sacrifice and servanthood and that these approaches can only reinforce this unhelpfully. This can be dangerous for women where Christian attitudes of service and self-sacrifice can be taken too far and therefore result in unhealthy oppression of women. Culture can certainly be a source of oppression and this was readily acknowledged by early missionaries—foot binding of women in China or *sati* in India being obvious examples. There are also more subtle examples, such as tribalism in the Majority World or "old boys' clubs" in the Western world, which can deeply embed male power. Moreover, we can become blinded by this as the prevailing culture and fail to see and name this oppression as sin. And then, as feminist theologian Serene Jones writes, "we must strain hard to see, given the powerfully destructive ways in which oppression structures our thinking and makes even the most profound forms of brokenness seem normal."[20] Oppression works like a blinder preventing us from seeing that we are caught in sin. Therefore relations of domination begin to abound; women become disempowered and invisible and so we have to be extremely careful that a missiology of emptiness and a missiology of hiddenness do not ultimately work against women. Sadly, we continue to see this throughout many cultures in our world. Marilú Rojas Salazar reminds us of the invisibility of women in Latin America in the Roman Catholic context. She quotes Brazilian theologian Ivone Gebara, whose critique of the Latin American Conference of Bishops, held in Aparecida in 2007, was, "we women were the great disappeared ones in Aparecida."[21] The official documents from the conference made no mention of indigenous women, religious women, feminist theology, nor women's organizations "that in Latin America have dedicated their labours to fight against the different faces of violence and to offer alternatives of survival."[22] Atola Longkumer, from India, claims that "discrimination, exclusion, marginalization and even violence" exist within the church.[23] She explains how a lack of gender analysis has led to a truncated understanding of the gospel so that an equal Christian community has not been created. This has led to "a position and participatory power that is not very different from the pre-Christian mission days for the Ao women despite education and Christianization."[24] This does beg the obvious question as to why Christian mission did not seem to challenge cultural practices that were discriminatory or harmful toward women.

And so while I would continue to make a plea for a missiology of emptiness and a missiology of hiddenness to be practiced by both women and men, I realize that context is vital and will mean important nuancing. If one is already invisible, excluded or oppressed then a missiology of emptiness and hiddenness may not be appropriate. If one is reading this from a position of relative power, then it is a very different story. However, I still believe this approach is what Jesus modeled to us all in his incarnation. We know that Jesus poured himself out for the sake of the world. We know that Jesus befriended disreputable people and refused to condemn the unrighteous. We know that Jesus loved women and children and the poor—the hidden ones, the little ones, the marginalized, the outsiders.

By contrast, so much of our current missiology is focused on the drive for growth, expansion, projects, strategies, and numbers. We have targets to meet, business plans to write, strategies to elaborate, conversions to count, projects to elaborate, ever bigger and more expensive conferences to attend.[25] Much of this language and worldview come from the worlds of the military and management—worlds of war and success. In fact there is even a term, "managerial missiology"[26]—a cold, reductionist term turning Christian mission into a manageable enterprise using information technology and marketing techniques. Concepts and programs such as "10-40" and the "4-14" windows, "Adopt-a-People," "AD2000 and Beyond," "homogeneous units" come from this approach. Escobar offers the following critique, "What I am seeing in the application of these concepts in the mission field is that missionaries 'depersonalize' people into 'unreached targets,' making them objects of hit-and-run efforts to get decisions that may be reported."[27] Some may argue that this is a contextual approach befitting North American culture but is this the kind of Kingdom we wish to inhabit? Where is the language that expresses our mission engagement in terms of weakness, vulnerability, relationships, service, compassion, meekness, and caring? What a contrast to the language of servanthood expressed by Indian Christian, P. T. Chandapilla, from his context as a minority Christian in a predominantly Hindu culture,

> Servanthood is entirely voluntary. Servanthood is for those like Jesus Christ, who laid aside his privileges, and who choose to act on it. There is no pressure, no recruitment, no inducement. True servanthood shows whether we are really sons and daughters of God. "He who is rich became poor." The benefactor becomes the beggar. The one who has everything opts for nothing. This is a paradox. Where this does not occur there is no servanthood.[28]

Belaynesh Bekele Abiyo explains that servanthood can be either an oppressive or life-giving metaphor for Ethiopian women. Ethiopian women understand servanthood as they are socialized into it from an early age. But Jesus' model of servanthood was not a passive one and the ensuing account of the resurrection provides hope for renewal and transformation. As Park Soon Kyung, a Korean woman theologian explains, servanthood can be a powerful witness to evil and a challenge to the powers and principalities of the world.[29] Perhaps we all need to have the courage to be weak and vulnerable, emptying ourselves to the point of death, as Jesus did.

## 3. A Missiology of Comforting, Consolation, and Healing

A missiology of comforting draws from the power of the Holy Spirit to comfort, transform and heal—both humanity and creation. The Holy Spirit, also known as the Comforter, is the one who comforts the broken, the afflicted, the suffering. God is a God of consolation who is with the HIV and AIDS sufferers, the abused women, the victims of Hiroshima or Rwanda, of war. Women and children are the victims of war and violence. Women struggle on to feed and protect their families, to live in reconciliation and peace, to bind up the wounded, to heal the brokenhearted. Women, as mothers, are always comforting their children. Anne Nasimiyu-Wasike writes that

Africa today needs a mother's love. African women as mothers have sustained and continued to nurture the life in Africa despite the ethnic wars, the military dictatorships, oppressive governments and economic hardships which deprive many people of basic necessities. . . . The woman of Africa has given her life for the love of her children but the man of Africa must join hands with women of Africa and follow the example of Jesus the mother.[30]

Traditionally, women have been more associated with the virtues of comforting, nurturing, and healing—certainly they are overrepresented in the caring professions. Whether this is thanks to nature or nurture (genes or socialization) is debatable but it does mean that women more often understand and practice a missiology of comforting. This is why we need a theology that does not mandate hierarchy in our approach to mission and where a Trinitarian understanding is helpful. The Trinitarian community of three divine persons modeling mutual submission is a far cry from hierarchical approaches that can sometimes lead to unhelpful practices of power, authority, and control.

Mission is comforting—bringing comfort to humanity in distress and to creation in distress. A good example is found in a Mother's Union (MU) group in Tanzania. The MU was founded in England in 1876 by Mary Sumner and now exists in 77 countries with 3.6 million members. It works to support family life and empower women in their communities through supporting the needs of families, tackling the causes of injustice, and providing a network to strengthen members in their Christian faith. "Heart and home of change" is the metaphor used by this group in Tanzania to speak of hospitality offered, widows and children being cared for, craftwork projects, prayers being offered, joys and sorrows shared, community development embodied. This group of women provide powerful, practical comforting, consolation and sustenance for their community, "the affirmed fellowship of love, the women who support you to leave an abusive husband and work to provide you with a house of your own, the receipt of needed food, the new family after losing your own."[31] Where women experience brokenness in so many ways—whether it is increasing family breakdown in the West, rape as an instrument of war to terrorize and humiliate women and whole communities,[32] or the daily grind of facing gender discrimination or racist structures in the workplace, mission carried out in the way of this Tanzanian MU group can offer healing and grace to broken and scarred women.[33] Another fascinating example can be found in this volume in the article by

Philomena Mwaura and Damaris Parsitau Seleina. They tell the story of SLIF (Single Ladies International Fellowship) in Nairobi. They explain that it "is dedicated to uplifting the lives of single women in Kenya by empowering them spiritually, socially, and economically, and by so doing, it addresses critical issues around inadequate healthcare, poverty, low self-esteem, loneliness, and marginalisation."[34] This is a ministry that provides comforting to single, separated, and divorced women, single mothers and widows. It is a ministry of support and encouragement and as with the MU it is a ministry that uses women's space for consolation, healing, transformation, and empowerment. This group enables women to rise above victimhood and to reclaim their self-esteem. Similarly, from a very different context in Japan, Haruko Nawata Ward elaborates the importance of the place of nunneries and the role which women catechists had in speaking out against injustice against women. "They helped women escape from abusive situations, and provided them with safe houses."[35]

However, it is also important to remember, as Atola Longkumer reminds us that "women-only" space can contribute to keeping women excluded and on the margins. Again, context is vital in determining the appropriate missiological reflection and response.

Chung Hyun Kyung claims that Asian women believe "in spite of"; in spite of lack of protection from their fathers and brothers who may beat them or sell them into child marriage or prostitution.[36] She writes, "Some Asian women have found Jesus as the one who really loves and respects them as human beings with dignity, while the other men in their lives have betrayed them."[37] In other words, women find consolation in their relationship with Jesus. They know that Jesus sides with silenced Asian women and can bring liberation and wholeness. Jesus is the one who can bring healing, solace, and renewal for women.

This is a reminder that women can offer very different images and understandings of God and this is necessary for a fully orbed appreciation of who God is. Perhaps women are more attuned to the female images of God in Scripture and also to the role models of women in the Scriptures—these can provide a healthy counterbalance to male-only imagery and language. Images of God as dance, God as Mother (in all aspects of suffering in childbirth as well as protecting her young), God as verb, God as relationship present us with other aspects of God's character. Feminist theologian, Janet Martin Soskice, reminds us that much of Jesus' ministry was spent in "turning the symbols," a king entering Jerusalem on a donkey for example. She asks, "Why in the Christian glossing of the Hebrew Bible should the unjust sufferings of innocent women not be read as prefiguring that of Christ? Is it only sufferings of men that can fit the template of the Christian saviour?"[38] Salazar also reminds us that to see the image of God as male only is idolatrous and that this creates problems for women. She asks the question that many feminists ask, can "a male saviour be the symbol of salvation for women when these women are living in their bodies the abuse and violence of men?"[39] She claims that we need a subversive love that not only denounces situations of oppression, but also can model a divine love that empties itself of privilege and power.

A missiology that embodies comfort, consolation, and healing may indeed be perspectives that women can bring to our hurting and wounded world today. Jesus proclaimed them when he read from the scroll of Isaiah at Nazareth where he announced freedom for those in captivity, release from oppression and good news for the poor (Luke 4:16-30); indeed, words of comfort, consolation and healing for those who have ears to hear.

## 4. A Missiology of Hospitality and Relationship

Christine Pohl reminds us in her superb book on hospitality, *Making Room, Recovering Hospitality as a Christian Tradition*, "The first formative story of the biblical tradition on hospitality is unambiguously positive about welcoming strangers."[40] Hospitality was considered an important duty and often we see the hosts becoming beneficiaries of their guests and strangers. So Abraham and Sarah entertained angels in Genesis 18, the widow of Zarephath benefited from Elijah's visit (1 Kings 17) and Rahab and her family were saved from death by welcoming Joshua's spies (Joshua 2). Ultimately Israel's obligation to care for the stranger is because of her experience as a stranger and alien. Hospitality is a good metaphor for mission and an appropriate concept for missiology because it implies invitation, warmth, sharing of food, relationship.

Nineteenth-century mission theory encouraged the formation of a pious Christian home as an "object lesson" for reforming home and family in mission contexts.[41] The use of "pious Christian home" as a mission theory meant that women could continue in their expected private sphere, without threatening the man's more public sphere, and also be engaged in mission service. In a similar vein, in her article on Presbyterian women in Guatemala, Karla Ann Koll explained that the women's societies served only to reinforce domesticity.[42] Dana L. Robert has argued that the idea of the Christian home has been a major force in Protestant mission, "a cornerstone of missionary thinking, it has been ignored in virtually all formal studies of mission theology."[43] Although this theory could reinforce traditional Victorian values of submission, public versus private space[44] and gender inequality, it could also provide "a platform for women's involvement in cultural change, social reform, self-sufficiency, and missiological innovation."[45] In a Christian home—at its best—women could experience a companionate marriage and respect from their husband in contrast to abuse, polygamy, and servitude to the husband's extended family. They could nurture and educate their children, practice philanthropy within their communities and thereby begin to effect some social transformation. The home is also the place where hospitality is offered and relationships nurtured. In the diaries and letters of missionary wives in nineteenth-century New Zealand, for example, hospitality and close relationships are key themes.

Michele Hershberger claims that offering hospitality helps us to see differently. As we welcome people into our homes, share food with them and spend time with them, our perspective begins to change. She writes that when we eat together we are "playing out the drama of life"[46] as we begin to share stories, let down our guard, welcome strangers, and see the other. Rebecca Nyegenye, chaplain at Uganda Christian University, Mukono, told me that in Uganda, hospitality goes with both elaborate meals and listening to the visitor. Ugandans believe that for any relationship to be strong, food and intentional listening must be shared. Listening is an important part of honoring the guest. In both hospitality and mission, listening to the other is the beginning of understanding and of entering the other's world.

A missiology of the house or a missiology of the kitchen table could be a necessary corrective to much of our missiology. This conjures up images of intimacy, homeliness, warmth, comfort, rootedness, safety, and relationship. However, these metaphors of hospitality and home can be problematic in some contexts. Christine Lienemann-Perrin alerts us to the ambiguities and complexities of this public/private separation for women. She writes, "We know that in all of our world's societies violence increases behind the excuse that what takes place in the home is of no public concern."[47] The home is sometimes not a safe place for women. Marilú Rojas Salazar reminds us that domestic violence is more common than we would like to think. "Home, for millions of women, has become a place more dangerous than the streets."[48] When violence against women is common in the home, it forms part of the educative system for the children and they grow up thinking this is normal. As Serene Jones reminded us, we then begin to believe that profound forms of brokenness are normal. Salazar claims that the church in Mexico invites women who suffer from domestic violence to "carry their cross" and to bear this abuse with the same patience as Christ. So rather than being a place of refuge, home can become a dangerous place for women, a place where women suffer and are brutalized by the men in their lives. This is a far cry from the nineteenth century vision of pious domesticity, and needs to be challenged and named for what it is—abuse and violence.

Again, hospitality is not a simple metaphor and plays out in different ways in different contexts. So while for some it may indeed mean invitation, warmth, sharing of food, relationship; for others it may mean ongoing stress and virtual impoverishment as hospitality is demanded and expected sometimes beyond the resources available. This begins to make it a more problematic metaphor for some. Belaynesh Bekele Abiyo reminds us that women in Ethiopia suffer as they overstretch themselves to offer hospitality for their husbands' benefit. Mercy A. Oduyoye comments more generally on the role of hospitality in Africa and how it can be oppressive for women,

> Women's experience of domestic hospitality is that of Sarah, a situation in which they work and the men take the credit (Gen. 18:1-15). Rebekah's hospitality to the servant of Isaac (Gen. 24:15-27) is traditional to Africa. . . . To illustrate the exploitation of women in men's hospitality to men, African women theologians recall Abraham passing Sarah off as his sister; Lot offering his virgin daughters in order to save his male guests (Gen. 19:1-8) and the horrible murder of the "Levite's concubine." (Judg. 19:22-30).[49]

And so hospitality becomes a burden and oppressive for the giver rather than life-giving and renewing. It is important to remember that what can be a life-giving and expansive metaphor for some can be problematic and constricting for others.

However, hospitality is still a powerful metaphor with which to think about mission. It begins with God and is an essentially outward looking practice and virtue. Hospitality involves listening, learning, seeing the other and negotiation of space by all parties. Generous hospitality can lead to reconciliation and genuine embrace of the other. Indeed, poverty may even be a good place to start with hospitality. Poverty of heart and mind creates space for the other. Poverty makes a good host—poverty of mind, heart, and even resources where one is not constrained by one's possessions but is able to give freely. Hospitality from the margins reminds us of the paradoxical power of vulnerability and the importance of compassion. "Hospitality . . . means primarily the creation of a free space where the stranger can enter and become a friend instead of an enemy. Hospitality is not to change people, but to offer them space where change can take place."[50] Immediately we can see the resonances for mission here. Mission, the divine invitation from God to enter into a loving relationship with God, is about allowing people the space to come to God in their own way; to become the person God created them to be. Mission is not about invading their space, forcing them to come to Christ in the manner of the *conquistadores*— vanquishing them in the name of Christ; nor is it imposing or transplanting Christianity to make them like us as was so often done in the colonial period.

This understanding is perhaps most powerfully expressed in the Eucharist, where this ritualized eating and drinking together re-enacts the crux of the gospel. As we remember what it cost Jesus to welcome us into relationship with God, we remember with sorrow the agony and the pain but at the same time we rejoice and celebrate our reconciliation and this new relationship made possible because of Christ's sacrifice and supreme act of hospitality. We rejoice in our new relationship with God, made possible through the Cross and we rejoice as we partake of this meal together in community. When we share in the Eucharist, we are not only foreshadowing the great heavenly banquet to come but we are also nourished on our journey toward God's banquet table. Jesus is, quite literally, the Host as we partake of his body and blood and we are the guests as we feed on him by faith with thanksgiving. In this way, the Eucharist connects hospitality at a very basic level with God and with the *missio Dei* as it anticipates and reveals God's heavenly table and the coming Kingdom.[51]

So what might our missiology look like if we adopted these perspectives of hospitality and relationship? I suggest that our missiology would be more humble, more modest and joyful. Our missiology might be done around the kitchen table over a meal. There would be fewer grand statements and plans,[52] fewer large conferences with important statements, less competitiveness. We would spend more time in relationships, more time feasting and feeding the stranger, more time listening to and learning from the other. This might lead to some surprising insights and challenging perspectives for the practice of mission.

# 5. A Missiology of Sight, Embrace, and Flourishing

The gifts of sight and insight are gifts of the Holy Spirit. Just as the women disciples were the first to see Jesus, our eyes have to be opened to recognize Jesus also. Once we can see Jesus, the Holy Spirit enables us to see the other person. Christian mission requires that we actively see and welcome the guest and stranger in our worlds.

Can we really talk about a missiology of sight? I think we can because sight and insight are important in Christian mission. If we had been able to "see the other" might the genocide in Rwanda never have happened? If we were able to "see the other" might the ethnic cleansing in Bosnia-Herzegovina, the civil war in Northern Ireland, the ignorance and apathy concerning Sudan and Congo, *apartheid* in South Africa, tribalism in Sri Lanka, violence and oppression in Burma and Zimbabwe, caste and class systems, oppressive colonialism—might all this have been avoided—if only we could see? Who are we blind to in our contexts, which prevents us from seeing the other person and, wittingly or unwittingly, means that we practice a missiology of exclusion or oppression rather than one of embrace? Might it be the homeless person, whom we have never seen before, whom we have always passed by in the street and never looked in the eye or exchanged a greeting. Might it be the young people whose music is so loud, whose language is incomprehensible, whose body-piercing and head shaving is so alien—have we ever stopped to look them in the eye, to appreciate their music, to consider the pressures they may be under—the bleak prospect of unemployment, broken homes, student loans, an uncertain future. Have we ever stopped to look them in the eye and tried to understand them in their context? Might it be those migrants who never learn our language, who never even try to integrate, who take over whole streets and suburbs in our cities—have we ever had them in our homes, offered them hospitality and tried to "see" their culture?

So a missiology of sight must encourage Christians to acknowledge the identity of the other—the other who is full of potential to be realized in relationship with Christ. The actual and the potential must be seen and acknowledged together. And in this encounter with the other, I too am confronted with the truth of myself and all that I am capable of becoming. When I embrace the other, in a small way I begin to die to myself and begin to see myself in the other. John V. Taylor comments, "But no less necessary to the Christian mission is the opening of our eyes towards other people. The scales fell from the eyes of the convert in Damascus precisely when he heard one of those whose very lives he had been threatening say, 'Saul, my brother, the Lord Jesus has sent *me to you*. I-Thou."[53] The gift of sight truly enables us to see the other person, to share our common humanity and to establish relationship. Therefore a missiology of sight that embraces the other, also acknowledges and welcomes the potential in the other. Mother Teresa saw this in her selfless giving and serving of the poor, the sick, and the dying in Calcutta. She knew that Jesus had sent her to them and she saw the potential in the other person. Therefore a missiology of sight that embraces the other can lead to human flourishing.

A further aspect of flourishing is care for creation. Creation suffered from Adam's refusal to safeguard Eden as a result of the Fall. Calvin DeWitt, professor of Environmental Studies comments, "Degradations of creation—beginning locally, extending regionally, and reaching globally—manifest an arrogation of Creation's Economy, a failure of people to be responsible stewards of God's gift."[54] He goes on to outline four biblical principles of stewardship: the conservancy principle: we should return the service of creation to us with service of our own; the safeguarding principle: we should safeguard the Lord's creation as the Lord safeguards us; the fruitfulness principle: we should enjoy the fruit of creation but not destroy its fruitfulness; and finally the Sabbath principle: we should provide for creation's Sabbath rests with no relentless pressing.[55] If we can care for creation, steward creation rather than dominate and exploit it for our own selfish purposes, then we will contribute to the sustaining and flourishing of the planet rather than the ruin of it. "As was expected of Adam, achieved by Noah, and taken on by Christ, we also become servants—servants of the garden, of humanity, of the whole creation."[56] Marilú Rojas Salazar writes about ecosophy, the wisdom of the *oikos* "which searches to learn from the wisdom of creation and its laws in order to live in harmony."[57] Feminist theologians have long seen the connection between exploitation of women and the domination of creation and therefore call for a re-imagination of our relationships within all of creation. "This movement is concerned not simply with the social, economic, and political equality of women with men but with a fundamental re-imagination of the whole of humanity in relation to the whole of reality, including non-human creation."[58] The World Evangelical Theological Commission issued a clarion call for the church "to proclaim the full truth about the environmental crisis in the face of powerful persons, pressures, and institutions which profit from conceal-ing the truth."[59] Creation care is indeed a vital part of mission and crucial for human and non-human flourishing in God's world.

## 6. Case Study

An interesting exercise might be to imagine what a women's mission society might look like. When some students were faced with this assignment, they came up with the following ideas: "A women's mission would be strong on nurture of members, it would make decisions by consensus rather than by voting, an all-women's mission would be characterized by humble service, there would be an emphasis on *doing* as much as on *telling*, there would be an impulse to cooperate with other like-minded groups."[60] These qualities did in fact characterize Interserve, founded in 1852 under the name Zenana Bible and Medical Mission, and was an all-women's mission for one hundred years. They were also found in the women's mission societies in early twentieth-century North America.[61] The existence of these Women's Mission Boards was relatively short-lived and by the early decades of the twentieth century they had merged and integrated with the General Boards, almost certainly to the detriment of the involvement of American women in mission.[62] The women succumbed to a variety of pres-sures: appeals to denominational loyalty, criticisms about dupli-cation of resources and inefficiency, assurances that they would be represented in decision-making structures and that their concerns would be acknowledged and served in the new "integrated" structures.[63] Unfortunately, the reality was very different. This has sadly resulted in a silencing of women and what women have to offer in the sphere of missiology. Ironically, at the beginning of this millennium Dana L. Robert, even wondered if the collapse of the women's missionary movement led to a decline in the mis-sion interest of mainline churches because of the removal of their greatest advocates of mission.[64]

And what about the role of the church? How might missiology be a study of the church as surprise? Argentinian theologian, C. Rene Padilla claims that the local congregation is the best agent for transformation because the deepest and most significant changes in people's lives take place through love expressed and experi-enced in community.[65] Hans Küng writes that the Church "takes over the reign of God in concentrated form: it becomes the voice of Jesus himself."[66] Do we experience the voice of Jesus and the love of God in and through church? Do our models and structures of church allow for transformation to take place among the community of disciples? The passages in Acts 2:44-45 and 4:32-35 are expressions of deep *koinonia,* including economic *koinonia,* made possible by Pentecost and the infilling of the Spirit. If this type of love, sharing, and solidarity were experienced and expressed by a local congregation, our communities and our world could look very different. Perhaps our local congregations could then become places of transformation with modest aspirations to offer comfort, consolation and healing, willing hospitality and genuine relationships, which would foster human flourishing. Perhaps then, missiology would indeed be the study of the church as surprise.

## 7. Conclusion

You will notice that I have grouped the perspectives—a missiology of emptiness and healing; of comforting, consolation and healing; of hospitality and relationship; and of sight, embrace and flourishing—and this is deliberate. Women see the connections, operate on different levels simultaneously, build bridges to reality, notice resonances and echoes, and tend to think holistically. It is not possible or appropriate to think of a single, dominating missiology. There is no overarching theory, no controlling metaphor, no final word. As I said at the beginning, missiology as a discipline is contingent, tentative, incomplete. Contexts vary, situations change and so our missiology needs constant refining and nuancing. There is no definitive missiology. Women have different perspectives from those which have been commonly on offer, perspectives worth heeding but which have been marginalized or not heard. Women's missiology is based on a real resistance to a male-dominated mission practice that can emphasize power, dominating control as well as endless activity and programs. So it is out of contexts such as this that women begin to reflect and imagine new ways of witnessing to the gospel. If Christianity were to be studied as a women's movement as Robert suggested in 2006—at least for the reason that women make up the majority of members of the world church—then it is only fair that women's perspectives be heard and celebrated; and then we shall begin to see face to face.

## Endnotes

1. I would like to thank Rosemary Dewerse for her helpful insights and editing. Rosemary is a PhD student at School of Theology, Auckland University, Aotearoa/NZ.

2. Dana L. Robert, "World Christianity as a Women's Movement," *International Bulletin of Missionary Research*, 30/4, (2006), 180.

3. For example, see Scott Moreau, "Missiology," in *Evangelical Dictionary of Theology*, ed. Walter A. Elwell (Grand Rapids: Baker Academic, 2001). "*Missiology* generally refers to the formal academic study of all aspects of the missionary enterprise. Inherent in the discipline is the study of the nature of God, the created world, and the Church as well as the interaction among these three. To study that interaction, of necessity it combines insights from the disciplines of biblical studies, theology, and the social sciences. Being identified with the missionary task, however, it must go beyond each of these disciplines to engage not only in understanding but in effecting change as part of the missionary endeavour." Or: "*Missiology*: 'the conscious, intentional, ongoing reflection on the doing of mission. It includes theory(ies) of mission, the study and teaching of mission, as well as the research, writing, and publication of works regarding mission' (Neely 2000, 633). '1. the study of the salvation activities of the Father, Son, and Holy Spirit throughout the world geared toward bringing the kingdom of God into existence, 2. the study of the worldwide church's divine mandate to be ready to serve this God who is aiming his saving acts toward this world' (*Verkuyl 1978*, 5)," quoted from *Missions Dictionary*, http://www.missiology.org/?p=24#M (December 13, 2011).

4. J. Andrew Kirk, *What is Mission? Theological Explorations* (London: Darton, Longman,Todd, 1999), 21.

5. Stephen B. Bevans, *An Introduction to Theology in Global Perspective* (Maryknoll: Orbis, 2009), 165.

6. Ibid., 5.

7. Paul Duane Matheny, *Contextual Theology, the Drama of our Times* (Eugene, OR: Wipf and Stock, 2011), 72.

8. Ivan Illich, quoted in David J. Bosch, *Transforming Mission: Paradigm Shifts in Theology of Mission* (Maryknoll: Orbis, 1992), 493.

9. Chun Chae Ok, "Integrity of Mission in the Light of the Gospel: Bearing the Witness of the Spirit: An Asian Perspective," Unpublished paper, 11th conference of the International Association for Mission Studies, Port Dickson, Malaysia, August, 2004.

10. See Colin Brown, ed., *The New International Dictionary of New Testament Theology, Vol 1*, (Exeter: Paternoster, 1976), 548.

11. Fiona Bowie, "Introduction: Reclaiming Women's Presence," in *Women and Missions: Past and Present Anthropological and Historical Perspectives*, ed. Fiona Bowie, Deborah Kirkwood and Shirley Ardener (Oxford: Berg, 1993), 1.

12. Ibid., 1.

13. Young Lee Hertig, "Without a Face, The Nineteenth Century Bible Woman and Twentieth Century *Jeondosa*," in *Gospel Bearers, Gender Barriers, Missionary Women in the Twentieth Century*, ed. Dana L. Robert (Maryknoll: Orbis, 2002), 185-99.

14. Ibid., 186.

15. Hertig, "Without a Face," 186.

16. Meehyun Chung, in this volume, 227.

17. Belaynesh Bekele Abiyo, in this volume, 148.

18. Chita Rebollido-Millan, in this volume, 261.

19. Ok, "Integrity of Mission."

20. Serene Jones, *Feminist Theory and Christian Theology, Cartographies of Grace* (Augsburg: Fortress, 2000), 109.

21. Marilú Rojas Salazar, "Mexico," in this volume, 297.

22. Ibid..

23. Atola Longkumer, "India," in this volume, 189.

24. Ibid., 198.

25. The Third Lausanne Congress on World Evangelization, held in South Africa in 2010, is one example. While the talk was of cooperation and representation, the language used by most speakers was gender-exclusive, only thirteen of forty-three main speakers were women, no women were on the Lausanne executive tasked with organizing the congress and Hwa Yung later estimated women made up only 27 percent of the total attendees. Meanwhile, Oceania was never given a voice from the main platform, nor were indigenous/aboriginal groups, Korea (a significant evangelical missionary-sending country), Pentecostals or the disabled. English was the dominant language used from the front. The congress itself, which 4500 delegates attended, cost $US17 million and has generated subsequent country, regional and international meetings, forums and gatherings. One wonders if the money could be better spent. See also Tim Stafford, "Who Got Invited to Cape Town and Why," http://blog.christianitytoday.com/ctliveblog/archives/2010/10/representing_th.html (March 12, 2011) and Allen Yeh, "Four Conferences on Four Continents: Cape Town 2010 (Epilogue)," http://www.scriptoriumdaily.com/2010/10/26/four-conferences-on-four-continents-cape-town-2010-epilogue/ (March 12, 2011).

26. "The belief that missions can be approached like a business problem. With the right inputs, the thinking goes, the right outcomes can be assured. Any numbers of approaches have been haled as the 'key' to world evangelization or to reaching particular groups—everything from contextualization to saturation evangelization. Most while successful up to a point, also have been shown to have limits. (Guthrie 2000,162, cf. Escobar 2000, 109-112)," quoted from: *Missions Dictionary*, http://www.missiology.org/?p= #M, (December 13, 2011).

27. Samuel Escobar, *The New Global Mission, The Gospel from Everywhere to Everywhere* (Downers Grove: IVP, 2003), 167.

28. Unpublished talk, Tertiary Students Christian Fellowship Conference, 1978, New Zealand.

29. See Chung Hyun Kyung, "Who is Jesus for Asian Women?" in *Liberation Theology, An Introductory Reader,* ed. Curt Cadorette, et al. (Maryknoll: Orbis, 1992), 127.

30. Quoted in Diane B. Stinton, *Jesus of Africa, Voices of Contemporary African Christology* (Maryknoll: Orbis, 2004), 157.

31. Eleanor Sanderson "Women changing: Relating spirituality and development through the wisdom of Mothers' Union members in Tanzania," *Women's Studies Journal,* 20/2, (2006), 95.

32. For example, see http://www.amnesty.org.uk/actions_details.asp?ActionID=534 (August 29, 2011) which relates the story of Justine Bihamba working to protect women from rape in the Congo.

33. See Jones, "Sin: Grace Denied," in *Feminist Theory,* 94-125.

34. Philomena Mwaura and Damaris Parsitau Seleina, in this volume, XX.

35. Haruko Nawata Ward, in this volume, 252.

36. Chung, "Who is Jesus," 124.

37. Ibid.

38. Janet M. Soskice, "Turning the Symbols," in *In Swallowing a Fishbone? Feminist Theologians debate Christianity,* ed. Daphne Hampson (London: SPCK, 1996), 31.

39. Marilú Rojas Salazar, in this volume, 297.

40. Christine Pohl, *Making Room, Recovering Hospitality as a Christian Tradition* (Grand Rapids: Eerdmans, 1999), 24 (cf. Genesis 18).

41. Diane Langmore, "The Object Lesson of a Civilized Christian Home," in *Missionary Lives Papua, 1874-1914*, ed. Robert C. Kiste, Pacific Island Monograph Series, No. 6 (Honolulu: University of Hawaii, 1989), 65–88.

42. Karla Ann Koll, in this volume, 330.

43. Dana L. Robert, "The 'Christian Home' as a Cornerstone of Christian Thought and Practice," in *Christian Missions and the Enlightenment of the West: The Challenges of Experience and History* (Boston: North Atlantic Missiology Project, June 1998), 36.

44. See Cathy Ross, "Separate Spheres or Shared Dominions," *Transformation* 23/4 (2006): 228-236.

45. Robert, "The 'Christian Home'," 37.

46. Michele Hershberger, *A Christian View of Hospitality, Expecting Surprises* (PA: Herald, 1999), 104.

47. Christine Lienemann-Perrin, in this volume, 38.

48. Rojas Salazar, in this volume, 302.

49. Mercy Oduyoye, *Introducing African Women's Theology* (Sheffield: Sheffield Academic Press, 2001), 46-47.

50. Henri Nouwen, *Reaching Out: The Three Movements of the Spiritual Life* (Glasgow: William Collins, 1976), 68f.

51. See Hershberger, *A Christian View*, 228-29 for further discussion on this.

52. International Bulletin of Missionary Research provides every year statistics on the number of plans to evangelize the world since 30 A.D. The total has reached 2,000 plans so far! *IBMR*, Vol 35, No 1, (Jan 2011), 29.

53. John V. Taylor, *The Go-Between God: The Holy Spirit and the Christian Mission* (London: SCM, 1972), 21.

54. Calvin B. de Witt, "To Strive to Safeguard the Integrity of Creation and Sustain and Renew the Life of the Earth (i)" in *Mission in the 21st Century. Exploring the Five Marks of Global Mission*, eds. Andrew Walls and Cathy Ross (London: DLT, 2008), 84-93 [86].

55. Ibid., 89-90.

56. Ibid., 93.

57. Marilú Rojas Salazar, in this volume, 297.

58. Quoted by Sandra Schneiders, "The 'Why' and 'What' of Christian Feminist Theology," in: *Introducing Feminist Theology*, ed. Anne Clifford (Maryknoll: Orbis, 2001), 27.

59. Summarizing Committee Report of the World Evangelical Theological Commission and *Au Sable* Institute Forum, in Mark Thomas, guest ed., *Evangelicals and the Environment: Theological Foundations for Christian Environmental Stewardship* (special issue), *Evangelical Review of Theology* 17(2) (1993), 122-133.

60. "Pioneers in Mission": http://www.interserve.org.nz/site/interserve/files/NZ_GO_text_%20files/Pioneers_In_Mission_GOmag_Oct08.rtf (January 12, 2010).

61. By 1900, forty-one of the ninety-four Mission Boards were Women's Boards. R. Pierce Beaver, *American Protestant Women in World Mission, A History of the First Feminist Movement in North America* (Grand Rapids: Eerdmans, 1980), 87-88.

62. According to women Beaver interviewed, they believe they now have less involvement in policy making and that missionary dynamism and zeal has declined. Beaver, *American Protestant Women*, 202-203.

63. Alice L. Hageman, "Women and Missions: The Cost of Liberation," in *Sexist Religion and Women in the Church, No More Silence!*, ed. Alice L. Hageman (New York: Association Press, 1974), 167-193.

64. See Dana L. Robert, "Women and Missions: Historical Themes and Current Realities," in *Twentieth Century Missions and Gender Conference* (unpublished paper presented at a conference at Boston University, March, 2000), 1-15.

65. See Carlos Rene Padilla, "Wholistic Transformation and the Local Church." (unpublished address given at Eastern University, USA, August, 2009).

66. Hans Küng, *The Church* (London: Burnes and Oates, 1967), 96.

# Whose Story Shapes the Present of the Past?

*Fulata Lusungu Moyo*

Project on Women in Church and Society is part of the WCC program on Ecumenism in the 21st Century. One of the searching questions we have been dealing with has to do with what it means to be a community of women and men in the face of different global challenges that threaten life in fullness. Life in mission today is about women (and men) united in love in action for justice, restoration and maintenance of dignity and creation. It is about women and men initiating movements of action to ensure that life is lived holistically as just and peaceable communities of women, men, and environment.

When we first met at Bossey in November 2008 at the beginning of a process that has brought to life this publication, it was clearly acknowledged that women have been the dynamism in the mission work. Whether missionary work was erroneously conceived as the enlightened West bringing Christ's light through Western cultures to the global south, as "dark corners," or as a movement of love in action to realize God's reign of justice, dignity, and peace; women have shared their love in action through their lived spirituality providing service in education, health, economy, ecology, and other developmental interventions. Yet since the mission historiography has mainly taken a male perspective, these women's stories have often not been captured in the published records. This current project therefore is one of those watershed initiatives at bringing to the book such ignored and "forgotten" narratives of heroism. The fact that authors in this volume come from the diverse contexts to share challenging stories of women and women's perspectives, gives renewed hope for possibility of equality and justice as a mission imperative in this twenty-first century, one hundred years after the first World Mission Conference in 1910.

According to Clayton Morrison, the editor of *Christian Century*, of the 1,200 delegates attending the conference in Edinburgh in 1910, there were only 200 women, who not only were seldom mentioned in the reports but generally also sat in the gallery halls above the proceedings and therefore were not an intrinsic part of the proceedings and decision making. This was despite the fact that many of the missionary-sending agencies were women's societies. The conference celebrating one hundred years of world missions (Edinburgh 2010) did not seem to improve much regarding women's presence and participation despite the fact that the keynote speaker was a woman and there were proportionately more women than there were a hundred years ago. Edinburgh 2010 did not seem to improve much regarding women's presence and participation despite the fact that the keynote speaker was a woman and there were proportionally more women than a hundred years ago. There were still many panels and presentations that excluded women. Women and mission was treated as a transversal and therefore sometimes not appearing as part of the major sections of the official record. This book therefore helps to rectify that by mainstreaming the women's voice and their perspectives to enrich the diverse perspectives to mission in this globalized world.

For WCC Women in Church and Society, it is such an honor to be associated with this important mission paradigm-shifting project. We hope that this book will find its rightful place in the ecumenical circles as it timely contributes to shaping ecumenical mission perspectives within this changing ecclesial landscape. I would highly recommend the resource book to all serious readers and leaders of mission, both women and men, young and old.

*Fulata Lusungu Moyo (Malawi) is Programme Executive for Women in Church and Society, World Council of Churches (WCC), Geneva, Switzerland.*

# Contributors

**Belaynesh Bekele Abiyo** was born 1979 in Doyoganu, Ethiopia. She is a member of the Ethiopia Evangelical Church Mekane Jesus (EECMY). She completed her studies of theology at the Mekane Yesus Theological Seminary in Addis Ababa in 2005 and at the Protestant Theological University of Kampen in the Netherlands with a Master Thesis in Cross Cultural Theology (2007). Belaynesh served as a school teacher and was an outreach area worker of the Mekane Yesus Church. She also gave an introductory course to Diakonia at the Mekane Yesus Seminary in Addis Ababa. Currently, Belaynesh is living in Switzerland where she prepares a doctoral project on "Liberating the Language to Liberate Humanity: Feminist Critical Approach toward Ethiopian Proverbial Philosophy."

**Meehyun Chung**, ordained minister of the Presbyterian Church in the Republic of Korea (PROK). She studied German Literature, Philosophy, and Protestant Theology in Seoul. In 1993 she received a doctor's degree in Basel, her thesis was published as *Karl Barth, Josef Lukl Hromadka Korea* (1995). In 2006 she was awarded the Karl-Barth prize of the Union of Protestant Churches within the EKD for her doctoral thesis and other articles. She served as Vice President for Ecumenical Association of Third World Theologians (EATWOT). Currently, she is the head of the Women and Gender Desk at mission21, Protestant Mission Basel, Switzerland. Recent publications include: (ed.), *Breaking Silence-Theology from Asian Women* (India: ISPCK, 2006); (ed.), *Weaving Dreams* (Berlin: Frank & Timme, 2009); *Another Discourse of Korean Feminist Theology*, (Seoul: Handl, 2007).

**Amélé Adamavi-Aho Ekué,** Protestant theologian originating from Togo. She is Professor of Ecumenical Ethics at the Ecumenical Institute Bossey/ Switzerland. Research areas comprise global Christianity (especially African Christianity), religion and violence, migration and changes of the ecclesial landscape, and gender theology. Recent publications include: "Migrant Christians: Believing Wanderers between Cultures and Nations," in: *Ecumenical Review* 61.4 (2009).

**Gulnar (Guli) Francis-Dehqani** was born in 1966 in Isfahan, Iran. She moved to England following the events of the 1979 Islamic Revolution and has, to date, been unable to return to Iran. A Nottingham University music graduate, she worked at BBC World Service radio and Domestic Radio's Religious Department. Her Ph.D from Bristol University was awarded in 1999, soon after which she was ordained in the Church of England. Guli has written and spoken in particular on the areas of feminist theology and interfaith studies. She is currently Curate Training Officer in the Diocese of Peterborough and lives in Oakham with her husband and three children.

**Karla Ann Koll**, a mission co-worker of the Presbyterian Church (USA), serves as professor of history, mission, and religions for the Latin American Biblical University (Costa Rica) and the Evangelical Center for Pastoral Studies in Central America (Guatemala). Her recent writings have focused on Central American Protestantism and short-term mission.

**Kwok Pui Lan,** William F. Cole Professor of Christian Theology and Spirituality at the Episcopal Divinity School, Cambridge, Massachusetts, USA. A pioneer in Asian feminist theology and postcolonial theology, she is the author or editor of fifteen books in English and Chinese. Professor Kwok's publications include: *Postcolonial Imagination and Feminist Theology* (Louisville: Westminster John Knox Press, 2006), *Introducing Asian Feminist Theology* (Cleveland: Pilgrim Press, 2000), *Discovering the Bible in the Non-Biblical World* (Maryknoll: Orbis Books, 1995), and *Chinese Women and Christianity, 1860–1927* (Atlanta: Scholars Press, 1992). She is also the editor of the major reference work *Women and Christianity* (London: Routledge, 2010).

**Christine Lienemann-Perrin**, Professor Emerita of Missiology and Ecumenical Studies at the Faculty of Theology, University of Basel, and part-time Professor for Ecumenical Theology at the University of Bern. Born in Switzerland 1946; doctorate (1976) and habilitation in Heidelberg (1990). She has done research work and given lectures in Congo/Kinshasa, South Africa, South Korea, Brazil, and Japan. Her publications deal with mission and interreligious dialogue, feminist missiology, ecumenical political ethics, and religious conversion.

**Atola Longkumer**, Associate Professor in the Department of Religions at Leonard Theological College, Jabalpur, MP, India. She is a member of the Baptist Church of Nagaland. She has published articles on Anti-Conversion Bill in India; Indigenous Theology; Gender and Comparative Mysticism; Christian Missions and Ethnography; Christian Missions and Women. She serves as the editor of *Sandeshharika* (Prophetess' Voice), a bi-annual journal on women and Indian Christians, published by Leonard Theological College, Jabalpur, MP, India.

**Chita Rebollido-Millan**, deaconess of the Methodist Church in the Philippines. She has served as the President of the World Federation of Methodist and Uniting Church Women (WFMUCW). She is also the School Director of two private schools: Calasiao and Lingayen Educational Centers. She received her Doctor of Philosophy in Educational Leadership and Management from De La Salle University. Among her recent publications are *Women in Philippine United Methodism*; *Spirituality: At the Core of Leadership among United Methodist Women Educational Leaders*. Apart from extensive publications on school materials, there are short story books to her credit.

**Philomena Njeri Mwaura,** Senior Lecturer in the Philosophy and Religious Studies Department and Director, Gender and Affirmative Action Implementation Center at Kenyatta University, Nairobi, Kenya. She is a former President of the International Association for Mission Studies, the Africa Region Co-coordinator of the Theology Commission of the Ecumenical Association of Third World Theologians and a member of the Circle of Concerned African Women Theologians. She is also a member of the Catholic Church. Mwaura has published extensively on various aspects of African Christianity and her recent publications include "Woman Lost in the Global Maze: Women and Religion in East Africa under Globalization," in Mary M. Fulkerson and Sheila Briggs, eds., *Oxford Handbook of Feminist Theology* (Oxford: Oxford University Press, 2011).

**Cathy Ross** is originally from Aotearoa/New Zealand. Her publications include: *Women with a Mission: Rediscovering Missionary Wives in Early New Zealand* (Auckland: Penguin, 2006); *Mission in Context: Explorations Inspired by J. Andrew Kirk* (Surrey:

Ashgate, 2012), co-edited with John Corrie; and *Mission in the 21st Century* (London: DLT, 2008), co-edited with Andrew Walls. She and her family have worked in Rwanda, Congo, and Uganda as mission partners with NZCMS. She has served as the Director of School of Global Mission, Bible College of New Zealand; and Manager of the Crowther Centre for Mission Education, CMS, Oxford. She is now Tutor in Contextual Theology at Ripon College, Cuddesdon and Lecturer in Mission at Regent's Park College, University of Oxford. She also serves as the General Secretary of the International Association for Mission Studies (IAMS).

**Marilú Rojas Salazar,** a member of the Catholic Church and a religious Missionary of Saint Therese of Lisieux, has a Masters degree in Theology from the Catholic University of Leuven, where she is currently undertaking her doctorate in Systematic Theology. She worked as a teacher in different institutions, seminaries, and religious houses in Mexico. She was a member of the Team of Theological Reflection (ERT) of the Conference of Religious Institutes of Mexico (CIRM). She belongs to the Association of European Theologians (ATE). Her research topic is on feminist theological method from the perspective of the Latin American eco-feminist theology.

**Afrie Songco Joye,** Professor (part-time), Union Theological Seminary, Philippines, is an ordained minister of The United Methodist Church with clergy membership at the California-Pacific Annual Conference, USA. With a doctorate in Theology and Religious Education from Claremont School of Theology, she has taught in seminaries in Taiwan, Hong Kong, Vietnam, and Malaysia as Visiting Lecturer/Professor. She served local churches in the Philippines as a deaconess, and in California as a pastor. Her areas of interest and advocacy work are: congregational studies, gender studies, social justice, the integrity of creation, Christian education as transforming power, mission and evangelism.

**Damaris Parsitau Seleina,** lecturer in African Christianities in the Department of History, Philosophy and Religious Studies at Egerton University, Njoro, Kenya. She has published widely and one of her latest publication is "God in the City: Pentecostalism as an Urban Phenomenon in Kenya," co-authored with Philomena Njeri Mwaura in Studia Historiae Ecclessiasticae Volume XXXVI (no 2) 2010.

**Heike Walz**, Rev. Dr., Junior-professor of Feminist Theology, Women's Studies, Religious and Mission Studies and Ecumenics at the Protestant University Wuppertal-Bethel (Germany). In 1998 she was ordained and served as Pastor of the Evangelical Church of the Palatinate (Germany). Her doctorate in theology (PhD) from University of Basel (Switzerland) was awarded in 2005. She was Extraordinary Professor of Systematic Theology at the *Instituto Universitario* ISEDET in Buenos Aires (Argentina) from 2005 until 2009. In 2004 she founded NGT: "Network for Dialogues on Gender and Theology between Women and Men." Her publications include liberation theologies, ecclesiology, women's theologies from the global South, postcolonial and gender theories. Recent publications are: "*... nicht mehr männlich und weiblich ...* "? *Ekklesiologie und Geschlecht in ökumenischem Horizont* (Frankfurt am Main: Lembeck, 2006); *Theologie und Geschlecht. Dialoge querbeet,* ed. with David Plüss (Wien: Lit, 2008); "*Madres* appear on the Public *Plaza de Mayo* in Argentina. Towards Human Rights as a Key for a Public Theology that carries on the Liberation Heritage," in *International Journal for Public Theology* vol. 3, no. 2 (2009).

**Haruko Nawata Ward,** Associate Professor of Church History, Columbia Theological Seminary, Decatur, GA, USA. She received her PhD in Reformation Studies at Princeton Theological Seminary, 2001. She is an ordained minister of Word and Sacrament, Presbyterian Church (USA). Her publications include: *Women Religious Leaders of Japan's Christian Century, 1549-1640* (Ashgate, 2009); and numerous journal articles and book chapters, such as "Jesuit Encounters with Confucianism in Early Modern Japan," *Sixteenth Century Journal* 40, no.4 (Winter 2009).

CPSIA information can be obtained at www.ICGtesting.com
Printed in the USA
LVOW10s2123140114

369401LV00032B/1523/P